ESSENTIALS OF

COMPARATIVE

POLITICS FOURTH EDITION

ESSENTIALS OF

COMPARATIVE

POLITICS

FOURTH EDITION

PATRICK H. O'NEIL

W. W. NORTON & COMPANY
New York • London

W. W. Norton & Company has been independent since its founding in 1923, when William Warder Norton and Mary D. Herter Norton first published lectures delivered at the People's Institute, the adult education division of New York City's Cooper Union. The firm soon expanded its program beyond the Institute, publishing books by celebrated academics from America and abroad. By mid-century, the two major pillars of Norton's publishing program—trade books and college texts—were firmly established. In the 1950s, the Norton family transferred control of the company to its employees, and today—with a staff of four hundred and a comparable number of trade, college, and professional titles published each year—W. W. Norton & Company stands as the largest and oldest publishing house owned wholly by its employees.

Editor: Ann Shin
Associate Editor: Jake Schindel
Manuscript Editor: Barney Latimer
Project Editor: Diane Cipollone
Electronic Media Editor: Lorraine Klimowich
Electronic Media Assistant Editor: Jennifer Barnhardt
Editorial Assistant: Caitlin Cummings
Marketing Manager, Political Science: Sasha Levitt
Production Manager: Eric Pier-Hocking
Photo Editor: Michael Fodera
Permissions Manager: Megan Jackson
Permissions Assistant: Bethany Salminen
Text Design: Faceout Studio
Art Director: Hope Miller Goodell, Chris Welsh
Composition: Jouve North America—Brattleboro, VT
Manufacturing: Quad Graphics—Taunton, MA

Library of Congress Cataloging-in-Publication Data

O'Neil, Patrick H., 1966-
  Essentials of comparative politics / Patrick H. O'Neil. — 4th ed.
      p. cm.
  Includes bibliographical references and index.
  ISBN 978-0-393-91278-4 (pbk.)
1. Comparative government.   2. State, The.   3. Capitalism.   4. Democracy.
  5. Post-communism.   I. Title.
JF51.O54 2012
320.3—dc23

                                                                      2012020079

W. W. Norton & Company, Inc., 500 Fifth Avenue, New York, N.Y. 10110
www.wwnorton.com
W. W. Norton & Company Ltd., Castle House, 75/76 Wells Street, London W1T 3QT
1 2 3 4 5 6 7 8 9 0

CONTENTS

5 DEMOCRATIC REGIMES 126

9 COMMUNISM AND POSTCOMMUNISM 256

10 LESS-DEVELOPED AND NEWLY INDUSTRIALIZING COUNTRIES 290

LIST OF MAPS

ABOUT THE AUTHOR

Patrick H. O'Neil is Professor of Politics and Government at the University of Puget Sound in Tacoma, Washington. He has a Ph.D. in Political Science from Indiana University. Professor O'Neil's teaching and research interests are in the areas of authoritarianism and democratization. His past research focused on Eastern Europe, and his current research interests are on the Middle East, particularly Iran. His publications include the books *Revolution from Within: The Hungarian Socialist Workers' Party and the Collapse of Communism* and *Communicating Democracy: The Media and Political Transitions* (editor).

PREFACE

The past twenty-five years has seen the dramatic transformation of comparative politics: the end of the Cold War and the collapse of the Soviet Union, the spread of democracy around the world, the rise of new economic powers in Asia, the deepening of globalization. For a time, many looked upon these changes as unmitigated progress that would bring about a decline in global conflict and produce widespread prosperity. Recently, however, there has been growing doubt, as the uncertainties of the future seem to portend more risk than reward, more conflict than peace. It is increasingly difficult to sustain the notion that a nation can function without a good understanding of the billions of people who live outside of its borders. Consider the Arab Spring: Will this help promote prosperity and peace in the Middle East, or unleash new authoritarian regimes and perhaps regional instability? We ignore such questions at our peril.

This textbook is meant to contribute to our understanding of comparative politics (the study of domestic politics around the world) by investigating the central ideas and questions that make up this field. It begins with the most basic struggle in politics—the battle between freedom and equality and the task of reconciling or balancing these ideals. How this struggle has unfolded across place and time represents the core of comparative politics. The text continues by emphasizing the importance of institutions. Human action is fundamentally guided by the institutions that people construct, such as culture, constitutions, and property rights. Once established, these institutions are both influential and persistent—not easily overcome, changed, or removed. How these institutions emerge, and how they affect politics, is central to this work.

With these ideas in place, we tackle the basic institutions of power—states, markets, societies, democracies, and nondemocratic regimes. What are states, how do they emerge, and how can we measure their capacity, autonomy, and efficacy? How do markets function, and what kinds of relationships exist between states and markets? How do societal components like nationalism, ethnicity, and ideology shape political values? And what are the main differences between democratic and nondemocratic regimes, and what explains why one or the other predominates in various parts of the world? These are a few of the questions we will attempt to answer.

Once these concepts and questions have been explored, subsequent chapters will apply them directly to various political systems—advanced democracies, communist and postcommunist countries, and newly industrializing and less-developed countries. In each of these, the basic institutions of the state, market, society, and democratic or nondemocratic regime all shape the relationship between freedom and equality. What basic characteristics lead us to group these countries together? How do they compare to one another, and what are their prospects for economic, social, and democratic development? Finally, we will conclude with a discussion of globalization, linking what we have studied at the domestic level to wider international forces.

There are two major changes to the Fourth Edition of this book. The first is the movement of the discussion of political violence to immediately following the discussion of non-democratic regimes. When first added to the textbook, the chapter was meant to address the events of 9/11 and its impact on the international community. However, the emphasis on both terrorism and revolution means that the chapter can serve as a good bridge between the discussion of democratic and non-democratic regimes and our discussion of advanced democracies, communist and postcommunist countries, and less-developed and newly industrializing countries. Especially given the momentous changes in the Middle East, shifting our emphasis back to the idea of revolution makes the chapter an important one, if in a different light than just a few years ago when revolutions seemed unlikely or far off, and thus of little merit to consider. A second change can be found in all chapters (excluding the first), which contain expanded "Institutions in Action" boxes that each address one important puzzle from around the world. These vary in their emphasis—for example, Chapter 4's box examines economic decline in Japan, while Chapter 6 assesses the differing paths of political change in South Africa and Zimbabwe—allowing for geographical diversity while tackling some of the major questions in comparative politics.

The format of this text is rather different from that of many comparative politics textbooks. Traditionally, these books have been built around a set of country studies, with introductory chapters for the advanced, postcommunist, and less-developed world. While such a textbook can provide a great deal of information on a wide range of cases, the trade-off is often a less thorough consideration of the basic grammar of comparative politics. We might know who the prime minister of Japan is but have less of an understanding of political culture, mercantilism, or state autonomy, all ideas that can help us make sense of politics across time and place. This text strives to fill this gap and can be used alongside traditional case studies to help draw out broader questions and issues. By grasping these concepts, arguments, and questions, students will better understand the political dynamics of the wider world.

This thematic approach to the essential tools and ideas of comparative politics is supported by a strong pedagogy that clarifies and reinforces the most important concepts. Key concepts lists and "In Focus" boxes in every chapter highlight important material that students will want to review. Numerous figures and tables illustrate important concepts and provide real world data related to the topic at hand. Timelines and thematic maps show important political developments over time and around the globe. The importance of institutions is emphasized by the "Institutions in Action" boxes discussed above.

Essentials of Comparative Politics is designed to offer instructors flexibility in creating the course that they want to teach. In addition to the core textbook, a corresponding casebook and a reader are also available. *Cases in Comparative Politics*, coauthored by Karl Fields, Donald Share, and myself, applies the concepts from *Essentials of Comparative Politics* to thirteen country studies. In *Essential Readings in Comparative Politics*, my coeditor Ronald Rogowski and I have selected key readings to accompany each chapter in the textbook. Norton also offers the textbook and casebook in e-book format. Support materials for instructors, including a Test Bank, PowerPoint lecture outlines, and a supplementary Image Bank, are also available at http://www.wwnorton.com/instructors.

Many people have contributed to this work. The text itself is inspired by Karen Mingst's *Essentials of International Relations*. When Norton released Mingst's book in 1999, I was struck by its concision and came to the conclusion that comparative politics would benefit from a similar kind of text. At Norton, Peter Lesser first encouraged me to submit a proposal for this textbook, and Roby Harrington encouraged me to develop the initial chapters, supported its publication, and provided important feedback at many stages. As editor, Ann Shin held me to a high standard of writing argumentation in the First Edition. For the Second and Third Editions, Peter Lesser and Aaron Javsicas took over editorial duties, helping to further improve the work. In this Fourth Edition, Jake Schindel guided me through a number of complicated revisions and edits that have improved the content and style. I am grateful to all four of them for their investment in this work.

In addition to the people at Norton, many academics have helped improve this work. Most important have been my colleagues at the University of Puget Sound, in particular Don Share and Karl Fields. Over the past few years Don, Karl, and I have team-taught introductory comparative politics, and it was my work with these two outstanding teachers and scholars that helped generate many of the ideas in this book. Don and Karl were also kind enough to use draft chapters of this text in their courses and provided a great deal of feedback and numerous suggestions. I am fortunate to have such colleagues.

Many thanks as well to those numerous reviewers who have provided useful critiques and suggestions that have improved this work, including Jason Arnold (Virginia Commonwealth University), Alex Avila (Mesa Community College), Caroline Beer (University of Vermont), Marni Berg (Colorado State University), Prosper Bernard, Jr. (College of Staten Island), Jeremy Busacca (Whittier College), Robert Compton (SUNY Oneonta), Bruce Dickson (George Washington University), Kenly Fenio (Virginia Tech), Sarah Goodman (University of California at Irvine), Ivy Hamerly (Baylor University), Yoshiko Herrera (University of Wisconsin at Madison), Tamara Kotar (University of Ottawa), Brian Kupfer (Tallahassee Community College), Michael Mitchell (Arizona State Univerity), Paul Rousseau (University of Windsor), Steve Sharp (Utah State University, Logan), and Stacey Philbrick Yadav (Hobart & William Smith Colleges).

Finally, I would like to thank the students of the University of Puget Sound for their questions and insights, the university administration for its support of this project, and my family for their patience.

Patrick H. O'Neil
Tacoma, Washington
May 2012

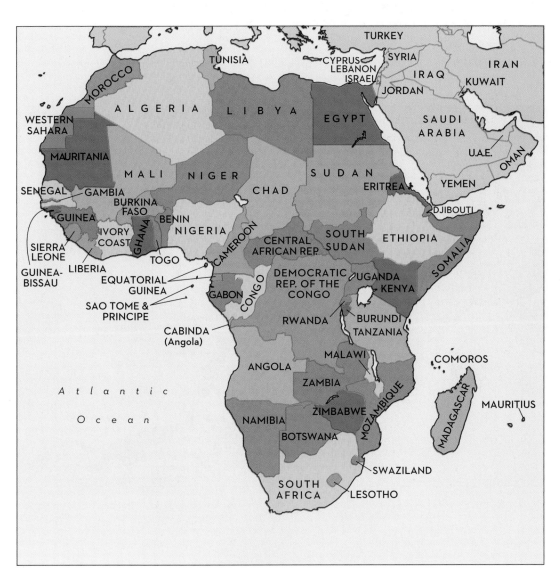

AFRICA

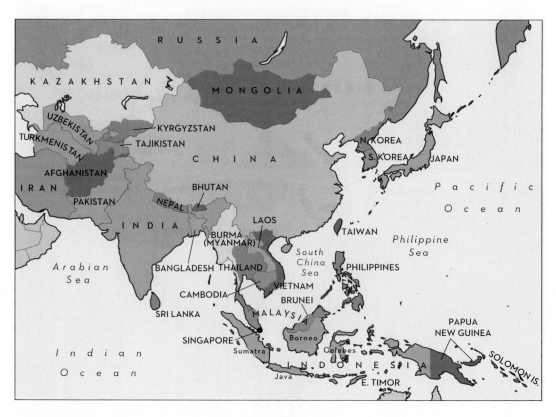

ASIA

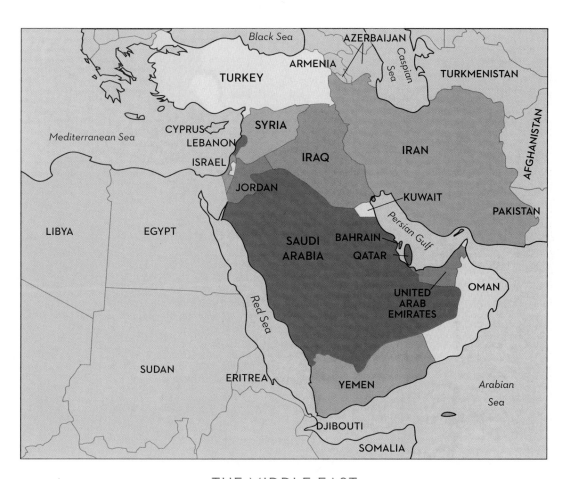

THE MIDDLE EAST

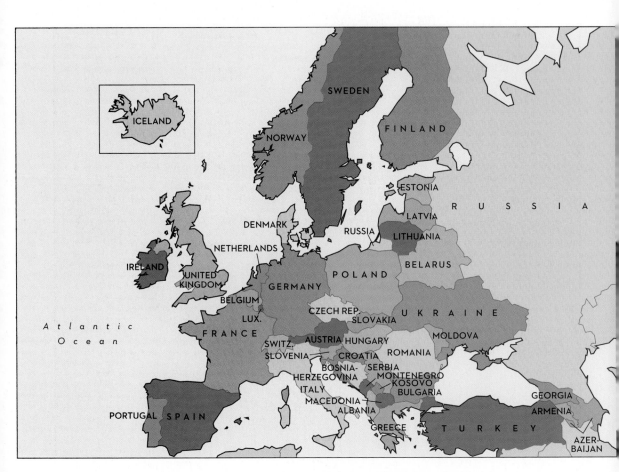

EUROPE

CENTRAL AND SOUTH AMERICA

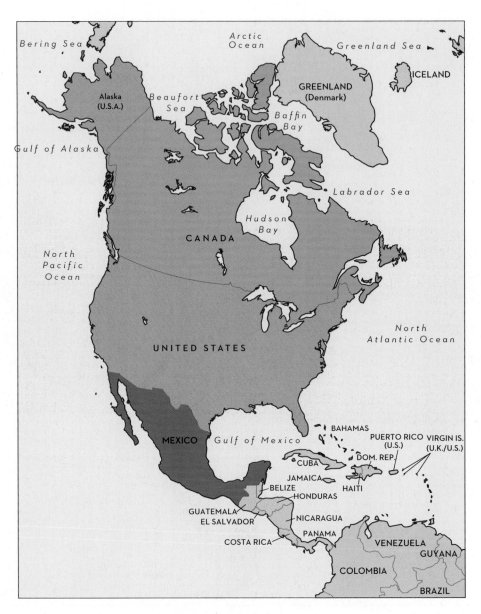

NORTH AMERICA

ESSENTIALS OF

COMPARATIVE

POLITICS FOURTH EDITION

1

Though when we think of institutions in politics we often think of formal examples such as legislatures or elections, informal institutions such as sports can command similar forms of power, authority, and legitimacy. Here, fans support their favorite teams at a soccer match in Germany.

INTRODUCTION

KEY CONCEPTS

- Comparative politics relies on a comparative method to construct and test hypotheses.

- There are long-running debates over whether we can make comparative politics more scientific—better at explaining or predicting politics.

- One concept that will guide our study is political institutions: self-perpetuating patterns of activity valued for their own sake.

- Two ideals that will guide our study are freedom and equality and we will look at how politics reconciles the two across countries.

During the past twenty-five years the world has seen an astonishing number of changes: the rise of new economic powers in Asia; the collapse of communism; revolutions across the Middle East; the return of religion to politics; the spread of information technology and social media; and the deepening of globalization. Many of the traditional assumptions and beliefs held by scholars, policy makers, and citizens have been overturned. New centers of wealth may reduce poverty, but we have seen how they may also increase inequality. Democracy may be an inexorable force, but it may founder on such obstacles as religious or economic conflict. Technological change may create new shared identities and sources of cooperation, but it can destabilize and fragment communities.

Debates over ethnic conflict illustrate these issues. Why does this form of political violence occur? Is it a response to inequality or political disenfranchisement? Is it a function of cultural differences, a "clash of civilizations?" Is it fostered or tempered by globalization? Perhaps the explanation lies somewhere else entirely, beyond our purview or comprehension. How can we know what is correct? How do we scrutinize a range of explanations and evaluate their merits? Competing assumptions and explanations are at the heart of political debates and policy decisions, yet we are often asked to choose in the absence of reliable evidence or a good understanding of cause and effect. To be better citizens, we should be better students of political science and **comparative politics**—the study and comparison of domestic politics across countries. Comparative politics can be contrasted with another related field in political science, **international relations**. While comparative politics looks at the politics inside countries (such as elections, political parties, revolutions, and judicial systems), international relations concentrates on relations between countries (such as foreign policy, war, trade, and foreign aid). There are of course many places where the two overlap, such as in ethnic conflict, which often spills over borders, or political change, which can be shaped by international organizations or military force. At the end of this book we will look at one specific area where the distinction between international relations and comparative politics has become blurred—globalization. For now, however, our discussion will concentrate on political structures and actions within countries.

This chapter will lay out some of the most basic vocabulary and structures of political science and comparative politics. These will fall under three basic categories: *analytical concepts* (assumptions and theories that guide our research), *methods* (ways to study and test those theories), and *ideals* (beliefs and values about preferred outcomes). Analytical concepts help us ask questions about cause and effect, methods provide tools to seek out explanations, and ideals help us compare existing politics to what we might prefer.

Our survey will consider some of the most basic questions: What is politics? How does one compare different political systems around the world? We will spend some time on the methods of comparative politics and how scholars have approached its study. Over the past century political scientists have struggled with the challenge of analyzing politics and have asked whether such analysis can actually be considered a science. Exploring these issues will give us a better sense of the limitations and possibilities in the study of comparative politics. We will consider comparative politics through the concept of **institutions**—organizations or activities that are self-perpetuating and valued for their own sake. Institutions play an important role in defining and shaping what is possible and probable in political life by laying out the rules, norms, and structures in which we live. Finally, in addition to institutions, we will take up the ideals of freedom and equality. If institutions shape how the game of politics is played, then the goal of the game is the right mix of freedom and equality. Which ideal is more important? Must one come at the expense of the other? Perhaps some other ideal is preferable to both? With the knowledge gained by exploring these questions, we will be ready to take on complex politics around the world.

What Is Comparative Politics?

Before we go any further, we must identify what comparative politics is. **Politics** is the struggle in any group for power that will give one or more persons the ability to make decisions for the larger group. This group may range from a small organization to the entire world. Politics occurs wherever there are people and organization; for example, we may speak of "office politics" when we are talking about power relationships in a business. Political scientists in particular concentrate on the struggle for leadership and power in a political community—a political party, elected office, a city, region, or country. Politics is the pursuit of authority to make decisions that will affect the community as a whole. It is therefore hard to separate the idea of politics from the idea of **power**, which is the ability to influence others or impose one's will on them. Politics is the competition for public power, and power is the ability to extend one's will.

In political science, comparative politics is a subfield that compares this pursuit of power across countries. The method of comparing countries can help us make arguments about cause and effect by drawing evidence from across space and time. For example, one important puzzle we will return to frequently is why some countries are democratic while others are not. Why have politics in some countries resulted in power being dispersed among more people, while in others power is concentrated in the hands of a few? Why is South Korea democratic while North Korea is not? Looking at North Korea alone won't necessarily help us understand why South Korea went down a different path, or vice versa. A comparison of the two, perhaps alongside similar cases in Asia, may better yield explanations. As should be clear, these are not simply academic questions. Democratic countries and pro-democracy organizations actively support the spread of like-minded regimes around the world, but if it is unclear how or why it comes about, democracy becomes difficult or even dangerous to promote. It is therefore important to separate ideals from our concepts and methods and not let the former obscure our use of the latter. Comparative politics can inform and even challenge our ideals, providing alternatives and questioning our assumption that there is one right way to organize political life.

The Comparative Method

If comparison is an important way to test our assumptions and shape our ideals, how we compare cases is important. If there is no criterion or guide by which we gather information or draw conclusions, our studies become little more than a collection of details. Researchers thus often seek out puzzles—questions about politics with no obvious answer—as a way to guide their research. From there, they rely on some **comparative method**—a way to compare cases and draw conclusions. By comparing countries or subsets within them, scholars seek out conclusions and generalizations that could be valid in other cases.

To return to our earlier question, let us say that we are interested in why democracy has failed to develop in some countries—a big puzzle if ever there was one. This question was central to debates in the West over going to war with Iraq and remains a contentious issue in the Middle East and elsewhere. We might approach the puzzle of democracy by looking at North Korea. Why has North Korean government remained communist and highly repressive even as similar regimes around the world have collapsed?

A convincing answer to this puzzle could tell scholars and policy makers a great deal and even guide our tense relations with North Korea in the future. Examining one country closely may lead us to form hypotheses about why a country operates as it does. We call this approach **inductive reasoning**—the means by which we go from studying a case to generating a hypothesis. But while a study of one country can generate interesting hypotheses, it does not provide enough evidence to test them. Thus, we might study North Korea and perhaps conclude that the use of nationalism by those in power has been central to the persistence of nondemocratic rule. In so concluding, we might then suggest that future studies look at the relationship between nationalism and authoritarianism in other countries. Inductive reasoning can therefore be a foundation on which we build greater theories in comparative politics.

Comparative politics can also rely on **deductive reasoning**—starting with a puzzle and from there generating some hypothesis about cause and effect to test against a number of cases. Whereas inductive reasoning starts with the evidence as a way to undercover a hypothesis, deductive reasoning starts with the hypothesis and then seeks out the evidence. In our example of inductive reasoning we started with a case study of North Korea and ended with some testable generalization about nationalism; in deductive reasoning we would start with our hypothesis about nationalism and then test that hypothesis by looking at a number of countries. By carrying out such studies, we may find a **correlation**, or apparent association, between certain factors or variables. If we were particularly ambitious, we might claim to have found cause and effect, or a **causal relationship**.[1] Inductive and deductive reasoning can help us to better understand and explain political outcomes and, ideally, could help us predict them.

Unfortunately, inductive and deductive reasoning, or finding correlation and causation, is not easy. There are seven major challenges comparativists face in trying to examine political features across countries. Let's move through each one of these challenges and show how they complicate the comparative method and comparative politics in general. First, political scientists have difficulty controlling the variables in the cases they study. In other words, in our search for correlations or causal relationships, we are unable to make true comparisons because each of our cases is different. By way of illustration, suppose a researcher wants to determine whether increased exercise by college students leads to higher grades. In studying the students who are her subjects, the researcher can control for a number of variables that might also affect grades, such as the students' diet, the amount of sleep they get, or any factor that might influence the results. By controlling for these differences and making certain that many of these variables are the same across the subjects with the exception of exercise, the researcher can carry out her study with greater confidence.

But political science offers few opportunities to control the variables because the variables are a function of real-world politics. Countries' economies, cultures, geography, resources, and political structures are amazingly diverse, and it is difficult to control for these differences. Even in a single-case study, variables change over time. At best, we can control as much as possible for variables that might otherwise distort our conclusions. If, for example, we want to understand why gun ownership laws are so much less restrictive in the United States than in most other industrialized countries, we would be well served to compare the United States with those that have similar historical, economic, political, and social experiences, such as Canada and Australia, rather than Japan or South Africa. This allows us to control our variables more effectively, but it still leaves many variables uncontrolled and unaccounted for.

A second, related problem concerns the interactions between the variables themselves. Even if we can control our variables in making our comparisons, there is the problem that many of these variables are interconnected and interact. In other words, many variables are tied together to produce particular outcomes, in what is known as **multicausality**. Variation in countries' gun control laws is unlikely to be explained by a single variable like a country's electoral system or the strength of its judicial system. The problem of multicausality also reminds us that in the real world there are often no single, easy answers to political problems.

A third problem is the limits to our information and information gathering. Although we have many uncontrolled and interconnected variables in the cases we study, we often have too few cases with which to work. In the natural sciences, research is often conducted with a huge number of cases—hundreds of stars or thousands of individuals, often studied across time. This breadth allows researchers to select their cases in such a way as to control their variables, and the large number of cases also prevents any single unusual case from distorting the findings. But in comparative politics, we are typically limited by the number of countries in the world—fewer than 200 at present, most of which did not exist a few centuries ago. Even if we study some subset in comparative politics (like political parties or acts of terrorism), our total number of cases will remain relatively small. And if we attempt to control for differences by trying to find a number of similar cases (for example, wealthy democracies), our total body of cases will shrink even further.

A fourth problem in comparative politics concerns how we access the few cases we do have. Research is often further hindered by the very factors that make countries interesting to study. Much information that political scientists seek is not easy to acquire, necessitating work in the field—that is, conducting interviews or studying government archives abroad. International travel requires time and money, and researchers may spend months or even years in the field. Interviewees may be unwilling to speak on sensitive issues or may distort information. Libraries and archives may be incomplete, or access to them restricted. Governments may bar research on politically sensitive questions. Confronting these obstacles in more than one country is even more challenging. A researcher may be able to read Russian and travel to Russia frequently, but if he wants to compare post-communism in Russia and China, it would be ideal to be able to read Chinese and conduct research in China as well. Few comparativists have the language skills, time, or resources to conduct field research in many countries. There are almost no comparativists in North America or Europe who speak both Russian and Chinese. As a result, comparativists often master knowledge of a single country or language and rely on deductive reasoning. Single-case study research can be extremely valuable, as it gives the researcher a great deal of case depth and the ability to tease out novel observations that may come only from close observation. However, such narrow focus can also make it unclear to researchers whether the politics they see in their case study has important similarities to the politics in other cases.

Fifth, even where comparativists do widen their range of cases, their focus tends to be limited to a single geographic region. The specialist on communist Cuba is more likely to study other Latin American countries than China or North Korea, and the specialist on China more likely to study South Korea than Russia. This isn't necessarily a concern, given our earlier discussion of the need to control variables—it may make more sense to study parts of the world where similar variables are clustered rather than compare countries from different parts of the world. This regional focus, however—often referred to as **area studies**—is not distributed evenly around the world. In spite of dramatic shifts in political power, population, and wealth, the largest share of comparative politics research continues to be on Western Europe—almost twice as much as there is on East Asia, which includes China, Japan, and South Korea.[2] Why? As mentioned earlier, some of this is a function of language; many scholars in the West are exposed to European languages at primary or secondary school, and in many European countries the use of English is widespread, thus facilitating research. Yet English is also widespread in South Asia, notably India, and in spite of this, there are relatively few comparativists outside India who study that country. While some of this may be changing among younger scholars, comparative politics remains uneven in its coverage and has been slow to widen its focus when new issues and questions arise.

Sixth, the problem of bias makes it even harder to control for variables and to select the right cases. This is a question not of political bias, though that can sometimes be a problem, but of how we select our cases. In the natural sciences, case selection is randomized as much as possible so that the cases under observation have not been chosen to support one hypothesis or another. But for the reasons mentioned above, such randomization is not possible in political science. Single-case studies are already influenced by the fact that comparativists study a country because they know its language or find it interesting. Yet even if we rely instead on deductive reasoning—beginning with a hypothesis and then seeking out our cases—we can easily fall into the trap of **selection bias.**

For example, say we want to understand revolutions and we hypothesize that the main cause is a rapid growth in inequality. How should we select our cases? Most of us would respond by saying that we should find as many cases of revolution as possible and then see whether they were preceded by an increase in inequality. But this is a mistake; by looking only at cases of revolution, we miss all the cases where inequality grew but revolution did *not* take place. Indeed, there may be many more cases of unequal growth without revolution than with it, disproving our hypothesis. So, we would do better to concentrate on what we think is the cause (growth in inequality) rather than on what we think is the effect. While this may seem the obvious choice, it is a frequent mistake among scholars who are often so drawn to particular outcomes that they start there and then work their way backward.

A seventh and final concern deals with the heart of political science—the search for cause and effect. Let us for the sake of argument assume that the half-dozen problems we have laid out can be overcome through careful case selection, information gathering, and control of variables. Let us further imagine that with these problems in hand, research finds, for example, that countries with a low rate of female literacy are less likely to be democratic than countries where female literacy is high. Even if we are confident enough to claim that there is a causal relationship between female literacy and democracy—a bold statement indeed—a final, and perhaps intractable problem looms. Which variable is cause and which is effect? Do low rates of female literacy limit public participation, empowering nondemocractic actors, or do authoritarian leaders (by and large men) take little interest in promoting gender equality? This problem of distinguishing cause and effect, known as **endogeneity**, is a major obstacle in any comparative research. Even if we are confident that we have found cause and effect, we can't easily ascertain which is which. On reflection, this is to be expected; one political scientist has called endogeneity "the motor of history," as causes and effects tend to evolve together, each transforming the other over time. Thus, early forms of democracy, literacy, and women's rights may well have gone hand in hand, each reinforcing and changing the others. This makes an elegant claim about cause and effect problematic, to say the least.[3]

IN FOCUS — Problems in Comparative Research

- Controlling a large number of variables

- Controlling for the interaction of variables (multicausality)

- Limited number of cases to research

- Limited access to information from cases

- Uneven research across cases and regions

- Cases selected on the basis of cause and not effect (selection bias)

- Variables may be either cause or effect (endogeneity)

Can We Make a Science of Comparative Politics?

We have so far elaborated many of the ways in which comparative politics—and political science in general—makes for difficult study. Variables are hard to control and can be interconnected, while actual cases may be few. Getting access to information may be difficult, and comparisons may be limited by regional knowledge and interests. What questions are asked may be affected by selection bias and endogeneity. All these concerns make it difficult to generate any kind of political science **theory**, which we can define as an integrated set of hypotheses, assumptions, and facts. At this point you may well have concluded that a science of politics is hopeless. But it is precisely these kinds of concerns that have driven political science, and comparative politics within it, toward a more scientific approach. Whether this has yielded or will yield significant benefits, and at what cost, is something we will consider next.

Political science and comparative politics have a long pedigree. In almost every major society there are masterworks of politics, prescribing rules or, less often, analyzing political behavior. In the West, the work of the philosopher Aristotle (384–322 B.C.E.) departed from the traditional emphasis on political ideals to conduct comparative research on existing political systems, eventually gathering and analyzing the constitutions of 158 Greek city-states. Aristotle's objective was less to determine the ideal political system than to understand the different forms of politics that actually existed and their relative strengths and weaknesses. With this approach, Aristotle conceived of an empirical (that is, observable and verifiable) science of politics with a practical purpose: statecraft, or how to govern. Aristotle was perhaps the first Westerner to separate the study of politics from that of philosophy.[4]

Aristotle's early approach did not immediately lead to any systematic study of politics. For the next 1,800 years, discussions of politics remained embedded in the realm of philosophy, with the emphasis placed on how politics should be rather than on how politics was actually conducted. Ideals, rather than conclusions drawn from evidence, were the norm. Only with the works of the Italian Niccolò Machiavelli (1469–1527) did a comparative approach to politics truly emerge. Like Aristotle, he sought to analyze different political systems—those that existed around him as well as those that had preceded him, such as the Roman Empire—and even tried to make generalizations about success and failure. These findings, he believed, could then be applied by statesmen to avoid their predecessors' mistakes. Machiavelli's work reflects this pragmatism, dealing with the mechanics of government, diplomacy, military strategy, and power.[5]

Because of his emphasis on statecraft and empirical knowledge, Machiavelli is often cited as the first modern political scientist, paving the way for other scholars. His writings came at a time when the medieval order was giving way to the Renaissance, with its emphasis on science, rationalism, secularism, and real-world knowledge over abstract ideals. The resulting work over the next four centuries reinforced the idea that politics, like any other area of knowledge, could be developed as a logical, rigorous, and predictable science.

During those centuries, a number of major thinkers took up the comparative approach to the study of politics, which slowly retreated from moral, philosophical, or religious foundations. In the late sixteenth and early seventeenth centuries, authors like Thomas Hobbes and John Locke followed in Machiavelli's footsteps, advocating particular political systems on the basis of empirical observation and analysis. They were followed in the eighteenth century by such scholars as Jean-Jacques Rousseau and Baron de Montesquieu, whose studies of the separation of power and civil liberties would directly influence the writing of the American Constitution and others to follow. The work of Karl Marx and Max Weber in the nineteenth and early twentieth centuries would further add to political science, with analyses of the nature of political and economic organization and power. All these developments reflected widespread changes in scholarly inquiry and often blended political ideals with analytical concepts and some attempt at a systematic method of study.

Thus, by the turn of the twentieth century, political science formally existed as a field of study, but it still looked much different from the way it does now. The study of comparative politics, while less focused on ideals or philosophy, resembled a kind of political journalism: largely descriptive, atheoretical, and concentrated on Europe, which still dominated world politics through its empires. There was little in this work that resembled a comparative method.

The two world wars and the rise of the Cold War would mark a turning point in political science and comparative politics, particularly in the United States. There were several reasons for this. First, there was a growing move among universities toward applying more rigorous methods to studying human behavior, whether in sociology, economics, or politics. Second, the world wars raised serious questions about the ability of scholars to meaningfully contribute to an understanding of world affairs. The creation of new countries, the rise of fascism, and the failure of democracy throughout much of interwar Europe were vital concerns, but political scholarship did not seem to shed enough light on these issues and what they meant for international stability. Third, the Cold War with a rival Soviet Union, armed with nuclear weapons and revolutionary ideology, made understanding comparative politics seem a matter of survival. Finally, the postwar period ushered in a wave of technological innovation, such as early computers. This generated a widespread belief that through technological innovation many social problems could be recast as technical concerns, finally to be resolved through science. The fear of another war was thus married with a belief that science was an unmitigated good that had the answers to almost all problems. The question was how to make the science work.

Although these changes dramatically transformed the study of politics, the field itself remained a largely conservative discipline, taking capitalism and democracy as the ideal. In comparative politics these views were codified in what was known as **modernization theory**, which held that as societies developed they would become capitalist democracies, converging around a set of shared values and characteristics. The United States and other Western countries were furthest ahead on this path, and the theory assumed that all countries would eventually catch up unless "diverted" by alternative systems such as communism (as fascism had done in past).

During the 1950s and 1960s, comparativists influenced by modernization theory expanded their research to include more cases. Field research, supported by government and private grants, became the normal means by which political scientists gathered data. New computer technologies combined with statistical methods were also applied to this expanding wealth of data. Finally, the subject of investigation shifted away from political institutions (such as legislatures and constitutions) and toward individual political behavior. This trend came to be known as the **behavioral revolution.** Behavioralism hoped to generate theories and generalizations that could help explain and even predict political activity. Ideally, this work would eventually lead to a "grand theory" of political behavior and modernization that would be valid across countries.

Behavioralism and modernization theory were two different things—modernization theory was a set of hypotheses about how countries develop, and behavioralism was a set of methods with which to approach politics. However, both were attempts to study politics more scientifically to achieve certain policy outcomes.[6] Behavioralism also promoted deductive, large-scale research over the single-case study common in inductive reasoning. It seemed clear to many that political science, and comparative politics within it, would soon be a "real" science.

By the late 1970s, however, this enthusiasm began to meet with resistance. New theories and sophisticated methods of analysis increased scholars' knowledge about politics around the world, but this knowledge in itself did not lead to the expected breakthroughs. The theories that had been developed, such as modernization theory, increasingly failed to match politics on the ground; instead of becoming more

Major Thinkers in Comparative Politics

Aristotle (384–322 B.C.E.)	First separated the study of politics from that of philosophy; used comparative method to study Greek city-states; in *The Politics*, conceived of an empirical study of politics with a practical purpose.
Niccolò Machiavelli (1469–1527)	Often cited as first modern political scientist because of his emphasis on statecraft and empirical knowledge; analyzed different political systems, believing the findings could be applied by statesmen; discussed his theories in *The Prince*.
Thomas Hobbes (1588–1679)	Developed the notion of a "social contract," whereby people surrender certain liberties in favor of order; advocated a powerful state in *Leviathan*.
John Locke (1632–1704)	Argued that private property is essential to individual freedom and prosperity; advocated a weak state in *Two Treatises of Government*.
Charles Louis de Secondat, Baron de Montesquieu (1689–1755)	Studied government systems; advocated the separation of powers within government in *The Spirit of Laws*.
Jean-Jacques Rousseau (1712–1778)	Argued that citizens' rights are inalienable and cannot be taken away by the state; influenced the development of civil rights; discussed these ideas in *The Social Contract*.
Karl Marx (1818–1883)	Elaborated a theory of economic development and inequality in *Das Kapital*; predicted the eventual collapse of capitalism and democracy.
Max Weber (1864–1920)	Wrote widely on such topics as bureaucracy, forms of authority, and the impact of culture on economic and political development; developed many of these themes in *Economy and Society*.

capitalist and more democratic, many newly independent countries collapsed in the face of violent conflict and revolution, to be replaced by authoritarianism that in no way reflected Western expectations or ideals. What had gone wrong?

Some critics charged that the behavioral revolution's obsession with appearing scientific had led the discipline astray by emphasizing methodology over knowledge and technical jargon over clarity. Others criticized the field for its ideological bias, arguing that comparativists were interested not in understanding the world but in prescribing the Western model of modernization. At worst, their work could be viewed as simply serving the foreign policy interests of the United States. Since that time, comparative politics, like all of political science, has grown increasingly fragmented. While few still believe in the old descriptive approach that dominated the earlier part of the century, there is no consensus about where scholarship is going and what research methods or analytical concepts are most fruitful. This lack of consensus has led to several main divisions and lines of conflict.

One area of conflict is over methodology—how best to gather and analyze data. We have already spoken about the problems of comparative methodology, involving selecting cases and controlling variables. Within these concerns there are also questions of how one gathers and interprets the data to compare these cases and measure these variables. Some comparative political scientists rely on **qualitative** evidence and methodology, such as interviews, observations, and archival and other forms of documentary research. Qualitative approaches are often narrowly-focused, deep investigations of one or a few cases drawing from scholarly expertise. However, some qualitative studies (such as work on modernization or revolution) do involve numerous cases spread out across the globe and spanning centuries. Either way, qualitative approaches are typically inductive, beginning with case studies in order to generate theory.

For some political scientists, a qualitative approach is of dubious value. Variables are not rigorously defined or measured, they argue, and hypotheses not tested through the use of a large sample of cases. Asserting that qualitative work fails to

IN FOCUS

Trends in Comparative Politics

TRADITIONAL APPROACH	Emphasis on describing political systems and their various institutions.
BEHAVIORAL REVOLUTION	The shift from a descriptive study of politics to one that emphasizes causality, explanation, and prediction; places greater emphasis on the political behavior of individuals than on larger political structures and on quantitative than on qualitative methodology; modernization theory predominant.

contribute to the accumulation of knowledge and is little better than the approach that dominated the field a century ago, these critics advocate **quantitative** methods instead. They favor a wider use of cases unbound by area specialization, greater use of statistical analysis, and mathematical models often drawn from economics. This quantitative methodology is more likely to use deductive reasoning, starting with a theory that can be tested with an array of data. Many advocates of qualitative research question whether quantitative approaches measure and test variables that are of any particular value, or simply focus on the (often mundane) things that can be expressed in numerical form.

A second, related debate concerns the theoretical assumptions of human behavior. Are human beings rational, in the sense that their behavior conforms to some generally understandable behavior? Some say yes. These scholars use what is known as **rational choice** or **game theory** to study the rules and games by which politics is played and how human beings act on their preferences (like voting, choosing a party, or supporting a revolution). Such models can, ideally, lead not only to explanation but also to prediction—a basic element of science. As you might guess, rational choice theory is closely associated with quantitative methods. And as with the critics of quantitative methods in general, those who reject rational choice theory assert that the emphasis on individual rationality discounts the importance of things like historical complexity, unintended outcomes, or cultural factors. In fact, some consider rational choice theories, as they do behavioralism, to be culturally American assumptions about self-interest, markets, and individual autonomy that do not easily describe the world.

As these debates have persisted, the world around us has continued to change. The Cold War came to an end, something that few scholars, regardless of methodology

---

IN FOCUS

Quantitative Method vs. Qualitative Method

QUANTITATIVE METHOD	Gathering of statistical data across many countries to look for correlations and test hypotheses about cause and effect. Emphasis on breadth over depth.
QUALITATIVE METHOD	Mastery of a few cases through the detailed study of their history, language, and culture. Emphasis on depth over breadth.

or theoretical focus, anticipated or even considered. Religion has reemerged as an important component in politics around the globe—a force that modernization theory (and research focused on Europe) told us was on the wane. New economic powers have emerged in Asia, coinciding with democracy in some cases but not in others. Terrorism has resurfaced, and many regimes have been swept away in the Middle East. It seems that many political scientists, whatever their persuasion, have had little to contribute to many of these issues—time and again, scholars have been caught off guard.

Where does this leave us now? In recent years there have been some signs of conciliation. Scholars recognize that careful (and sloppy) scholarship and theorizing is possible with both qualitative and quantitative methods. Inductive or deductive reasoning can generate valuable theories in comparative politics. Rational choice and historical or cultural approaches can contribute to and be integrated into each other. One finds more mixed-method approaches that use both quantitative and qualitative research. As a result, some scholars have spoken optimistically of an integration of mathematics, "narrative" (case studies), and rational choice models, each contributing to the other. For example, large-scale quantitative studies of political activity can be further elucidated by turning to individual cases that investigate the question in greater detail.[7] Other scholars go even further, albeit in a somewhat different direction, suggesting that political science will be transformed by the integration of new findings in biology and neuroscience, making many of the above debates irrelevant.

For now, at least, the evolution away from models that describe politics and toward those that analyze it and compare its role in different countries—inductively, deductively, qualitatively, and quantitatively—is hard to see. Despite hopeful changes, half of the articles in American comparative politics journals remain primarily descriptive and focused on a single country.[8] We still have a long way to go from questions that describe *what* politics is like to more provocative questions that ask *why* it is the way it is.

A final observation is in order as we bring this discussion to a close. Irrespective of methodology or theory, many have observed that political science as a whole has lost touch with real-world concerns, become inaccessible to laypersons, and failed to speak to those who make decisions about policy—whether voters or elected leaders. In the past few years there has been an increasing emphasis on reconnecting political science to central policy questions and also on reengaging political ideals, something largely discarded over time as "unscientific."

This new emphasis is not a call for comparativists' research to be biased in favor of a particular ideal; rather, comparative politics should not simply be about what we can study or what we want to study but also about how our research can reach people, empower them, and help them be better citizens and leaders. After decades of asserting that political science should have an objective and scientifically neutral approach, this call for greater relevance and contribution to the ideals of civic life represents a change for many scholars, but relevance and rigor are not at odds. They are in fact central to a meaningful political science and comparative politics.

A Guiding Concept: Political Institutions

A goal of this textbook is to provide a way to compare and analyze politics around the world in the aftermath of recent changes and uncertainties. Given the long-standing debates within comparative politics, how can we organize our ideas and information? One way is through a guiding concept, a way of looking at the world that highlights some important features while deemphasizing others. There is certainly no one right way of doing this; any guide, like a lens, will sharpen some features while distorting others. With that said, our guiding concept is institutions, which were defined at the beginning of this chapter as organizations or patterns of activity that are self-perpetuating and valued for their own sake. In other words, an institution is something so embedded in people's lives as a norm or value that it is not easily dislodged or changed. People see an institution as central to their lives, and, as a result, the institution commands and generates legitimacy. Institutions embody the rules, norms, and values that give meaning to human activity.

Consider an example from outside politics. We often hear in the United States that baseball is an American institution. What exactly does this mean? In short, Americans view baseball not simply as a game but as something valued for its own sake, a game that helps define society. Yet few Americans would say that soccer is a national institution. The reason is probably clear: soccer is not perceived as indispensable the way that baseball is. Whereas soccer is simply a game, baseball is part of what defines America and Americans. Even Americans who don't like baseball would probably say that America wouldn't be the same without it. Indeed, even at the local level, teams command such legitimacy that when they merely threaten to move to another city their fans raise a hue and cry. The Brooklyn Dodgers moved to Los Angeles in 1958, yet many in New York still consider them "their" team half a century later. For many Canadians, while baseball is important, hockey is a national institution, thought of as "Canada's Game" and an inextricable part of Canadian identity and history. In Europe and much of the world, soccer reigns as a premier social institution, and teams provoke such fervent loyalty that fan violence is quite common. As a result of their legitimacy and apparent indispensability, institutions command authority and can influence human behavior; we accept and conform to institutions and support rather than challenge them. Woe betide the American, Canadian, or European who derides the national sport!

Another example is directly connected to politics. In many countries, democracy is an institution: it is not merely a means to compete over political power but a vital element in people's lives, bound up in the very way they define themselves. Democracy is part and parcel of collective identity, and some democratic countries and their people would not be the same without it. Even if they are cynical about democracy in practice, citizens of democracies will defend the institution when it is under threat and even die for it. In many other countries, this is not the case: democracy is absent, poorly understood, or weakly institutionalized and unstable. People in such countries do not define themselves by democracy's presence or absence, and so democracy's future there is more insecure. However, these same people might owe a similar allegiance to a different set of institutions, such as their ethnic group or religion. Clearly, there is no single, uniform set of institutions that holds power over people all around the world, and understanding the differences among institutions is central to the study of comparative politics.

What about a physical object or place? Can that, too, be an institution? Many would argue that the World Trade Center was an American institution—not just a set of office buildings but structures representing American values. The same thing can be said about the Pentagon. When terrorists attacked these buildings on September 11, 2001, they did so not simply to cause a great loss of life but also to show that their hostility was directed against America itself—its institutions, as they shape and represent the American way of life, and its relation to the outside world. Like the World Trade Center and the Pentagon, the city of Jerusalem is a powerful cultural and national institution, in this case reflecting the identity and ideals of two peoples, the Israelis and Palestinians. Both groups claim it as their capital, and for both the city holds a key historical, political, and religious significance.

The examples above raise the distinction between formal and informal institutions. When we think of **formal institutions**, we assume that they are based on officially sanctioned rules that are relatively clear. But there are also **informal institutions**—unwritten and unofficial rules, but no less powerful as a result. And of course, institutions can be a combination of both.

Because institutions are embedded in each of us, in how we see the world and what we think is valuable and important, it is difficult to change or eliminate them. When institutions are threatened, people will rush to their defense and even re-create them when they are shattered. This bond is the glue of society. However, one problem that institutions pose is this very "stickiness," in that people may come to resist even necessary change because they have difficulty accepting the idea that certain institutions have outlived their value. Thus, while institutions can and do change, they are by nature perseverant.

Politics is full of institutions. The basic political structures of any country are composed of institutions: the army, the police, the legislature, and the courts, to name a few. We obey them not only because we think it is in our self-interest to do so but also because we see them as legitimate ways to conduct politics. Taxation is a good example. In many Western democracies, income taxes are an institution; we may not like them, but we pay them nonetheless. Is this because we are afraid of going to jail if we fail to do so? Perhaps. But research indicates that a major source of tax compliance is people's belief that taxation is a legitimate way to fund the programs that society needs. We pay, in other words, when we believe that it is the right thing to do, a norm. By contrast, in societies where taxes are not institutionalized, tax evasion tends to be rampant; people view taxes as illegitimate and those who pay as suckers. Similarly, where electoral politics is weakly institutionalized, people support elections only when their preferred candidate wins, and they cry foul or riot when the opposition gains power.

Institutions are a useful way to approach the study of politics because they set the stage for political behavior. Because institutions generate norms and values, they favor and allow certain kinds of political activity and not others, making a more likely "path" for political activity (what is known as path dependence). As a result, political institutions are critical because they influence politics, and how

IN FOCUS

Institutions

- Are organizations or patterns of activity that are self-perpetuating and valued for their own sake.

- Embody norms or values that are considered central to people's lives and thus not easily dislodged or changed.

- Set the stage for political behavior by influencing how politics is conducted.

- Vary from country to country.

- Are exemplified by the army, taxation, elections, and the state.

political institutions are constructed, intentionally or unintentionally, will have a profound effect on how politics is conducted.

In many ways, our institutional approach takes us back to the study of comparative politics as it existed before the 1950s. Prior to the behavioral revolution, political scientists spent much of their time documenting the institutions of politics, often without asking how those institutions actually shaped politics. The behavioral revolution that followed emphasized cause and effect but turned its attention toward political actors and their calculations, resources, or strategies. The actual institutions were seen as less important. The return to the study of institutions in many ways combines these two traditions. From behavioralism, institutional approaches take their emphasis on cause-and-effect relationships, something that will be prevalent throughout this book. However, institutions are not simply the product of individual political behavior; they powerfully affect how politics functions. In other words, institutions are not merely the result of politics; they can also be an important cause.

As recent events have shown us, there is still a tremendous amount of institutional variation around the world that needs to be recognized and understood. This textbook will map some of the basic institutional differences between countries, acknowledging the diversity of institutions while pointing to some features that allow us to compare and evaluate them. By studying political institutions, we can hope to gain a better sense of the political landscape across countries.

A Guiding Ideal: Reconciling Freedom and Equality

At the start of this chapter, we spoke about analytical concepts (such as institutions), methods (such as inductive or deductive, quantitative or qualitative), and political ideals. Politics was defined as the struggle for power people engage in to make decisions for society. The concept of institutions gives us a way to organize our study by investigating the different ways that struggle can be shaped. Yet this raises an important question: People may struggle for political power, but what are they fighting for? What is it they seek to achieve once they have gained power? This is where ideals come in, and we will concentrate on one core debate that lies at the heart of all politics: the struggle between freedom and equality. This struggle has existed as long as human beings have lived in organized communities, and it may be that these are more than ideals—they are a part of our evolutionary history as we transitioned from small, nomadic bands to larger, settled communities.

Politics is bound up in the struggle between individual freedom and collective equality and in how these ideals are to be reconciled. Since "freedom" and "equality" can mean different things to different people, it is important to define each term. When we speak of **freedom**, we are talking about an individual's ability to act independently, without fear of restriction or punishment by the state or other individuals or groups in society. At a basic level it connotes autonomy; in the modern world it encompasses such concepts as free speech, free assembly, freedom of religion, and other civil liberties. **Equality** refers to a material standard of living shared by individuals within a community, society, or country. The relation between equality and freedom is typically viewed in terms of justice or injustice—a measurement of whether our ideals have been met.

Freedom and equality are tightly interconnected, and the relation between the two shapes politics, power, and debates over justice. What is unclear, however, is whether one must come at the expense of the other. Greater personal freedom, for example, may imply a smaller role for the state and limits on its powers to do such things as redistribute income through welfare and taxes. As a result, inequality may increase as individual freedom trumps the desire for greater collective equality. This growing inequality can in turn undermine freedom if too many people feel as though the political system no longer cares about their material needs. Even if this discontent is not a danger, there remains the question of whether society as a whole has an obligation to help the poor—an issue of justice. The United States, as we shall see, has one of the highest degrees of both personal freedom and economic inequality in the world. Should this be a cause of concern? Is it right?

Alternatively, a focus on equality may erode freedom. Demands for greater material equality may lead a government to take greater control of private property and personal wealth, all in the name of redistribution for the "greater good." Yet when economic and political powers are concentrated in one place, individual freedom may be threatened since people control fewer private resources of their own. In the Soviet Union, under communism, for example, all economic power was held by the state, giving it the ability to control people's lives—where they lived, the education they received, the jobs they held, the money they earned. Levels of inequality were in turn quite low.

Is the balance between freedom and equality a zero-sum game, in which the gain of one represents the loss of the other? Not necessarily. Some would assert that freedom and equality can also reinforce each other, with material security helping to secure certain political rights, and vice versa. In addition, while a high degree of state power may weaken individual freedom, the state also plays an important role in helping to define individual freedom and protect it from infringement by other individuals. Finally, the meaning of freedom and equality may change over time, as the material world and our values change. For some, managing freedom or equality necessitates centralized political power. Others view such power as the very impediment to freedom or equality. We will look at these debates more closely when we consider political ideologies in subsequent chapters.

In short, politics is driven by the ideal of reconciling individual freedom and collective equality. This inevitably leads to questions of power and of the people's role in political life. How much should any individual or group be allowed to influence others or impose their will on them? Who should be empowered to make decisions about freedom and equality? Should power be centralized or decentralized, public or private? When does power become a danger to others, and how can we manage this threat? Each political system must address these questions and in so doing determine where political power shall reside, and how much shall be given to whom. Each political system creates a unique set of institutions to structure political power, shaping the role that the people play in politics.

In Sum: Looking Ahead and Thinking Carefully

Politics is the pursuit of power in any organization, and comparative politics is the study of this struggle around the world. Over the past centuries, the study of politics has evolved from philosophy to a field that emphasizes empirical research and the quest to explain politics and even predict political change. This approach has limitations: in spite of the earlier desire to emulate the natural sciences, comparative politics, like political science as a whole, has not been able to generate any grand or even smaller theories of political behavior. Yet the need to study politics remains as important as ever; dramatic changes over the past quarter century have called on comparativists to shed light on these developments and concerns.

Political institutions can help us organize this task. Since institutions generate norms and values, and different configurations of institutions lead to different forms of political activity, they can help us map the political landscape. Specifically, they can show how political activity attempts to reconcile the competing values of individual freedom and collective equality. All political groups, including countries, must reconcile these two forces, determining where power should reside.

In the chapters to come, we will return to this question of freedom and equality and to the way in which these values influence, and are influenced by, institutions.

A final thought before we conclude on how to use all this information. Much of our discussion in this chapter has been about the controversies over how best to study politics—What method? What concepts? What role for ideals? In all of this it may seem that we have gained little understanding of how to "do" political science well. If scholars can't agree on the best way to analyze politics, what hope do we have of making sense of the world? The work by the political scientist and psychologist Philip Tetlock provides some insight. Tetlock conducted a long-term survey of a number of scholars and policy makers, asking them to forecast the likelihood of specific world events (such as a revolution in a particular country or a war between rivals). He also conducted psychological surveys of those same individuals, hypothesizing that certain personal characteristics, rather than ideological or methodological differences, would be most strongly correlated with the ability to predict political events. The result? Tetlock divides his subjects into two basic categories, borrowed from the late philosopher Isaiah Berlin: hedgehogs and foxes. Hedgehogs know one big thing; they tend to look for a single overarching explanation that can explain many different political events and are more likely to reject information that runs counter to their beliefs. Foxes are less confident in their views, which consist of many small ideas cobbled together and subject to frequent revision. As you might suspect, hedgehogs are much worse predictors of world events and are more interested into trying to fit the world into their preconceptions than revise their beliefs on the basis of new information.[9]

We would do well to consider these findings. The most fruitful approach to comparative politics is to be skeptical not simply of others—that's the easy part— but also of what we believe and take for granted. We should be ready to reconsider our beliefs in the face of new evidence and arguments and to remember that every explanation in this book is conjecture, subject to revision if we can find new or contradictory evidence. With this approach, by the end of this course you will be able to draw your own conclusions about the contours of politics and what combination of values might construct a better political order.

So, drop your assumptions about how the world works, and let's begin.

For Further Reading

Aristotle, *The Politics*. T. A. Sinclair, trans. (New York: Viking, 1992).

RS> Bartels, Larry M. "Some Unfulfilled Promises of Quantitative Imperialism." *Rethinking Social Inquiry: Diverse Tools, Shared Standards*, Second Edition. Henry Brady, David Collier, eds. (Lanham, MD: Rowman & Littlefield Publishers, 2010).

Bueno de Mesquita, Bruce. *The Predictioneer's Game* (New York: Random House, 2009).

Katznelson, Ira and Helen V. Milner, eds. *Political Science: The State of the Discipline* (New York: Norton, 2002).

RS> King, Gary, Robert O. Keohane, and Sidney Verba. *Designing Social Inquiry: Scientific Inference in Qualitative Research* (Princeton, NJ: Princeton University Press, 1994).

RS> Lichbach, Mark I. and Alan S. Zuckerman, eds. *Comparative Politics: Rationality, Culture, and Structure* (New York: Cambridge University Press, 1997).

Machiavelli, Niccolò. *The Prince*. W. K. Marriott, trans. (New York: Knopf, 1992).

RS> Rogowski, Ronald. "How Inference in the Social (But Not the Physical) Sciences Neglects Theoretical Anomaly." *Rethinking Social Inquiry: Diverse Tools, Shared Standards*, Second Edition. Henry Brady, David Collier, eds. (Lanham, MD: Rowman & Littlefield Publishers, 2010).

Tetlock, Philip. *Expert Political Judgment* (Princeton, NJ: Princeton University Press, 2005).

 Visit StudySpace for quizzes and other review material.
www.norton.com/studyspace

- **Vocabulary Flashcards of All Key Terms**
- **Chapter Review Quizzes**
- **Complete Study Reviews and Outlines**

RS >
Reader Selection

Highlighted selections are included in *Essential Readings in Comparative Politics*, Fourth Edition.

2

FEDERALISM is a process of building confidence for the Iraqi citizen entity.

One way in which states are defined is by their distribution of power. Following the U.S. invasion in 2003, Iraq introduced federalism as a way to overcome significant ethnic, national, and religious differences.

STATES

KEY CONCEPTS

- The state, a central institution in comparative politics, is a means of centralizing violence over a territory.

- Regimes guide states by serving as the fundamental rules and norms of politics.

- Government is the leadership in charge of running the state.

- Political legitimacy can take several forms: charismatic, traditional, and rational-legal.

- States can vary in autonomy and capacity, and this can shape their power at home and abroad.

We begin our study of the basic institutions of politics by looking at the state. This discussion is often difficult for North Americans, who are not used to thinking about politics in terms of centralized political power. Indeed, for Americans the word *state* typically conjures up the idea of local, not centralized, politics. But for most people around the world, *state* refers to centralized authority, the locus of power.[1] In this chapter, we will break down the basic institutions that make up states and discuss how states manage freedom and equality and distribute power toward achieving their authority. The chapter will define what states are and what they comprise, distinguishing a state from a government and a regime.

We will also consider their origins. For most of human history, politics was built on organizations other than states, and myriad forms of authority existed around the world. Yet now only states remain. What caused them to come into existence?

Once we have discussed the nature and origins of the state, we will look at some different ways in which states can be compared. This discussion will analyze the different forms of legitimacy that give states their power and the varying degrees of this power. Can we speak of states as weak or strong? If so, how would we measure their strength or weakness? To answer this question, we will make a distinction between state capacity and state autonomy and examine how this might differ across cases and policy areas. Here, we consider states as a cause, a force that can shape other institutions. With these ideas more clearly in hand, we will return to our theme of individual freedom and collective equality and consider the future of the state.

Defining the State

What exactly do we mean by *state*? Political scientists, drawing on the work of the German scholar Max Weber, typically define the **state** as the organization that maintains a monopoly of violence over a territory.[2] This definition of what a state is and does may seem severe, but a bit of explanation should help flesh out this concept. One of the most important elements of a state is what we call **sovereignty**, the ability to carry out actions and policies within a territory independent of external actors and internal rivals. In other words, a state needs to be able to act as the primary authority over its territory and the people who live there, passing and enforcing laws, defining and protecting rights, resolving disputes between people and organizations, and generating domestic security.

To achieve this, a state needs power, typically (but not only) physical power. If a state cannot defend its territory from outside actors such as other states, then it runs the risk that those rivals will interfere with its authority, inflicting damage, taking its territory, or destroying the state outright. Similarly, if the state faces powerful opponents within its own territory, such as organized crime or rebel movements, its rules and policies may be undermined. Thus, to secure control, a state must be armed. To protect against international rivals, states need armies. And in response to domestic rivals, states need a police force. In fact, the word *police* comes from an old French word meaning "to govern."

A state is thus a set of institutions that seeks to wield the most force within a territory, establishing order and deterring challengers from inside and out. In so doing, it provides security for its subjects by limiting the danger of external attack and internal crime and disorder—both of which threaten the state and its citizens. In some ways, a state (especially a nondemocratic one) is a kind of protection racket—demanding money in return for security and order, staking out turf, defending those it protects from rivals, settling internal disputes, and punishing those who do not pay.[3]

But most states are far more complex than mere entities that apply force. Unlike criminal rackets, the state is made up of a large number of institutions that are engaged in the process of turning political ideas into policy. Laws and regulations, property rights, health and labor, the environment and transportation are but a few policy areas that typically fall under the responsibility of the state. Because of these responsibilities, the state serves as a set of institutions (ministries, offices, army, police) that society deems necessary to achieve basic goals. When there is a lack of agreement on these goals, the state must attempt to reconcile different views and seek (or impose) consensus.

The public views the state as legitimate, vital, and appropriate. States are thus strongly institutionalized and not easily changed. Leaders and policies may come and go, but the state remains, even in the face of crisis, turmoil, or revolution. Although destruction through war or civil conflict can eliminate states altogether, even this outcome is unusual and states are soon re-created. Thus, the state is defined as a monopoly of force over a given territory, but it is also the set of political institutions that helps create and implement policies and resolve conflict. It is, if you will, the machinery of politics, establishing order and turning politics into policy. Thus, many social scientists argue that the state, as a bundle of institutions, is an important causal variable in economic development, the rise of democracy, and other processes.[4]

Beyond *state*, a few other terms need to be defined. First, we should make a distinction between a state and a **regime**, which is defined as the fundamental rules and norms of politics. More specifically, a regime embodies long-term goals that guide the state with regard to individual freedom and collective equality, where power should reside, and how power should be used. At the most basic level, we can speak of a democratic regime or a nondemocratic one. In a democratic regime, the rules and norms of

---

IN FOCUS — The State Is . . .

- The monopoly of force over a given territory.
- A set of political institutions to generate and carry out policy.
- Typically highly institutionalized.
- Sovereign.
- Characterized by such institutions as an army, police, taxation, a judiciary, and a social welfare system.

politics give the public a large role in governance, as well as certain individual rights and liberties. A nondemocratic regime, in contrast, limits public participation and favors those in power. Both types of regimes can vary in the extent to which power is centralized and in the relationship between freedom and equality. The democratic regime of the United States is not the same as that of Canada; China's nondemocratic regime is not the same as Cuba's or Syria's. Some of these regime differences can be found in basic documents such as constitutions, but often the rules and norms that distinguish one regime from another are informal, unwritten, and implicit, requiring careful study. Finally, we should also note that in some nondemocratic countries where politics is dominated by a single individual, observers may use *regime* to refer to that leader, emphasizing the view that all decisions flow from that one person. As King Louis XIV of France famously put it, *L'état, c'est moi* ("I am the state"). However, the term *regime* is not inherently negative any more than *rules* or *norms*.

Regimes are an important component of the larger state framework. Regimes do not easily or quickly change, although they can be transformed or altered, usually by dramatic social events such as revolutions and national crises. Most revolutions, in fact, can be seen as revolts not against the state or even the leadership but against the current regime—to overthrow the old rules and norms and replace them with new ones. For example, France refers to its current regime as the Fifth Republic. Ever since the French Revolution overthrew the monarchy in 1789, each French republic has been characterized by a separate regime, embodied in the constitution and the broader political rules that shape politics. In another example, South Africa's transition to democracy in the 1990s involved a change of regime as the white-dominated system of apartheid gave way to one that provides democratic rights to all South Africans. The recent uprisings

IN FOCUS — A Regime Is . . .

- Norms and rules regarding individual freedom and collective equality, the locus of power, and the use of that power.

- Institutionalized, but can be changed by dramatic social events such as a revolution.

- Categorized at the most basic level as either democratic or authoritarian.

- Often embodied in a constitution.

in the Middle East sought, and in several cases achieved, the destruction of existing regimes, though it is unclear what forms the new regimes will take.

In summary, if the state is a monopoly of force and a set of political institutions that secure the population and generate policy, then the regime is defined as the norms and rules that establish the proper relation between freedom and equality and the use of power toward that end. If the state is the machinery of politics, like a personal computer, one can think of a regime as its software, the programming that defines its capabilities. Each computer runs differently, and more or less productively, depending on the software installed. Over time software becomes outdated and unstable, and machines crash. However, countries and regimes are not like consumer electronics that we can simply throw away or upgrade. No matter how hard we try to erase old political institutions, many aspects of them tend to persist. This is a particularly big obstacle to reforming or transforming states and regimes; building democracy, reducing corruption, or ameliorating ethnic conflict all involve changing existing, deeply embedded institutions.

Our third term related to the concepts of state and regime is the most familiar one: *government*. **Government** can be defined as the leadership that runs the state. If the state is the machinery of politics, and the regime its programming, then the government operates the machinery. The government may consist of democratically elected legislators, presidents, and prime ministers, or it may be made up of leaders who gained office through force or other nondemocratic means. Whatever their path to power, governments all hold particular ideas regarding freedom and equality, and they all attempt to use the state to realize those ideas. But few governments are able to act with complete autonomy in this regard. Democratic and nondemocratic governments must confront the existing regime that has built up over time. Push too

IN FOCUS   Government Is . . .

- The leadership or elite in charge of running the state.

- Weakly institutionalized.

- Limited by the existing regime.

- Often composed of elected officials, such as a president or prime minister, or unelected officials, such as a monarch.

hard against an existing regime, and resistance, rebellion, or collapse may occur. For example, Mikhail Gorbachev's attempt to transform the Soviet Union's regime in the 1980s contributed to that country's dissolution.

In part because of the power of regimes, governments tend to be weakly institutionalized—that is, the public does not typically view those in power as irreplaceable or believe that the country would collapse without them (Figure 2.1). In democratic regimes, governments are replaced fairly frequently, and even in nondemocratic settings rulers are continuously threatened by rivals and their own mortality. Governments come and go, whereas regimes and states may live on for decades or centuries.

Finally, the term **country** can be taken as shorthand for the combined political entities defined so far—state, regime, government—as well as for the people who live within that political system. We will often speak about various countries in this textbook, and when we do, we are referring to the entire political entity and its citizens.

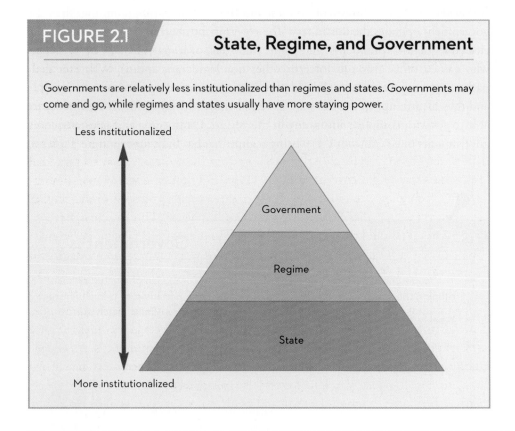

FIGURE 2.1 **State, Regime, and Government**

Governments are relatively less institutionalized than regimes and states. Governments may come and go, while regimes and states usually have more staying power.

Less institutionalized

Government

Regime

State

More institutionalized

The Origins of Political Organization

So far we have noted that modern politics is defined by states, which monopolize force and generate and realize policy. This political machinery is directed by a particular regime and by the government in power. Governments generate short-term goals regarding freedom and equality, which are in part based on an existing regime that provides an institutionalized set of political norms and values. This combination, linking state, regime, and government, is relatively new in human history, though, to be clear, as long as there have been human beings (around 200,000 years) there has been some form of human organization. In our earliest stages, we were likely organized by families and tribes. Genetic research suggests that the modern human population outside Africa derives largely from a group of a few hundred individuals who rapidly migrated outward less than 100,000 years ago, displacing other archaic human populations around the world as they went. Groups descended from this relatively small band also traveled by sea (at least 60,000 years ago, and perhaps much earlier). These developments suggest organization, some technological sophistication, and the ability to pass knowledge from generation to generation.

By 8000 B.C.E., agriculture, animal domestication, and sedentary communities emerged in the Middle East, allowing for more complex political systems to form; from about 4000 B.C.E., if not earlier, cities of several thousand people emerged. Technological sophistication led to specialization, consumer goods, and trade; agricultural surplus helped increase population density; and from these developments came issues of inequality and personal freedom. Those with economic surpluses sought to protect their riches from theft. Those without surpluses sought a greater share of the group's resources. And both feared attack by outside groups or internal competitors that might covet their lands, crops, and homes. It was human innovations like technology, trade, and agriculture that probably first led to the conflict between the individual and the collective. Who gets what? Who has the right to do what? And how should these decisions be made and enforced? Having to reconcile freedom and equality in turn raises questions about where power should reside and toward what end. Alongside the city, the state emerged to answer these questions.

There are several things in this account that remain unclear. What was the sequence of urbanization and state building? Our discussion above suggests that communities formed, settled, and then built political institutions, but we could also imagine early forms of political leadership that helped establish sedentary communities. An endogenous explanation—that both were institutionalized simultaneously—may make the most sense. Further questions concern the role of centralization, consensus, and coercion. Did loose communities form and slowly centralize because of the economic opportunities this provided? Did communities perhaps develop for primarily defensive reasons? Were these systems constructed through consensus or coercion?

In the absence of evidence, philosophers have long debated these questions. Some, like the philosopher Thomas Hobbes, believed that human beings voluntarily submitted to political authority to overcome anarchy, which ensures neither freedom nor equality. In return for giving up many of their rights, people gained security and a foundation upon which to build a civilization. In contrast, Jean-Jacques Rousseau believed that human beings were in essence "noble savages" who were instinctively compassionate and egalitarian. It was civilization and the rise of the state that corrupted them by institutionalizing a system of inequality. These competing visions provide different interpretations of civilization and political organization, but both emphasize that sovereignty emerged through a "social contract" between rulers and ruled.

For a long time, scholars have debated whether Rousseau or Hobbes provided a more accurate view of early state development. Recent research, however, indicates that neither was correct. Many scholars assumed that humans lived relatively solitary lives—what one calls "primordial individualism"—before modern forms of political organization took hold, but we now know that family and tribal organization has a much older past. In addition, while warfare was possibly a driver of political organization, it may have broken out less between individuals, as was often assumed, than between rival groups. As human populations expanded, tribes battled one another for resources and territory. Pre-state societies were probably much more violent than states are now. By some estimates, anywhere from a quarter to over half of the male population died at the hands of others, and the expansion of pre-state societies coincided with the extermination of many large species around the world that were apparently hunted to extinction. The widespread taking of life appears to have begun with the emergence of modern humans, long before the rise of the state.

States, then, appear to have emerged out of this history of violence. As one group conquered others, political organizations brought new peoples and territories under control. Such organizations also allowed for more effective defense, especially in urbanized communities that could build city walls and stockpile weapons. In short, where the inherent conflict between people intersected with agricultural technology, population density, and urbanization, state building followed. Whereas we once speculated that technological innovation, civilization, and human political organization were the sources of violence, the opposite now appears to be true.[5]

Complex organizations began to emerge about 8,000 years ago in the Middle East, bearing the hallmarks of politics that exist to this day, such as taxation, bureaucracy, laws, military force, and leadership. Some of these political units were relatively small, such as the city-states that emerged in ancient Greece some 2,700 years ago. In other cases, large and highly sophisticated empires emerged, as in

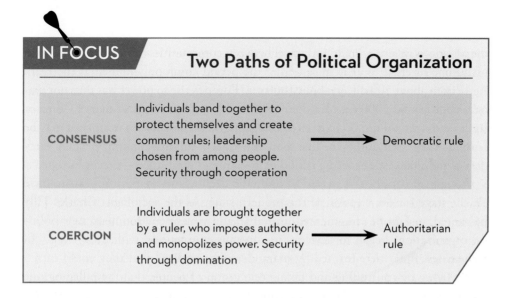

Two Paths of Political Organization

CONSENSUS — Individuals band together to protect themselves and create common rules; leadership chosen from among people. Security through cooperation → Democratic rule

COERCION — Individuals are brought together by a ruler, who imposes authority and monopolizes power. Security through domination → Authoritarian rule

China, South America, the Middle East, and Africa. Across these political systems, economic relations were based on agricultural production, while specialized goods and trade were secondary activities. And unlike modern countries, these early political systems often did not have defined borders.

The Rise of the Modern State

The diversity of early political systems eventually gave way to the modern state, which first took shape in Europe. Why the modern state emerged in Europe and came to dominate the world is uncertain, but it may in part be due to historical chance and the curious advantage of backwardness. Two thousand years ago, Europe, like other parts of the world, was dominated by a single, large empire—in this case, the Roman Empire. Spanning thousands of miles across western Europe, North Africa, and Egypt, the Roman Empire developed a complex political system that tied together millions of people and generated an advanced infrastructure of cities, laws, trade, knowledge, and roads. After a thousand years, however, the Roman Empire eventually declined, succumbing to the pressures of overexpansion and increased attacks by rival forces. In the fifth century C.E., Rome itself was sacked by invaders.

As the Roman Empire collapsed, the complex political institutions and the other benefits that had extended across its territory largely disappeared, particularly in western Europe. The security generated by imperial control evaporated, replaced by roving bands of marauders. Roads and the other basic forms of infrastructure that people depended on eroded. Rules and regulations fragmented and lost their power. The knowledge and technology accumulated under the empire were lost or forgotten, and the advanced system of trade and travel between communities came to an end. Much of Europe reverted to anarchy, entering the period commonly known as the Dark Ages, from about 500 C.E. to about 1000 C.E. Europe's rise to power was thus not pre-ordained; around 1000 C.E., Europe's total wealth was less than half that of China or India, and it would not begin to close this gap until the nineteenth century. It may be hard to believe, but during the first thousand years of this millennium, virtually every part of the globe experienced a period of growth and innovation—except Europe.[6]

Yet, paradoxically, this period of dramatic decline and anarchy appears to have set the stage for the creation of the modern state. As the sociologist Charles Tilly has noted, in Europe's fragmented, unstable, and violent environment, new political organizations began to develop, in constant competition with their rivals.[7] In some cases, these were formed by marauders who realized that they could earn a better living by controlling and taxing one group of people than by pillaging one place and moving on to the next. Warlords staked out small areas of land that they could easily defend and consolidated control over these regions, fighting off rival groups. In other cases, the people banded together to defend themselves. As Tilly and others have concluded, the modern state emerged from and in reaction to what was essentially organized crime: armed groups staking out turf, offering protection, and demanding payment in return. The constant warfare among these numerous rivals, which created a competitive and fluid environment, seems to have generated a kind of rapid organizational evolution. Groups that could quickly adapt in response to new challenges and challengers survived, while less successful groups were conquered and disappeared.

Not only history but also geography has played a role in the rise of the modern state. The physiologist Jared Diamond has argued that Europe's rapid political evolution owed something to the continent's proximity to Asia and the Middle East, which gave it access to new plants, animals, and technological innovations that were unavailable to peoples in the Americas or Africa. China, which also benefited from its ability to import a range of foreign goods and technologies, had by the third century B.C.E. developed one of the most sophisticated political organizations of the time, at least a thousand years before Europe. Why then did China not come to rule the world instead of Europe, and why did "Europe" come to mean a collection of rival states while "China" came to mean a single enormous country? One explanation may involve the centralization of the Chinese empire, which was facilitated by the absence of significant internal geographic boundaries, the related ethnic and cultural homogenization of the population, and the absence of major neighboring political rivals. This led to an early and highly developed state—though its lack of major competitors eventually limited its organizational evolution. In contrast, Europe's weaknesses—ethnic and linguistic fragmentation, numerous rival actors, and geographic boundaries—hindered political centralization. That said, we should not be too deterministic in explaining these outcomes. Across many centuries China faced upheavals and warfare. At numerous points in history this violence could have led to the permanent fragmentation of China into a collection of states similar to Europe—albeit with a thousand-year head start in technology, bureaucracy, and education.[8]

Out of the constant warfare of the European Dark Ages emerged the first modern states, which possessed three important advantages over alternative forms of political organization. First, states encouraged economic development. Before and during the Dark Ages, most Europeans lived under an economic system based on subsistence agriculture. Property such as land tended to be monopolized by those in power rather than owned by those who worked it. Warlords could tie the people to the land (through serfdom) and extract their labor and levy heavy taxes on those who produced nonagricultural goods. However, such economic conditions were counterproductive for society as a whole: individuals had little incentive to produce if the fruits of their labor were simply taken by others. Rulers who created laws, regulations, and infrastructure that permitted and respected private property and individual profit found that production grew, giving the ruler more resources to tax or borrow (and with which to make war). Property rights thus became a hallmark of state development.[9]

Second, states encouraged technological innovation. Some rulers who pursued such innovation to increase their economic and military power recognized that, like private commerce and trade, new technologies would stimulate economic development by providing new goods and services. When technological innovation was harnessed to commerce, economic development grew dramatically. These rulers viewed technological change not as a threat to their power but as a means to expand it. Many of the technologies that made Europe powerful as it set off to conquer the world—gunpowder, advanced mathematics, modern mapmaking, paper, astronomy—originated in other parts of the world. But the Europeans absorbed these innovations and put them to new use. What mattered most was not who made the discoveries but how these discoveries were encouraged or used by the state. Whether this application of innovation was a function primarily of intense European competition or of cultural values is still a source of debate (see Chapter 3).[10] Whatever the reason, technological innovation, combined with state power, set the stage for modern politics.

A third advantage was domestic stability, which increased trade and commerce and permitted the development of infrastructure. Finally, and related to this, people's ability to travel more freely within the territory of their country encouraged interaction and the emergence of a shared identity. The state, through printed documents, education, and legal codes, also contributed to the standardization of language. People in Europe began to see themselves as having a common identity comprised of shared values. Instead of defining themselves primarily by their trade, clan, religion, or town, people began to see themselves as, for example, English, French, or German. Ethnicity proved to be a powerful asset to the state, for it in turn fostered nationalism. This will be discussed in detail in the next chapter.

Although the modern state offered all these advantages, by around 1500 modern states covered only 20 percent of the globe, the rest ruled by alternative forms of centralized organization or none at all. But this was soon to change. Well-organized and armed with advanced technologies, growing national identity, and economic resources, the states of Europe began to rapidly accrue power. As economic power grew, so did the ability of the state to manage ever greater numbers of people and ever more territory. Increased finances and state organization also allowed for the development of major militaries. Able to conquer and control larger pieces of land, states began to defeat and absorb their European rivals. Spiritual rivals also lost political power. The Thirty Years' War (1618–48), in part a struggle between Roman Catholicism and Protestantism, culminated in the Treaty of Westphalia in 1648. Under this treaty, the authority of the pope over Europe's people was radically curtailed. Without this rival spiritual authority, states were free to direct religion within their own territory, subordinating the spiritual to the political. State sovereignty as we understand it today is often dated from the Treaty of Westphalia.

European states now began to expand their economic, technological, and military powers beyond their own shores. During the seventeenth and eighteenth centuries, Spain and Portugal took control of large parts of the Americas, while the Dutch, French, and British expanded state power into Asia. By the nineteenth century, nearly all of Africa had similarly been divided up among European states and incorporated into their respective empires.

The organizational structure of the state was thus imposed around the world by force. Yet as European control receded in the twentieth century, the structure of the state remained—indeed, states grew in number as the lands and peoples subjugated by Europe gained sovereignty. Although peoples all around the world resisted and eventually threw off European domination, they viewed the state as a superior—or at least inevitable—form of political evolution, and they adopted it for their own purposes. The world thus became a world of states. States established international boundaries and rules and were the primary actors in domestic and international politics around the world. Countries like Venezuela or Nigeria threw off colonial rule, but they retained and expanded the state institutions originally imposed by imperialism.

The rapid spread of states may be viewed as the triumph of a form of organization that allowed groups of people to destroy political rivals, no matter how sophisticated. But this has not come without cost. Whereas Europe took several hundred years to create the modern state, much of the world has been forced to take up this form of organization and its institutions more quickly. And the historical paths

Timeline of Political Organization

8TH–7TH CENTURIES B.C.E.	Beginning of Greek city-states; centralization of political power in Europe
6TH–5TH CENTURIES B.C.E.	Establishment of Roman republic; first development of democracy in Athens
5TH–3RD CENTURIES B.C.E.	Unification of China under Qin Dynasty
2ND–1ST CENTURIES B.C.E.	Roman conquest of Greece
1ST–2ND CENTURIES C.E.	Roman Empire expands across Europe and into the Middle East; zenith of centralized imperial power in Europe
3RD–4TH CENTURIES C.E.	Internal decline of Roman Empire; beginning of European Dark Ages; development stagnates
5TH–6TH CENTURIES C.E.	Rome sacked by the Visigoths; widespread strife among competing European warlords
7TH–8TH CENTURIES C.E.	Rise of Islamic Empire from Southern Europe to Central Asia
9TH–10TH CENTURIES C.E.	Viking raids across Europe
11TH–12TH CENTURIES C.E.	European crusades into Middle East; warfare begins to consolidate Europe into distinct political units
12TH–13TH CENTURIES C.E.	Period of rapid innovation and development: mechanical clock invented; paper, compass adopted from Asia and the Middle East
13TH CENTURY C.E.	Rise of Ottoman Empire in Southern Europe, North Africa, and the Middle East
14TH–15TH CENTURIES C.E.	Voyages of exploration and early imperialism; early European states centralize
16TH–17TH CENTURIES C.E.	Scientific revolution; modern states develop; modern identities of nationalism and patriotism develop

of Africa, Asia, and South America were radically different from that of Europe. Many of the new states in these continents have lacked the resources, infrastructure, shared national identities, and capital that much older states developed over a thousand years. Consequently, these newer states often face significant challenges, such as establishing sovereignty over territories where a multitude of peoples, languages, religions, and cultures may coexist—problems that most European states solved only over the course of centuries and at the cost of many lives lost in wars and revolutions.[11] For better or worse, although Europe no longer directly rules over much of the earth, it has left us with the legacy of the state.

Comparing State Power

It is clear from the preceding discussion that political evolution has been a lengthy and somewhat arbitrary process. Where conditions allowed for human beings to settle permanently, complex forms of political organization emerged, with features that reflect the modern struggle over freedom, equality, and the allocation of power. But only over the past few centuries has the modern state taken shape, forging new political, economic, and social institutions that have made it so powerful. States quickly eradicated every other form of political organization and now lay claim to all corners of the earth.

Still, not all states are the same. As we have observed, some states are powerful, effective, prosperous, and stable; others are weak, disorganized, and largely incapable of effective action. Moreover, a single state can have a commanding presence in one area but be ineffectual in another. What explains this range? How do we understand differences in what we might call "stateness"—that is, in the power of states? To answer this question and make effective comparisons, we need a few more conceptual tools with which to work.

Legitimacy

The first concept, **legitimacy**, can be defined as a value whereby something or someone is recognized and accepted as right and proper. A legitimate institution or person, therefore, is widely accepted and recognized by the public. Legitimacy confers authority and power. In the case of states, we know that they wield a great deal of force. But is that the only reason that people recognize their authority? In the absence of legitimacy, states must rely largely on coercion to retain their power. However, where there is legitimacy, people obey the law even when the threat of punishment is slight. We may pay our taxes, stand at the crosswalk, or serve in the military not because we fear punishment or seek immediate reward but because we assume that the state has the authority to ask these things of us. As states provide security and other benefits, they can engender a sense of reciprocal responsibility to the state. Legitimacy thus creates power that relies not on coercion but on consent. Without legitimacy, a state would have to use the continuous threat of force to maintain order—a difficult task—or expect that many of its rules and policies would go unheeded. As one scholar puts it, in the absence of legitimacy "the state can never be anything but a predatory imposition upon many or most citizens."[12]

Legitimacy is therefore a critical component of stateness. Legitimacy, however, does not depend on freedom or equality; a society may be largely unfree or unequal and still view its state as legitimate, no matter how difficult we might imagine that to be.

How then does a state become legitimate? Let us turn again to Max Weber, who argued that political legitimacy comes in three basic forms: traditional, charismatic, and rational-legal.[13] Traditional legitimacy rests on the idea that someone or something is valid because "it has always been that way." In other words, this legitimacy is built on the idea that certain aspects of politics are to be accepted because they have been built over a long period of time. They are viewed as part of the historical identity of the people themselves. **Traditional legitimacy** often embodies historical myths and legends as well as the continuity between past and present. Rituals and ceremonies all help to reinforce traditional legitimacy by providing actions and symbols that are ancient, unique, and dramatic. A long-standing monarchy, where one family retains power over generations, is a good example of a traditionally legitimate institution. However, traditional is not the same as outdated. Even a modern institution, like an elected office or a regime, can develop traditional legitimacy if it is in place long enough. In short, traditional legitimacy is built on history and continuity. Its legitimacy comes in part from the simple fact that it has the weight of history on its side. Change becomes difficult to imagine if an institution has existed "since time immemorial."

Charismatic legitimacy is in many ways the opposite of traditional legitimacy. When we use the word *charisma* in everyday conversation, we often mean someone who is good-looking or charming. But this is a much-reduced version of the term's original meaning, sometimes rendered as "the gift of grace." Instead of relying on the weight of history and the continuity of certain roles or values, charismatic legitimacy is based on the power of ideas or beliefs. Charisma is typically embodied by individuals who can move and persuade the public through ideas and the manner in which they present them. Some individuals possess a certain magnetism that binds who they are to what they say. Jesus and Muhammad are perfect examples of charismatic figures who could gather huge followings through the power of their ideas which they asserted were transmitted to them from God. Although in its origins *charisma* indicated this spiritual link, in modern politics charisma can encompass secular ideas as well. Adolf Hitler was clearly a charismatic figure, who wielded ideas and language to articulate the need for war and genocide.

As you can imagine, charismatic legitimacy is not institutionalized and thus is fairly tenuous, since it commonly dies with the individual who possesses it. But charismatic legitimacy can be transformed into traditional legitimacy through the creation of rituals and values that are meant to capture the spirit and intent of the charismatic leader's power. Religions, monarchies, even constitutions and regimes can be examples of this. Weber called this kind of institutionalization "the routinization of charisma."

In contrast to the first two forms of legitimacy, **rational-legal legitimacy** is based not on history or rituals (traditional legitimacy) or on the force of ideas and those who present them (charismatic legitimacy) but rather on a system of laws and procedures that are presumed to be neutral or rational. Leaders or political officials gain legitimacy through the rules by which they come to office. People abide by the decisions of those in power because those individuals are abiding by existing institutionalized rules. In this case, it is not the individual leaders who are important, or even their values or ideas, but the offices they hold. Once they leave office, they lose much of their authority. This can be contrasted with traditional or charismatic legitimacy, where authority tends to reside with individuals rather than a set of rules.

The world of modern states is built on a rational-legal foundation. States rely on bureaucracies, paperwork, and thousands of individuals to make daily decisions on a wide range of issues. Ideally, the public accepts these decisions as the proper way to get things done, and it presumes that these decisions are reasonably fair and predictable. For example, if there are elections, the people accept the outcome even if their preferred candidate loses, and they obey those who won. The 2000 presidential election in the United States is a perfect example of rational-legal legitimacy. After weeks of bitter disputes over who had won the election, the Supreme Court's intervention effectively ended the battle, and the Democratic candidate, Al Gore, agreed to abide by the outcome. In spite of denunciations by some that the election was illegitimate, the majority of Americans accepted George W. Bush as their president, even if they had not voted for him (and the majority of voters had not). What's more, legitimacy is not confined to political actors within the state; our own individual legitimacy as citizens comes from a rational-legal foundation: our driver's licenses, identification numbers, passports, or voter registration cards all confer a certain form of authority and power—from the state to the citizen.

Although modern states are built on rational-legal legitimacy, traditional and charismatic legitimacy have not disappeared. In almost any country, one can see variations in the mix of traditional, charismatic, and rational-legal legitimacy. Political leaders in many countries throughout modern history have wielded a great deal of charismatic power and have sometimes become the centers of large "cults of per-

Three Types of Legitimacy

TYPE	CHARACTERISTICS	EXAMPLE
TRADITIONAL LEGITIMACY	Built by habit and custom over time, stressing history; strongly institutionalized	Monarch (Queen Elizabeth II)
CHARISMATIC LEGITIMACY	Built on the force of ideas and the presence of the leader; weakly institutionalized	Revolutionary hero (Vladimir Lenin)
RATIONAL-LEGAL LEGITIMACY	Built on rules and procedures and the offices that create and enforce those rules; strongly institutionalized	Elected executive (Barack Obama)

sonality," which we will explore further in Chapter 6. These cults portray the leader as the father (or, occasionally, the mother) of the nation and imbue him or her with almost superhuman powers. Charismatic leadership, and the power that it places in the hands of one individual, can corrupt, as we have seen in the case of Kim Jong-Il and his son, Kim Jong-Un. But some charismatic figures, political leaders like Mohandas K. Gandhi, who fought for independence from British rule in India, or Nelson Mandela, who struggled to end apartheid in South Africa, have dramatically changed the course of politics for the better.

Traditional power can similarly be found in a wide variety of countries. The United Kingdom, Japan, Saudi Arabia, and more than forty other countries still have monarchs. The powers of most, though not all, of these monarchs are now quite limited, yet even constitutional monarchs remain important symbols and attract national and sometimes even international attention. Families can have a similar legitimacy in politics. In India, Indira Gandhi of the Congress Party (no relation to Mohandas) served as prime minister for 15 years, in the 1960s, 1970s, and 1980s. Upon her death, her son Rajiv became prime minister. After his death, his wife, Sonia, became head of Congress. Her son, Rahul, now serves in the legislature and is seen as a possible future prime minister. Not just individuals and families but also rules and regulations can gain a kind of traditional legitimacy if they function for so long that people can't imagine doing things any other way. The U.S. Constitution, for example, is not only a set of rules for conducting politics; it is also considered a sacred symbol of what makes the United States unique and powerful. Is it difficult to modify the Constitution because of the procedures involved, or because a resistance has developed over time to tinkering with this "sacred" document? If the latter is true, then it is not simply rational-legal legitimacy but also traditional legitimacy that binds American politics together.

To summarize, legitimacy is a central component of stateness. Traditional legitimacy stresses ritual and continuity; charismatic legitimacy, the force of ideas as embodied in a leader; rational-legal legitimacy, laws and rules. Whatever its form, legitimacy makes it possible for the state to carry out its basic functions. Without it, states find it very difficult to function. If the public has little faith in the state, it will frequently ignore political responsibilities, such as paying taxes, abiding by regulations, or serving in the armed forces. Under these conditions, the state has only one tool left to maintain order: the threat of force. While we might assume that violent states are somehow inherently powerful, states that use the most coercion against their citizens are often the most weakly institutionalized, for without violence, they cannot get the public to willingly comply with the rules and duties set forth.

Centralization or Decentralization

In addition to enjoying various kinds and levels of political legitimacy, states are defined by different distributions of power. As we noted in Chapter 1, individual freedom is typically associated with the decentralization of power, whereas collective equality usually accompanies a greater centralization of power.

State power can be centralized or decentralized in a couple of different ways, the first of which is the dispersal of power within the state. Under **federalism**, powers such as taxation, lawmaking, and security are devolved to regional bodies (such as states in the United States and India, *Länder* in Germany, and provinces in Canada) and to local legislatures that control specific territories within the country. These powers are defined in the national constitution and therefore not easily constricted or eliminated by any government. Here the argument is that federalism helps represent local interests as well as check the growth of central power (which may be viewed as a threat to democracy). We should note that federalism need not be uniform; some countries, like Spain, Russia, and India, rely on **asymmetric federalism**, whereby power is divided unevenly between regional bodies. Some regions are given greater power over taxation or language rights than others, a more likely outcome in a country with significant ethnic divisions. In **unitary states**, by contrast, political power is concentrated at the national level, and local authority is limited. The central government is responsible for most areas of policy. Territorial divisions in unitary states like China, Japan, and France have less bearing on political power. If federalism reflects a view that overcentralization is unrepresentative or dangerous, the argument for a unitary state is that local interests can be represented without recourse to regional political institutions. Federalism may weaken state efficiency by dispersing power among too many competing authorities, and exacerbate, rather than weaken, ethnic or regional conflict.

In recent years there has been a greater tendency toward decentralization in many states. This process, called **devolution**, has become popular for a number of reasons. In some cases, devolution has been viewed as a way to increase state legitimacy by moving political power closer to the people, a concern as states have grown larger and more complex over time. In other cases, devolution has been seen as a way to resolve problems like ethnic or religious differences by giving greater local powers to regions where they are predominant. This has sometimes meant the elimination of unitary government; in 2005, Iraq became a federal country for the first time in its history; Nepal abolished its monarchy in 2007 and in 2011 finalized a new federal constitution with 14 provinces. Often devolution does not lead to outright federalism but nevertheless results in a significant movement of power downward from the central state. We will speak more about devolution in subsequent chapters.

Power, Autonomy, and Capacity

At the most basic level we can make a distinction between **strong states** and **weak states**. Strong states are those that are able to fulfill basic tasks: defend their territory, make and enforce rules and rights, collect taxes, and manage the economy, to name a few. In contrast, weak states cannot execute such tasks very well. Rules are haphazardly applied, if at all; tax evasion and other forms of public noncompliance are widespread; armed rivals to the state, such as rebel movements, organized crime, or other states, may control large chunks of territory or the economy. State officials themselves, having little faith in their offices or responsibilities, may use their jobs simply to fill their own pockets through corruption and theft. Economic development is certain to be much lower as a result of this unstable political environment. In general, weak states are not well institutionalized and lack authority and legitimacy. At an extreme, the very structures of the state may become so weak that they break down. When this occurs, a country is commonly termed a **failed state** (see Table 2.1).[14] Before 2001 Afghanistan was typically viewed as a failed state, and it remains one today, with only limited power that must be backed up by international force. But a failed state does not necessarily mean complete anarchy. Piracy off the coast of Somalia (considered one of the world's "most failed" states) is seen as a natural outgrowth of state failure, but one study suggests that piracy thrives when state power is weak but not wholly absent, allowing pirates to rely on functioning markets and infrastructure on land. As the authors put it, even criminals need some degree of law and order.[15] States can fail to different degrees, in different areas, and in different ways.

TABLE 2.1

Top Twenty Failed States

FAILED STATE INDEX, 2010

RANK	TOTAL	COUNTRY	MOUNTING DEMOGRAPHIC PRESSURES	REFUGEES	AGGRIEVED COMMUNAL GROUPS
1	113.4	Somalia	9.7	10.0	9.5
2	110.3	Chad	9.2	9.5	9.4
3	108.7	Sudan	8.5	9.6	9.9
4	108.2	Congo (D. R.)	9.7	9.6	8.3
5	108.0	Haiti	10.0	9.2	7.3
6	107.9	Zimbabwe	9.3	8.2	9.0
7	107.5	Afghanistan	9.1	9.3	9.3
8	105.0	Central African Republic	8.9	9.6	8.6
9	104.8	Iraq	8.3	9.0	9.0
10	102.8	Cote d'Ivoire	8.1	8.5	8.7
11	102.5	Guinea	8.2	7.7	7.9
12	102.3	Pakistan	8.8	9.2	9.3
13	100.3	Yemen	8.7	8.4	8.6
14	99.9	Nigeria	8.3	6.0	9.6
15	99.1	Niger	9.8	6.6	7.8
16	98.7	Kenya	8.8	8.5	8.7
17	98.6	Burundi	9.1	8.7	8.2
18	98.3	Guinea Bissau	8.7	7.2	5.4
19	98.3	Myanmar	8.2	8.0	8.7
20	98.2	Ethiopia	9.1	8.2	8.4

Note: Areas are ranked on a 10 point scale, with 10 representing the worst conditions.

Source: Foreign Policy, June 21, 2010, www.foreignpolicy.com/articles/2010/06/21/2010_failed_states_index_interactive_map_and_rankings (accessed 2/10/12).

BRAIN DRAIN	UNEVEN ECONOMIC DEVELOPMENT	POVERTY AND ECONOMIC DECLINE	DELEGITIMIZATION OF THE STATE	DETERIORATION OF PUBLIC SERVICES	VIOLATIONS OF HUMAN RIGHTS AND WEAK RULE OF LAW	UNSTABLE MILITARY SECURITY	FACTIONALIZED ELITES	EXTERNAL INTERVENTION
8.2	8.4	9.3	9.8	9.4	9.7	10.0	9.8	9.7
8.0	8.9	8.5	9.8	9.6	9.3	9.2	9.8	9.1
8.2	9.1	6.4	9.4	9.0	9.7	9.6	9.9	9.5
7.7	9.2	8.7	9.0	8.9	9.2	9.6	8.8	9.5
8.9	8.8	9.2	9.4	10.0	8.0	8.4	8.8	10.0
9.3	9.2	9.0	9.3	9.0	9.2	9.0	9.6	7.8
7.2	8.4	8.0	9.7	8.5	8.8	9.8	9.4	10.0
5.8	8.9	8.1	9.1	9.0	8.6	9.7	9.1	9.6
8.9	9.0	7.0	8.7	8.0	8.6	9.5	9.6	9.3
7.9	8.0	7.7	9.5	8.4	8.6	8.6	9.1	9.7
8.3	8.4	8.6	9.4	8.7	9.2	9.3	9.2	7.6
7.5	8.5	6.6	8.6	7.3	8.7	9.4	9.1	9.3
6.9	8.3	7.7	8.6	8.7	7.7	9.3	9.3	8.2
7.7	9.0	7.3	9.0	9.0	8.6	9.1	9.5	6.9
6.2	7.9	8.9	8.9	9.5	8.2	8.0	8.6	8.7
7.6	8.5	7.0	8.9	7.8	7.7	7.9	8.8	8.5
6.2	8.1	8.5	8.2	8.8	8.0	7.7	8.2	9.0
7.4	8.1	8.7	9.2	8.4	7.8	9.3	9.2	8.8
6.0	9.0	7.9	9.7	8.3	9.0	8.5	8.3	6.7
7.2	8.2	7.7	7.5	8.4	8.5	7.9	9.0	8.1

In short, speaking of states as merely weak or strong fails to capture the complexity of state power. In fact, we get stuck in a loop of circular logic if we simply argue that if a state can do something it must be strong and if it can't it must be weak. American elected officials can wage large-scale wars around the globe but can't ban handguns, whereas for Canada just the opposite is true. Which one, then, is weak or strong? Comparative politics builds on the categories of weak and strong states through the use of two other terms: *capacity* and *autonomy*. **Capacity** is the ability of the state to wield power in order to carry out the basic tasks of providing security and reconciling freedom and equality. A state with high capacity is able to formulate and enact fundamental policies and ensure stability and security for both itself and its citizens. A state with low capacity is unable to do these things effectively. High capacity requires not just money but also organization, legitimacy, and effective leadership. Roads get paved, schools get built, regulations are created and followed, and those who break the law are punished.

In contrast, **autonomy** is the ability of the state to wield its power independently of the public or international actors. This is closely related to the idea of sovereignty. In the case of sovereignty we are speaking of a state's formal and legal independence. In the case of autonomy, we are speaking of the informal, practical ability to act on that independence. In other words, if an autonomous state wishes to carry out a policy or action, it can do so without having to consult the public or worry about strong public or international opposition that might force it to reverse its decision. A state with a high degree of autonomy may act on behalf of the public, pursuing what it believes are the best interests of the country, irrespective of public opinion. A state with a low degree of autonomy will act largely at the behest of private individuals, groups, or other states and will be less able to disobey the public will or the demands of well-organized groups. Scholars sometimes describe states with low autonomy as "captured" by certain interests that control specific issues or policies.

The concepts of capacity and autonomy help us to evaluate differences in state power. Strong states with a high degree of capacity and autonomy may be able to execute major policies relatively easily. A case in point is China's construction of the Three Gorges Dam, the world's largest such project, which the state carried out despite technical challenges, enormous cost, and international criticism for its possible environmental impact. High capacity and autonomy, however, may come at the expense of individual freedom. By contrast, states with high capacity but lower autonomy may have widespread powers but are more subject to public intervention. The United States and Canada are good examples of states with lower autonomy, facilitated by their federal structure. Individual freedom may be high, but this can constrain central authority and consequently hinder national policy making. States with high autonomy but low capacity, meanwhile, may have few limits on

State Autonomy and Capacity

	HIGH AUTONOMY	LOW AUTONOMY
HIGH CAPACITY	State is able to fulfill basic tasks, with a minimum of public intervention; power highly centralized; strong state.	State is able to fulfill basic tasks, but public plays a direct role in determining policy and is able to limit state power and scope of activity.
	Danger: Too high a level of capacity and autonomy may prevent or undermine democracy.	Danger: State may be unable to develop new policies or respond to new challenges owing to the power of organized opposition.
LOW CAPACITY	State is able to function with a minimum of public interference or direct control, but its capacity to fulfill basic tasks is limited.	State lacks the ability to fulfill basic tasks and is subject to direct public control and interference—power highly decentralized among state and nonstate actors; weak state.
	Danger: State is ineffectual, limiting development, and slow development may provoke public unrest.	Danger: Too low a level of capacity and autonomy may lead to internal state failure.

their decision making but lack the ability to realize those policies effectively. Russia falls into this category: during the last decade the state has become more centralized and autonomous, but it still does not have the capacity to successfully promulgate and enforce regulations and rights. Finally, states may lack both autonomy and capacity. This is true of many less-developed countries, such as those in Africa that have been "captured" by elites or certain ethnic or religious groups and are largely unable to fulfill some of the most important national tasks, like encouraging economic development and ensuring public education.

In short, speaking of state power in terms of autonomy and capacity can help us better understand stateness: what states are and are not able to do, and why. However, we should note that the degree of a state's autonomy and capacity may vary widely depending on the issue at hand. An observer of China may conclude that this state enjoys high autonomy and capacity. However, China's corruption, widespread disregard of regulations, and numerous public protests indicate that

Why Has Pakistan Slid Toward State Failure?

Since 2001, there has been a great deal of international concern regarding Pakistan. Bordering Afghanistan and India, it displays many of the hallmarks of a typical failing state (see Table 2.1). The quality of education and health care is extremely low. The level of corruption is among the highest in the world. The judicial system is unresponsive to the public, and the military and intelligence institutions appear unaccountable to government officials. The country suffers from the world's third-largest number of terrorist deaths after Iraq and Afghanistan, and large swaths of the country's border with Afghanistan are not effectively under state control. The killing of Osama Bin Laden, who had been living for several years in a home in Pakistan a short distance from a military academy, raised serious questions inside and outside the country: were segments of the Pakistani military or intelligence involved in sheltering him, or were they unaware of his presence? As observers inside and outside Pakistan commented, both answers are disturbing. Many of Pakistan's issues of state capacity and autonomy are not unique; however, they are of particular concern to the international community because Pakistan supports guerrilla and terrorist activity in Afghanistan and possesses nuclear weapons.

The broad problem, as numerous scholars have expressed, is that a failing Pakistani state may also be an "irrational" one. In the study of international relations, many scholars assume that states are "rational" in the sense that they focus primarily on national security. However, this also assumes that states are able to coordinate with and control their governments. Without some centralized authority, rational-ity may give way as different segments of the state pursue contradictory and competing goals. Because central authority is weak, Pakistan lacks the ability to gain control over the violence that occurs within its borders. Terrorist attacks have been frequent in some parts of the country, where the state lacks sovereign control, while in other regions the military and intelligence sectors have essentially usurped power and do not appear to be accountable to the government. Such state fragmentation can breed risky behavior, as individual leaders or segments of the state vie for power or their own short-term interests. There is clear evidence that military and intelligence forces in Pakistan have supported terrorist attacks inside India, which have brought the two countries to the brink of war; in addition, while the United States views Pakistan as a key ally in its war against the Taliban, it is evident that the Taliban finds support among elements inside the Pakistani state. Most worrisome, it is unclear who has effective control over Pakistan's nuclear weapons or how secure these weapons are. Although Pakistan has become the second-largest recipient of U.S. foreign aid (nearly $3 billion a year), there is little sign that this aid has done much to stop the erosion of Pakistan's state capacity.

How did Pakistan end up this way? This is an excellent question for comparative politics and clearly a critical one. It is also quite puzzling, especially when we compare Pakistan to its neighbor, India. In 1947, as India gained independence from British rule, Muslim leaders demanded their own independent state of Pakistan, so that they would not be a perpetual minority under Hindu rule. Upon independence (known as Partition), both countries faced similar kinds of opportunities and problems, including poverty, weak states, linguistic and regional differences, and democratic institutions inherited from the British. If anything, Pakistan would seem to have had more going for it; it was built on a common religious identity and was wealthier than India. Yet now Pakistan has just two-thirds of India's wealth, with a weaker state that has been under military rule for most of its history. Perhaps we have constructed our puzzle in the wrong way: that Pakistan would succumb to military rule and state failure is not the mystery, as this has been the fate of many poor countries. Perhaps the puzzle is why India escaped this trap. We examine India's ascent in more detail in the next chapter.

There are some institutional factors, though, that scholars believe help explain Pakistan's specific trajectory. First, while the Indian state attained independence with limited disruption, in the newly created Pakistan a state had to be constructed largely from scratch. Second, Pakistan's birth was almost immediately followed by a war with the much larger India over disputed territory. This subsequently led to an emphasis on building a new state with a strong military force, which ultimately became stronger than the central government. Politics in Pakistan were further complicated by the huge number of refugees from India. Though a minority, these refugees dominated the state and military and were less inclined toward democracy, which would allow them to be outvoted by the nonrefugee majority. Finally, the initial ruling party, the Muslim League, had been built around the struggle for Indian independence, and after this goal was accomplished with Partition it lacked a strong leadership or set of ideological values on which to institutionalize a new regime. This combination of a weak state,

Pakistanis rally to express their support of the military following the U.S. raid that killed Osama Bin Laden.

regime, and government left the military a powerful but largely unaccountable force, and it became the primary institution of sovereign power and national identity. In the absence of accountability, the Pakistani military has both grown and fragmented, increasing its control over the state but remaining unable to solidify that control into effective state capacity. At its core, the state is a monopoly of violence, but in the absence of nonmilitary political institutions, this monopoly can be just as destabilizing as its absence.[16]

1. In what way has Pakistan struggled to meet the definition of a state (and thus might be considered failing)?

2. What kinds of political institutions does Pakistan lack (or have weak versions of) that have led to continued military rule?

3. What is meant by describing Pakistan as an "irrational" state?

its autonomy and capacity are in many areas circumscribed. Japan's state capacity was long seen as a model for successful development, but its sluggish response to the 2011 earthquake raised questions in this regard. North Korea and Iran suffer from limited economic development and from international sanctions, yet can make progress on sophisticated nuclear technology—no small feat. Autonomy and capacity, therefore, are useful concepts for comparing states, but the degree to which an individual state possesses them depends on the issue or task at hand.

Finally, we are left some big questions: Why are some states more centralized or decentralized? Why do they have more or less capacity or autonomy? Some of the answers lie in history, particularly the nature of international threats and how they affected the relation between taxation (needed to pay for wars) and representation (how much say people have in how the state conducts itself). Cultural norms regarding freedom and equality may also play a role. For more recently founded states, however, such idiosyncratic and historical explanations are not particularly useful. Can international or domestic actors engineer more viable and effective states, such as in Afghanistan, Pakistan (see the "Institutions in Action" box, p. 50) or Iraq? Is there an ideal mix of different forms of legitimacy, centralization, autonomy, and capacity? Scholars and policy makers are still debating this issue, which we will take up in subsequent chapters.

In Sum: Studying States

This chapter began by defining the state as a monopoly of force but also as the set of institutions charged with transforming freedom and equality from ideas into concrete action. The kinds of decisions made toward this end are shaped by regimes and governments. Regimes are the fundamental rules and norms of politics, providing long-term goals regarding individual freedom and collective equality and the location and use of power toward those goals. Governments, in contrast, are the political elites in charge of running the state. Influenced and constrained by the existing regime, they attempt to formulate policy that may then be executed by the state. These represent the most basic facets of states everywhere—and, indeed, states are everywhere. Although similar political organizations have existed for thousands of years, only within the past few centuries did modern states arise in Europe and quickly come to dominate the globe. States are the main political players in the world today.

The universal presence of states, and variations in their stateness, compels comparativists to find some way to study and evaluate them. One way is by assessing their legitimacy; different kinds of legitimacy—traditional, charismatic, and rational-legal—create their own kinds of authority and power. The other is by assessing the dispersal of power; states may be weaker or stronger, with more or less capacity and autonomy, depending on how power is distributed within the state and between the state and the public. Too much power in the hands of the state risks tyranny; too little power risks anarchy. Finding the right mix is not simply a technical question but one that shapes how states and societies reconcile freedom and equality. This debate over freedom and equality ranges far beyond the boundaries of the state itself. As we shall see in the chapters that follow, it is influenced by ethnic and national identity; by culture and ideology; by economic institutions and the interaction between states and markets; and by democratic and nondemocratic practices.

Since the dawn of humanity, people have relied on some form of political organization to construct a relationship between individual freedom and collective equality. For the past few centuries, modern states have been the dominant expression of that relation. We might thus conclude that states now represent an end point in human intellectual and organizational evolution. But why should this be so? It seems logical that in the future new forms of political organization will displace states, just as states displaced empires, city-states, and other institutions. Perhaps challenges to states—environmental, economic, or cultural—will overwhelm many of them and they will revert to earlier forms, such as empires and city-states. Or perhaps technological innovation will make old forms of political centralization weak or irrelevant, binding humans in communities where sovereignty is virtual, not physical. Perhaps the core debate over freedom and equality that has stretched over millennia will be reconciled once and for all, changing the very nature of politics as we understand it. These questions may seem unanswerable, more amenable to fortune-telling than to research. But as we shall see, they lie at the heart of ideas and conflicts that have transformed the world in the past and may dominate our future.

For Further Reading

Diamond, Jared. *Guns, Germs, and Steel: The Fates of Human Societies* (New York: W. W. Norton, 1997).

Evans, Peter, Dietrich Rueschemeyer and T. Skopol, eds. *Bringing the State Back In* (New York: Cambridge University Press, 1985).

RS> Fukuyama, Francis. *The Origins of Political Order: From Prehuman Times to the French Revolution* (New York: Farrar, Straus, and Giroux, 2011).

Gat, Azar. *War in Human Civilization* (New York: Oxford University Press, 2006).

Gilley, Bruce. *The Right to Rule: How States Win and Lose Legitimacy* (New York: Columbia University Press, 2009).

RS> Herbst, Jeffrey. "War and the State in Africa." *International Security* 14, no. 4 (Spring 1990).

Keeley, Lawrence. *War Before Civilization: The Myth of the Peaceful Savage* (New York: Oxford University Press, 1997).

RS> Krasner, Stephen D. "Sovereignty." *Foreign Policy* (January/February 2001).

Landes, David. *The Wealth and Poverty of Nations: Why Some Are So Rich and Some So Poor* (New York: W. W. Norton, 1999).

Maddison, Angus. *Contours of the World Economy, 1–2030 AD* (New York: Oxford University Press, 2007).

Olson, Mancur. "Democracy, Dictatorship, and Development." *American Political Science Review* 87, no. 3 (September 1993).

RS> Rotberg, Robert I. "The New Nature of Nation-State Failure." *The Washington Quarterly* 25, no. 3 (Summer 2002).

Tilly, Charles. *Coercion, Capital, and European States: 990–1990* (Oxford, UK: Blackwell, 1990).

RS> Weber, Max. "Politics as a Vocation." *Max Weber: Essays in Sociology*. H. H. Garth and C. Wright Mills, eds., trans. (New York: Oxford University Press, 1958).

RS>
Reader Selection

Highlighted selections are included in *Essential Readings in Comparative Politics*, Fourth Edition.

Visit StudySpace for quizzes and other review material.
www.norton.com/studyspace

- Vocabulary Flashcards of All Key Terms
- Chapter Review Quizzes
- Complete Study Reviews and Outlines

3

4° CONGRESSO
PARTIDO DO
TRABALHA
REFORMA ESTA
Um novo Bra
Uma nova

Political attitudes and ideologies help shape our political identity. Brazil's Workers' Party, pictured here in 2010, is a social democratic party (a type of ideology). As it has evolved over time it has shed much of its original radicalism (a type of attitude).

NATIONS AND SOCIETY

KEY CONCEPTS

- Ethnic identity defines how individuals identify with their community.

- National identity binds people through common political aspirations such as sovereignty.

- Citizenship and patriotism define our legal and emotional relationship to the state.

- Ethnic and national conflict can stem from clashes between these different identities and their goals.

- Political attitudes are views regarding the pace and scope of any political change.

- Political ideologies are specific values held by individuals regarding the fundamental goals of politics.

- Political culture constitutes the basic norms for political activity in a society.

Society is a broad term that refers to complex human organization, a collection of people bound by shared institutions that define how human relations should be conducted. From country to country and place to place, societies differ in how individuals define themselves and their relationships to one another, to government, and to the state. Each relationship is unique; for all the surface similarities that may exist between societies, each country views itself and the wider world around it in a distinct way. These differences make comparative politics a rich field of study but also a frustrating one, as social scientists seek to find similarities that are often few and far between.

In this chapter, we will look at the ways in which people identify themselves and are identified, both as individuals and as groups, and how these identifications relate to politics and the state. We will start with the concepts of ethnic and national identity, two of the most basic ways in which individuals and groups define themselves. What does it mean to be part of an ethnic group? How is such a group defined? What is the difference between an ethnic group and a nation? We will also make a distinction between ethnicity, nationality, and citizenship. A related question arises in the distinction between nationalism and patriotism: What is the difference between being patriotic and being nationalist? We will answer these questions by looking at some examples and tracing their historical origins. Throughout recent history, the world has seen violent domestic and international conflicts connected to national and ethnic identities. Why do such conflicts occur? Are they a natural and inevitable part of human organization, or are such conflicts manufactured by political leaders to serve their own purposes? In this chapter, we will also look at some of the effects of conflict between different ethnic and nationalist identities.

From there we will move on to a discussion of political attitudes and ideologies. Whereas ethnicity, nationality, and citizenship are group identities, political attitudes and ideologies are the values individuals hold and the positions they take with regard to freedom and equality. How should these values and positions be reconciled, and to what end? One thing we will see is that although there are only a few basic political attitudes and ideologies, which can be broadly compared across countries or regions, their relative strength or influence differs dramatically from country to country, and we'll discuss why this is the case.

Before we move ahead, we should ask whether identities like ethnicity, nationality, or ideology are a fixed part of our nature. Scholars have answered this question in different ways. At one end, many social scientists argue that identities exist independent of any biological functions and are a set of "social constructions" that have largely emerged in the modern era. At the other end, many evolutionary psychologists emphasize the role that biological functions (such as kin recognition and genetic similarity) have played in building human identities for tens of thousands of years.[1] These views appear diametrically opposed, and their supporters are often dismissive of each other. But there clearly is room for integration—a view that recognizes an underlying human instinct to sort groups by preference and to elevate one over another, and that notes how modern politics has helped shape that instinct into particular political identities. Whatever their approach, social scientists have grown skeptical that ethnicity or nationalism will become a thing of the past or that collective identities will somehow no longer be a central part of defining who we are. Let us consider some of the most powerful societal institutions that shape comparative politics.

Ethnic Identity

People identify themselves in many ways. One way that they do so is by ethnicity, as when they speak of themselves as German or Irish, Kurdish or Zulu, Latino or Ukrainian Canadian. When we use the term **ethnic identity** or **ethnicity**, we emphasize a person's relation to other members of society. Ethnic identity is a set of institutions that bind people together through a common culture. These institutions can include language, religion, geographic location, customs, appearance, and history, among other things. As these distinct attributes are institutionalized, they provide members of a group with a shared identity that is passed down from generation to generation. This process is called "ascription"—the assigning of a particular quality at birth. People do not choose their ethnicities; they are born into them, and their ethnic identity remains largely fixed throughout life. Ethnicity provides social solidarity and can generate greater equality as well. Groups with a high degree of ethnic solidarity may also be more willing to redistribute resources within the group and, conversely, less willing to share resources with groups that are ethnically different. Related research has focused on the relationship between trust, inequality, and ethnic diversity.[2]

Each ethnic group is characterized by a set of institutions that embody norms and standards of behavior, and a single society can be broken up into numerous ethnic groups. For example, Singaporean society is made up of ethnic Chinese, Malays, and Indians. Most countries in the world are not ethnically homogeneous; rarely are society and ethnicity one and the same. Societies are made up of various ethnic groups, in some cases only a few, in other cases tens or even hundreds, each with its own particular identity. It is important to note that ethnicity is at its core a social, not a political, identity; people may identify themselves with an ethnic group without drawing any particular conclusions about politics on that basis. Ethnicity and the solidarity it provides are not inherently political, though they can become so.

Although we have listed a number of attributes that often define ethnic differences, there is no master list of differences that automatically define one group as ethnically different from another. In Bosnia, for example, the main ethnic groups— Croats, Serbs, and Muslims—speak the same language and are similar in numerous

- A set of specific attributes and societal institutions that makes one group of people culturally different from others.

- Often based on customs, language, religion, or other factors.

- Ascriptive, generally assigned at birth.

- Not inherently political.

other ways. What divides Bosnians is primarily religion: Croats are mostly Roman Catholic, Serbs are Eastern Orthodox Christian, and Muslims practice Islam. Yet we speak of Germans as a single ethnic group, even though some are Catholic and some are Protestant. Why are ethnic groups in Bosnia divided by religion, while in Germany such divisions don't produce different ethnic groups? In an even more confusing case, that of Rwanda, the Hutu and Tutsi ethnic groups cannot be easily distinguished by any of the factors we have listed. Both speak the same language, practice the same religions, live in the same geographic regions, and share the same customs. To most outside observers, there is no real ethnic difference between the two, and even Hutus and Tutsis cannot easily distinguish between one another, since they rely on such vague distinctions as diet. That is not to say that ethnicity is therefore a fiction because it has no single, neat origin. Ethnicity exists when people acknowledge and are acknowledged by outsiders as belonging to a distinct group. In the case of Rwanda, even though ethnic distinctions between Hutu and Tutsi are unclear, ethnic conflict in the 1990s led to the deaths of several hundred thousand civilians. Though ethnic distinctions may be difficult to observe, these ascriptive identities can have powerful effects.

National Identity

In contrast to ethnicity, which may be constructed in a unique manner from group to group and is not an inherently political concept, the idea of a **nation**—a group that desires self-government through an independent state—is largely consistent from case to case and is inherently political. If ethnic identity is a set of institutions that bind people together through a common culture, then **national identity** is an institution that binds people together through common political aspirations.

IN FOCUS

National Identity Is . . .

- A sense of belonging to a nation (a group that desires self-government through an independent state) and a belief in its political aspirations.

- Often (but not always) derived from ethnic identity.

- Inherently political.

- The basis for nationalism: pride in one's people and belief that they have a unique political destiny.

Among these, the most important are self-government and sovereignty. National identity implies a demand for greater freedom through sovereignty, as in a colony's revolt against its colonial master. It also involves a demand for equality, such as a secessionist movement that argues that independence would eliminate unequal treatment of one group by another. Pakistan's secession from India in 1947, Kosovo's declaration of independence from Serbia in 2008, and the "Free Tibet" movement reflect one group's aspiration toward greater freedom (from another, dominant group) and toward equality with others in the international system (through the creation of a sovereign state).

As you can see, national identity often—but not always—develops from ethnic identity. For example, an ethnic group may chafe against the political system under which it lives; its members may feel that they lack certain rights or freedoms. As a result, some leaders may argue that the ethnic group should have greater political control and that the group's interests would be better served if it controlled its own political destiny. The interaction between ethnicity and national identity can be seen in recent developments in Canada. There, the French-speaking population of the province of Québec constitutes its own ethnic group, quite distinct from the English-speaking citizens of the rest of Canada (as well as from their own French ancestors). By the 1960s, this ethnicity began to develop into a sense of national identity, as some in Québec argued for separation from Canada, where they saw themselves as a minority whose unique concerns were not taken into consideration. Such arguments actually led to national referenda on the issue of secession in 1980 and 1995. In the latter case, the proposal that Québec secede failed by little more than 1 percent of the vote. Over 15 years later, surveys suggest that nearly half of French speaking Québecois continue to support independence.[3]

National identity can create **nationalism**, a pride in one's people and the belief that they have their own sovereign political destiny that is separate from those of others. In Québec we find a people uncertain of whether they are just an ethnic group or also a nation—a group that desires self-government through an independent state. This lack of clarity between ethnicity and national identity is also evident in other groups, such as the Scots in the United Kingdom, some but not all of whom support the nationalist cause of independence. In other words, although ethnic identity often leads to a political identity built on nationalism, this is not always the case. Just as groups can vary in the strength of their ethnic identification, people may also vary in the degree of their nationalism. Indians and South Africans have strong ethnic identification across numerous groups but at the same time a high degree of national identity; in the more homogeneous Germany and Japan, national pride is far lower, reflecting the disastrous results of extreme nationalism in both countries in the past.

If we can have ethnicity without its leading to national identity, can we have national identity without ethnicity? Must ethnicity always be the source of nationalism? At first glance, it would seem logical that without ethnicity there is no foundation for national identity; people would lack a common source of solidarity and a set of institutions on which to build national pride. But like ethnicity, nationality lacks a "master list" of defining attributes. In the case of the United States, it is easy to conclude that there is no single American ethnic group. But is there an American nation? Some might say no, because nationalism is often assumed to require an ethnicity on which political aspirations can be built. Yet Americans are bound by certain common historical symbols, such as flags, anthems, a constitution, and common cultural values (recall our discussion of baseball in Chapter 1). One could thus argue that even in the face of great ethnic diversity, the United States is indeed a nation, whose people are bound together by, among other things, a sense of pride in certain democratic ideals. Finally, we should emphasize that nationalism is not inherently bad, as is often believed. Nationalism carries in it a tension with those who are outside the group, but it can also be seen as a vehicle for much of what we consider modern civilization.

Citizenship and Patriotism

Our final form of identification is citizenship. So far, we have noted that ethnicity is not inherently political, although it may develop a political aspect through nationalism. At the other end of this spectrum, citizenship is a purely political identity, developed not out of some unique set of circumstances or ascribed by birth but rather developed explicitly by states and accepted or rejected by individuals. **Citizenship** can be defined as an individual's or group's relation to the state; those

- An individual's relation to the state; the individual swears allegiance to the state, and the state in turn provides certain benefits or rights.

- Purely political and thus more easily changed than ethnic identity or national identity.

- The basis for patriotism: pride in one's state and citizenship.

who are citizens swear allegiance to that state, and that state in return is obligated to provide rights to those individuals or the members of that group. Citizenship can also convey certain obligations, such as the duty to serve in the armed forces or pay taxes. Citizens are therefore defined by their particular relation to one state rather than to one another. Although citizenship is often gained at birth, it has qualities quite separate from those of ethnic or national identity.

Citizenship is a potentially more inclusive or flexible concept than national or ethnic identity. Like those two identities, however, citizenship can vary in clarity and power. Citizenship may confer a host of benefits, such as education and health care, or relatively few, depending on the state. In addition, one state may not necessarily grant citizenship to all those born on its territory, while another may allow citizenship in more than one country. Matters can be further complicated if citizenship is founded on ethnic or national identity. In an extreme example, in the 1950s, South Africa's apartheid regime created internal "homelands" for blacks as a means of stripping them of their South African citizenship. Many Palestinians lack any citizenship, living in areas under Israeli occupation or as refugees in nearby countries.

Citizenship, in turn, can give rise to **patriotism**, or pride in one's state. People are patriotic when they have pride in their political system and seek to defend and promote it. When we think of patriotism, some of the things that may come to mind are our flag, important historical events, wars, anthems—anything that people associate with politics and the state. It can be hard to separate the definitions of patriotism and nationalism. National identity is bound up in the quest for sovereignty, as is patriotism. As a result, the two can closely overlap. However, they can also be quite distinct: there may be a high degree of national identity without patriotism. Returning to the Palestinians, they have a strong sense of national identity but, for now, no state of their own—hence, the term *patriotism* does not apply to them. An ethnic minority's sense of nationalism may be confined to the political aspirations of its own members, and as a result that group may have a low level of patriotism—that is, of pride in their state, which they do not see as their own. The United States (along with India or Canada) may be a case where there is not one clear sense of nationalism, as we argued above, but rather strong patriotism that emphasizes pride in the state. Since patriotism emphasizes the state, those states that are weak or illegitimate often have difficulty instilling patriotism in their citizens. This makes tasks like defending the state in times of war very difficult. Being a citizen does not automatically make you patriotic, nor does a strong ethnic or national identity.

To sum up, ethnicity, nationality, and citizenship are institutions that define groups in different ways and that carry different political implications. Ethnic identity is built on social attributes that are unique to a group of people, such as language or culture, whereas national identity implies political aspirations, specifically sovereignty. Although a dominant ethnic identity often leads to a national identity and nationalism, it does not always do so, nor does the absence of a dominant ethnicity necessarily prevent nationalism from developing. Finally, citizenship is an identity built on a relation to the state. As should be clear, none of these identities is exclusive; all of us possess different combinations of ethnicity, national identity, and citizenship, with each contributing to how we see the world and our role within it.

Ethnic Identity, National Identity, and Citizenship: Origins and Persistence

Now that we have distinguished among these three identities, it is worth considering their origins: Where did they come from and why do they exist? From our earlier discussion we might assume that before the modern era people lacked clear identities. In truth, for thousands of years communities defined themselves by culture, language, and gods, often contrasting themselves with "barbarians"—people who were different and therefore, in their view, uncivilized. However, the specific concepts of ethnic and national identity are relatively recent, having emerged in Europe toward the end of the eighteenth century. Citizenship, too, has relatively recent origins: although the concept can be traced back to ancient Athens and to the Roman Empire, it disappeared with the fall of Rome, only resurfacing centuries later.

The emergence (or reemergence, in the case of citizenship) of these identities had much to do with the formation of the modern state.[4] As states took form in Europe in the fifteenth and sixteenth centuries, asserting sovereign control over people and territory, people could travel greater distances, enjoying the security provided by the state. This mobility in turn increased commerce, which was often centered around the city where the state leadership was based. These fortified capitals served as centers for trade, information, and new social relations. Such inter-action in turn fostered increased homogeneity. Languages and dialects began to merge into a common tongue, further standardized by the state through educa-tion and documentation. Common cultural and religious practices also developed, often created or supported by the state (as during the Protestant Reformation in the sixteenth century). Social institutions began to take shape that were meaning-ful to a majority of a country's population. People could now identify themselves not only by village or profession, clan or tribe, but also, more abstractly, by the institutions they shared with many thousands of other people across space and time. These institutions formed the foundation for ethnic identity. People in turn slowly began to identify with each other primarily on the basis of broad cultural institutions—as, for instance, German or French or English.

Growing ethnic identity was thus tightly connected to state development. Moreover, state leaders also saw this development as something that could serve their own interests. By encouraging the formation of a single ethnic identity, the state could in turn claim that it existed to defend and promote the unique inter-ests and values of its people. The state came to be portrayed as the institution that embodied the people's collective identity.

In the linked development of ethnic identity and of the state, we can see the seeds of national identity, which became a potent force in the eighteenth century. National identity, when added to ethnic identity, powerfully asserts that the state is legitimate because it maintains national values and that the people and the state are united in the quest to chart an independent political future. The development and fusion of ethnic and national identities radically transformed states. On the basis of the idea that the people and their state were bound together in common cause, states could mobilize the public in ways never before possible. Most important, countries with a strong sense of nationalism could raise mass armies and generate tax revenue, as people would sacrifice their resources and very lives for the glory and destiny of their nation.

The thought that individuals would fight and die for an abstract political con-cept marked a radical change in human history. In Europe, Napoleonic France became the first country able to use such nationalist sentiment to its own advan-tage, raising a huge volunteer army that would conquer much of Europe. Both threatened and inspired by such nationalist fervor, other European peoples and states in turn forged their own national identities and aspired to independence and self-government. This transformation gave rise to the idea of a **nation-state**, a sovereign state encompassing one dominant nation that it claims to embody and represent. Within a hundred years, most of the multiethnic empires that domi-nated Europe would be destroyed, replaced by nation-states that were dominated by distinct ethnic groups and political identities.

Finally, the development of ethnic and national identities paved the way for the concept of citizenship. As societies viewed themselves first in ethnic and then in national terms, their relation to the state began to change. If the state was the instrument of national will, some extended this logic to conclude that state and people must be bound by mutual accountability and obligation in the form of a social contract, as we mentioned in Chapter 2. How far this citizenship should be extended and what rights it should entail have come to be central concerns for all societies and states.

With the rise of European imperial power, the institutions of ethnic and national identity and citizenship began to spread around the world. Just as states now lay claim to almost all the earth, so too have nearly all human beings become identified by some ethnicity, some nationality, some form of citizenship. In some cases, this has been the foundation for political stability, economic development, and democracy; at the other extreme, where identities are weakly held or come into conflict, the result is civil strife. Why these conflicts emerge and how to prevent them from becoming violent can be a matter of life and death.

Ethnic and National Conflict

Why are some countries able to forge consensus between different ethnic and national identities, whereas in other countries such differences lead to seemingly irreconcilable conflict? Why is it that different identities can coexist peacefully and then suddenly clash? Political scientists have a range of often contending explanations for such forms of conflict, a debate that has intensified rapidly over the past two decades as ethnic and national conflicts have grown in number and intensity. Before we discuss these debates, we should clarify our terms.

Ethnic conflict can be defined as conflict between ethnic groups that struggle to achieve certain political or economic goals at each other's expense. Each may hope to increase their power by gaining greater control over existing political institutions like the state or government. By contrast, groups involved in **national conflict** seek to gain (or prevent the other from gaining) sovereignty, clashing with one another over the quest to form an independent state. In both of these cases, violence is a common tool, using, bypassing, or destroying the coercive powers of the state.

Around the world, we can find examples of ethnic and national conflict as well as cases where both are present. Afghanistan, for example, has seen frequent ethnic conflict, but this is not national; most Afghan groups are seeking not independence but greater power over each other. Ethnic conflict in Kenya and Nigeria over the past decade has similarly pitted rival ethnic groups against one another over contested presidential elections. In contrast, the American Revolution can be seen as a national rather than an ethnic conflict. The American colonies broke away from Great Britain to form a separate country, but this separation was based more on conflicts over political rights and the desire for sovereignty than on a strong "American" identity. And finally, conflicts can be both ethnic and national, such as in Yugoslavia and the Soviet Union in the 1990s, where various ethnic groups seceded to create their own nation-states.

Why do such conflicts break out in the first place? Scholars emphasize different factors, which can be grouped by where they place the primary cause: society, the economy, or politics. Societal explanations tend to emphasize such issues as ethnic heterogeneity—the number of ethnic groups and their degree of integration or polarization. Economic explanations concentrate on the struggle for resources (natural or otherwise) between groups, as well as the general level of poverty across a country as a whole. A political explanation emphasizes the state and regime, such as the relative capacity or autonomy of the state and the degree and form of democratic or nondemocratic regimes. Of course, these three categories bleed into one another, and in the case of actual conflicts it can be hard to distinguish cause from effect. Still, we can see how each explanation can give us a way to think about ethnic and national conflict. For example, in Africa we see a great deal of ethnic heterogeneity, particularly across the central part of the continent, and these correspond to several major conflicts, as in Nigeria, Kenya, and Sudan (see Figure 3.1). In a number of these cases, ethnic clashes are influenced by the presence of natural resources. Congo is a horrific example. Although ethnic divisions were less pronounced there than in other countries, when ethnic conflict spilled over from Rwanda in the 1990s, this sparked battles over gold and diamonds in a war that left anywhere from 2–5 million people dead—the worst conflict since World War II. Finally, political difficulties abound in much of Africa: borders drawn by colonial powers that do not conform to major ethnic divisions; weak states that are often "captured" by one dominant ethnic group that benefits disproportionately from that control and dominates the military; authoritarian systems that prevent effective participation or conciliation. Any one of

IN FOCUS | Views of Ethnic and National Conflict

- Societal explanations emphasize such issues as ethnic heterogeneity.

- Economic explanations emphasize poverty and the struggle for natural or other resources.

- Political explanations emphasize state capacity or autonomy and the type of regime.

FIGURE 3.1

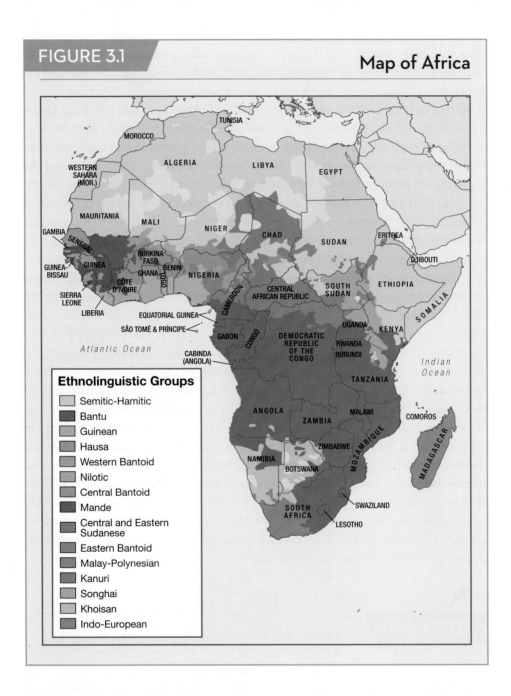

Map of Africa

these three areas can contribute to ethnic conflict, and when all are present they can create a dangerous synergism.[5]

How do we prevent ethnic and national conflicts or bring them to an end? In part this depends on the nature of the conflict, and whether the struggle is based on demands for greater equality or on some territorial demand, like autonomy or secession. It may be possible to create institutions that make the majority of players feel that the political system is fair and serves their needs. One example of power sharing can be devolution; as we discussed in the last chapter, federal structures, asymmetric or otherwise, can provide ethnic groups with greater rights and autonomy. Representative structures (such as presidencies or legislatures) and electoral systems can make a difference as well, something we will address in detail in Chapter 5. However, not all scholars are convinced that power-sharing institutions, even when carefully crafted, work well. One concern is that such structures may "freeze," or institutionalize, group divisions and conflicts. The challenge, then, is to build institutions that can meet existing group demands while remaining flexible enough to foster cooperation and integration across these divides.[6]

Political Attitudes and Political Ideology

We have spent some time discussing ways in which people's identities are shaped by their membership in larger ethnic or national groups. But such groups do not completely define our political identity. We also hold individual views regarding the ideal relation between freedom and equality. In the rest of this chapter, we will divide these views into two categories: political attitudes and political ideology. Political attitudes are concerned with the speed of political change and the methods used to achieve it. Political ideology comprises the basic values held by an individual about the fundamental goals of politics regarding freedom and equality. Political attitudes focus on the specific context of political change in a given country, while political ideologies are more universal, since they assume that there is one ideal way to balance freedom and equality.

Where do political attitudes and ideologies come from? These views are not defined by birth or by the state, although they may be influenced by either. Nor are the boundaries between such views as clear or evident as are those that define ethnicity, national identity, or citizenship. At the same time, they do not simply materialize out of thin air. Ideologies are built over time out of a set of ideas, and attitudes are articulated in response to the institutional conditions around us. More fundamentally, it may be that attitudes and ideologies—our individual or group preferences regarding freedom, equality, and the degree of change needed to achieve them—stem from basic human traits that balance our need to establish order and our need to embrace change. While our own political views may not be inherited, having such views in the first place is central to what makes us human.

How Has India Held Together?

In Chapter 2, we addressed the question of why Pakistan has been unable to institutionalize democracy and has slid toward state failure. In that discussion, we made some comparisons to India, as they were both part of a single country under British rule until 1947. Both countries faced similar challenges, including poverty, ethnic diversity, a weak state, and linguistic and regional differences. In fact, in a number of these areas it can be argued that India was at a greater disadvantage.

Upon independence, India was forced to contend with several major religious divisions, including those between Hindus, Muslims, Christians, and Sikhs; at least ten major languages; hundreds, if not thousands, of caste divisions (hereditary classes); and the sheer size of the country, the seventh largest in the world geographically and the second largest in population (then and now). In the course of Partition, approximately 15 million people moved between India and Pakistan, a situation that led to hundreds of thousands of deaths from ethnic violence.

Following Partition, India continued to face internal threats to its stability and sovereignty. For example, ownership of the Indian state of Jammu and Kashmir was contested with Pakistan because of the state's overwhelmingly Muslim population. Many Indian Kashmiris have continued to seek greater autonomy within India, unification with Pakistan, or outright independence. Adherents of the Sikh religion (established in India in the fifteenth century) similarly agitated for greater rights and complained of discrimination in a Hindu-majority country. This eventually culminated in a separatist movement for an independent Sikh state and a violent conflict between government forces and Sikh separatists in the 1980s. After that uprising was crushed, Indian prime minister Indira Gandhi was assassinated by her own Sikh bodyguards. While Sikh separatism has abated, violent conflict from and toward the Muslim community has increased. In the past two decades, riots and acts of terrorism have left several thousand dead. Hindu fundamentalism has also increased, led by the Bharatiya Janata Party (BJP), which opposes secularism and seeks a regime built around Hindu nationalism.

Given these difficulties, we can well wonder how this country has managed to stay intact, let alone democratic. Numerous scholars have tackled this question, and their answers reflect many of the points we have mentioned in the chapter about the role of identity in shaping and defining political institutions.

Instead of founding the newly independent India on a strong, unified national identity, the country's leaders attempted to accommodate as many religious, ethnic, and cultural differences as possible. Indian identity in the new constitution was built around citizenship rather than ethnicity. English, alongside Hindi, was established as a national language of government, allowing for greater integration while not giving any single Indian language political dominance. Religious holidays for all major groups were officially recognized. To meet local demands, a system of asymmetric federalism (see Chapter 2) devolved power differently across states, and some state borders were drawn based on local identities. Finally, central executive and legislative institutions that would give any one group a chance to dominate the government—such as a presidency—were avoided. As a result, some scholars have concluded that India has managed to create multiple and complementary identities that have strengthened, not weakened, democracy. Rather than a nation-state, India can be seen as a state-nation, with multiple nations given varying degrees of autonomy under one central state.[7] This is quite the opposite of Pakistan, where the state has not succeeded in effectively drawing diverse groups into a functioning political system.

These explanations are valuable not only in answering the puzzle of India's national and democratic success, but also in providing insights into our question of how to craft institutions to prevent or resolve ethnic and national conflict elsewhere in the world. They also have implications for the question of how homogenous societies (like those in Europe) might deal with increasingly diverse populations.

That said, we should not conclude that India's solution is perfect. As we noted above, ethnic and national conflict continues in India, and one can argue that conflict between Hindus and Muslims has intensified over time. This conflict is exacerbated by the rise of the BJP, which argues that India's secular multiculturalism weakens national identity. Many Muslims feel disenfranchised from Indian democracy, because of Hindu nationalism and Muslims' continuing exclusion from economic and political power.

In addition, it has been argued that devolving economic and political power, especially to poor regions, creates more opportunities for corruption—a major prob-

Standing before a statue of Gandhi, a group of protestors call for the creation of a new state within India—Telangana.

lem in India, and one frequently seen as an obstacle to growth. Local power is also a significant check on central state power. While we might assume that this check is a positive component of democracy, it also can create a barrier to implementing national policies. One question raised by modern India's political history is whether stability in such a diverse country comes at a cost: a reduction in state autonomy and capacity. This is not a small concern in a country with major ambitions and significant deficiencies.

1. How do India's political institutions accommodate the country's profound ethnic diversity?

2. What is an example of an ethnic conflict in India? What is an example of a national conflict? How do they differ?

3. In what ways are state stability and state autonomy and capacity at odds in India?

Political Attitudes

Political attitudes describe views regarding the necessary pace and scope of change in the balance between freedom and equality. The attitudes are typically broken up into the categories of radical, liberal, conservative, and reactionary and are often arrayed on a spectrum, from left to right.

Radicals are placed on the extreme left. **Radicals** believe in dramatic, often revolutionary change of the existing political, social, or economic order. Radicals believe that the current system is broken and cannot simply be improved or repaired but must be scrapped in favor of a new order. As a result, most radicals do not believe in slow, evolutionary change. Politics will be improved, they believe, only when the entire political structure has been fundamentally transformed, remaking the political institutions of government, regime, and state. As a result, some radicals may be more inclined to favor violence as a necessary or unavoidable part of politics. The institutions of the old order, in some radicals' view, will not change willingly; they will have to be destroyed. These views are not held by all or even most radicals, however. Many may argue that radical change can be achieved through peaceful means, by raising public consciousness and mobilizing mass support for wide-ranging change.

Liberals, like radicals, believe that there is much that can be improved in the current political, social, and economic institutions, and liberals, too, support widespread change. However, instead of revolutionary transformation, **liberals** favor evolutionary change. In the liberal view, progressive change can happen through changes within the system; it does not require an overthrow of the system itself. Moreover, liberals part from radicals in their belief that existing institutions can be instruments of positive change. Liberals also believe that change can and sometimes must occur over a long period of time. They are skeptical that institutions can be replaced or transformed quickly and believe that only constant effort can create fundamental change.

IN FOCUS   Political Attitudes Are . . .

- Concerned with the speed and methods of political change.

- Generally classified as radical, liberal, conservative, or reactionary.

- Distinct from political ideologies.

- Particularistic: relative to the specific context of a given country. A view that is "radical" in one country may be "conservative" in another.

Conservatives break with both radicals and liberals in this view of the necessity of change. Whereas radicals and liberals both advocate change, disagreeing on the degree of change and the tactics needed to achieve it, **conservatives** question whether any significant or profound change in existing institutions is necessary. Conservatives are skeptical of the view that change is good in itself and instead view it as disruptive and leading to unforeseen outcomes. They see existing institutions as key to providing basic order and continuity; should too much change take place, conservatives argue, the very legitimacy of the system might be undermined. Conservatives also question the extent to which the problems that radicals and liberals point to can ever really be solved. At best, they believe, change will simply replace one set of problems with another, and, at worst, it will create more problems than it solves.

Reactionaries are similar to conservatives in their opposition to further evolutionary or revolutionary change, yet, unlike conservatives and like radicals, they view the current order as fundamentally unacceptable. Rather than a transformation of the system into something new, however, **reactionaries** seek to restore political, social, and economic institutions. Reactionaries advocate a restoration of values, a change back to a previous regime or state that they believe was superior to the current order. Some reactionaries do not even look back to a specific period in history, but instead seek to return to an envisioned past ideal that may never have existed. Reactionaries, like radicals, may in some cases be more willing to use violence to advance their cause.

The left-right continuum on which political attitudes are typically placed gives the impression that the farther one travels from the center, the more polarized politics becomes. By this logic, then, radicals and reactionaries are miles apart from one another, with nothing in common (Figure 3.2, top). But our preceding discussion indicates that in many ways this is incorrect. Viewing left and right as extending along a single continuum is misleading, for the closer one moves toward the extremes, the closer the attitudes become. In other words, the continuum of left and right is more aptly portrayed as a circle, bringing the two ends, radical and reactionary, close together (Figure 3.2, bottom). And in fact, radicals and reactionaries have much in common. Both believe in dramatic change, though in different directions, and both contemplate the use of violence to achieve this change. Although their ends may be quite different, the means of both groups can often be similar. Just as liberals sometimes become conservatives and vice versa, radicals and reactionaries often cross over into each other's camps. For example, many reactionary fascists in Europe became supporters of radical communism after World War II. Some extreme forms of contemporary environmentalism exhibit both reactionary and radical elements.

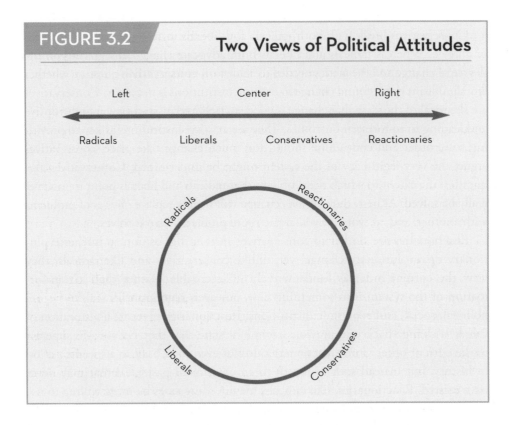

FIGURE 3.2 **Two Views of Political Attitudes**

Left — Center — Right

Radicals — Liberals — Conservatives — Reactionaries

Radicals — Reactionaries — Liberals — Conservatives

You may have noticed that our discussion of the spectrum of political attitudes has not provided any specific examples of political issues, such as welfare, civil liberties, or national defense—common sources of political division that separate right from left in most industrialized democracies. But these policy areas are the concern of political ideology, the basic beliefs about how politics should be constructed. It is important to emphasize again that ideology and political attitudes are not interchangeable. The attitudes of radicals, liberals, conservatives, and reactionaries often take on different ideological content in different societies, depending on the context. What might be considered radical in one country could be conservative in another.

Consider some examples. In the United States, Canada, and Western Europe, radicals are viewed as those who seek to fundamentally transform or overthrow the current capitalist democratic order, replacing it with a system of greater economic and social equality. Liberals in these countries are sympathetic to some of these ideas but believe in pursuing gradual changes within the current system, engaging democratic institutions. Conservatives believe that the current economic and social structures are as good as they are likely to be and that change is unlikely to improve the state of humanity, and might make it worse. Reactionaries, meanwhile, would not only reject the radical and liberal critique of the status quo but would favor a restoration of greater inequality or hierarchy between people. The foregoing is a simplified but accurate description of how political attitudes are manifested in North America and much of the West.

These same political attitudes would manifest themselves quite differently in a country such as China, however. Despite dramatic economic reforms, China still has a nondemocratic regime dominated by a communist party. A Chinese radical, defined as someone who seeks the destruction of the current system, would advocate the overthrow and replacement of communist rule, perhaps by a democracy like those found in the West. Students who were active in the Tiananmen Square protests for democracy in 1989 were frequently described or condemned by observers and the Chinese government as "radicals" because of their demands for sweeping political changes. Chinese liberals are also likely to support these changes, although they would favor a process of gradual change within the existing political system. Chinese conservatives, skeptical of institutional change, resist calls for democratic reform. They may support market reforms, but they do not view these steps as leading down an inevitable path to democracy. Finally, Chinese reactionaries strongly oppose any reforms that might jeopardize communist rule. These "neo-Maoists," as they are sometimes referred to, favor a return to earlier, "purer" communist values and policies, rolling back changes and restoring their communist ideal.

Clearly, American or Western European radicals would have little to say to Chinese radicals; they are united by their attitudes toward the scope and speed of political change, but their political values and goals—their ideologies—are dramatically different. Indeed, Chinese radicals might have more in common with American or European conservatives in terms of their ideological values, which we will discuss next. Chinese reactionaries, on the other hand, might have more in common with American or Western European radicals. Context matters.

Political Ideology

The importance of context in understanding political attitudes might lead one to conclude that comparing political attitudes in one country to those in another is difficult: what is radical in one country might be conservative in another. To move past these particularistic differences between countries, political scientists also speak about political ideologies. Like much of modern politics, the concept of ideology is relatively recent: the term was first used during the French Revolution to speak of a "science of ideas."[8] This meaning reflects the fact that ideologies emerged with the construction of modern secular states as a means to guide politics. Ideologies were thus viewed as alternatives to traditional sets of values such as religion; they were seen as based on rational thought rather than spiritual notions of good and evil. For our purposes, **political ideologies** are defined as sets of political values held by individuals regarding the fundamental goals of politics. Instead of being concerned with the pace and scope of change in a given context, as political attitudes are, ideologies are concerned with the ideal relation between freedom and equality for all individuals and the proper role of political institutions in achieving or maintaining this relation. Supporters of each ideology work to ensure that their values become institutionalized as the basic regime. In the modern world, there are five primary ideologies.

Liberalism as an ideology (rather than as a political attitude) places a high priority on individual political and economic freedom. Adherents of a liberal ideology believe that politics should seek to create the maximum degree of liberty for all people, including free speech, the right of association, and other basic political rights. This goal requires a state with a low degree of autonomy and capacity so that it can be easily controlled or checked by the public should it begin encroaching on individual rights. For liberals, the lower the ability of the state to intervene in the public's affairs, the greater the scope and promise of human activity and prosperity. As Thomas Jefferson said, "the legitimate powers of government extend to such acts only as are injurious to others. But it does me no injury for my neighbor to say there are twenty gods, or no God. It neither picks my pocket nor breaks my leg."[9]

It is from these ideas of liberalism that we take our current definition of democracy, which is often called **liberal democracy**—a system of political, social, and economic liberties, supported by competition, participation, and contestation (such as voting). To be sure, liberals do recognize that if everyone is left to their own devices, not all individuals will succeed and there will inevitably be great economic inequality between the wealthiest and the poorest. Liberals argue that in spite of this shortcoming a high degree of freedom will produce the greatest amount of gen-

IN FOCUS

Political Ideologies Are . . .

- Sets of political values regarding the fundamental goals of politics.

- Exemplified by five dominant modern ideologies: liberalism, communism, social democracy, fascism, and anarchism.

- Universalistic: not specific to one country or time.

- Distinct from political attitudes.

eral prosperity for the majority. As a final point, we should note that liberalism as an ideology and liberalism as a political attitude are very different things (see "The Different Meanings of the term *Liberalism*").

Communism differs greatly from liberalism in its view of freedom and equality. Whereas liberalism enshrines individual freedom over equality, communism rejects the idea that personal freedom will ensure prosperity for the majority. Rather, it holds that in the inevitable struggle over economic resources, a small group will eventually come to dominate both the market and the state, using its wealth to control and exploit society as a whole. Prosperity will not be spread throughout society but will be monopolized by a few for their own benefit. The gap between rich and poor will widen, and poverty will increase. For communists, liberal democracy is "bourgeois democracy"—of the rich, by the rich, and for the rich. Such institutions as free speech and voting are meaningless when a few control the wealth of society.

To eliminate exploitation, communism advocates that the state control all economic resources in order to produce true economic equality for the community as a whole. This goal requires a powerful state in terms of both autonomy and capacity, able to restrict those individual rights (such as owning property or opposing the current regime) that would hinder the pursuit of economic equality. Individual liberties must give way to the needs of society as a whole, creating what communists would see as a true democracy. In the Soviet Union, from 1917 to 1991, this communist ideology was the political regime, as it has been in China since 1949 (though much less so since the 1980s).

Social democracy (sometimes called **socialism**) draws from ideas connected to both communism and liberalism to form its own distinct ideology. Social democracy accepts a strong role for private ownership and market forces while still maintaining

IN FOCUS

The Different Meanings of the Term *Liberalism*

- As a political attitude: favoring slow, evolutionary change

- As a political ideology outside North America: favoring free markets and individualism, accepting greater inequality

- As a political ideology in North America: favoring a greater state role in limiting inequality; many outside the region would call this ideology "social democracy"

- As a political economy: favoring a limited state role in the economy an emphasis on economic equality. A state with strong capacity and autonomy is considered important to social democrats to ensure greater economic equality through specific policies like job protection or social benefits like medical care, retirement, and higher education. This commitment to equality means that social democracy may limit freedom more than liberalism does, through such mechanisms as regulation or taxation. However, social democracy recognizes the importance of individual liberty as complementary to freedom. In much of Europe, social democracy, rather than liberalism, is the guiding political regime. Many environmental parties, which seek to balance human and environmental needs, also have social democratic influences.

Fascism is hostile to the idea of individual freedom and also rejects the notion of equality. Instead, fascism rests on the idea that people and groups can be classified in terms of inferiority and superiority, justifying a hierarchy among them. Whereas liberals, social democrats, and communists all see inherent potential in every person (although they disagree on the best means to unleash this potential), fascists do not. Fascism conceives of society as an organic whole, a single living body, and the state as a vital instrument to express national will. State autonomy and capacity must therefore be high, and democracy, no matter how it is defined, is rejected as anathema, just as freedom and equality are rejected. No fascist regimes currently exist in the world, although fascism is well remembered from the Nazi regime that ruled Germany from 1933 to 1945.

Anarchism departs from these other ideologies quite drastically. If liberalism, communism, and fascism differ over how powerful the state should be, anarchism rejects the notion of the state altogether. Anarchists share with communists the belief that private property leads to inequality, but they are opposed to the idea that the state can solve this problem. As the Russian anarchist Mikhail Bakunin (1814–76) once stated, "I am not a communist, because communism unites all the forces of society in the state and becomes absorbed in it . . . while I seek the complete elimination of the principles of authority and governmental guardianship, which under the pretense of making men moral and civilizing them, has up to now always enslaved, oppressed, exploited, and ruined them."[10]

Thus, like liberals, anarchists view the state as a threat to freedom and equality rather than as their champion, but they believe that both individual freedom and equality can be achieved only if the state is eliminated entirely. Without a state to reinforce inequality or limit personal freedom, argue anarchists, people would be able to cooperate freely as true equals. Given that we live in a world of states, anarchism is the only one of the five primary ideologies that has never been realized. However, anarchist ideas played a role in the Russian Revolution (1917) and in the Spanish Civil War (1936–39). In North America, some versions of libertarianism come close to an anarchist view in their hostility to the state, though libertarians differ from anarchists in their emphasis on private property.

Political ideologies differ according to what they consider the proper balance between freedom and equality to be and what role the state should have in achieving that balance. Building on the preceding chapters' discussion of freedom and equality and state strength, Figure 3.3 shows how liberalism, social democracy, communism, fascism, and anarchism try to reconcile freedom and equality with state power. These values are not particularistic, like political attitudes, but are universal in their outlook. And although ethnic and national identities and citizenship may draw the lines of conflict between groups, ideologies and attitudes shape

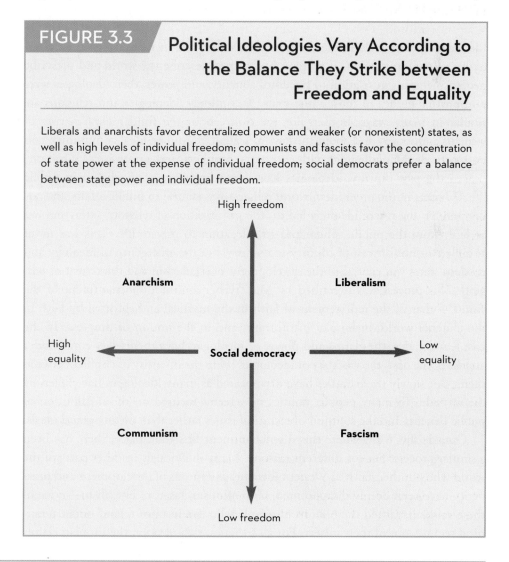

FIGURE 3.3
Political Ideologies Vary According to the Balance They Strike between Freedom and Equality

Liberals and anarchists favor decentralized power and weaker (or nonexistent) states, as well as high levels of individual freedom; communists and fascists favor the concentration of state power at the expense of individual freedom; social democrats prefer a balance between state power and individual freedom.

the arena of political conflict within groups. How much change should there be? How fast should it occur? Should it be achieved through peaceful or violent means? What end should it serve? This is the essence of political life, as ideologies rise and fall in prominence, compete peacefully or violently, and pass from the scene as new ones take their place. In 200 years, such ideologies as liberalism and social democracy may make no more sense than monarchism does today.

Religion, Fundamentalism, and the Crisis of Ideology

Ideologies emerged alongside the modern secular state in many ways as an alternative or rival to religion. If religion had helped describe the world and prescribe people's behavior in relation to freedom, equality, and power, then ideologies were nonspiritual guides to those same ends. Accordingly, ideologies and religions are similar in many ways: both make assertions about the fundamental nature of humans and society and about the keys to a good life and an ideal community, and both provide their adherents with core texts, prophets, and a promise of salvation.

For the past century, ideologies have increasingly replaced religion in public life. Whereas in the premodern world religion was central to public affairs, including politics, the rise of ideology led to "the privatization of religion"—the removal of faith from the public sphere and its relegation to private life. This was never complete or uniform from country to country, but the emergence of ideology and modern states was central to the development of secularism and the retreat of religion. This process was described by Max Weber as "the disenchantment of the world"—that is, the replacement of faith in the mystical and spiritual by faith in the material world, in human institutions, and in the notion of progress. In the past few decades, the claims and power of ideologies have themselves come under attack. In the past, the vibrancy of ideologies lay in the intensity of conflict between them. But slowly these battles have disappeared as many ideologies have fallen by the wayside. To many people, politics now seems focused on the distribution of public benefits and the solution of technical issues rather than on any grand ideals.

Outside the West, where this disenchantment first took place, there has been a similar process, but for different reasons. Many individuals in other parts of the world who put their faith in Western ideology as a means of development and prosperity have been deeply disappointed. Communism, fascism, liberalism—none of these values has lifted the billions of people who live in poverty and under tyrannical regimes out of their misery. For all societies, rich or poor, the utopian claims

Ideology and Political Attitudes

IDEOLOGY	TENETS	CORRESPONDING POLITICAL ATTITUDE IN NORTH AMERICA
LIBERALISM	Favors a limited state role in society and economic activity; emphasizes a high degree of personal freedom over social equality.	Conservative
COMMUNISM	Emphasizes limited personal freedom and a strong state in order to achieve social equality; property is wholly owned by the state and market forces are eliminated; state takes on task of production and other economic decisions.	Radical
SOCIAL DEMOCRACY	Supports private property and markets but believes that state has a strong role to play in regulating the economy and providing benefits to the public; seeks to balance freedom and equality.	Liberal
FASCISM	Stresses a low degree of both personal freedom and equality in order to achieve a powerful state.	Reactionary
ANARCHISM	Stresses the elimination of the state and private property as a way to achieve both freedom and equality for all; believes that a high degree of personal freedom and social equality is possible.	Radical

associated with many ideologies—that modernity, science, and rationalism would usher in a golden age—have been discredited. As a result, many people have sought to make religion a powerful force in their lives again. This can affect politics in a number of ways. When religions become most intensely political, fundamentalist ideas and organizations emerge within them.

We should be clear about what we mean by *fundamentalism*. As with many politically charged words, *fundamentalism* is bandied about indiscriminately, often used to describe any strong view that repels us. Some scholars even think the term should be restricted to its original use—a description of a particular kind of movement among Protestant Christians in the nineteenth century. But in spite of these problems or concerns, the term is useful and can describe a similar pattern across many religions.

The scholar Bruce Lawrence has defined fundamentalism as "the affirmation of religious authority as holistic and absolute, admitting of neither criticism nor reduction; it is expressed through the collective demand that specific creedal and ethical dictates derived from scripture be publicly recognized and legally enforced."[11] Following from this, **fundamentalism** can be viewed as an ideology that seeks to unite religion with the state or, rather, to make faith the sovereign authority—that is, to create a theocracy. This definition implies several things. First, fundamentalism is not the same as religiosity, puritanism, or religious conservatism. For example, Orthodox Jews or the Amish are by definition not fundamentalists; any group that retreats from public life and politics hardly fits our definition. The belief that spirituality should merely take on a greater role in politics or society, a movement seen in many places around the world, is also not fundamentalism. Second, fundamentalism is not a premodern view. As we mentioned earlier, in the premodern world, religion played a central role in public life. The rise of the modern state pushed faith into the private realm, replacing it in part with ideology. But fundamentalism seeks not to return faith to a premodern role but rather to restructure religion as an ideology—to make faith the sole foundation for a modern regime, a concrete and inerrant guide for politics in the contemporary world.

To that end, fundamentalists base their beliefs on the failures of ideology. Through ideology, people sought to create heaven on earth, believing that they could deny the authority of God and seize control of their own destinies. The result has been, in the fundamentalists' view, not only greater human misery but also spiritual malaise. Fundamentalists believe that even those who have benefited materially are still truly disenchanted, spiritually empty, and morally adrift, forced to fill their lives with mindless distractions—consumption, entertainment, sex—to avoid confronting this terrible truth. Fundamentalism, religion as a form of ideology, is thus a very modern phenomenon.[12]

As a political attitude, fundamentalism can appear reactionary or radical or a combination of the two. Fundamentalists will often claim they want to return to a golden age of faith, but they also seek to solve the problems of the modern world, not simply turn back the clock. This mixture of reactionary and radical attitudes also explains why fundamentalism is often associated with violence. However, we should be clear that only a small number of fundamentalists embrace such an approach. We will delve into this issue in depth in Chapter 7 when we consider political violence. To reiterate, we should not confuse religiosity or piety with fundamentalism, or fundamentalism with violence.

How does fundamentalism approach the relation between freedom and equality? Even within fundamentalist trends in a single religion, there is a great diversity of ideas. Some fundamentalist views emphasize collective equality and reject individual freedom in favor of submission to God; others posit an expression of individual freedom made possible through a political system based on faith and are less concerned with inequalities between people. There are also views that reject both freedom and equality in favor of hierarchy and the domination of believers over nonbelievers or the more faithful over the less so. Some forms of fundamentalism see the possibility of a religiously correct state; for others, that very notion of the state is incompatible with faith. It is thus a mistake to think of fundamentalism as a single ideology; rather, it is a pattern that recurs across many religions and that has produced various ideological forms. In some cases, these forms remain nebulous and attract few adherents. In other cases, the ideologies are well defined and exercise significant political power. As the politics of fundamentalism continues to develop, this aspect of the "return of God" may prove to be one of the most important developments in comparative politics.[13]

Political Culture

Our final area of consideration in this chapter is political culture. First we need to understand what is meant by "culture" in general; if society is a group of people bound by shared institutions, as it was defined at the start of this chapter, then **culture** is the content of the institutions that help define a society. Culture acts as a kind of social road map, providing norms and priorities that guide people as they organize their lives. While ethnicity, nationality, and citizenship define which group an individual belongs to, culture is the repository for the activities and ideas that the group considers proper and normal. **Political culture**, in turn, refers to a society's norms for political activity.

The study of culture in political science has changed over time. In the past, social scientists tended to treat them indistinguishably. The economic and political development of countries was often explained as a function of cultural or religious factors. For example, Weber famously argued that a "Protestant work ethic," linked to religious values, fostered the accumulation and investment of wealth that was critical in sparking the Industrial Revolution. A related argument has stressed that Protestantism's emphasis on private property and individualism also contributed to the emergence of democracy in Europe—in contrast to Catholicism, whose religious values were more authoritarian and anticapitalist. However, over time these kinds of arguments lost favor for several reasons. First, as we noted in the previous section, from the beginning of the twentieth century religion lost much of its authority in the developed world as ideologies and secular regimes grew in power. Second, modernization theory argued that culture in general was undergoing a process of transformation, such that as states modernized, they would develop shared secular values. Inasmuch as there were different cultures, they were, like faith in God in general, remnants of a premodern era that would be swept away by material and technological progress. Given enough time and money, every society would eventually wind up looking like Western Europe. Third, even for those who advocated cultural explanations for politics, there was the problem of how to measure and compare culture.

But if God has returned as a subject of study, so has culture. As in the past, culture and religion are often interlinked—political scientists and social psychologists who define major cultural differences still do so largely on the basis of religion (though they make other important distinctions, such as ideological legacies). As you can imagine, this resurgent interest is not without controversy—the idea that culture strongly influences politics goes against decades of scholarship that emphasized modernization and secularization. The best example of this debate has been the work of Samuel Huntington, who caused a firestorm with his 1996 book *The Clash of Civilizations and the Remaking of World Order*.[14] In it, he argued that with the end of the Cold War, cultural differences were now the main fault lines defining international relations. Huntington was praised and pilloried, and for nearly two decades scholars have been trying to confirm or reject his arguments. If we can get past the controversy, there are important puzzles to explore. Why are some countries richer than others? Why are some more unequal? Why are some more democratic? Why are some more prone to political violence? Can culture explain these differences?

IN FOCUS

Political Culture Is . . .

- The basic norms for political activity in a society.
- A determining factor in what ideologies will dominate a country's political regime.
- Unique to a given country or group.
- Distinct from political attitudes and ideologies.

In short, the study of political culture has resurfaced in political science, but there is still a great deal of confusion about what conclusions we can draw from it. Some of the best research we have in this regard is the work of Ronald Inglehart, who for three decades has been conducting public-opinion research in nearly 80 countries around the world. His data, known as the World Values Survey, allows us to track differences in beliefs across countries, cultures, and time. Inglehart finds that at the national level, countries can be mapped in terms of their particular values; as he and his co-author, Christian Wetzel, assert, "a society's heritage—whether shaped by Protestantism, Catholicism, Islam, Confucianism, or communism—leaves a lasting imprint on a society's worldview."[15] Even as countries modernize, their cultural heritage continues to influence their society and politics.

With this idea in mind, let's tackle one of the most controversial cultural questions: whether Islam is incompatible with democracy (as Huntington claimed might be the case). Table 3.1 provides answers from a number of important Muslim countries in the Middle East, North Africa, and Asia. The questions posed in the survey focus on the religiosity of those in government, the influence of religious leaders, and the general preference for democratic leadership. The United States and India are added for comparison. There is widespread support for religious individuals in government office; however, whether religious leaders should influence politics and government is another matter. In only one country (Morocco) is there majority support for religious leaders influencing the public vote. If we look at the fourth question, we get yet another set of answers. Three countries (Turkey, Indonesia, and Jordan) are opposed to the influence of religious leadership on government, while three (Malaysia, Morocco, and Iran) support it. Support for democratic leadership is similarly diverse. Survey findings from the United States and India show a lower demand for government leaders to be religious, but the answers regarding the influence of religious leaders and democratic leadership are in the same range as in Muslim countries. Surveying the data, Inglehart and his colleagues conclude there is not a significant difference between Muslim and Western countries in their support for democracy; however, there is greater support for a *societal role* for religion in Muslim countries, which can in turn affect other political issues, such as gender equality or sexual and reproductive freedoms. Beyond Islam, the persistence of religion's role in social institutions can be found across all world cultures.[16]

In short, modernization theory and political-culture theory can both be right: as societies modernize, their important political institutions and values are likely to undergo transformation. But other social values may be much more resistant to change, however developed a country may be. This should not surprise us—as we have noted, institutions are sticky. Culture and development will continue to shape each other in ways we do not expect.

In Sum: Society and Politics

Societies are complex and often difficult to unravel. In looking at how societal organization shapes politics, we have found that individuals have a number of identities that they hold simultaneously: ethnicity, national identity, citizenship, political attitude, ideology, and political culture. Ethnicity provides a group identity, binding individuals to a group, providing solidarity, and separating them from

TABLE 3.1

Religion, Politics, and Democracy (% in agreement)

	GOVERNMENT LEADERS AND RELIGION		RELIGIOUS LEADERS AND GOVERNMENT		DEMOCRACY
	Politicians who do not believe in God are unfit for office	It is better if more people with strong religious beliefs are in public office	Religious leaders should not influence how people vote	Religious leaders should not influence government	It is better to have a strong leader who does not have to bother with parliament and elections
Turkey	55	48	72	69	59
Indonesia	88	83	78	57	24
Malaysia	64	58	54	46	60
Morocco	54	61	39	38	27
Iran	75	68	60	44	73
Jordan	69	64	72	64	19
Iraq	87	52	52	n/a	21
United States	32	42	61	49	33
India	49	38	67	65	63

Source: World Values Survey, 2005–08.

others. National identity provides a political aspiration for that group, a desire for freedom through self-government, while citizenship establishes a relation between that group and a state. Although each of these identities can be clearly defined, they are often strongly connected and in some cases blend into each other. Such identities may bind people together, but they can be the source of conflict when different groups see each other as threats to their freedom and equality.

Whereas group identities establish differences between groups as a whole, an individual is positioned within a group by political attitudes, ideologies, and culture. These three identities shape an individual's view of the ideal relation between freedom and equality in society and the scope and pace of political change.

Society's role in politics is clearly complicated, shaped by an array of factors that affect the ongoing debate over freedom and equality. Not long ago, many social scientists dismissed social identities such as nationalism and religion as outdated forms of identification that were giving way in the face of modernization and individualism. However, most now believe that collective identities are more resilient than was once thought and that they may in fact sharpen in the face of new societal challenges. Politics is not simply a sum of individual actions but the product of a rich array of institutions that overlap one another, giving our lives meaning and informing our ideas, viewpoints, and values. We will consider this idea further in the next chapter as we turn to a new set of institutions and ideas that shape the struggle over freedom and equality: those concerned with economic life.

For Further Reading

RS> Alesina, Alberto and Eliana La Ferrara. "Ethnic Diversity and Economic Performance." *Journal of Economic Literature* 43, no. 3 (September 2005).

RS> Baldwin, Kate and John D. Huber. "Economic vs. Cultural Differences: Forms of Ethnic Diversity and Public Goods Provision." *American Political Science Review* 104, no. 4 (2010).

Bendix, Reinhard. *Nation-Building and Citizenship* (Berkeley: University of California Press, 1964).

Boix, Carles and Susan C. Stokes, eds. *The Oxford Handbook of Comparative Politics* (New York: Oxford University Press, 2007).

RS> Fearon, James D. and David D. Laitin. "Ethnicity, Insurgency, and Civil War." *The American Political Science Review* 97, no. 1 (2003).

RS> Hobsbawm, Eric. "Nationalism." *The Age of Revolution* (London: Weidenfeld & Nicholson, 1962).

Huntington, Samuel P. *The Clash of Civilizations and the Remaking of World Order* (New York: Simon and Schuster, 1996).

Horowitz, David. *Ethnic Groups in Conflict* (Berkeley: University of California Press, 2000).

Lawrence, Bruce. *Defenders of God: The Fundamentalist Revolt against the Modern Age* (New York: Harper and Row, 1989).

Norris, Pippa and Ronald Inglehart. *Sacred and Secular: Religion and Politics Worldwide* (New York: Cambridge University Press, 2004).

Stepan, Alfred, Juan Linz, and Yogendra Yadav. *Crafting State-Nations: India and Other Multinational Democracies* (Baltimore: Johns Hopkins University Press, 2011).

Tilly, Charles, ed. *The Formation of National States in Western Europe* (Princeton: Princeton University Press, 1975).

RS>
Reader Selection

Highlighted selections are included in *Essential Readings in Comparative Politics*, Fourth Edition.

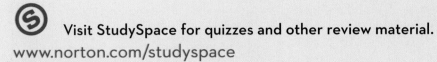

Visit StudySpace for quizzes and other review material.
www.norton.com/studyspace

- Vocabulary Flashcards of All Key Terms
- Chapter Review Quizzes
- Complete Study Reviews and Outlines

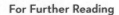

4

Different political-economic systems produce varying levels of freedom, equality, wealth, and human development. Here, a Holiday Inn overlooks shanty housing in Gujerat, India. As India liberalizes its economy, both its wealth and level of inequality have grown.

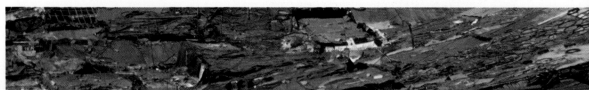

POLITICAL ECONOMY

KEY CONCEPTS

- All states are involved in the management of markets and property.

- States provide public goods, which are shared by society to some collective benefit.

- Different political-economic systems reconcile freedom and equality through such things as social expenditures, taxation, regulation, and trade.

- Different states and political-economic systems can be compared through levels of human development, wealth, and inequality.

- Political-economic systems have become increasingly liberal over the past three decades.

Like politics, economies are made up of many different institutions—rules, norms, and values—that strongly influence how the economic system is constructed. People often think about economic systems as somehow "natural," with functions akin to the law of gravity. In reality, an economy relies on an array of institutions that enable individuals to exchange goods and resources with one another. Moreover, economic institutions, like political ones, are not easy to replace or change once they have been constructed. They become self-perpetuating, and people have a hard time imagining life without them.

Economic institutions directly influence politics, and vice versa. The economy is one of the major arenas in which the struggle over freedom and equality takes place. Some view the economy as the central means by which people can achieve individual freedom, whereas others view the economy as the central means by which people can achieve collective equality. Inevitably, this struggle involves the government, the state, and the regime. How the balance between freedom and equality is struck directly influences such things as the distribution of wealth, the kinds of economic activity and trade that citizens may conduct, and the overall degree of security and prosperity that people enjoy. In short, the interactions between political and economic institutions in any country will have a profound impact on the prosperity of every citizen. The study of how politics and economics are related and how their relationship shapes the balance between freedom and equality is commonly known as **political economy.**

In this chapter, we will address these issues through an investigation of the relationship between freedom and equality. We will start by asking what role states play in managing an economy. There are several different areas in which states commonly involve themselves in economic life; depending on such things as the dominant ideology and regime, the scope and impact of these actions can vary dramatically. Just as there are different ideologies concerning the ideal relationship between the state and society, as we saw in Chapter 3, there are different ideological views regarding the ideal relationship between the state and the market, each of which leads to a different political-economic system. Once we have compared these differing views, we will consider how we might measure and compare their relative outcomes. In the process, we will look at some of the most common standards by which wealth and its distribution can be measured. Finally, we will consider the future of the relationship between state and market and how their interaction shapes the balance between freedom and equality.

The Components of Political Economy

Before we compare the different types of relationships between states and economies around the world, we should familiarize ourselves with the basic components of political economy. All modern states are strongly involved in the day-to-day affairs of their economies, at both the domestic and the global level. In shaping the economy to achieve their stated ideological goals, states and regimes use a variety of economic institutions.

Markets and Property

The most fundamental components of political economy are markets and property. When people speak of markets, the first thing that may come to mind is a physical place where individuals buy and sell goods. For as long as human beings have lived in settled communities that were able to produce a surplus of goods, there have been markets. Markets are closely connected to the rise of cities; people would settle around markets, and markets would often spring up around fortifications, where commerce could be conducted with some sense of security. Such markets are still common in much of the world.

When social scientists speak of markets, they are speaking of the interaction of supply and demand, though without a specific location. **Markets** are the interactions between the forces of supply and demand, and they allocate resources through the process of those interactions. As these two forces interact, they create values for goods and services by arriving at specific prices. What is amazing about markets is that they can be so decentralized. Who decides how many cars should be built this year? Or what colors they should be? Or the cost of this textbook? These decisions are made not by any one person or government but by millions of individuals making decisions about what they will buy and sell. If I produce a good and set its price at more than people are willing to pay, I will not be able to sell it and turn a profit. This will force me to either lower my price or go out of business. Similarly, if I have a good that no one wants, I must change it or face economic ruin. Sellers seek to create products that people will desire or need, and buyers seek to buy the best or the most goods at the lowest price. Because more than one seller or producer typically exists for a product, this tends to generate competition and innovation. Sellers seek to dominate a market by offering their goods at the cheapest price or by offering a good that is innovative and therefore superior to any alternative.

In short, markets are communities of buyers and sellers constantly interacting through the economic choices they make. At the same time, market forces typically require the state to enforce contracts, sanction activity, and regulate supply and demand where necessary. For example, by setting a minimum wage, a state is controlling to some extent the price of labor. By making certain drugs or prostitution illegal, the state is attempting to stamp out a part of the market altogether. Yet these goals are not always easily achieved. Minimum wages can be subverted by relying on illegal immigrants, and "black" or underground markets appear where drugs and prostitution are illegal. While markets rely on states, they also have a life of their own, and each state must decide in what way and to what extent it will sustain and control the market.

- Sellers seek to create products that will be in demand.

- Buyers seek to buy the best or most goods at the lowest price.

- Markets are the medium through which buyers and sellers exchange goods.

- Markets emerge spontaneously and are not easily controlled by the state.

Property is a second element critical to any economy. **Property** refers to the ownership of the goods and services exchanged through markets. Property can refer to land, buildings, businesses, or personal items, to name some of its most common forms. In addition, a certain set of property rights can accompany ownership, such as the right to buy and sell property or the right not to have it taken away by the state or other citizens without a good reason (just cause) and compensation. As with market forces, property rights must be regulated by the state. Without state power functioning in a fair manner, property is insecure.

In many people's minds, property has a physical presence. I can see a car, buy it, own it, and sell it when I want a new one. However, property is not always tangible. Intellectual property, for example, refers to ownership of a specific type of knowledge or content—a song, a piece of software code, or a treatment for diabetes. As economic developments center more and more on such intangible forms of information and knowledge, the concept of property and property rights becomes as fuzzy as that of markets, with no physical entity to make transactions clearer. Anyone who has downloaded a song, a movie, or software from the Internet knows exactly what we are speaking of.

Like the role states play in regulating markets, the role they play in constructing and enforcing property rights, both between people and between the state and society, varies from state to state. States may fail to enforce the rights of individuals to protect their own property from other individuals—by neglecting to enact or uphold laws against counterfeiting or theft. States may also assume certain property rights for themselves, claiming ownership over property such as airwaves, oil, land, or businesses. It is important to understand that property rights do not automatically come into being. In fact, many less-developed countries enjoy a wealth of property but have a poverty of property rights, as these states are unable or unwilling to establish and enforce such rules. We will speak about this more in Chapter 10.

Public Goods

We have so far described property as goods that individuals acquire or use through the market for their own benefit. But there are limits to what property and the markets can achieve. In some cases, their interaction does not produce benefits that society desires. Take, for example, transportation. Forms of transportation infrastructure do exist in the private realm, such as toll roads or passenger ferries, and these private forms have a long history that predates the state. But most modern societies question the moral and practical implications of allowing these goods to belong only to a few. The privatization of such goods may limit economic development: a network of privately held roads might impede trade or fail to reach certain parts of the population. Because of such concerns, all states provide some level of public goods; indeed, the core definition of a state itself—a monopoly of violence—is the underlying public good on which all markets and property rest.

Public goods can be defined as those goods, provided or secured by the state, that are available for society and indivisible, meaning that no one private person or organization can own them. Unlike private goods, with their inherent link to individual freedom, public goods can generate greater equality, as the public is able to share broadly in their benefits.[1]

In many countries, roads, national defense, health care, and primary education are public goods, and everyone in the country may use them or benefit from their existence. But states do differ greatly in the extent to which they provide public goods, in large part because of the role of ideology in the relationship between states and markets. In the United States, health care is not a public good; it remains in private hands, and not everyone has equal access to it. In Canada, however, health care is a public good, provided by the state in the form of publicly owned hospitals and universal benefits for all citizens. In Saudi Arabia, Brazil, Mexico, Norway, and Iran, oil is a public good, owned by the state; revenue from its sale is spread (although not equally) among society. In Cuba, most businesses are owned by the state, making them public goods as well. The goods and profits of these firms belong not to a private owner but to the state, to be distributed as the government sees fit.

Social Expenditures: Who Benefits?

This discussion of public goods leads us to the broader subject of **social expenditures**— the state's provision of public benefits, such as education, health care, and transportation, or what is commonly called "welfare" or the "welfare state." For many

Americans the very word *welfare*, like taxes, has an inherently negative connotation; it calls up images of free riders living off the hard work of others. In many countries the redistribution of wealth in this manner can be controversial, with critics asserting that social expenditures lead to counterproductive behavior. High unemployment benefits, they argue, may discourage people from seeking work. Moreover, alternative forms of social security that people have relied on in the past, such as the family, the community, or churches, could be weakened by too broad a welfare system. None of these arguments is necessarily true, or true for all countries. We'll talk more about this in a moment.

However valid these arguments may or may not be, one practical problem for many countries is that social expenditures can be very costly, especially where the population is aging and paying less in taxes while drawing more social expenditures. In recent years, many countries have sought to control the growth of social expenditures, but this is easier said than done. We will explore this issue further in Chapter 7 as we consider the problem in the advanced democracies in particular.

Who benefits from social expenditures? Strictly defined, social expenditures are provided by the state to those who find themselves in circumstances where they require greater care: the unemployed, the elderly, the poor, and the disabled. Such expenditures can include health care, job training, income replacement, and housing. However, many forms of social expenditures are public goods that are more widely used. For example, a national health-care system treats employed and unemployed, wealthy and poor alike. Highways, public higher education, and cultural institutions such as museums may primarily benefit the well-off. In fact, if we look at social expenditures more broadly, we find that in many countries they mostly benefit the middle class, not the poor. In this sense, the modern welfare state is less a structure whereby the middle class and the rich are taxed to benefit the poor than one in which the middle class and the rich are taxed for services that benefit themselves.

Taxation

Over the past fifty years, states have become increasingly responsible for providing public goods and social expenditures. How do states pay for these expenses? One major source of funds is taxation. As with social expenditures, taxation generates passionate opinions: some view it as the means by which a greedy state takes the hard-earned revenues of its citizens, stunting economic growth, whereas others see it as a critical tool for generating a basic level of equality. Regardless of one's opinion of taxation, states are expected by societies to provide a number of public goods and services, and for most countries taxation is the key source of revenue. The other option is to borrow money from domestic and international lenders.

How much tax is collected varies from country to country. Figure 4.1 illustrates this variation, showing that in some countries taxes consume a large portion of a country's **gross domestic product (GDP)**, defined as the total market value of goods and services produced by one country in a year. Many European countries with large social expenditures tend to have high overall tax rates to fund those expenses. In addition, countries differ in where this revenue comes from. Some countries rely on high personal taxation while others rely on taxes on businesses or goods and services. All countries struggle with finding the right mix and level of taxation, aiming to extract needed funds and reinvest them in a way that will generate development and prosperity.

Money, Inflation, and Economic Growth

It should be getting clearer that many political-economic processes are tightly interlinked. States must form a relationship with markets and property, deciding what goods and property should remain in private hands, what should be public, and what kinds of rights exist for each. They must also determine the level and forms of social expenditures needed to ensure a basic standard of living and security for all citizens. This distribution requires funds, and states must typically draw on the public's resources through taxation. But a successful and productive tax base needs a dynamic and growing economy. So while the state is charged with managing markets, property, and public benefits, it also has a hand in fostering economic growth.

One basic way the state fosters growth is through the creation and management of money. Money is nothing more than a medium of exchange; unlike wealth, which consists of property that has value, money is an instrument with which people conduct economic transactions. Money represents only a tiny fraction of the wealth in the world, most of which is tied up in houses, factories, land, and other property. But without money, economic transactions are difficult. States thus play a critical role in providing money as a means to secure and stimulate economic transactions.

Long ago, money did not exist. As complex political systems began to take shape, however, they established some basic monetary relationships through a monetary system, which typically rested on metals that held some intrinsic value, like gold and silver. Within the past century, however, money has lost its intrinsic worth, and people have come to base their faith in a state's currency on their trust

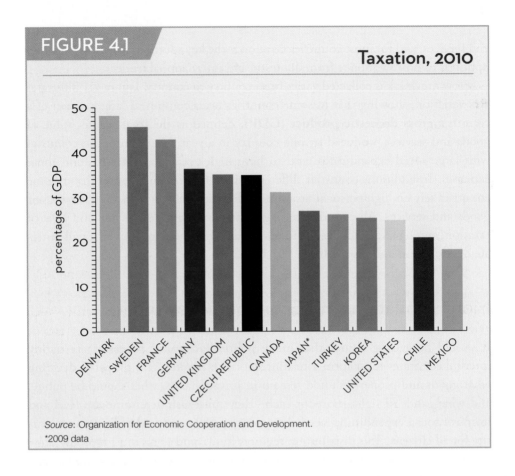

FIGURE 4.1

Taxation, 2010

percentage of GDP

DENMARK · SWEDEN · FRANCE · GERMANY · UNITED KINGDOM · CZECH REPUBLIC · CANADA · JAPAN* · TURKEY · KOREA · UNITED STATES · CHILE · MEXICO

Source: Organization for Economic Cooperation and Development.
*2009 data

in that state. People accept payments in dollars or euros or yen because they know that others will accept them in turn. A society trusts its currency only so long as it trusts its state.

Because states control money, they have a great deal of influence over their domestic economies. Part of this power comes through what is known as a **central bank**, an institution that controls how much money is flowing through the economy, as well as how much it costs to borrow money in that economy. One of the main ways a central bank influences these two areas is by changing a national interest rate—that is, the rate charged to private banks when they need to borrow funds from the central bank or one another. When the central bank lowers the interest rate charged to banks, those banks in turn typically lower their own interest rates for businesses and individuals. Loans become less expensive and saving becomes less lucrative, prompting people to borrow more and spend more. This in turn increases the amount of money active in the economy and stimulates economic growth. If the central bank raises interest rates, on the other hand, people are likely to borrow less and save more to take advantage of the higher interest their savings can earn. The money supply in the economy contracts as a result, and economic growth is likely to slow. Thus, during the first half of 2008 the U.S. Federal Reserve (the U.S. central bank) cut interest rates six times in an effort to stave off an economic downturn. As of 2011, it sat at one quarter of one percent (.25%). In 1980, by contrast, it was 17 percent.

The actions the central bank takes are closely tied to two other important factors in any economy: inflation and deflation. **Inflation** can be defined as an increase in the overall prices in the economy when demand outstrips supply. Although small levels of inflation are not a problem, inflation can become problematic when it is too high. Wages and savings lose their value, and workers and those on fixed incomes, such as the retired, find that their money buys less and less. People press for higher wages or benefits to offset higher prices, and this feeds inflation further. Central banks can try to control inflation by raising interest rates, making credit more expensive, thereby reducing spending and lowering prices. However, the prices of many things, like oil, are beyond a state's control. States can also be the cause of inflation if the government, unable to cover its expenses, is forced to borrow money at ever-higher interest rates to attract lenders. This can lead to very high inflation.

In extreme cases, countries can experience **hyperinflation**, defined as inflation that is higher than 50 percent a month for more than two months in a row (the inflation rate in North America and Europe over the past decade ranged between 1 and 4 percent per year). When governments find themselves lacking the tax revenues to cover basic expenditures and are unable to borrow from lenders, they may decide to print money to cover their debts, expanding the money supply. At the same time, such circumstances are often accompanied by a public belief that there is no longer a strong state to support the currency—a collapse of legitimacy. Under such conditions, normal economic processes fail. Zimbabwe is an extreme example. Over the past decade its government, having largely disrupted its agricultural economy and thus its tax base, began to cover expenses by printing money. By 2008, inflation reached 231,000,000 percent. The largest bank notes issued were for 100 trillion Zimbabwean dollars—about 30 U.S. dollars. Hyperinflation typically leads to currency collapse, as people increasingly refuse to accept the devalued currency as payment and switch to other means of transaction, from foreign currency to barter.

The dangers of inflation might lead us to conclude that tight control over the money supply should be a government's first economic priority. But there are problems at the other end of the spectrum as well. Under some conditions, especially recently, states face the danger of **deflation**, when too many goods are chasing

- Controls the amount of money in the economy.
- Controls the cost of borrowing money.
- Lowers interest rates to stimulate the economy.
- Raises interest rates to check inflation.

too little money. Dropping prices might sound like a good thing, but they can be devastating if businesses are unable to make a profit, leading to unemployment, less spending, and even more deflation. This has been a serious problem in Japan, which has suffered deflation almost every year since 1998, and has been a concern in North America and Europe since 2008. Heavy levels of debt by banks, consumers, and states, as well as related unemployment, have led to a tightening in spending. Central banks have set their lending rates extremely low, in the hope of stimulating borrowing, spending, and growth. However, they have had limited effect. States can certainly harm or hurt economies, but markets also have a life of their own.[2]

Regulation

So far, our discussion has dealt with the state's role in markets and property—what is to be provided, by whom, and at what cost. But states must concern themselves not only with economic output but also with the means by which that output is created. As with public goods, moral and technical issues often affect a state's approach in this area. Are some economic processes inherently counterproductive to creating goods and services? What about economic processes that can result in a detrimental impact on society, such as pollution? Whose rights are primary in these circumstances, citizens' or businesses'? These concerns draw states into the realm of economic regulation. **Regulations**—rules or orders that set the boundaries of a given procedure—may take a number of different forms. First, regulations may be fundamentally economic in nature. Such regulations may control prices for certain goods or services, such as food or energy. Economic regulations may also control what firms may operate in what markets. National rail systems, for example, have functioned in many countries as either a private or state **monopoly**—in other words, a market controlled by a single producer. A second set of regulations can be described as essentially social in nature. In contrast to economic regulations that focus on how businesses function in the market, social regulations deal more with managing risk, such as safety and environmental standards. Naturally these kinds of regulations overlap; for example, environmental regulations can strongly affect what firms may enter the market.

Trade

States must grapple with the challenge of regulating economic production not just within their country but between their citizens and the outside world. In most economies, markets are not only local; goods and services come from all over the world. States can influence the degree of competition and access to goods within their own country by determining what foreign goods and services may enter the domestic market.

The way in which a state structures its trade can have a profound impact on its own economic development. States have a number of tools to influence trade: **tariffs**, which are basically taxes on imported goods; **quotas**, which limit the quantity of a good coming into the country; and other **nontariff regulatory barriers**, which may create health, packaging, or other restrictions and whose purpose is to protect its citizens and make it difficult or expensive for foreign goods to be sold in the local market. For example, in Canada, 35 percent of all music on AM and FM radio must be of Canadian origin, and for television programs, 60 percent must be Canadian. Airlines that fly only within the United States must be American owned.

Why regulate trade? States may favor tariffs as a way to generate revenue, and they and local manufacturers may see such barriers as a way to stimulate or protect

IN FOCUS / Arguments over the Regulation of Trade

WHY REGULATE TRADE?	WHY NOT?
■ To generate state revenue	■ To promote competition
■ To foster local industry	■ To keep the costs of goods low
■ To protect local jobs	■ To stimulate domestic innovation in areas of comparative advantage
■ To keep wealth in the country	

local industries and firms. Those who oppose trade barriers argue that trade leads to more competition, innovation, and **comparative advantage**—the ability to produce a particular good or service more efficiently than other countries.

We've covered a great deal in this section, so let's quickly review what we have discussed. The most basic building blocks of political economy are markets and property, and states are involved in creating and enforcing rules that govern both. States help fashion markets and define property, and they use taxation in part to provide public goods and services. States can influence the growth of an economy through interest rates and, through regulation and trade, what is produced and where. All these responsibilities are part of a complex web of cause and effect that can shape freedom, equality, and the generation of wealth. Which mixture of policies across these areas will result in economic prosperity and state power? States have taken radically different approaches to the ideal relationship between state and market, leading to a variety of distinct political-economic systems around the world—all of which are currently under challenge.

Political-Economic Systems

A **political-economic system** can be defined as the actual relationship between political and economic institutions in a particular country, as well as the policies and outcomes they create. Various types of political-economic systems view the ideal relationship between state and market, and between freedom and equality, in different ways. Political-economic systems are often classified as liberalism, social democracy, communism, or mercantilism. Three of these political-economic systems match the political ideologies we discussed in Chapter 3. This should not be too surprising: political-economic systems can be seen as the attempt to realize an abstract ideology in the form of real economic institutions and policies. There is always a disjuncture, however, between theory and practice. For example, some subscribers to a liberal ideology would say that existing "liberal" political-economic systems around the world do not live up to liberal ideals. Many communists similarly condemned the communist political-economic system that was practiced in the Soviet Union as a betrayal of "true" communist thought. In addition, the ideologies of fascism and anarchism do not have a political-economic counterpart to speak of. The fascist political-economic systems that arose in the 1930s were destroyed by World War II, and anarchism has never been effectively realized.

These basic classifications simplify the complexity of political economy. In reality, of course, there are many different variations within these categories. Each of these categories strikes a different balance between state power and the economy, thereby shaping markets and property, public goods and social expenditures, taxation, regulation, and trade.

Liberalism

Recall from Chapter 3 that, as a political ideology, liberalism places a high priority on individual political and economic freedom and advocates limiting state power in order to foster and protect this freedom. Liberalism assumes that individuals are best suited to take responsibility for their own behavior and well-being. Liberal scholars such as Adam Smith put their faith in the market and in private property: if people are allowed to harness their own energies, sense of entrepreneurialism, and, yes, greed, they will generate more prosperity than any government could produce through "top-down" policy making and legislation.

For liberals, then, the best state is a weak one, constrained in its autonomy and capacity. Other than securing property rights, the state should have a limited involvement in the economy. Public goods should be located only in critical areas such as defense and education to prevent "free riding" and to encourage individual responsibility. Unemployment should be accepted as an inevitable, even desirable part of market flexibility. Taxation should be kept to a minimum so that wealth remains in the hands of the public. Regulation should be light, and trade should be encouraged to stimulate competition and innovation. Overall, the state should act as a sort of night watchman, intervening to defend the public only when crises arise. These conditions describe the liberal tenet of **laissez-faire** (French for "let do"), which holds that the economy should be allowed to do what it wishes. This is what we typically think of as **capitalism**—a system of private property and free markets.

When the government's role is minimal, liberals believe, economic growth will be maximized. Moreover, under such conditions, people will enjoy the greatest amount of personal and political freedom. Liberals would in fact maintain that democracy requires a free market. If too much economic and political power is concentrated in the hands of the state, they believe, this monopoly would endanger democracy. Thus, weak states are best; as Adam Smith, one of the fathers of liberal ideology, argued in 1755, "Little else is requisite to carry a state to the highest degree of opulence from the lowest barbarism but peace, easy taxes, and a tolerable administration of justice: all the rest being brought about by the natural course of things."[3]

Liberalism as a political-economic system, then, is defined by its emphasis on individual freedoms over collective equality and on the power of markets over the state. As you might imagine, the United States is typically touted as a paragon of liberal values. Regulations are often weaker and social expenditures and taxation lower than in other industrialized democracies, and the American public is largely skeptical of state power and embraces capitalism. But the United States is not the only country in the liberal camp. The United Kingdom, the intellectual wellspring for much of liberal thought, is also viewed as a liberal country, as are Canada, Australia, and New Zealand (all, like the United States, former British colonies). Many other countries around the world have over the past twenty years embraced the "neoliberal" economic model and are noted for their relatively low levels of government regulation, taxation, and social expenditures. However, even though these countries can all be classified as liberal, they vary in a number of ways, such as the range of public goods they provide, like higher education and unemployment or retirement benefits. In addition, even though liberal ideology would argue that a free market and democracy are inseparable, we find countries with liberal political-economic systems that nevertheless restrict democratic rights. Singapore and Bahrain are regularly noted for having some of the freest economic systems in the world, and yet individual political and civil rights are restricted in each. In 2011, Bahrain cracked down against its Shia Muslim majority population after pro-democracy protests, killing and arresting many protestors. In the 1980s, Chile, while suffering under military dictatorship, was lauded as a paragon of economic liberalism. Critics of liberalism often highlight this contradiction, pointing out that the free market can sit easily with political repression. We will discuss this contradiction further when we turn to authoritarianism in Chapter 6.

Social Democracy

In Chapter 3, we noted that social democracy draws from liberalism and communism in an attempt to temper the extremes of too much freedom and too much equality. Like liberalism, social democracy functions on a foundation of capitalism—private property and open markets—rejecting communists' call for revolution and the state appropriation of private property and wealth. Most notable among early social democratic thinkers was Edward Bernstein (1850–1932). In his 1898 work *Evolutionary Socialism*, Bernstein rejected Karl Marx's belief in inevitable revolution, concluding instead that democracy could evolve into socialism through the ballot box rather than through the gun.[4]

Rejecting revolution and embracing democracy, social democracy accepts a role for private property and market forces, but it remains more cautious than liberalism about their ultimate benefits to society. Unchecked economic development produces great inequality, social democrats argue, by concentrating wealth in the hands of a very few. This in turn can polarize society, pitting owners against laborers, rich against poor, city against countryside. In this way of thinking, the state is seen not as a threat to society or the economy but as a creator of social rights, otherwise lost in the vicissitudes of the market.

State power can thus manifest itself in a number of ways. According to social democracy, a wide array of public goods, such as health care, pensions, and higher education, should be made available by the state. The need for competition should not stand in the way of strong state regulation or even ownership of certain sectors of the economy, and trade should similarly be managed in such a way that it does not endanger domestic businesses and jobs. Finally, the goal of equality requires a higher level of social expenditures to ensure basic benefits for all. Taxes make these social expenditures possible while also redistributing wealth from the rich to the poor. Thus, taxes tend to be higher in a social democratic system, and capitalism more constrained.

As with liberalism, social democracies are not all of one type. For example, social democratic systems can vary in labor flexibility. Jobs may be highly regulated in terms of hours worked and conditions of termination, or firms may be able to fire workers more easily and hire at full or part time. Unemployment benefits may be generous, or more limited and contingent on retraining or government work schemes. Tax rates and the redistribution of income can also be quite varied; taxes as a percentage of GDP are not significantly different in the liberal United Kingdom and social democratic Germany, though in general social democratic systems rely on higher taxes.[5]

Another element found in some social democratic systems is **neocorporatism**, a system of policy making involving the state, labor, and businesses. In the liberal

IN FOCUS

How Do Social Democracies Seek To Achieve Greater Equality?

- Through taxes, which make high levels of social expenditure possible while redistributing wealth from rich to poor.

- Through trade, which is promoted but balanced with preserving domestic industry and jobs.

- Through government regulation and even ownership of important sectors of the economy.

Contributors to the Theories of Political Economy

SYSTEM	THINKER	CONTRIBUTION
LIBERALISM	Adam Smith	*The Wealth of Nations* (1776), considered one of the first texts on modern economics. Articulated the idea that economic development requires limited government interference.
MERCANTILISM	Friedrich List	*National System of Political Economy* (1841). Rejected free-trade theories of liberalism, arguing that states must play a strong role in protecting and developing the national economy against foreign competitors.
COMMUNISM	Karl Marx	*Das Kapital* (1867). Asserted that human history is driven by economic relations and inequality and that revolution will eventually replace capitalism with a system of total equality among people.
SOCIAL DEMOCRACY	Edward Bernstein	*Evolutionary Socialism* (1898). Rejected Marx's belief in the inevitability of revolution, arguing that economic equality can be achieved through democratic participation.

model, economic decisions are made through the competitive interaction of business and labor; workers demand higher wages or better safety conditions, striking or quitting their jobs when necessary, and employers hire, fire, and negotiate with workers as they see fit. The state plays a limited role in these relations. In contrast, a neocorporatist system relies on a limited number of associations that represent a large segment of business and labor. These associations, such as trade unions and business associations, are in turn recognized by the state as legitimate representatives of their members, and together these associations and the state forge agreements on such important economic policy issues as wages, unemployment compensation, and taxation. The result, supporters argue, is a system that is much less prone to conflict and that provides a greater role for both business and labor in state economic policies.

Finally, social democratic systems often involve themselves in the economic system through partial or total state ownership of firms, which they consider to be public goods. Until 2002, the French state owned more than 40 percent of the auto manufacturer Renault (it now owns around 15 percent); and in Sweden, all iron mines are owned by the state, having been purchased from private businesses decades ago. Social democratic systems are most common in Europe (particularly Scandinavia) where states have more autonomy and capacity in order to actively manage the economy.[6] Liberals criticize such systems as costly and a drag on innovation and competition; social democrats respond that their system avoids the excesses of liberalism while still encouraging entrepreneurial activity.

Communism

Whereas social democracy departs from liberalism in its attempt to balance individual freedom and collective equality, the political-economic system of communism chooses effectively to eliminate individual freedom to achieve equality. We will discuss communism in much greater detail in Chapter 8, when we look at communist and postcommunist countries; for now we will focus on its basic political-economic institutions. Communist thinkers such as Karl Marx began with the premise that capitalism, with its private property and free markets, cannot truly serve the needs of society as a whole. Communists view private property and markets as a form of power that inevitably leads to one person or group gaining control over others. Economic competition between people creates exploitation and the development of social classes in which a small group of the wealthy dominate and benefit from the labor of the poor majority. Both domestically and internationally, this exploitation opens an ever-wider gap between those who control the economy and those who merely labor in it. Such inequalities, Marx argued, will inevitably lead to a revolution, through which a single communist party will take control of the state on behalf of all people.

Communist systems use the state to transform markets and property. Private property is fully nationalized, placed in the hands of the state on behalf of the people. In other words, the entire economy becomes a public good, existing for the benefit of all. In addition, market forces are eliminated by the state; almost all private transactions take place illegally, on the black market. Under communism, economic decision making is entrusted entirely to the state, which is assumed to be the only institution that can rationally allocate resources fairly. This requires a large bureaucracy to determine what needs to be made and how it should be distributed.

Because communist states centralize all economic decision making and ownership, many of the essential tasks of states in other political-economic systems are fundamentally different under communism. Taxation takes an indirect form through fixed prices and wages; any profit produced by a worker or a firm goes to the state for public

Political-Economic Systems

	LIBERALISM	SOCIAL DEMOCRACY	COMMUNISM	MERCANTILISM
ROLE OF THE STATE IN THE ECONOMY	Little; minimal welfare state	Some state ownership, regulation; large welfare state	Total state ownership; extensive welfare state	Much state ownership or direction; small welfare state
ROLE OF THE MARKET	Paramount	Important but not sacrosanct	None	Limited
STATE CAPACITY AND AUTONOMY	Low	Moderate	Very high	High
IMPORTANCE OF EQUALITY	Low	High	High	Low
HOW IS POLICY MADE?	Pluralism	Corporatism	State/party	State
POSSIBLE FLAWS	Inequality	Expense	Authoritarianism	Inefficiency
EXAMPLES	U.S., UK, former British colonies	Europe (Germany, Sweden)	Cuba, Soviet Union, North Korea	Japan, South Korea

expenditures. Labor is allocated by the state—in other words, the state decides who will work and where. Competition is eliminated, and regulations, although present, may be much weaker, since the state winds up regulating itself. Social expenditures are extensive, with all basic services, including health care, education, retirement, and even leisure activities owned and provided by the state. Finally, trade is highly restricted; the only imports are those the state deems necessary because they cannot be produced domestically. State capacity and autonomy are extremely high; the state can operate without interference from either the public or private economic actors.[7]

As you would expect, supporters of private property and market forces argue that states with communist political-economic systems lack the ability to effectively centralize all the economic decisions that are the normal product of a decentralized market. Moreover, placing all economic power in the hands of the state would essentially make democracy impossible. If there are no property rights left with the people and if all economic decisions are made by the state, there is no separation between public and private. States wind up controlling the fates of people—where they live and work, what they earn, what they may buy. In response, communists would say that what they offer is total equality for all; their system emphasizes equality over individual freedom, while liberalism does the opposite. And even if such a system is inefficient, its supporters might argue, better that economic resources are wasted in the attempt to provide for all than squandered on luxuries for a wealthy few, as seen in market economies.

Mercantilism

The final political-economic system, **mercantilism**, stands quite apart in the debate over freedom and equality that separates liberalism, social democracy, and communism. Whereas all three systems we have studied so far emphasize some mix of freedom and equality, mercantilism focuses on the needs of the state. National economic power is paramount and the domestic economy is an instrument to generate that power. Mercantilist states focus in particular on their position in the international system, for they believe that economic weakness undermines national sovereignty.[8]

Although this system may seem a strange outlier in the debate over the proper balance between freedom and equality, since it seems to emphasize neither, mercantilism is the oldest of the four political-economic systems we have covered. Historically, most states engaged in mercantilist practices. The building of empires, in particular, was an outgrowth of mercantilism, a way in which a state could use its political power to gain control over resources and markets, shutting out its rivals. The British Empire's policy that its colonies trade only with the home country is a good example of mercantilist practices at work. More recently, mercantilism has been used to great effect in Asia.

One way that mercantilist states attempt to achieve state economic power is through an active industrial policy. Economic ministries seek to direct the economy toward certain industries and away from others through such policies as taxation and subsidies. In some cases, they may rely on partial or full state ownership of specific industries (sometimes called **parastatals**), attempting to create or control businesses that are viewed as critical for international competitiveness.

Another, complementary method is the use of tariffs, nontariff barriers, and other trade regulations. Here the rationale is that foreign goods drain away wealth and promote an increased dependence on foreign economies. High tariff barriers are a common way to shield and promote domestic industry. After World War II,

How Do Mercantilist States Seek To Achieve Economic Power?

- By directing the economy toward certain industries and away from others through the use of subsidies and taxation.

- Through partial or full state ownership of industries that are considered critical (parastatals).

- With the strong use of tariffs, nontariff barriers, and other regulations.

- By limiting social expenditures and thereby keeping taxation to a minimum.

- With low interest rates set by the central bank to encourage borrowing and investment.

the Japanese government relied on its Ministry of International Trade and Industry to steer the economy toward exports such as electronics and automobiles. High tariff barriers kept foreign competition at bay, and subsidies were provided to certain industrial sectors, such as producers of semiconductors. South Korea and Brazil followed a similar set of policies; Brazil, for example, sought to create its own domestic computer industry through such policies.

In its emphasis on state power, mercantilism does not typically focus on social expenditures in the way that social democracy does. Welfare benefits tend to be much lower. Indeed, there is a logic to this policy: a low level of benefits can encourage higher public savings, which can in turn be borrowed by the state or businesses. Lower levels of expenditure are also likely to translate into lower taxes. State capacity and autonomy tend to be higher in mercantilist political-economic systems, though markets and private property remain.

Supporters of mercantilism cite its ability to direct an economy toward areas of industrial development and international competitiveness that the market, left on its own, might not pursue. For developing countries, such direction is particularly attractive, and Japan and South Korea are cited as exemplars of mercantilism's strengths.[9] Critics of mercantilism observe that, as with communism, states are ill-suited to decide a country's industrial path, and the result is often inefficient industries that survive only because they are protected from outside competition. In addition, the tight relationship between private property and the state is a recipe for corruption, which may drag down development. In the past, mercantilism was often associated with nondemocratic and even fascist regimes. However, South Korea and postwar Japan are countries whose mercantilism did not preclude democracy.

Political-Economic Systems and the State: Comparing Outcomes

Having gained an understanding of the different political-economic systems used around the world and the different ways they approach their tasks, we should next consider how to compare these systems. There are various indicators we can use; they are by no means the only means to make comparisons and draw conclusions, but they are useful tools for our purposes.

Measuring Wealth

One basic criterion for comparison is a country's level of economic development. The most common tool that economists use to measure economic development is gross domestic product, or GDP, which we earlier defined as the total market value of all goods and services produced in a country over a period of one year. GDP provides a basic benchmark for the average per capita income in a country. However, GDP statistics can be quite misleading. For one thing, a given amount of money will buy more in certain parts of a country than in others. A salary of $40,000 a year will go a lot further in Boise, Idaho, than it will in New York City, where the cost of living is much higher. The same problem arises when one compares countries: people may earn far more in some countries than they do in others, but those raw figures do not take into account the relative costs of living in those countries. Moreover, as exchange rates between national currencies rise or fall, countries can look richer or poorer than they are. To address these difficulties, economists often calculate national GDP data on the basis of what is known as purchasing-power parity. **Purchasing-power parity (PPP)** attempts to estimate the buying power of income in each country by comparing similar costs, such as food and housing, using prices in the United States as a benchmark. When these data are factored in, comparative incomes change dramatically, as shown in Table 4.1. For example, without PPP, Sweden's national income is much higher than Canada's, but when the cost of living in each country is factored in through PPP, their economies are revealed to be of similar size. Incomes in poorer countries such as China and India rise quite dramatically when PPP is taken into account.

Although GDP can be a useful way to measure wealth, it has limitations. One major problem is that it fails to capture much about the quality of life in a country, such as crime levels, mortality rates, and the health of the environment. Other elements of GDP provided by the state, such as health care or education, are hard to measure—meaning that social democratic countries, whose economies are greatly devalued using PPP, would appear to be much richer if these public goods were factored in. Many economists thus call for a revision if not the outright scrapping of GDP and its replacement with some other form of measurement.[10] Until that happens, we have other ways to determine the outcome of different political-economic systems.

Measuring Inequality and Poverty

Perhaps the most problematic aspect of GDP is that these data do not tell us how wealth is distributed among a population. One sophisticated approach to this problem is the **Gini index**, a mathematical formula that measures the amount of economic inequality in a society. Complete equality is given a Gini ranking of zero, and complete inequality gets a ranking of 100. Thus, the greater the Gini index number, the greater the inequality in a given economy. Some recent Gini coefficients are given in Table 4.1. If we look at these few cases, we note that the relationship between wealth and inequality is not automatic—more wealth does not make a country more or less equal. Second, political-economic systems do matter. Social democratic countries tend to have the lower Gini ratings, which is not surprising given their emphasis on equality. Liberal political-economic systems are more unequal, but levels of income disparity vary widely among them, from Canada and Ireland at the low end of the spectrum to the United States and Singapore at the high. Mercantilist and postcommunist countries show a similar range.

The most unequal countries in the world are very poor. However, inequality is not the same thing as poverty. Poverty tends to be measured in terms of absolute wealth; organizations like the World Bank establish benchmarks for world poverty rates—typically less than $1 per person per day. In contrast, inequality is a measure of relative wealth. Thus, an entire society can become more materially wealthy and grow more unequal at the same time. Australia has become wealthier and more equal since the 1990s; South Africa has grown wealthier and more unequal.

What are the trends for inequality and poverty worldwide? Some have calculated that a Gini coefficient for the world—a measure of total global inequality for all people—would stand at around 70, a figure that has probably not moved since the 1980s. At the same time, in many specific countries, such as China, India, and the United States, inequality has increased. And as for poverty, data indicate that it has fallen worldwide as a percentage of the world

TABLE 4.1	Economic Size and the Distribution of Wealth		
COUNTRY	GDP PER CAPITA (IN U.S. $)	GDP PER CAPITA (PPP, IN U.S. $) takes cost of living into account	GINI INDEX AND YEAR (100 = COMPLETE INEQUALITY)
Sweden	63,000	41,700	23 (2005)
Canada	51,600	41,000	32 (2005)
United States	50,300	50,300	45 (2007)
France	44,600	35,800	33 (2008)
Germany	44,300	38,800	27 (2006)
United Kingdom	41,300	36,800	34 (2005)
Japan	46,500	36,000	38 (2008)
South Korea	24,400	33,100	31 (2009)
Russia	15,800	18,000	42 (2009)
Mexico	11,100	15,800	48 (2008)
Brazil	13,100	12,300	57 (2005)
South Africa	7,900	11,300	65 (2005)
Iran	5,800	11,600	45 (2006)
China	5,300	9,200	42 (2007)
India	1,500	4,000	37 (2004)
Nigeria	1,800	2,700	44 (2003)

Source: International Monetary Fund and Central Intelligence Agency. GDP data is estimated for 2012.

population since the 1980s, from a third to less than 20 percent. Most of this reduction has occurred in Asia, particularly China and India. In Africa, poverty has declined as well, but at a much slower rate. However, as the world population grows, the absolute number of people in poverty continues to grow. In short, the conclusions you draw about poverty and inequality depend on what data you examine.[11]

Human Development Index (HDI)

Poverty, inequality between people and within countries—how can we make sense of any of this if we simply want to know whether people are better off? There is another measurement that might help. The **Human Development Index (HDI)**, created by the United Nations Development Program, not only looks at the total amount of wealth in a society and its distribution but also gives equal weight to income, health (life expectancy), and educational indicators. By looking at such data, we can consider whether the wealth generated in a country is actually used in a way that provides a basic standard of living for all through public or private means. Nearly all countries in the world are ranked on the HDI; in 2010, Norway was ranked at number one, and Zimbabwe (recall our discussion of hyperinflation) came in at the very bottom.

The HDI does show a strong correlation between standard of living and a country's GDP, as shown in Table 4.2. The countries with the highest national incomes also show the highest levels of education and life expectancy in the world. Interestingly, among the top twelve ranked on the index, we find social democratic systems such as Sweden and Norway right alongside more liberal countries such as the United States, Canada, and Australia and more mercantilist ones such as Japan and South Korea. But these findings are not quite as clear if we unpack their components of income, education, and health. In Table 4.2 each of these indicators has been evaluated separately, showing very different sets of rankings. The United States does well in education and income, but its health ranking lags far behind that of other wealthy countries. The United Kingdom does similarly poorly, while Japan's health ranks highly, even above that of social democratic states. However, Japan

---

IN FOCUS
Measuring Wealth

GROSS DOMESTIC PRODUCT (GDP)	Measures total production within a country, regardless of who owns the products.
PURCHASING-POWER PARITY (PPP)	Takes cost of living and buying power into account.
GINI INDEX	Assesses inequality.
HUMAN DEVELOPMENT INDEX (HDI)	Assesses health, education, and wealth of population.

TABLE 4.2

Measuring Wealth, Equality, and Prosperity

COUNTRY	UN HUMAN DEVELOPMENT RANKING	UN HEALTH RANKING	UN EDUCATION RANKING	UN INCOME RANKING	UN GENDER-EQUALITY RANKING
United States	4	29	5	9	55
Canada	8	11	13	14	15
Sweden	9	9	15	17	2
Germany	10	20	7	19	8
Japan	11	1	21	22	16
South Korea	12	25	6	28	19
France	14	6	25	23	13
United Kingdom	26	26	37	20	41
Mexico	56	43	70	57	77
Russia	65	122	63	53	50
Iran	70	99	89	72	116
Brazil	73	81	93	75	98
China	89	75	107	94	20
South Africa	112	164	80	78	138
India	121	133	132	126	124
Nigeria	142	173	134	143	153

Source: United Nations.

does less well in education given its overall HDI. Finally, we can add in another important variable calculated by the United Nations but not included in the HDI: gender equality. If we look at all the relevant indicators (maternal mortality, female education, fertility rates, labor-force participation, and share of seats in the legislature), our rankings are again quite different. The United States does particularly poorly, given its HDI, as does the United Kingdom, and, less surprisingly, Iran. In contrast, countries whose past communist regimes showed a strong commitment to gender equality, like Russia and China, have shown higher gender-equality rankings. China's is particularly striking given its overall level of development.[12]

Happiness

Given the rather technical nature of our discussions so far, it may seem strange to speak of happiness as an indicator that we can use to compare political-economic systems. But when we think about it, happiness is at the core of human activity, the result of the interaction between freedom and equality. From philosophers to evolutionary psychologists, there is a common argument that the pursuit of personal happiness is one of the central motivations that drive human behavior. If that is the case, happiness can be a useful indicator of political-economic development, and it is one to which social scientists have recently paid more attention.

At the most basic level, we can observe that in general richer countries are happier than poorer ones. This is logical; people in extreme poverty have little security and few resources to advance their lives. Past that level of poverty, however, there has been a long-standing debate over the sources and levels of happiness around the world. This debate can be seen in terms of absolute versus relative happiness. For example, in the case of extreme poverty, we can view happiness as an absolute good—enough money to eat is quite likely to increase happiness. However, many psychologists have argued that beyond basic human needs, much happiness is neither sustained nor absolute. Similarly, according to the "Easterlin paradox," developed by the social scientist Richard A. Easterlin, when standards of living rise past a certain level (perhaps $10–15,000 per capita GDP), happiness stagnates. After that level, it is argued, relative income—one's wealth relative to those around one—is a stronger predictor of one's happiness than one's overall standard of living.[13]

However, not all scholars agree that one's level of happiness is a function of one's relative wealth. While economic growth may generate greater "happiness returns" in poor countries, some studies indicate that richer countries, too, continue to see a modest growth in happiness. But is a country's happiness shaped only by its overall level of development? If we look at Table 4.3, we see some interesting variations. First, wealth is not necessary to happiness. It is true that the unhappiest countries in the world are the most desperately poor, and that most of the happiest countries in the world are wealthy states. But there are important exceptions. Costa Rica, Panama, Brazil, Colombia, the Dominican Republic, and Venezuela all rank within the top twenty happiest countries. These are all countries with modest

TABLE 4.3	Measuring Happiness, 2000–09

NATION	SATISFACTION WITH LIFE (SCALE 0–10)	NATION	SATISFACTION WITH LIFE (SCALE 0–10)
Costa Rica	8.5	Egypt	5.7
Denmark	8.3	Nigeria	5.7
Mexico	7.9	India	5.5
Norway	7.9	Russian Federation	5.5
Canada	7.8	Morocco	5.4
Panama	7.8	Serbia	5.4
Sweden	7.8	Belarus	5.2
Australia	7.7	Pakistan	5.0
Brazil	7.5	Ukraine	5.0
New Zealand	7.5	Palestine	4.9
Venezuela	7.5	Iraq	4.7
United States	7.4	Lebanon	4.7
Germany	7.1	Bulgaria	4.4
United Kingdom	7.1	Georgia	4.3
Japan	6.5	Liberia	4.3
Saudi Arabia	6.5	Rwanda	4.3
China	6.3	Afghanistan	4.1
Indonesia	6.3	Cameroon	3.9
Republic of Korea	6.0	Haiti	3.9
Iran	5.9	Kenya	3.7
Syrian Arab Republic	5.9	Sierra Leone	3.5
Tunisia	5.9	Zimbabwe	3.0
South Africa	5.8		

Source: World Database of Happiness, http://worlddatabaseofhappiness.eur.nl (accessed 2/7/2012).

levels of development (less than $15,000 per capita GDP at PPP) and high levels of economic inequality. If they have anything in common, it is culture and geography. Every country in the Americas, except Haiti, is among the top half of happy countries in the world. In contrast, most postcommunist countries fall in the bottom half, in some cases further down the list than very poor countries.

Russians and Hungarians are no happier than Indians, even though their income is approximately five times higher. They also have among the highest suicide rates in the world. Many countries in Asia, such as Japan, Taiwan, and South Korea, are less happy than we might expect if we assumed that GDP or HDI was the most important predictor of happiness. If these puzzles can be explained, the answers would seem to lie in culture rather than in levels of wealth and development. This imperfect fit between wealth and happiness is important to consider alongside the Easterlin paradox. Extreme poverty produces misery, and many rich countries are happy. However, levels of wealth, inequality, and development do not correlate with happiness as neatly as we would expect.[14]

The Rise and Fall of Liberalism?

We've covered a lot of ground in this chapter, laying out variations in the relationships among property, markets, the state, and political-economic systems. From there, we laid out some different tools for making comparisons, such as GDP, the Gini index, the Human Development Index, and measurements of happiness. In this discussion we've had glimpses of change in the international system but have not addressed this directly. Where do we seem to be heading?

For at least a century, our four major models of political economy have rivaled one another as they have sought to strike the ideal relationship between freedom and equality. At the dawn of modern capitalism, mercantilism was a dominant force, central to the establishment of empires and industries. At the same time, liberalism began to emerge as a challenge to mercantilism, particularly in the United Kingdom and its former colonies. But by the early twentieth century, liberalism was in turn threatened by fascist and communist regimes. Many believed that these regimes, coupled to powerful states, were superior to a liberalism faltering under global depression. Even when fascism was defeated, communism continued to spread worldwide, social democracy came to define much of Europe, and mercantilism drew adherents in many less-developed countries.

Yet as we stand at the beginning of the twenty-first century, the world is a quite different place. Communism has effectively vanished, even in places like China, where market forces now drive the economy, something we will discuss in Chapter 8. Mercantilism, too, has been scaled back or dismantled in many developing countries, a trend we will consider in Chapter 9. For the past two decades, social democracy and liberalism have appeared to be the only viable political-economic systems, but even the countries using these systems have been undergoing further **economic liberalization**—cutting taxes, reducing regulation, privatizing state-owned businesses and public goods, and expanding property rights—something we'll talk about more in Chapter 10.

Table 4.4 compares the levels of economic change around the world consistent with liberalism, taking into account such factors as government expenditures, price

TABLE 4.4	Levels of Economic Liberalization, 1980–2009		
COUNTRY	1980	2005	2009
Canada	7.7	8.0	7.8
United Kingdom	6.7	8.0	7.7
United States	8.0	8.1	7.6
Germany	7.4	7.6	7.5
Japan	7.1	7.5	7.4
South Korea	5.7	7.3	7.3
France	6.2	7.0	7.2
Sweden	6.0	7.4	7.2
Mexico	5.7	7.0	6.7
Russia	N/A	6.4	6.6
South Africa	6.1	6.8	6.5
China	4.2	6.1	6.4
India	5.4	6.6	6.4
Brazil	4.5	6.3	6.2
Iran	3.8	6.3	6.2
Nigeria	3.8	6.0	6.1

Note: 10 = most liberal.

Source: Fraser Institute.

INSTITUTIONS IN ACTION

What Explains Japan's Economic Decline?

In 1979, the social scientist and Japan expert Ezra Vogel published his highly influential book *Japan as Number One*. Implicit in this title is an important puzzle: how did Japan industrialize so rapidly, both before and after World War II, to earn the title "number one" in the global economy? Vogel and others drew on several explanations, often used in combination. A cultural argument spoke to Japan's "Confucian work ethic" or "Asian values," which stressed harmony and hierarchy; an institutional argument emphasized the wisdom of a political-economic system that gave the state a great deal of power in guiding the economy; a geopolitical argument asserted that a Cold War alliance with the United States following World War II gave Japan a huge political and economic foothold. These factors created "Japan, Inc.," a mercantilist powerhouse extolled as a new model for development that could outperform North America and Europe. Other developed countries were urged to follow Japan's lead and become more like it—in fact, Vogel's subtitle for his book was "Lessons for America." He felt that unless the other industrialized states embraced the Japanese model, their decline relative to Japan was all but inevitable.

Why does this concern seem so far-fetched now? How did we get from the puzzle of Japan's fast ascent in the 1960s through the 1980s to the puzzle of its rapid decline in the 1990s through the present? One difficulty in making sense of Japan's rise and fall is that often the same explanations are used to explain these two, very different, paths. With that in mind, recent analyses have pointed to a number of factors that illustrate the particular

context of Japanese institutions and their failure to adapt to a changing environment. After World War II, Japan retained much of the mercantilist structure it had built up before the war, including large industrial conglomerates working in coordination with the state and a single dominant political party. Japanese business was given open access to the U.S. market—a decision made by the United States to help rapidly rebuild Japan as a Cold War ally. The combined power of a bureaucratic and a corporate elite reinforced hierarchical cultural institutions. These factors all worked in tandem to produce rapid economic growth and national wealth. This rapid growth in turn produced an asset "bubble," the result of prices for stocks and real estate dramatically outstripping their underlying value. Eventually, confidence in such fevered growth gave out, and Japan's bubble collapsed.

But bubbles are not unique to Japan; we have just seen similar forces at work in the United States and parts of Europe (see Chapters 8 and 11). But many of the actions taken by Japan in response to the crisis now seem unwise. For example, when unprofitable firms faced bankruptcy, many were repeatedly given loans even though it was unlikely they could repay them. The government similarly spent a tremendous amount of money on public infrastructure, such as roads, bridges, and sea walls, that was not useful enough to justify the cost, creating enormous public debt (currently the highest in the world). Why?

An important factor to consider is the tight linkage between businesses, the state, and the ruling party—and the institutional inertia that prevented them from adjusting to changing circumstances. As we saw earlier in this chapter, mercantilist systems generally place little value on promoting equality. Yet postwar Japan could boast a highly equal society (in the 1980s, its Gini index rating was around 32) despite low tax rates and limited welfare benefits. This was because, in the absence of state welfare, social expenditures were either borne by businesses (offering lifetime employment) or imposed on the family (women were typically expected to stay at home to care for children and the elderly).

Thus, when economic difficulties finally did hit Japan, the state continued to support unprofitable firms and public investments because key constituencies benefited from the expenditures they provided and because no strong public-welfare institutions were in place to help deal with growing problems like unemployment. This ongoing support of obsolete institutions that provided a form of welfare meant not only that old firms were not allowed to fail but also that new, innovative firms could not easily emerge to take their place. This would also explain why Japan has lost so much ground as a producer of cutting-edge technology; students may find it hard to believe that Sony was once the leading global brand in sophisticated electronics, the Apple of its day. Finally, the pressure on families resulting from the weak welfare state has dramatically reduced the fertility rate. This has led to a shrinking workforce and aging society, which has caused further economic problems.[15]

What broader lessons can we draw from this case? First, any set of political-economic institutions may work well under particular conditions but become increasingly out of sync with broader changes over time. Pundits and politicians now speak of China as "number one," often without considering what institutional barriers, as well as advantages, it may face in the future. The danger that political-economic institutions can go

Japan built numerous seawalls to support its construction industry. However, they failed to protect many communities from the 2010 tsunami, and in fact may have instilled a dangerously false sense of security.

out of sync also applies to the United States; its ongoing attempt to come out of recession will be an important test of how flexible its liberal economic model truly is. Second, institutions can produce a "feedback loop" that can compound problems. The pressure on families resulting from the weak welfare state, for example, has led to fewer children and an aging population, which in turn has created an increased burden on the state and less dynamic economy. China, which also has a weak welfare system and a rapidly aging workforce, faces a similar problem. In short, if we make comparisons across cases and over time, we are less likely to assume that the future is simply an extrapolation of what we see in the present.

1. How has Japan's mercantilist system shaped its political-economic institutions?

2. What role have cultural factors played in Japan's rise and decline?

3. Why have Japan's current political-economic and cultural institutions been ill-suited for solving its economic crisis?

controls, taxes, individual property rights, and trade. Changes in these areas that limit the power of the state over private property and market forces are what we view as economic liberalization. The ratings in the table are given on a 10-point scale, with 10 being the most liberal and 1 being the least. The study concludes that from 1980 to 2005, there was a steady move toward greater economic liberalization, from an average global score of 5.5 in 1980 to 6.7 in 2005.[16] Economic liberalization grew, in some cases dramatically, around the world.

So is this the century of liberalism? Some qualifications are in order. First, in spite of the increasing liberalization of many economic systems, most industrialized democracies still largely adhere to social democratic ideology. The United States is very much an outlier in such areas as health care, retirement, and education. Many argue, however, that while centralized public goods like health care are missing, even the United States has a huge welfare state, albeit one "hidden" in its complicated array of taxes and tax breaks.[17] Second, in spite of increased liberalization, many countries that have traditionally relied on the social democratic model have continued to maintain both social expenditures and good economic growth (though this may come under threat from globalization and changing demography, which we will consider in later chapters).

Third and most important, since 2008 the global economy has seen one of the worst downturns since the Great Depression of the 1930s, battering liberalism and its adherents. To many, the economic crisis has been a direct result of growing and excessive global liberalization, which led states to relinquish their regulatory responsibilities and contributed to frenzied economic growth that eventually collapsed as housing prices and stock markets fell. The steep economic decline that has followed has undermined many of the arguments of liberalism—for example, that the economic pursuits of each individual will contribute to overall prosperity. As long as economic difficulties continue, it will be hard for supporters of liberalism to argue that the state is an obstacle to development. We will speak of this more in our final chapter, on globalization.

The ideological battering that liberalism has taken is compounded by actions on the ground. In response to the economic crisis, states around the globe have actively intervened in their economies, nationalizing banks, supporting declining industries, and creating new policies to regulate the economy. As we see in Table 4.4, in many countries liberalization has reversed; according to the Fraser Institute, which compiled these data, this is true for the world as a whole. A slew of scholars and pundits have declared that liberalism is in "freefall" or even that we face "the end of the free market."[18] This sounds not unlike what was heard in the 1930s, including the hyperbole of decline. Even if we discount such language, it is easy to imagine that liberalism will come under increasing stress as richer countries struggle with their economic problems and rising countries like China become more important economic actors. Shifts in international power may transform domestic political economies worldwide, as they have always done in the past.

In Sum: A New Economic Era?

As we have seen, states play a large role in the domestic and international economies. They must manage markets and property with an eye toward generating societal wealth and revenue so that basic political tasks can be funded. This is no small task, as it goes to the heart of freedom and equality: How should freedom and equality be reconciled through economic policy, and what mixture of the two will create the most wealth? Different political-economic systems give very different answers to those questions. Economic liberalism has weathered various challenges to emerge as the dominant system in much of the world. As we shall see in the coming chapters, this "triumph" of liberalism has occurred alongside political liberalization, as many nondemocratic regimes around the globe have given way to democracy.

At the same time, the past few years have raised serious questions about the limits of liberalism, as various countries have faced sustained economic difficulties. And as we look ahead, we will discuss how the end of communism has introduced important and unforeseen factors into the political-economic system, and we will examine globalization and demographic change. A great deal of change is on the horizon, and we'll spend much of the upcoming chapters trying to get a better glimpse of what may lie ahead.

For Further Reading

RS> Acemoglu, Daron. "Root Causes: A Historical Approach to Assessing the Role of Institutions in Economic Development." *Finance and Development* (June 2003).

RS> Banerjee, Abhijit and Lakshmi Iyer. "History, Institutions, and Economic Performance: The Legacy of Colonial Land Tenure Systems in India." *American Economic Review* 95, no. 4 (September 2005).

Bernstein, Edward. *Evolutionary Socialism: A Criticism and Affirmation* (New York: Schocken, 1961).

Easterlin, Richard A. *Happiness, Growth and the Life Cycle* (New York: Oxford University Press, 2011).

Leblang, David. "Familiarity Breeds Investment: Diaspora Networks and International Investment." *American Political Science Review* 104, no. 3 (August 2010).

List, Friedrich. *The National System of Political Economy* (New York: Kelley, 1966).

RS> Mankiw, N. Gregory. "The Trilemma of International Finance." *The New York Times*, 10 July 2010.

Milanovic, Branko. *The Haves and the Have-Nots: A Brief and Idiosyncratic History of Global Inequality* (New York: Basic Books, 2011).

RS> North, Douglass C. "Institutions." *Journal of Economic Perspectives* 5, no. 1 (winter 1991).

Olson, Mancur. *The Logic of Collective Action: Public Goods and the Theory of Groups* (Cambridge: Harvard University Press, 1965).

Roubini, Nouriel and Stephen Mihm. *Crisis Economics: A Crash Course in the Future of Finance* (New York: Penguin, 2010).

RS> Smith, Adam. *An Inquiry into the Nature and Causes of the Wealth of Nations*. Edwin Cannan, ed. (Chicago: Chicago University Press, 1976).

RS >
Reader Selection

Highlighted selections are included in *Essential Readings in Comparative Politics*, Fourth Edition.

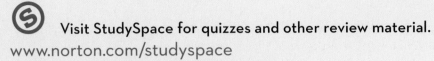

Visit StudySpace for quizzes and other review material.
www.norton.com/studyspace

- Vocabulary Flashcards of All Key Terms
- Chapter Review Quizzes
- Complete Study Reviews and Outlines

Political participation is a vital component of a democratic regime. Here, Moncef Marzouki, human rights activist and interim president of Tunisia, shows his inked finger after voting in that country's first democratic election in 2011. Fingers were inked to prevent voter fraud.

DEMOCRATIC REGIMES

KEY CONCEPTS

- Democracy is political power exercised either directly or indirectly through participation, competition, and liberty.

- There are various, and competing, explanations for why democracy has emerged in some cases and not in others.

- Executive, legislative, and judicial institutions can vary dramatically across democracies in their construction and degree of power.

- Democracies can be classified as parliamentary, presidential, or semipresidential systems.

- Electoral systems can be classified as plurality, majority, or proportional systems, or a combination thereof.

For most of human history, societies have not been organized in a way that we would consider democratic. But in the last two centuries, revolution, war, and the destruction of rival ideologies have paved the way for democracy around the globe. From the perspective of those already living in a democratic society, the spread of this political system may appear natural or inevitable. But why would democracy be an attractive or effective form of government? How does democracy actually work? Does democracy by definition reconcile freedom and equality in a single way, or does it allow for different mixtures of the two?

This chapter will speak to these questions in some detail as we consider the origins, structures, strengths, and weaknesses of democracy. We will begin by defining democracy, and then trace democracy's origins. Next we will consider the various institutions that represent the core "goods" of democracy: participation, competition, and liberty. As we shall see, there is no one relationship among these three. Various democracies construct them differently, shaping freedom, equality, and the locus of power. Finally, we will consider some of the challenges to democracy around the world as we move into the next set of chapters.

Defining Democracy

Before we proceed, we must nail down our terminology. The word *democracy* has an inherently positive connotation for many people: things that are "democratic" are good; things that are "undemocratic" are bad. Of course, in reality, this is far from the truth: a university is not a democratic institution, but that does not mean that it is necessarily deficient. Because of the word's symbolism, however, many individuals and organizations describe themselves as democratic but define the term in very different ways. For example, in Chapter 3 we noted that for communists, democracy means collective equality and not individual freedom. Countries such as China thus see themselves as "true" democracies, which they define as featuring, among other things, full employment, universal education, and the elimination of economic classes. These societies see democracy in the United States and Europe as little more than the struggle among a small elite. Naturally, capitalist countries view communist systems, with their single-party control and lack of civil liberties, as anything but democratic. As you can see, each side uses different criteria to define democracy.

How can we make any comparisons if democracy is in the eye of the beholder? One way to begin is to go back to the origin of the word. *Democracy* comes from the Greek words *demos*, meaning "the common people," and *kratia*, meaning "power" or "rule." Based on this origin, we can define democracy at its most fundamental as a system in which political power resides with the people. The people, in turn, may exercise that power either directly or indirectly, and the exercise of power typically takes three forms: participation, through means such as voting and elections; competition, such as that between political parties; and liberty, such as freedom of speech or of assembly. **Democracy**, then, can be fully defined as political power exercised either directly or indirectly through participation, competition, and liberty.

This definition is subjective; it clearly emphasizes individual freedom and is in keeping with the ideology of liberalism. Indeed, many political scientists use the more specific term **liberal democracy** to indicate that they are referring specifically to a political system that promotes participation, competition, and liberty. Liberal democracies are rooted in the ideology of liberalism, with its emphasis on individual rights and freedoms.[1] But liberal democracy is not found only where a liberal ideology and a liberal political-economic system are predominant. Many liberal democracies have social democratic regimes, which place a much higher emphasis on collective welfare than on individual rights, curtailing individual freedoms in favor of greater equality. But social democracies nevertheless continue to respect the basic liberal democratic tenets of participation, competition, and liberty. Mercantilism, too, emphasizes a strong role for the state, resulting in fewer personal freedoms, but this has not prevented countries such as India, Japan, Taiwan, and South Korea from developing liberal democratic institutions. In each case, we find the basic rights of participation, competition, and liberty, though to different degrees. This in turn affects the degree of state autonomy and capacity.

Finally, it is important to remember what is not being said here about democracy. This book does not claim that a particular kind of democracy, or even democracy itself, is the best way to organize politics. It is only presenting democracy as a particular system of institutions that have developed over time and out of liberal thought. Each person must decide whether the particular goals enshrined in liberal democracy are the most important and whether society is best served by being organized in this manner.

Origins of Democracy

We now have an understanding of the most basic elements of democracy, but this still does not explain why it has come about and where it comes from. Some elements of democratic participation can be found in many societies around the world, dating back thousands of years. But liberal democratic institutions and practices have their roots in ancient Greece and Rome, each contributing to modern democracy in different ways.

Athenian and other early Greek democracies are important because they provide the foundation for the concept of public participation. Typically found in small communities, ancient Greek democracy allowed the public (excluding women, children, foreigners, and slaves) to participate directly in the affairs of government, choosing policies and making governing decisions. In this sense, the people were the state.[2] In contrast, the Roman Empire laid out the concept of **republicanism**, which emphasized the **separation of powers** within a state and the representation of the public through elected officials (as opposed to the unaccountable powers of a monarchy or the direct participation of the people). Thus, while Greece gives us the idea of popular sovereignty, it is from Rome that we derive the notion of legislative bodies like a senate. In their earliest forms, neither Greek democracy nor Roman republicanism would be defined as liberal democracies by today's standards. Both emphasized certain democratic elements but restricted them in fundamental ways. As political rights and institutions have expanded over the centuries, republicanism and democracy—Roman and Greek thought and practices—have become intertwined to produce the modern liberal democratic regime we know today.

The discussion above may lead us to conclude that the development of democracy was a long unbroken line from Greece to today. But that was not the case. Roman republicanism was quite different from Greek participatory democracy, and in time both collapsed. Yet democratic institutions and practices slowly reemerged, most notably in thirteenth-century England. At that time, English nobles forced King John to sign the Magna Carta, a document that curbed the rights of the king and laid the foundation for an early form of legislature, a key element of republicanism. In addition, the Magna Carta asserted that all freemen (at the time, only members of the aristocracy) should enjoy due process before the law; this assertion set the stage for the idea of liberty. The Magna Carta states:

> No freeman shall be taken, imprisoned, . . . or in any other way destroyed . . . except by the lawful judgment of his peers, or by the law of the land. To no one will we sell, to none will we deny or delay, right or justice.

Although the Magna Carta was limited in its goals and application, it presented the idea that no individual, not even the king, was above the law. This concept thrived in England over the centuries as democratic practices expanded and an ever-greater proportion of the public was given political rights. The emergence of democracy in England was thus incremental, developing across centuries.

Was there something special about England that allowed democracy to flourish there in the first place? As noted in Chapter 2, European states emerged out of centuries of conflict as rival warlords slowly concentrated their holdings and extended their power. For various reasons, in England neither the state nor the feudal elite was able to get the upper hand, leading to a relative balance of power. This may have been facilitated by the defensive benefits of being an island; the need to maintain a large army to unify and defend the country was much lower for isolated England than for the many other European states. Ocean trade, too, provided revenue through port duties, which meant less need for a strong state to

Two Forms of Democracy

DIRECT DEMOCRACY	Public participates directly in governance and policy making; historically found in small communities such as ancient Athens.
INDIRECT DEMOCRACY	Public participates indirectly through its elected representatives; the prevalent form of democracy in the modern age.

squeeze taxes from the public. The result was a relatively clear separation of power that facilitated individual freedom. This in turn would eventually give shape to the ideology of liberalism. It is no accident that an ideology that emphasized individual freedom and private property emerged in a country where the state capacity and autonomy were not excessive. The public, able to gain the upper hand against the state early on in England's political development, could check attempts by the state to increase its power. This public power paved the way for an expansion of rights over time, culminating in modern liberal democracy.[3]

Contemporary Democratization

This historical background helps us understand the emergence of democracy, but for scholars of contemporary politics, it does not provide much guidance. Why is South Africa a democracy when neighboring Zimbabwe is not? Why did Russia not institutionalize democracy after the collapse of communism? Competing explanations for democratization and democratic institutionalization have fallen in and out of favor over time. Some of this may be a function of improved scholarship, but it may also be that explanations that were accurate at one time lose their explanatory power as the world changes.

Modernization and Democratization

One of the most prominent theories argues that democratization is correlated with, if not caused by, modernization. As we recall from Chapter 1, the behavioral revolution in political science was strongly connected to modernization theory, which posited that as societies became more modern, they would inevitably become more

Milestones in the Rise of Democracy

18TH CENTURY B.C.E.	Babylonian ruler Hammurabi establishes the earliest-known legal code.
6TH CENTURY B.C.E.	Autocratic rule overthrown and first democracy established in Athens.
5TH CENTURY B.C.E.	Democracy collapses in Athens as it is undermined by war and economic crisis.
1ST CENTURY B.C.E.	Roman philosopher Cicero writes of res publica, or "affairs of the people," viewing the public as an important source of political power.
5TH–10TH CENTURIES C.E.	European dark ages: power in Europe is fragmented, fostering intense competition among rulers and setting the stage for the emergence of the nation-state.
1215	English Magna Carta establishes an early precedent for the rule of law.
1646	Treaty of Westphalia asserts the right of European states to choose their own religion, enforcing the notion of state sovereignty.
1689	Bill of Rights is passed in England, establishing parliamentary supremacy.
1690	English philosopher John Locke writes *Two Treatises of Government*, arguing that government's job is to protect "the right to life, liberty, and the ownership of property."
1762	Jean-Jacques Rousseau writes *The Social Contract*, arguing that if a government fails to serve its subjects, the populace has the right to overthrow it.
1787	U.S. Constitution and Bill of Rights codify the separation of powers and civil rights.
1832–84	Reform Acts in the United Kingdom expand voting rights to much of the male population.
1893	New Zealand is the first country to grant women the right to vote.
1945	Defeat of the Axis powers eliminates fascism as a threat to democracy in Europe and Japan.
1948	United Nations approves the Universal Declaration of Human Rights, setting the stage for the internationalization of civil rights.
1989–91	Soviet Union disintegrates, leading to democratization in Russia and Eastern Europe.
1994	First democratic elections in South Africa, ending racial restrictions on voting.

democratic. Why? Modernization is associated with better education, a weakening of older traditional institutions that stressed authority and hierarchy, greater gender equality, and the rise of a middle class. To sum up, modernization theory suggests that as societies become better educated and more economically sophisticated they need and desire greater control over the state to achieve and defend their own interests.

In the 1970s, this theory fell out of favor as democracy failed in many countries in Latin America while development in Asia leapt forward alongside nondemocratic regimes. It seemed that modernization at best was irrelevant to the development of democracy and at worst could destabilize existing institutions and lead to political violence (see Chapter 7) and democratic failure. Scholars no longer make sweeping claims that modernization inevitably leads to democracy. However, some note that while democracy can emerge in a variety of circumstances, wealth and ongoing economic development are critical to the institutionalization and long-term survival of any democracy.[4]

Elites and Democratization

We noted above that modernization theory has risen, fallen, and risen again in prominence over time. In the past, modernization theory implied that democratization was almost automatic once a country developed a strong middle class and reached a certain standard of living. This argument, however, did not explain how this change would come about. We can also point to countries where standards of living have risen, such as the oil states of the Middle East, but democracy has not followed. What explains this?

One answer may lie in the role of those in power, the political elites. For the past several decades, many scholars who had turned away from modernization theory concentrated instead on the strategic motivations of those in power, and on what would lead them to hang on to or surrender power. Much of this work tended to describe rather than explain political change, but of late these arguments have gained new life by drawing on some of the earlier ideas of modernization theory. Central to modernization theory is the idea that a middle class is essential for democratization—a significant segment of the population with the economic resources necessary to advance and demand their own rights. Similarly, overall poverty can be an obstacle to democracy—where people have little, they have little to fight for. But the distribution of wealth may be more important. Where economic assets are concentrated in the hands of those in power, political change is much less likely if they believe that it would divest them of their wealth. Think, for example, of countries where there are significant natural resources, such as oil, controlled by those in power—something we spoke about in our discussion of ethnic and national conflict in Chapter 3. Those with control over these assets may be loath to give them up. But sources of wealth are not fixed; natural resources may decline, an economy may stagnate. Those in power may no longer see much value in clinging to power, especially if they believe that they can take some wealth with them in exchange for stepping aside.[5] In short, economic development is important, but the nature of the resources that fuel it can determine how likely it is that democracy will emerge. We will speak of this in much greater detail in the next chapter, on nondemocratic regimes.

Society and Democratization

A somewhat different view of democratization emphasizes not the importance of political elites but the political power of society itself. Elite-based theories can give us a sense of why leaders may be more or less willing to surrender power to the public, but not why the public would demand power in the first place. Likewise, modernization theory, though it explains how societies might change in a direction more in tune with democratic institutions, does not provide a clear sense of why society would want to move in this direction. Scholars more interested in the role of society have in the past stressed the importance of public organization or, specifically, what is called **civil society**. Basically, civil society can be defined as organized life outside the state, or what the French scholar Alexis de Tocqueville called the "art of association."[6] Civil society is a fabric of organizations, not necessarily political, created by people to help define their own interests, whatever they may be: environmental groups, churches, sports teams, fraternal organizations, and the like. Under the right circumstances, they serve as a vehicle for democratization by allowing people to articulate, promote, and defend what is important to them. Where civil society has been able to take root, it is argued, democratization is more likely, as it provides the ideas and the tools of political action and mobilization that allow small-scale democratic practices to spread. Indeed, the term *civil society* gained currency in reference to movements in Eastern Europe in the 1970s that organized independent of communist rule.[7] Where civic association can emerge, it may create a powerful incentive for democratic change, even if that is not the original intent. Modernization may help foster civil society, and civil society in turn may pressure elites for change—and these elites may or may not acquiesce, depending on their incentives to do so.

International Relations and Democratization

So far, our discussion of democratization has focused on variables inside the country in question. Can international factors also play a role? We can think of extreme cases, such as the occupation of Japan and Germany after World War II, or of Iraq and Afghanistan more recently. But scholars believe that the international community also plays a role in less overt ways. Modernization resulting from foreign investment, globalization, and trade may push democratization forward. In addition, international pressure or incentives may cause elites to favor democracy; some have suggested that the institutionalization of democracy in Eastern Europe came about partly because democracy was a prerequisite for membership in the European Union. Civil society, too, can be strengthened by the transmission of ideas across borders by education, media, and nongovernmental organizations; some argue that this factor was key to Egypt's recent revolution. How influential the international community may be in each case probably depends on a number of factors, including the degree to which that society is open to and dependent on the outside world. North Korea's isolation means that there is little contact between that society and those beyond its borders. The vast size of China's economic resources means that the international community has far fewer tools it can use to press for change within that country.

Culture and Democratization

Our last argument is a familiar one. In Chapter 3 we spoke of the idea of political culture, which is essentially the argument that there are differences in societal institutions—norms and values—that shape the landscape of political activity. Political culture may influence the preference for certain kinds of policies as well as the particular relationship between freedom and equality. Some scholars take this idea much further, arguing that there is in essence a culture of democracy, emerging from historical, religious, and philosophical foundations. In this view, for example, it is not modernization that leads to individualism and democracy; it is a Western democratic and individualist practice that gave rise to modernity.

If this argument is true, then democratization is less likely to be found the farther one travels from the West, where historical developments forged strong national identities, as well as a commitment to democracy in its own right. As we have discussed earlier, such arguments make many scholars uncomfortable, both because they are difficult to test and because they smack of stereotyping and determinism.

They also have a questionable track record; not long ago, countries whose cultures were dominated by hierarchical Roman Catholicism, such as Spain, Portugal, Italy and many Latin American nations, were seen as unlikely to democratize—until they did. Similar arguments are deployed regarding Islam, as we discussed in Chapter 3.

To summarize, there are numerous explanations for why democratization takes place in some cases and not others. While scholars tend to favor one of these explanations over the others, we see that most if not all of these factors play some role in each case of democratization. Modernization can set the stage for political activity and awareness, which can find its organizational expression in civil society. Elites may be influenced by economic conditions at home and international inducements or sanctions. Even culture may encourage certain kinds of identities and ideas that catalyze democracy or get in its way. In the end, changing domestic and international conditions may mean that what leads to democracy now may be unrelated to how it comes about in the future. Politics is not a physical law, unchanging across time and space.

Institutions of the Democratic State

We now have an understanding of the basic definition of liberal democracy and some of the explanations for how it emerged in the past and present. Next we should spend some time looking at how liberal democracies are constructed. As we shall see, liberal democratic institutions vary dramatically. Legislatures differ greatly from country to country, as do executives, and the legislative-executive relationship in each country is unique. Each judiciary, too, plays a distinct role in the democratic process. There is tremendous variation in the range and number of political parties, and this in part is shaped by the myriad electoral systems used around the world. Even what we consider basic civil rights and civil liberties differ from one liberal democracy to another. There is no one way, no right way, to build a liberal democracy. Let's look at some of the major ways in which each institution differs from country to country before we consider several of their most common combinations.

Executives: Head of State and Head of Government

We begin with what is the most prominent office in any country, the **executive**, the branch that carries out the laws and policies of a state. When we think of this office, what often comes to mind is a single person in charge of leading the country and setting a national agenda, as well as leading foreign policy and serving as commander in chief in times of war. But in fact, the executive comprises two distinct roles. The first is **head of state**, a role that symbolizes and represents the people, both nationally and internationally, embodying and articulating the goals of the regime. Conducting foreign policy and waging war are also sometimes considered parts of the head of state's duties. In contrast, the **head of government** deals with the everyday tasks of running the state, such as formulating and executing domestic policy, alongside a cabinet of ministers who are charged with specific policy areas (such as education or agriculture). The distinction, then, is between direct policy management and international and symbolic functions. This distinction is an old one that goes back to the days when monarchs reigned over their subjects, leaving ministers in charge of running the country.

Countries combine or separate these two roles to different degrees. Heads of government are usually referred to as prime ministers: they serve as the main executive over the other ministers in their cabinet. They may serve alongside a head of state, who may be a monarch or a president. A country may also combine the two roles, as in the United States, where the president is both head of state and head of government. The balance of power between the head of state and that of government differs from country to country, as we will learn shortly.

Legislatures: Unicameral and Bicameral

The **legislature** is typically viewed as the body in which national politics is considered and debated; it is charged with making or at least passing legislation. As with executives, legislatures vary in their political powers and construction; the major distinction is between bicameral and unicameral systems. As you might guess from their names, **bicameral systems** are legislatures that contain two houses, whereas **unicameral systems** are those with one house. Small countries are more likely to have unicameral systems, though the majority of liberal democracies are bicameral. Bicameral systems can be traced back to predemocratic England and other European states, where two or more chambers were created to serve the interests of different economic classes. Even as feudalism gave way to liberal democracy, the idea of bicameralism remained, for two major reasons. First, in some countries an upper chamber was retained as a check over the lower house, often reflecting a fear that a popularly elected lower house, too close to the people's current mood, would make rash decisions. Thus, upper houses can often amend or veto legislation originating in the lower house. One can also see this concern in tenure: members of upper houses often serve for longer terms than members of lower houses. A related element is federalism; federal states typically rely on an upper house to represent local interests, with members able to oversee legislation particularly relevant to local

Branches of Government

BRANCH	FUNCTIONS, ATTRIBUTES, AND POWERS
EXECUTIVE	Head of state / head of government Parliamentary, presidential, and semipresidential systems Term length may be fixed (president) or not (prime minister)
LEGISLATIVE	Lawmaking Unicameral or bicameral
CONSTITUTIONAL COURT	Determines the constitutionality of laws and acts Judicial review (abstract and concrete)

policies. In some cases, local legislatures may even appoint or elect the members of that upper chamber, again reflecting a desire to check a directly elected lower house. In the United States, the Senate was indirectly elected by local legislatures until 1913. However, there are many unitary (non-federal) liberal democratic systems that also have bicameral legislatures. Legislatures may wield a great deal of power over the executive, serving as the prime engine of policy or legislation, or take a back seat to executive authority. Moreover, the balance of power between upper and lower houses differs from country to country and issue to issue, though generally speaking upper houses are weaker than lower houses.

Judiciaries and Judicial Review

The judiciary is the third major institution central to liberal democracies. All states rely on laws to prescribe behavior and lay out the rules of the political game. At the core of this body of laws lies a constitution, which is the fundamental expression of the regime and the justification for subsequent legislation and the powers of executives, legislatures, and other political actors. In nondemocratic systems, constitutions may count for little, with the state acting as it sees fit. In liberal democracies, however, constitutional power is central to maintaining what we refer to as the **rule of law**—the sovereignty of law over the people and elected officials. As a result, judicial institutions are important components in upholding law and maintaining its adherence to the constitution.

As with executives and legislatures, judiciaries vary greatly across liberal democracies—not simply in their authority but also in how laws are interpreted and reviewed. Most (but not all) liberal democracies have some form of **constitutional court** charged with ensuring that legislation is compatible with the constitution. This is a relatively new development; in 1950, only a third of liberal democracies provided for **judicial review**, whereas now nearly 90 percent do. Alongside this rise in judicial review is the growth in the sheer number of rights that are protected under the constitution. This correlation makes sense; as constitutions define more rights, there is a greater need for judiciaries to rule on them.[8]

How these judiciaries function with regard to the constitution varies from country to country. In most countries the right of judicial review is explicitly written into the constitution. However, in a few, such as the United States and Australia, this right is implicit and has become institutionalized in the absence of any specific provision in the constitution. Another variation is in the authority and division of high courts. In some countries, like the United States, Canada, Japan, and Australia, there is a combined appellate and constitutional court. In other words, a single high court serves as a court of appeals (to which lower court rulings can be appealed) and as a court of constitutional review. Because of this dual function, trials can be an important source of constitutional interpretation. In other countries, such as Brazil, there are two separate high courts—a final court of appeals and a constitutional court. This greatly limits the influence of trials on constitutional interpretation,

Judicial systems also vary in their powers and how those powers are wielded. We might imagine that unified constitutional and appellate courts are by their nature more powerful than those in which the two bodies are separate. Yet other important variations can shape judicial authority as much if not more. Judicial review can take different forms—most specifically, "concrete" or "abstract." In **concrete review**, courts can consider the constitutionality of legislation when this question has been triggered by a specific court case; for example, in the case of separate appellate and constitutional courts, a case before a court of appeal may be forwarded to the constitutional court if the court of appeal believes there is a constitutional issue at stake. In **abstract review**, a constitutional court may rule on legislation without a specific court case. This is typically initiated upon request by one or more elected officials, such as members of the national or local legislatures. Courts can also differ in the timing of their review. In some countries, constitutional review may occur only after a piece of legislation is passed; in others, the constitutional court may give a ruling beforehand. Finally, courts differ in the appointment and tenure of their judges; these are typically fixed terms (the United States' lifetime tenure is an anomaly). The combination of these factors can radically affect the power of the courts in the democratic process.

Models of Democracy: Parliamentary, Presidential, and Semipresidential Systems

With our overview of state institutions in hand, let's look at the main differences in how some of these institutions can be constructed in relation to one another. Described below is a generalized portrait of these systems; in reality, there are numerous variations within these basic categories.

Parliamentary Systems

Parliamentary systems can be found in a majority of democracies around the world. Parliamentary systems comprise two basic elements: first, prime ministers and their cabinets (the other ministers that make up the government) come out of the legislature; and second, the legislature is also the instrument that elects and removes the prime minister from office. In these cases, there is a division of power and roles between a head of government and a head of state, with the overwhelming majority of power residing with the head of government (the prime minister). In contrast, the head of state may be a president who is directly elected by the public or indirectly elected by the legislature, or a monarch who has inherited the office. Their powers are typically little more than ceremonial, particularly in the case of monarchs. They may hold some reserve powers such as the ability to reject legislation or forward it to a constitutional court if it is seen as undemocratic. Even in these cases, however, the powers of the president or monarch are rarely exercised.

The prime minister is elected from the legislature and therefore reflects the balance of power between parties in the legislature. Typically, he or she is the head of the party in the lower house that holds the largest number of seats. Indeed, in most parliamentary systems the prime minister continues to hold a seat in the lower house of the legislature, as do other members of her or his cabinet. This tight connection between the executive and the legislature means that while there is a separation of power and responsibility between them, these two branches of government do not check and balance each other's power to the degree that they do in presidential systems. A party with a majority of seats in the legislature can choose its own prime minister and cabinet with little concern for other parties. However, when a party holds a plurality of seats—that is, more seats than any other party but fewer than 50 percent of them—it must commonly forge a coalition government with one or more other parties. In such a government, the prime minister will come from the largest party, while other members of the cabinet come from the coalition parties. When the largest party lacks a majority, it is also possible for a coalition of smaller parties to form a government and select the prime minister, in effect shutting out the largest party.

It is important to note that in these systems the public does not directly elect their country's leader. That task is left to the parties. As a result, the length of time the prime minister serves in office is uncertain. Members of the legislature are voted in and out of office in direct elections, but prime ministers usually serve in office for as long as they can command the support of their party and its allies. Prime ministers sometimes remain in office for many years—in the United Kingdom, Tony Blair was prime minister for a decade. Yet prime ministers can often be removed relatively easily through what is known as a **vote of no confidence**. Parliaments typically retain the right to dismiss a prime minister at any time simply by taking a vote of confidence; in such a vote, the absence of majority support for the prime minister will bring down the government. Depending on the constitution, this may trigger a national parliamentary election, or a search for a new government

IN FOCUS

Parliamentary, Presidential, and Semipresidential Systems

TYPE	EXECUTIVE POWERS AND RELATIONSHIPS
PARLIAMENTARY	Indirectly elected prime minister holds executive power as head of government; directs cabinet, formulates legislation and domestic and international policies. Serves for an unfixed term, and may be removed by a vote of no confidence. Head of state (president or monarch) is largely ceremonial.
PRESIDENTIAL	Directly elected president holds majority of executive power as head of state and government. Directs cabinet and formulates legislation and international and domestic policies. Serves for a fixed term and cannot be easily removed from office.
SEMIPRESIDENTIAL	Directly elected president and indirectly elected prime minister share power. President helps set policy while prime minister executes it. President also manages foreign policy. Which office holds more power depends on the country.

and prime minister from among the parties. Prime ministers also hold the right to call elections. While the constitution may specify that elections must be held within a specific timeframe (such as every four or five years), prime ministers can often schedule these elections when they imagine it will serve their party best.

In parliamentary systems, legislatures and judiciaries often take a back seat to the prime minister, who along with the cabinet is the main driver of legislation and policy. Especially when the prime minister enjoys a majority in the parliament, the house's role may be limited to debating policy that comes down from the cabinet. Upper houses, too, typically have little say in the selection or removal of the prime minister, and what powers they may have in rejecting legislation can often be overturned by the lower house. Judicial systems are frequently much weaker under these conditions as well. In parliamentary systems, the idea of checks and balances is subordinated to a concentration of power that guarantees greater political autonomy. In addition, the fusion of the prime minister's power with that of the lower house, and the weakness of the upper house, means that fewer opportunities arise for real constitutional conflicts that would empower constitutional courts. Finally, in some cases heads of state and upper houses themselves have certain powers of constitutional review, further limiting the opportunity for independent judicial power.

Presidential Systems

Presidential systems make up a minority of democratic systems around the world. In this system, the president is directly elected by the public for a fixed term and has control over the cabinet and the legislative process. The positions of head of state and head of government are typically fused in the presidency. Here we see a significant difference between parliamentary and **presidential systems**. In the former, prime ministers and their cabinets come from the legislature and must command a majority of support to stay in office. In presidential systems, however, the president and legislature serve for fixed terms, typically between four and seven years. Election dates may not be altered easily. Nor can presidents or legislatures be removed by anything resembling a vote of no confidence. Only in the case of malfeasance can elected officials lose their seats.

The way in which this institutional relationship affects government is profound. First, as a directly elected executive, the president is able to draw on a body of popular support in a way in which no member of a legislature, or even a prime minister, can. Only a president can say that she or he has been elected by the whole of the people in a single national vote (even if the reality is more complicated than that). Second, as the head of the state and the government, the president serves as an important national symbol as well as the overseer of policy. Third, the president is able to choose a cabinet, many or perhaps all of whom are not members of the legislature. Unlike prime ministers, presidents need not be concerned that their cabinets are comprised of party leaders. Nor need a president be concerned with coalition government. Since the president is directly elected, minority parties have no effective control over the executive. Fourth, and related to this, the president's power is not directly beholden to the legislature, and vice versa. Neither one has the ability to easily remove the other, creating a much stronger separation of powers between executive and legislature. This separation of powers is also more likely to lead to checks and balances and divided government. Presidents and legislative majorities can be from different parties, and even when they belong to the same party, the separation of these institutions means greater independence from each other. President and legislature can easily check each other's ability to pass legislation in a way unlikely in a parliamentary system. Presidentialism can in fact weaken political parties, since their leaders are concerned with winning a single national and directly elected office. To become prime minister, by contrast, one must work one's way up through the ranks of the party. Finally, the conflict between an independent legislature and president may pave the way for a more active judiciary, drawing it into disputes between the president and legislature, as has often been the case in the United States. There are relatively few presidential democracies around the world. The United States is the most typically cited example. Presidentialism is also common in Latin America.

Semipresidential Systems

Our final variant is an interesting hybrid between parliamentary and presidential systems that has become more widespread over the past fifty years (though it still remains far less common than presidential and parliamentary systems). In this model, power is divided between the head of state and the head of government, with a prime minister and a directly elected president both exercising power. Presidents enjoy fixed terms while prime ministers remain subject to the confidence of the legislature and, in some cases, the confidence of the president as well. How power is divided between these two offices depends on the country. In some cases, the prime minister is relatively independent from the president; while the president exercises important powers, his or her control over the prime minister is limited. In other cases, the prime minister is beholden to both the legislature and the president, giving the president greater authority over the selection, removal, and activity of the prime minister. In both cases, the president holds power independently of the legislature yet shares powers with a prime minister. **Semipresidential systems** tend to reflect the old distinction between "reign" and "rule" that existed under monarchies. Presidents will often set forth policy but expect the prime minister to translate those policy ideas into legislation and to ensure that it is passed. Presidents will also take the lead in foreign policy and serve as commander in chief, representing the country in international relations. The most prominent semipresidential systems, like the French, place the preponderance of power in the hands of the president, with the prime minister playing a supporting role. In semipresidential systems the role of the judiciary varies. The independence of constitutional courts is often limited by the fact that they are appointed by the president. At the same time, however, conflicts between presidents and prime ministers, and a lack of clarity over which executive has what power, have on a few occasions created opportunities for more judicial authority. Since the collapse of communism, semipresidentialism has spread into several former Soviet republics, most notably Russia, and it is also the form of government in a few countries in Asia such as South Korea and Taiwan.

Parliamentary, Presidential, and Semipresidential Systems: Benefits and Drawbacks

Having reviewed these three systems, it makes sense to ask which is the best system of governance. Of course, that depends on how one defines "best"; each system has certain advantages and drawbacks. That said, scholars have made some arguments about how effective, democratic, or stable these systems may be.

Advocates of parliamentary systems point out that the fusion of power between the executive and legislature promotes greater efficiency by reducing the chances of divided government and deadlock. The prime minister's office, even when beholden to several parties in a coalition government, can normally promulgate and pass legislation relatively quickly, without having to take into consideration the narrow interests of individual legislators or smaller parties. In fact, prime ministers can use the vote of no confidence to their own advantage, threatening, for example, to make a vote against individual pieces of legislation an effective vote of no confidence—should the legislature vote against the legislation, the prime minister will call for new elections. Critics assert that the efficiency made possible by parliamentary systems—the prime minister's ability to generate and quickly pass legislation—comes at the cost of a weaker separation of powers. Legislatures may

Parliamentary, Presidential, and Semipresidential Systems: Benefits and Drawbacks

TYPE	BENEFITS AND DRAWBACKS
PARLIAMENTARY	Benefits: Prime minister has confidence that he or she can get legislation passed. Prime minister may also be more easily removed by the legislature through a vote of no confidence.
	Drawbacks: Public does not directly select prime minister and may feel that it has less control over the executive and the passing of legislation.
PRESIDENTIAL	Benefits: President is directly elected and can draw on a national mandate to create and enact legislation.
	Drawbacks: President and legislature may be controlled by different parties, leading to divided government. Office does not allow for power sharing, and president may not be easily removed from office except through elections.
SEMIPRESIDENTIAL	Benefits: Directly elected president and indirectly elected prime minister share power and responsibilities, creating both a public mandate (presidency) and an indirectly elected office that may be supported by a coalition of parties (prime minister).
	Drawbacks: Conflict possible between prime minister and president over powers and responsibilities.

have far fewer opportunities to influence the passage of legislation or effectively express the voters' specific interests, since legislation is more a top-down than a bottom-up process. The voters' distance from government decision making can apply to the executive as well, since that individual is directly accountable only to the legislature. Greater efficacy may thus mean weaker public oversight and control over elected officials.

Presidentialism has its own problems. The chief benefit of this system is the public's ability to directly select its leader, who serves for a fixed term. But this can generate difficulties. Unlike prime ministers, who must keep the confidence of their party (or parties, in the case of coalition governments), presidents are not dependent on their parties in this way. Even if a president loses the confidence of the public, he or she cannot be replaced except through new elections. Presidents also enjoy (or suffer from) the separation of power from the legislature, which can lead to divided government. Whether checks and balances are a benefit or a hindrance to democracy is open to debate. Several prominent scholars have asserted that presidentialism is a more unstable system, since it limits power sharing and also lacks the mechanism through which legislators and executives can be easily removed from office. The result can be more polarized, and therefore unstable, politics. We might conclude, then, that semipresidentialism would be the best of both worlds, but its track record is limited and mixed. In many cases, power still becomes concentrated in the presidential office, and, in some cases, like Russia, presidents can use their office to dismantle democracy.

Political Parties

James Madison once wrote that "in every political society, parties are unavoidable."[9] Observers have offered several reasons why this is the case. Parties are important organizations that bring together diverse groups of people and ideas under the umbrella of an ideological mandate. These organizations serve two functions. By bringing different people and ideas together, they help establish the means by which the majority can rule. Without political parties that provide candidates and agendas for politics, the political process would be too fragmented, and it would be impossible to enact policy or get much else done. But political parties remain relatively loose, containing various factions built around differing issues. This heterogeneity helps limit a "tyranny of the majority," since parties are often diverse enough that they are unable to fully dominate politics even when they hold a majority of power. Parties in liberal democracies are thus homogeneous enough to create majority rule but too weak to facilitate a tyranny of the majority, so long as open and regular elections create the opportunity to turn the ruling party out of power.

Political parties also create the means by which politicians can be held accountable by the electorate and fellow political elites. By articulating an ideology and a set of goals, parties ensure that their members work toward those goals. Voters are able to evaluate politicians on the basis of their fulfillment of a party's policy platform. A party can thus serve as a political symbol, a shorthand for a set of ideas and objectives, and voters can distill a complex set of beliefs and preferences into the decision of whether to vote for party A or party B. Countries exhibit a variety of party systems, shaped by a number of factors. Some countries have seen the virtual dominance of two or even one party over a long period of time—Sweden's Social Democratic Party and Japan's Liberal Democratic Party were able to control government for much of the postwar era. In other countries, such as Italy, power has moved back and forth between a handful of parties on a regular (sometimes

- Political parties encourage democratic competition by gathering diverse groups under an ideological mandate while simultaneously preventing domination by any one group.

- The separation of powers between different branches of government prevents abuses of power by any one branch.

yearly) basis, creating greater instability. In some parliamentary systems, like Italy's, coalition governments are the norm, while in others coalition governments are rare. There are so many reasons for this difference, specific to each case, that we can't make easy generalizations. One factor that accounts for the diversity in party politics, however, is the diversity in **electoral systems**.

Electoral Systems

We have discussed why there are political parties, but we must look more closely at why certain countries have more parties than others, and why each party exhibits its particular ideological content. There might be no single answer to this—the fortunes of political parties rise and fall over time. But as we look around the world, we see a tremendous diversity in the ways that members of the public cast their votes, how those votes are applied, and, as a result, how many and what kinds of parties enter the legislature.

All democracies divide their populations geographically into a number of electoral groups or **constituencies**—a geographic area that an elected official represents. These constituencies are allocated a certain number of legislative seats. The total number of constituencies varies widely from country to country: Norway is broken up into 19 constituencies that correspond to the country's 19 counties, whereas in Nigeria 360 constituencies elect members of the country's lower house. How these boundaries are drawn matters, too. For example, if an ethnic or religious minority is concentrated in one constituency, it has more political power than it would have if it were divided across a number of constituencies. Also, different districts may have very different population sizes but the same number of legislative seats, giving those in less populated districts more power. How governments draw electoral boundaries can thus have a huge impact on who gets elected and is often a source of great contention in new (and old) democracies.

A second distinction is how votes are cast and counted.[10] There are essentially two broad forms of electoral systems in use in liberal democracies today. The first is made up of plurality and majority systems, often called **single-member-district (SMD)** systems for reasons that will become clear in a moment, and the second, **proportional representation (PR)** systems. Let us consider each one in turn.

A minority of democratic countries around the world, including the United Kingdom, Canada, the United States, India, Nigeria, and several other former British colonies, rely on plurality-based SMD systems, also called "**first past the post**" systems. In these systems, as in all SMD systems, electoral constituencies are single-member districts, which means that there is only one representative for that constituency. In plurality-based SMDs, the candidate who receives the most votes—whether a majority or plurality—wins the seat. In SMD systems, the votes cast for other candidates are "wasted"; that is, if a candidate for whom a vote is cast does not win, his or her votes do not count toward any other candidate's electoral bid. The SMD system's "winner take all" approach can amplify the political power of some parties while weakening the political power of others.

Political scientists have long argued that under SMD systems most people are unwilling to vote for smaller parties. Since such parties are unlikely to win a plurality of the votes, voters feel that a vote cast for a small party will be wasted and that they would be better off giving their vote to a stronger party that has a chance of coming in first.[11] As a result, an SMD system is much more likely to produce a legislature dominated by two parties, as in the United States, Canada, and the United Kingdom, and marginalize or eliminate smaller parties.

By way of illustration, let's look at the outcome of the 2010 elections for the House of Commons (the lower legislative house) in the United Kingdom. As Table 5.1 shows, the Conservative Party won 36 percent of the vote and 47 percent of the seats; the Labour Party won 29 percent of the votes and 39 percent of the seats. The Liberal Democrats, meanwhile, garnered 23 percent of the vote but won only 9 percent of the seats. In other words, in spite of polling nearly as well as the Labour Party, the Liberal Democrats did not win in as many constituencies as Labour. The importance of this winner-take-all system, built around single-member districts, can also be seen clearly in the case of smaller parties. Some parties with only one or two percent of the vote, like the Scottish National Party, Sinn Fein, Plaid Cymru, and the Democratic Unionist Party, gained between 3 and 8 seats, while parties with an equally large share of the vote, like the United Kingdom Independence Party or the British National Party, got no seats whatsoever. Why? In the case of the first four, these are regional parties in Scotland, Wales, and Northern Ireland whose voters were concentrated in a few local constituencies. In contrast, the United Kingdom Independence Party and the British National Party are ideologically based parties whose supporters are scattered across constituencies.

In addition to determining the distribution of power across parties, SMD systems can affect power within the parties themselves. In SMD elections, voters are choosing between individual candidates within a constituency as much as they are choosing from among parties. Voters may be more interested in what a candidate has to say about their local needs than in party ideology, and individual candidates may therefore act more independently of their party if they believe that is what will get them elected. This is especially likely to be the case under presidential systems. When there is a directly elected president, voters do not have to worry about their party winning a majority of seats in the legislature so that it can choose the prime minister. National politics thus becomes more driven by local politics.

It is possible to alter the impact of SMDs with a small modification in the electoral rules. Majority-based SMD systems, for instance, function largely the same way plurality-based systems do, except that certain mechanisms ensure that the winner is elected by a majority of the voters in the district. The simplest way to do this is by having two electoral rounds: after the first round, the top two vote getters go on to a runoff election. This is the system used in France. In a more complicated variation, a majority can be generated by having voters rank candidates by preference. If no candidate wins an outright majority, the candidate with the lowest number of first preferences is eliminated, and her or his ballots are then reassigned on the basis of the second preferences on those ballots. The elimination of the lowest-ranking candidates continues until one candidate has a majority. This system, called alternative, preferential, or instant-runoff voting, is currently used in Australia. Advocates have supported its adoption in the United States and Canada.[12] Supporters believe that this system would increase the chances for smaller parties to gain office, since voters would worry less about wasting their vote. In 2011, the United Kingdom

TABLE 5.1 — Electoral Systems and Outcomes: The United Kingdom and South Africa

PLURALITY SINGLE-MEMBER DISTRICT: UNITED KINGDOM, HOUSE OF COMMONS, 2010

PARTY	PERCENTAGE OF VOTES WON NATIONALLY	PERCENTAGE OF SEATS WON IN LEGISLATURE/NUMBER OF SEATS WON
Conservative Party	36	47 (307)
Labour Party	29	40 (258)
Liberal Democrats	23	9 (57)
United Kingdom Independence Party	3	0
British National Party	2	0
Scottish National Party	1.7	0.9 (6)
Democratic Unionist Party	0.6	1.2 (8)
Sinn Fein	0.6	0.8 (5)
Plaid Cymru	0.6	0.5 (3)
Green Party	1	0.1 (1)

(Continued)

held a referendum on whether to switch to alternative voting. This was strongly supported by the Liberal Democrats, who believed that they would do much better under such a system. However, more than two-thirds of voters opposed the change.

Quite different from plurality- and majority-based SMD systems is proportional representation (PR), which is used in some form by a majority of democracies around the world. PR generally attempts to decrease the number of votes that are wasted, thus increasing the number of parties in the legislature. Instead of relying on SMDs, PR relies on **multimember districts (MMDs)**; in other words, more than one legislative seat is contested in each district. In PR systems, voters cast their ballots

TABLE 5.1

Electoral Systems and Outcomes: The United Kingdom and South Africa (*Continued*)

PROPORTIONAL REPRESENTATION: SOUTH AFRICA, NATIONAL ASSEMBLY, 2009

PARTY	PERCENTAGE OF VOTES WON NATIONALLY	PERCENTAGE OF SEATS WON IN LEGISLATURE/NUMBER OF SEATS WON
African National Congress	65.9	66 (264)
Democratic Alliance	16.7	16.8 (67)
Congress of the People	7.4	7.5 (30)
Inkatha Freedom Party	4.5	4.5 (18)
Independent Democrats	0.9	1.0 (4)
United Democratic Movement	0.8	1.0 (4)
Vryheidsfront Plus	0.8	1.0 (4)
African Christian Democratic Party	0.8	0.8 (3)
United Christian Democratic Party	0.4	0.5 (2)
Pan Africanist Congress	0.3	0.3 (1)
Minority Front	0.2	0.3 (1)
Azanian People's Organization	0.2	0.3 (1)
African People's Convention	0.2	0.3 (1)

for a party rather than for a candidate, and the percentage of votes a party receives in a district determines how many of that district's seats the party will gain. In a simple theoretical version, a party that won 17 percent of the vote in a district would receive 17 percent of that district's seats; if it won 100 percent of the vote in a district, it would receive all the seats. The ways in which votes are counted and applied are complex and can profoundly affect how seats are distributed among competing parties. Yet overall, in comparison to plurality and majority SMD systems, PR enables even a small percentage of the vote to win representation. The 2009 elections in South Africa, also detailed in Table 5.1, show how the number of votes under PR can correspond much more closely to the percentage of seats won in the legislature. Small parties that would not have won a single seat under plurality- or majority-based SMD systems are represented in the South African National Assembly.

Because PR is based on multimember districts, elections are not centered on competitions between individuals, as in SMD systems. Instead, political parties draw up in advance a list of their candidates for each electoral district, often proposing as many candidates as there are seats. If a district has ten seats and a party wins 50 percent of the vote in that district, the party will send the first five candidates on its party list to the legislature. Political parties themselves decide who will be placed on their party list and at what rank, with the most senior members listed at the top. A candidate would want to be listed as high on the list as possible to gain a seat even if the party gets a small share of the district vote.

Unlike voters in plurality or majority systems, who tend to support only parties with a chance of winning a large share of votes in a district, PR voters are more willing to vote for small parties, since they stand a better chance of winning at least some seats in the legislature. Even if a party wins less than 10 percent of the vote, it may well gain seats, as the 2009 South African elections showed. As a result, countries with PR systems are likely to have many more parties in the legislature. Israel's legislature, for example, has 12 parties, some of which are coalitions of several smaller parties. Some PR systems try to limit the number of small parties by establishing a minimum percentage of the vote that parties need to receive to gain seats in the legislature; in Germany and several other countries, the threshold is five percent. Of course, this also leads to wasted votes, since voters choosing parties that do not make it over the threshold will not have their votes count. Still, the number of wasted votes tends to be much smaller in PR than in SMD systems.

Finally, party discipline and ideology may be more pronounced in a PR system, for two reasons. First, the diversity of parties is related to their need to carve out distinct ideological spaces. This is different from SMD systems, in which parties want to reach as many people as possible in order to win a plurality or majority. Second,

PR may lead to more internally disciplined parties, since those who do not follow the party rules can be dropped from the party lists in the next election. Where PR is combined with a parliamentary system, party discipline may be even greater, since it can make the difference between stable government and a vote of no confidence.

Which system is more representative: SMD or PR? Supporters of PR note that it wastes fewer votes and in so doing allows for a greater range of interests to be expressed politically. These can include the interests of groups defined by existing societal distinctions such as religion and ethnicity; one way to resolve ethnic conflict, we noted in Chapter 3, is to use institutions like PR to allow ethnic groups to advance their causes. PR can also encourage the sharpening and expansion of different ideological views, increasing the competition of ideas and providing a means by which new issues can enter the system. Environmental parties, for example, were able to form and make an impact in many PR systems as early as the 1970s, while they remain marginal forces in SMD systems. In addition, when combined with the parliamentary form of government, PR often makes it necessary for parties to form coalitions to muster a majority of votes, thus building consensus across a range of views. Finally, PR's use of party lists can also make it easier for the parties themselves to expand the representation of underrepresented groups, such as women and minorities, by placing them high on their party lists.[13]

Those who favor SMD systems emphasize the benefits of single-member districts and winner-take-all elections. Under such systems, individuals can more easily connect with their elected representatives than they can under PR. As we mentioned earlier, since SMD voters express their support or rejection of particular candidates, these candidates form ties to their constituents that are as close as those to their party, if not closer. SMD supporters would note that as Russia has moved away from democracy in recent years, it has moved from a mixed system of SMD and PR (see below) to pure PR, in order to eliminate independent candidates who were critical of the government. Supporters also note that an SMD system allows for the creation of large parties that are able to muster the majorities needed to govern without being held hostage by smaller, often fringe parties. The flip side of party diversity under PR, critics argue, may be fragmentation and political instability.

Given that SMD and PR systems both have advantages and disadvantages, some countries have combined the two. For example, Germany, Hungary, Japan, and Mexico use what is known as a **mixed electoral system** that combines plurality or majority SMDs with PR. Voters are given two votes—one for a candidate and the other for a party (these two votes can be divided on one ballot paper itself, or voters may participate in two separate elections, one for the PR candidates and one for the SMD candidates). Candidates in the SMDs are elected on the basis of

Electoral Systems

SINGLE-MEMBER DISTRICTS	Votes cast for individuals	Candidate with the largest share wins seat or majority	Fewer and larger parties
PROPORTIONAL REPRESENTATION (MULTIMEMBER DISTRICTS)	Votes cast for parties	Seats divided among parties on basis of share of vote	More smaller parties
MIXED SYSTEM	Votes cast both for parties and for individuals	Some seats filled by individual races, some by party outcome	Mixed outcome

plurality or majority, while in the PR segment of the election, votes are allocated proportionally. The percentage of seats allotted for each electoral method varies from country to country. For example, in Germany, the seats in the lower house of the legislature are divided evenly between SMDs and PR, whereas in Japan, the breakdown is 60 percent SMD and 40 percent PR. Under this system, voters not only get two votes but also have the option to split their choice, voting for a candidate from one party with their SMD vote while choosing a different party with their PR vote. For example, in Germany one might vote for the large, left-wing Social Democratic Party on the plurality SMD portion of the ballot (since only a large party is likely to get the plurality of votes needed to win) while reserving the PR portion of the ballot for the smaller, environmentalist Green Party.

Finally, we should consider what bearing, if any, electoral systems have on executive-legislative relations. First, parliamentary systems that rely on SMDs are less likely to have coalition governments, since small parties are less likely to get into office and single parties are often able to command a majority of seats in the legislature. PR in parliamentary systems may make coalition governments more likely; this can broaden the range of participation but also increase the likelihood for government instability inherent in managing so many contending interests. Second, the electoral system used for the legislature is unconnected to the form of executive-legislative relations. A presidential or parliamentary system may use PR or SMD for the legislature. A country could change its constitution so that the executive position changes from president to prime minister without changing its electoral system, or it could switch from PR to SMD (or vice versa) without having to modify its executive structure.

Referendum and Initiative

In addition to shaping how a voter's participation is counted, electoral systems can affect policy. Although voting is typically used to choose parties or candidates for office, many countries offer the public the option of voting directly on particular policy issues. Such a ballot is commonly known as a **referendum**. In contrast to the more indirect impact that elections have on politics, referenda allow the public to make direct decisions about policy. There is no constitutional provision for national referenda in the United States and Canada (although they exist in some local and state governments in those countries), but they are used in many other democracies. Italy and New Zealand have used national referenda to dramatically restructure their electoral and legislative systems, and in Switzerland, where the political system comes closer to the idea of direct democracy than in any other country, many of the most important national decisions are regularly made by referenda. Constitutions and constitutional reforms are often put to referenda, and some European countries use referenda to approve changes in their relationship with the European Union. These referenda may be called by the government, with the formal power to do so often resting with the head of state. In addition, in some countries citizens themselves may collect signatures to put a question to a national vote in what is known as an **initiative**. Such direct participation can help legitimize the democratic process, but some are concerned that national votes place too much power in the hands of an uninformed public, weakening representative democracy.[14]

Civil Rights and Civil Liberties

The last component of liberal democracy is liberty itself. To speak of liberty, we must go beyond democratic process and speak about the substance of democracy: civil rights and civil liberties. **Civil rights** typically refers to the promotion of equality, whereas **civil liberties** refers to the promotion of freedom, though the two overlap. Civil rights and liberties include free speech and movement, the right to religious belief, the right of public assembly and organization, equal treatment under the law, the prevention of inhumane punishment, the right to a fair trial, the right to privacy, and the right to choose one's own government. These rights and liberties depend on the rule of law—on legal institutions that everyone is subject to, rulers and ruled, and that uphold laws that support liberty.

Democratic constitutions around the world vary in the number of rights they articulate and the kinds of rights they emphasize. Despite the numerous discrepancies

Why Did Hungary Write a New Constitution?

We have spoken at length in this chapter about the origins and forms of democracy around the world. It is easy to think of democracy as an inexorable process driven forward naturally by social evolution. From this perspective, tyrannical leaders, cultural anachronisms, or economic difficulties block the progress of democracy, and when these obstacles are removed the emergence and institutionalization of democracy is inevitable. While this remains a strong assumption among some scholars and people in liberal democracies, others note that democracy is a set of specific relationships between people and states that form often by accident. While these relationships can become institutionalized, they can just as easily unravel. This view is a challenge both to the concept of democracy as a form of global social evolution and to the notion of the "stickiness" of political institutions that we have advocated in this text.

Hungary may serve as a cautionary tale about the relative instability of democratization and constitutions. Hungary's historical experience with democracy has been fairly limited. In the twentieth century, it went from monarchy to dictatorship to a brief fascist regime and then to forty years of communism. In spite of this, it was a fairly developed country with a high standard of living and a resilient civil society that mounted continuous challenges to communist rule (including a failed revolution in 1956) when it lay behind the iron curtain. Hungary was one of the countries whose protests set in motion the rapid collapse of communism and the rise of democracy across Eastern Europe in the late 1980s and early 1990s, and one of the first former communist countries to join the European Union. Many scholars of the region (including this author) viewed Hungary as an exemplar of democratic development after communism.[15] Twenty years later, however, many view Hungary's democracy as becoming less institutionalized, not more.

Since the collapse of communism, Hungary had been operating under a version of the old communist-era constitution, substantially modified to provide for participation, competition, and liberty. These provisions included an extremely strong constitutional court. The constitution helped facilitate democratization and seemed well institutionalized. However, in 2012 it was scrapped in favor of an entirely new document, written rapidly and behind closed doors by the ruling party (known as Fidesz) without input from the public or opposition parties. There were a number of notable changes. The preamble of the new constitution speaks of the role of Christianity as part of Hungarian national identity, and it explicitly rejects the legitimacy (and, presumably, legal precedents) of the previous constitution. The new constitution also delineates the government's responsibility for Hungarians living outside the country's borders, implying that Hungary has some form of sovereignty over these citizens of neighboring countries (Hungarians living in Romania and Slovakia comprise one of the largest ethnic minorities in Europe).

While we might dismiss such language as largely symbolic, there are more specific concerns. Among them is the concern that the new constitution significantly weakens the once-powerful constitutional court, concentrating power into the hands of the legislature and executive, and also reduces the independence of the central bank. The European Union, the United States, and the International Monetary Fund, as well as other actors, have expressed a great deal of concern about the new constitution, with some worried that it will undermine Hungary's relatively new democratic order. In the view of the Council of Europe, the very "principle of democracy itself is at risk."[16]

Why did Hungary pass an entirely new constitution? As we noted, Hungary was an early actor in ending communism in Eastern Europe, following lengthy negotiations between the Communist Party and opposition groups. This led to the substantial modification of the communist-era constitution as a precursor to (rather than following) the first democratic elections. Hungary was the only country in Eastern Europe that did not write a wholly new constitution as part of its transition. Nor was the Communist Party swept away by mass protests, as elsewhere; in fact, the Communist Party not only helped amend the constitution but also reinvented itself along social democratic lines and returned to power in 1994. While at the time this transition was hailed as a model of pragmatic political change, it also helped foster a polarized politics.

For opposition parties like Fidesz, the transition from communism had never fully taken place, and they saw it as their duty to bring that about. After Fidesz and its coalition partner, the Christian Democrats, won a two-thirds legislative majority in 2010, they had the votes needed to overturn the constitution. Fidesz presented this new constitution as the decisive break with communism. Critics argue that Fidesz specifically sought to rewrite the political rules in a way that would help consolidate its political control—hence the constitution's provisions to weaken the constitutional court. At the same time, embedding particular values into the constitution—through references to the nation, Christianity, and family—was an effort to institutionalize the ideological values of Fidesz. In short, many observers view this process as an attempt to consolidate Fidesz's political victory, weakening checks in the political system while infusing the constitution with the party's own values.

What are the long-term repercussions of these changes? Given that the new constitu-

"We are the power": Protestors in Hungary demonstrate against Hungary's new constitution, 2011.

tion has only recently come into force, it is hard to say. The Hungarian government has already faced significant international criticism for its new media laws, which allow the government to fine the media for press coverage it finds unbalanced or "immoral." When the current coalition eventually leaves office, whoever comes to power will confront this new constitution. If they lack a two-thirds majority, they will be unable to modify it. If they do possess sufficient votes, there will be a natural temptation to rewrite the constitution once again to serve the new government's objectives. Either way, the result may be a less-stable constitution and democracy—an unexpected outcome for a country once viewed as a pioneer of postcommunist democracy.

1. Why might Hungary's not having written a new constitution upon democratization made the regime more vulnerable?

2. How does Hungary's new constitution potentially undermine certain democratic principles and institutions?

3. In Hungary's case, how might elections and the regular changing of power actually make for a less stable demcracy?

between democratic constitutions, they can all be characterized by which of two basic kinds of rights they emphasize. In the first case, individuals are considered the primary vehicle of democratic rights, and their rights are defended from intrusion by the state and other individuals. The South African constitution goes quite far in this regard, asserting that "the state may not unfairly discriminate directly or indirectly against anyone on one or more grounds, including race, gender, sex, pregnancy, marital status, ethnic or social origin, color, sexual orientation, age, disability, religion, conscience, belief, culture, language and birth." This was in fact the first constitution to explicitly deal with rights having to do with sexual orientation. At the same time, the constitution bans "advocacy of hatred that is based on race, ethnicity, gender or religion," which some would regard as a violation of individual free speech. Similarly, Germany's constitution has strong provisions for individual rights, but it also asserts, "Parties that, by reason of their aims or the behavior of their adherents, seek to undermine or abolish the free democratic basic order . . . shall be unconstitutional."

In the second case, democratic rights are seen as institutions created and defended by the state. Thus, some democratic constitutions speak at length about social or economic institutions as rights, such as universal education, health care, and retirement benefits. Such rights are particularly strong in social democratic regimes. For example, the second article of the Swedish constitution states that "the public institutions shall secure the right to employment, housing and education, and shall promote social care and social security, as well as favorable conditions for good health." The Brazilian constitution states that among its fundamental objectives are national development and the eradication of poverty, and it includes such provisions as a minimum wage, overtime, and annual vacations. Other constitutions enshrine state control over natural resources, or the obligation of the state to preserve the natural environment. What are the limits of individual rights and liberties, and what is the acceptable balance between individual rights and the role of the state in meeting society's needs? These vary across country, case, and time, meaning that the concept of liberty will continue to evolve.

In the above discussion, we see that liberty is not simply the absence of controls over our scope of action—a negative freedom. Rather, liberty is also something that must be created, institutionalized, and defended—a positive freedom. The state, government, and regime are thus central to fostering and furthering liberty. But it would be a mistake to conclude that liberty flows only from the state, a gift to the people. Recall our opening discussion of democratization. Domestic and international institutions, culture, civil society, modernization, committed leaders, and other factors can open the space for democratic change. The challenge becomes vesting that space with liberty—with the institutionalization of civil rights and civil liberties that fuels democratic participation and competition. Where liberty is weak or absent, the trappings of democracy may be in place but repression will remain the norm. This will be the focus of our next chapter, as we turn to nondemocratic regimes.

In Sum: Future Challenges to Democracy

As we have seen, democracy is one way to maintain a balance between individual freedom and collective equality, a form of government whose origins this chapter has traced back thousands of years. In its modern, liberal form, democracy emphasizes individual freedom through participation, competition, and liberty. Participation, often through elections, helps provide the public a means of control over the state and the government; competition ensures an open arena of ideas and prevents too great a centralization of power; and liberty creates norms for human freedom and equality. When these elements are institutionalized—valued for their own sake, considered legitimate by the public—democracy is institutionalized, and we can speak of the existence of a rule of law. No one can claim that they stand above the democratic regime.

In the next chapter, we shall consider politics when this is not the case. In nondemocratic regimes, all those things we have taken for granted are weakly institutionalized or absent. Participation, competition, liberty, and the rule of law are circumscribed, with the preponderance of power resting in the hands of a few elites who are not accountable to the public. How do these systems come about? How do they differ? Are their days numbered, or will democracy continue to struggle against nondemocratic actors and institutions for the foreseeable future? We will discuss these questions further.

For Further Reading

Acemoglu, Daron and James A. Robinson. *Economic Origins of Dictatorship and Democracy* (New York: Cambridge University Press, 2007).

Dalton, Russell J. *The Good Citizen* (Washington: CQ Press, 2008).

Duverger, Maurice. *Political Parties: Their Organization and Activity in the Modern State* (New York: Wiley, 1964).

de Tocqueville, Alexis. *Democracy in America*, Vol. 2. Henry Reeve, trans. (New York: Henry G. Langley, 1845).

RS> Lijphart, Arend. "Constitutional Choices for New Democracies." *The Global Resurgence of Democracy*. Larry Diamond and Marc F. Platter, eds. (Baltimore: Johns Hopkins University Press, 1996).

MacPherson, C. B. *The Life and Times of Liberal Democracy* (New York: Oxford University Press, 1977).

RS> Putnam, Robert D. "Tuning In, Tuning Out: The Strange Disappearance of Social Capital in America." *PS: Political Science & Politics* (December 1995).

RS> Schmitter, Philippe C. and Terry Lynn Karl. "What Democracy Is . . . and Is Not." *Journal of Democracy* (Summer 1991).

RS> Stepan, Alfred, Juan J. Linz and Yogendra Yadav. The Rise of "State-Nations." *Journal of Democracy* 21, no. 3 (2010).

RS> Zakaria, Fareed. *The Future of Freedom* (New York: Norton, 2003).

RS >
Reader Selection

Highlighted selections are included in *Essential Readings in Comparative Politics*, Fourth Edition.

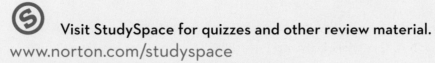

Visit StudySpace for quizzes and other review material.
www.norton.com/studyspace

- Vocabulary Flashcards of All Key Terms
- Chapter Review Quizzes
- Complete Study Reviews and Outlines

6

Many nondemocratic regimes rely on a large secret police force for domestic surveillance and intimidation. Romania, like other post-communist countries, has debated whether these files should be made public.

NONDEMOCRATIC REGIMES

KEY CONCEPTS

- Nondemocratic regimes are often divided between authoritarianism and totalitarianism.

- As with democracy, there are various and competing theories for the emergence and perseverance of nondemocratic regimes.

- Coercion, co-optation, and personality cults are common means through which nondemocratic regimes maintain their power.

- Types of nondemocratic regime include personal and monarchical, military, one-party, theocratic, and illiberal/hybrid.

- The general trend worldwide has been away from nondemocratic regimes, though there remain a large number of illiberal regimes.

"Man is born free, but everywhere he is in chains," wrote Jean-Jacques Rousseau in 1762. Since his time, democracy has emerged and flourished in many places throughout the world. However, according to Freedom House, an American nongovernmental organization that monitors and promotes democratic institutions around the world, over half the world's population still lives in societies defined as either "partly free," where significant personal liberties and democratic rights exist in theory but are not institutionalized and are subject to restriction, or "not free," where the public has little in the way of civil liberties or opportunity for political participation.[1] In neither case can these regimes be described as democratic.

In this chapter, we will look at the internal dynamics and origins of nondemocratic regimes. After defining these regimes and their relationship to freedom and equality, we will look at their origins, addressing the puzzle of why nondemocratic regimes are the norm in some countries but not in others. Behind this puzzle lies the broader question of the origins of nondemocratic rule, which mirrors our discussion in Chapter 5 on competing explanations for democratization. What variables are associated with nondemocratic rule? This discussion of the possible sources of nondemocratic regimes will lead us into an examination of how nondemocratic rulers maintain their hold on power. Nondemocratic regimes display a great diversity; nevertheless, we can identify and contrast a number of common features. Finally, we will consider the future of nondemocratic rule. At the end of the Cold War, many assumed that liberal democracy was the wave of the future. In recent years, however, nondemocratic rule has shown an ability to adapt and thrive. The "wave of democracy" may be facing a reverse tide. Whether this is true, and what its implications would be, will be the final consideration of our chapter.

Defining Nondemocratic Rule

One challenge to studying nondemocratic regimes is that they constitute what we could call a "residual category." Unlike democratic regimes, which can be defined and identified, nondemocratic regimes represent a wide array of different kinds of systems, many of which bear little resemblance to one another. This in turn leads to a proliferation of terms that are often used interchangeably and indiscriminately: autocracy, oligarchy, dictatorship, tyranny. Even more confusing, in some cases nondemocratic regimes may resemble democracies more closely than they do other nondemocratic regimes. As a result, we tend to speak of nondemocratic regimes in terms of what they deny their citizens, the very things that define democracy: participation, competition, and liberty. We will often use the term **authoritarianism** to cover many of these different forms of nondemocratic rule.

If we want to speak of nondemocratic regimes as more than simply the absence of democracy, however, we need a definition to work with. Scholars define **nondemocratic regimes** as those in which a political regime is controlled by a small group of individuals who exercise power over the state without being constitutionally responsible to the public. In nondemocratic regimes, the public does not play a significant role in selecting or removing leaders from office; thus, political leaders in nondemocratic regimes have much greater leeway to develop policies that they "dictate" to the people (hence the term *dictator*). As one can imagine, nondemocratic regimes by their nature are built around the restriction of individual freedom. At a minimum, they eliminate people's right to choose their own leaders, and they also restrict to varying degrees other liberties, such as freedom of speech or of assembly. Nondemocratic regimes' relationship to equality is less clear. Some nondemocratic regimes, such as communist ones, limit individual freedom in order to produce greater economic equality. Others seek to provide neither freedom nor equality, existing only to enhance the power of those in control.[2]

There are various kinds of nondemocratic regimes. Nondemocratic leaders do not necessarily rule in a capricious or arbitrary manner; indeed, nondemocratic regimes can have a strong institutional underpinning of ideology. As ideologies, fascism and communism, for instance, explicitly reject liberal democracy as an inferior form of social organization, favoring instead a powerful state and restricted individual freedoms. This ideology provided the norms that fascist and communist nondemocratic leaders followed in places like Nazi Germany and the Soviet Union. But other nondemocratic regimes are not ideological and may even be anti-ideological, asserting that the leadership speaks for "the people." In other cases, few if any substantial political ideas are evident among those in power, whose rule is predicated simply on power for power's sake and the benefits that come with it. In these cases, it becomes difficult even to speak of a regime, since we are not talking about a set of institutionalized rules and norms for political activity. In this case the term *regime* is often used pejoratively by critics, coupled with a leader's name (such as the "Saddam Hussein regime" in Iraq). This terminology reflects the critics' view that all decisions flow from the ruler, unfettered by political institutions of any sort. The leader, in essence, is the regime.

Totalitarianism and Nondemocratic Rule

Before we continue, we should examine a tricky and often misused term that is applied to a range of nondemocratic regimes: *totalitarianism*. Totalitarianism, which should not be confused with authoritarianism, connotes violence and terror, and so the word is often used in a partisan way to label a political system that we particularly dislike. This problem of definition goes back to the earlier part of the last century. Many scholars used the term totalitarianism to describe Nazi Germany and the Soviet Union and its satellite states; others countered that when the term was used in a way that equated fascism and communism it was being applied more for political reasons than in an attempt at objective classification. Some thus called for abandoning the term altogether, claiming that it had no real scholarly utility. However, totalitarianism remains a valuable term, especially if used consistently and judiciously.

What then is the difference between totalitarianism and other forms of nondemocratic rule? There are several important elements. **Totalitarianism** is a form of nondemocratic rule with a highly centralized state whose regime has a well-defined ideology and seeks to transform and fuse the institutions of state, society, and the economy. The main objective of totalitarianism, unlike those of other nondemocratic regimes, is to use power to transform the total institutional fabric of a country to meet an ideological goal. Finally, because of the ambitious goals of totalitarianism, violence and the resulting terror often becomes a necessary tool to destroy any obstacle to change.[3] Violence and terror not only destroy enemies of the totalitarian ideology but also, as the political philosopher Hannah Arendt pointed out, shatters human will, eliminating individuals' ability to create, much less aspire to, freedom.[4] Because they achieve these effects, terror and violence are commonly used to break down existing institutions and remake them in the leadership's own image. This is not to say that all violent regimes are totalitarian. The central issue is to what end violence is used. Totalitarianism often emerges when those who have come to power profess a radical or reactionary political attitude that rejects the status quo and sees dramatic, often revolutionary change as indispensable and violence as a necessary or even a positive force toward that goal.

Many countries in history have been controlled by leaders with totalitarian aspirations, but few of these leaders have been able to put their theories into practice. The Soviet Union under the rule of Josef Stalin, from the 1930s to the 1950s, is commonly viewed as totalitarian: most domestic institutions were radically restructured, most aspects of private life were controlled by the state and the

Totalitarian Regimes . . .

- Seek to control and transform all aspects of the state, society, and economy.

- Use violence as a tool for remaking institutions.

- Have a strong ideological goal.

- Have arisen relatively rarely.

Communist Party, and millions were imprisoned and executed toward those ends. Nazi Germany is also typically seen as a totalitarian regime, although in some areas, such as the economy, changes were relatively few. Other fascist regimes, such as Italy during World War II, lacked the capacity and power to be totalitarian, even though they openly aspired to be so. Similarly, while China during the Cultural Revolution of the 1960s experienced widespread violence against people and institutions, the fragmentation of the Communist Party and the state was quite different from totalitarianism. As we see, even when it is more precisely defined, *totalitarian* is a difficult word to apply, making it liable to subjective, rather than objective, use.

Today, only communist North Korea can properly be described as totalitarian, dominated by an elaborate ideology that covers all aspects of life and is backed by violence, widespread fear, and the absence of even small personal freedoms. By way of comparison, a country such as Iraq under Saddam Hussein, although highly oppressive, could not be described as totalitarian because it lacked a strong ideology and in many ways was less centralized than outsiders imagined. Saddam Hussein's primary goal as Iraq's leader was to maintain and expand his own political power as an end in itself. In spite of this, critics often described Iraq as a totalitarian society. Similarly, Iran is frequently described as a totalitarian system, but though one might describe the current regime as embodying a "totalist" ideology, large swaths of the state, society, and economy function with varying degrees of independence.

To sum up, nondemocratic rule is a political regime in which power is exercised by a few, unbound by public or constitutional control. The public lacks not only the right to choose its own leaders but also other personal liberties that those in power may see as a threat, such as freedom of speech or assembly. Totalitarianism is distinguished from other forms of nondemocratic rule by its totalist ideology, which seeks the fundamental transformation of most domestic institutions and the potential use of violence toward that end.

Origins and Sources of Nondemocratic Rule

Now that we have defined nondemocratic regimes, we might consider their emergence and perseverance. In the last chapter we spoke about some of the competing explanations for why democracy comes about. In a number of these explanations, the discussion was built on the ways in which authoritarian rule can give way to democracy. Let's return to these arguments, with an emphasis on nondemocratic perseverance rather than decline. As always, there is no single or dominant explanation for nondemocratic regimes, and the explanatory power of any theory may be limited by space or time.

Modernization and Nondemocratic Rule

Recall that one of the central assertions of the behavioral revolution was that with modernization, societies would become more urban, educated, and politically sophisticated, creating the basic conditions that would catalyze democracy. And indeed, there is a strong correlation between societies that lack modern institutions and nondemocratic rule. Societies that are poor and poorly developed are less likely to have democracy for a number of reasons, which we noted in Chapter 5. One important explanation is the role of the middle class. According to the common political science dictum "no middle class, no democracy," modernization is necessary for the development of an urban, educated middle class that has specific political, social, and economic interests that it can articulate and advance, helping to generate demands for democratic rule. The absence of a middle class is more likely to result in a polarization between those few in power and a wider population that is weakly organized.

Yet modernization can sometimes lead to nondemocratic rule—even replacing existing democratic regimes. Contrary to our expectations, modernization can be a disruptive and uneven process. Urban areas may experience a sudden transformation of institutions and norms while rural areas lag behind; technology like telephones and Internet access, as well as infrastructure such as roads and schools, may be enjoyed by some and unavailable to others. Disruptive shifts in economic institutions (such as from agricultural to industrial) and social institutions (such as changes in gender relations or increased secularism) can generate instability. Modernization can also trend backward, with increased inflation or unemployment, weakening economic development and destabilizing the political order. Where a sufficient number of individuals feel disoriented by change, political movements and leaders may emerge who promise to restore "order" and reconcile the tensions between old institutions and new. This can bring down a democratic regime if it appears unable to resolve these tensions or avoid the pitfalls of modernity. Paradoxically, these nondemocratic movements are often driven by the direct beneficiaries of modernization, such as students and urban intellectuals, who have gained the organizational and ideological tools to articulate a political vision alternative to the status quo.

Nondemocratic regimes run the spectrum of levels of wealth and modernization. We may think of nondemocratic countries as necessarily poor. Yet Singapore and many Gulf states are commonly cited as modern and economically advanced societies where nondemocratic regimes are highly institutionalized (we can also think of countries, like India and South Africa, that are democracies yet relatively poor). Regime type and poverty do not correlate neatly, though it has been suggested that a country above $7000 per capita GDP at PPP is more likely to be an institutionalized democracy.

Elites and Nondemocratic Rule

In our discussion above, we've noted that the absence or destabilizing effects of modernization may be a factor in the emergence of authoritarianism. Much of this argument assumes that modernization is strongly correlated with wealth, as agricultural societies become more industrial and developed. However, modernization and wealth do not take into account inequality. As we saw in Chapter 4, countries can vary dramatically in their levels of financial equality, and we can imagine that in highly unequal societies, those who monopolize economic power will also monopolize political power.

In particular, elites may be less willing to share power when they fear losing their economic opportunities in the process. In fact, the longevity of nondemocracy may be due precisely to the fact that rivals for power seek control specifically so that they can enrich themselves. The state under these conditions becomes a tool to siphon off resources and maintain control. Regimes that have increased inequality this way may be particularly loath to surrender power, not only because they may be forced to give up their assets but also because they may lose their lives in retribution. The threat of revolution may make these systems particularly unlikely to provide much in the way of participation, competition, or liberty.

One variant of this argument that has gained currency of late is the "resource trap" theory of development. Since natural resources, such as oil, gas, and minerals, might be a source of great wealth, the puzzle is why so many resource-rich countries are undeveloped or nondemocratic. According to this theory, the existence of natural resources is a barrier to modernization and democracy, for several related reasons. Resources in the ground give leaders the wealth necessary to run the state without taxation. This means those in power need not bother themselves with the taxation-and-representation trade-off; since they do not need to tax the people, they can effectively ignore their political demands. Even worse, natural resources tend to stunt the development of a modern economy and middle class, since neither is of concern (and may in fact be a threat) to those in power. Finally, since natural resources are not portable, those in power know that should they give up power, they would not be able to take these assets with them. The result is that wealth is highly concentrated in the hands of those in power. Under these conditions, nondemocratic rule can effectively subsidize itself, so long as the resources last and have a market. Oil is the most obvious example of a resource trap, but diamonds, gold, or timber could also serve this function.

Society and Nondemocratic Rule

This discussion returns us to the idea of civil society. Recall that we defined civil society as a fabric of organizations created by people to help define their own interests. These organizations are not necessarily political, and, in fact, the vast majority of them have no specific political content. Sports teams, groups of collectors and enthusiasts, and religious and other organizations all form civil society. It is commonly argued that civil society is crucial to democratic life because it allows individuals to organize, articulate their preferences, and form networks that cross economic, social, or political divides. Civil society is thus commonly viewed as a crucible for democratic action, laying the groundwork for democratic institutions.

Conversely, many authoritarian systems are characterized by the absence of civil society. This can result from those in power taking steps to absorb, monitor, or destroy any form of independent action not sanctioned by the state. Civil society may also have little precedent in society or be hindered by ethnic or other societal divisions that dissuade people from forming organizations across institutional barriers. The result can be a society that views the state as the primary arena for social organization and therefore focuses more on winning control over the state than on building strong institutions outside it. Interestingly, this emphasis on the state can sometimes go hand in hand with what is known as populism. **Populism** is not a specific ideology and in fact draws much of its power from an anti-institutional approach. But generally, populism carries within it the view that elites and established institutions do not fully represent the will of the people and that a new move-ment, free from ideology and often led by a charismatic leader, can usher in a new order. While populism commonly takes on an antigovernmental, anti-institutional orientation, it often assumes that people need to "take back" the state and set it on the correct path. Populism need not lead to an antidemocratic outcome; however, we can see how it can destabilize democratic practices and provide a foundation for antidemocratic leaders to come to power.

Finally, civil society may emerge alongside a nondemocratic regime but itself take on nondemocratic tendencies, especially where more-democratic forms of civil society have been repressed by the state. Many countries have an array of active organizations with antidemocratic tendencies, such as groups that advocate pre-ferred rights for one ethnic or religious group over another. More civil activity can undermine democracy if many nonstate groups view the political process as legiti-mate only if it meets their specific needs and marginalizes others.

International Relations and Nondemocratic Rule

International influences can contribute to nondemocratic rule, most obviously through occupation. After World War II, the occupation of Japan and Germany led to democratization, but in Eastern Europe, Soviet control brought an end to democratic movements and eliminated much of civil society. Western imperialism has also contributed to nondemocratic rule in various ways. Borders badly drawn by imperial powers, as we discussed in Chapter 2, have created many countries with sharp ethnic and religious divisions that make consensus building difficult and authoritarianism an effective way for one group to monopolize power over others. Imperial institutions can similarly foster authoritarianism by contributing to such things as uneven modernization and weak state autonomy and capacity. Even after the end of Western imperialism, during the Cold War, both the Soviet Union and the United States backed authoritarian rulers against democratic forces in order to maintain or expand their influence. The United States played a significant role in overthrowing the democratically elected government in Iran in 1953, fearing that the prime minister was tilting toward the Soviet Union. The Soviet Union crushed revolts in Hungary in 1956 and Czechoslovakia in 1968. China and Russia have more recently become important supporters of nondemocratic regimes in Africa and the Middle East through investment and by building diplomatic support for them in the international community. Iran and Venezuela, too, have sought to use their oil wealth to support like-minded regimes.

Culture and Nondemocratic Rule

Let us return to the idea of political culture, which argues that there are differences in societal institutions—norms and values—that shape the landscape of political activity. In previous chapters we discussed the controversial idea that there may be a culture of democracy or liberty that is a precondition for institutionalized democracy, and that certain societies may, for whatever reason, hold these values while others do not. By extension, it could be argued that there are nondemocratic political values as well. Challenging modernization theory, which essentially equates "Western" and "modern," some scholars argue that culture is much more fixed than modernization theory holds it to be; they believe that modernization will not necessarily cause cultures to Westernize—that is, to adopt such values as secularism, individualism, and liberal democracy. Nondemocratic rule in this view is not the absence of democracy—it is its own set of values.

One common argument in this regard is that democracy is a unique product of interconnected historical experiences in Europe, such as Christianity (particularly Protestantism), the emphasis on individualism and secularism, the development of the nation-state, modern ideologies, early industrialization, and the development of capitalism, among others. These factors, the argument goes, allowed for the creation of democracy as a regime built on liberal values that emphasize freedom—what we typically call "Western" values. In contrast, some (both inside and outside the Muslim world) have asserted that Islam views political power and religious power as one and the same. Laws are handed down by God to be observed and defended, and that democracy is essentially anathema to the will of God. Cultural arguments can also be found in what has been called the "Asian values" debate. Proponents of the idea of Asian values argue that Asia's cultural and religious traditions stress conformity, hierarchy, and obedience, which are more conducive to a political regime that limits freedom in order to defend social harmony and consensus. The philosophy of Confucianism is frequently cited in this regard, with its emphasis on obedience to hierarchy and its notion of a ruler's "mandate from heaven." According to Confucianism, the ruling elite stands as a parental figure over the people, acting in the public's best interests but not under its control. As the former Malaysian prime minister Mahathir Mohamad, one of the major proponents of "Asian values," has put it, "When citizens understand that their right to choose also involves limits and responsibilities, democracy doesn't deteriorate into an excess of freedom. . . . These are the dangers of democracy gone wrong, and in our view it is precisely the sad direction in which the West is heading."[5]

As we have noted, there are many both inside and outside societies with Islamic or Confucian traditions who reject the idea that there is a culture of nondemocratic

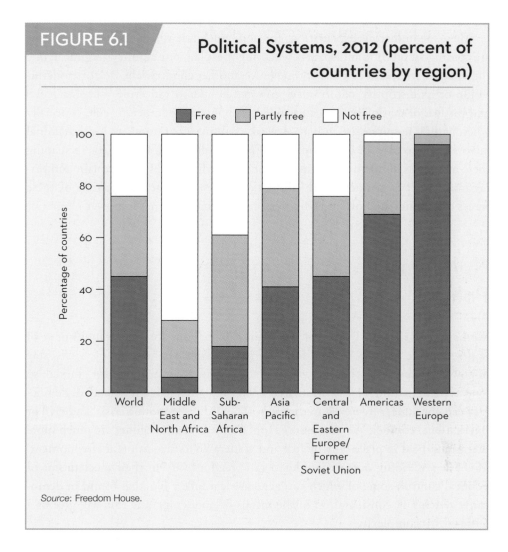

FIGURE 6.1

Political Systems, 2012 (percent of countries by region)

Free   Partly free   Not free

Percentage of countries

100

80

60

40

20

0

World | Middle East and North Africa | Sub-Saharan Africa | Asia Pacific | Central and Eastern Europe/ Former Soviet Union | Americas | Western Europe

Source: Freedom House.

rule. These societies and the peoples within them, it is argued, are far too diverse to represent one set of values. Differences in history, religion, social structure, and other institutions have led to an array of contrasting and overlapping ideas that are in a continuous process of interaction and reinterpretation. Confucian thought, just like the Bible in the West or the Koran in Islamic countries, can be interpreted in very different ways. As we saw in our discussion of political culture in Islam in Chapter 3, surveys show a wide variation across Muslim countries in how people view democracy and the separation of faith and state. Cultural arguments may inform the content of nondemocratic or democratic institutions, but we should be wary of making sweeping arguments about culture and regime type.

There are numerous explanations for nondemocratic rule, and these arguments are contingent on time and space—what might explain one country's regime at one time may be irrelevant at another time or for another country. The lack of modernization or its disruptive nature may reinforce nondemocratic rule. Elite strategies and the fear of sharing power can also help support nondemocratic rule, especially when natural resources are in play. A weak civil society at home and international factors can also play an important role. Finally, culture can be a factor in shaping the contours of nondemocratic institutions, but whether this can explain authoritarianism itself is a much more contentious question. The intersection of these forces can illuminate how and why nondemocratic rule comes to power.

Nondemocratic Regimes and Political Control

We have so far covered some of the main explanations for the establishment of nondemocratic regimes. In addition, we should consider how these systems stay in power. In liberal democracies, we take the system of government for granted; so long as participation, competition, and liberty are provided and defended, democracy can continue, often even in the face of inequality, economic crisis, and civil or international conflict. We may assume that nondemocratic regimes are much more precarious, held in place only by fear and vulnerable to revolution at any moment. This is a misleading image. Nondemocratic regimes vary in their mechanisms of political control, some of which can generate legitimacy like that found in democratic systems. A consideration of the means of nondemocratic rule will give us a sense of this complexity.

Coercion and Surveillance

One feature that we initially, and perhaps primarily, associate with nondemocratic regimes and especially with totalitarianism is the use of coercion. Coercion can be defined as compelling individuals by threatening their lives or livelihoods. Compliance with regime goals is often enforced through the threat or use of force against the population, sending a clear signal that those who oppose the regime or government will be dealt with harshly: they will face the loss of their job or access to certain resources, arrest, detention without trial, torture, and death. In an extreme example, in the 1970s several nondemocratic regimes in Latin America used "death

Nondemocratic Means of Control

- Coercion: public obedience is enforced through violence and surveillance.

- Co-optation: members of the public are brought into a beneficial relationship with the state and government, often through corporatism or clientelism.

- Personality cult: the public is encouraged to obey the leader based on his or her extraordinary qualities and compelling ideas.

squads" made up of police or military troops to target individuals suspected of harboring political views opposed to the regime. These individuals were abducted by the death squads and murdered, frequently after torture. In some cases, their bodies were dumped in the open as a warning to others who dared to question the regime; in other cases, the victims simply joined the thousands of "disappeared," individuals abducted and never seen again.

In other regimes, violence has been used even more indiscriminately. When Stalin consolidated his totalitarian rule in the Soviet Union in the 1930s, he carried out what are known as "purges," widespread arrests that decimated the ranks of the Communist Party and the state bureaucracy. Former leaders of the 1917 revolution, city mayors and local party bosses, high-ranking officers in the army and navy, university professors, scientists, diplomats, and many others were detained, tortured, coerced into confessing during "show trials," forced to implicate others in their supposed crimes, and either sent to forced labor camps or executed. The targets of the purges were not limited to the party or the state; writers, artists, students, farmers, and workers were also among those accused of political sabotage and anti-Soviet views. It is not known how many died in these purges; estimates range from 5 to 20 million. Undoubtedly, in the vast majority of these cases, the victims were innocent; yet this was unimportant to Stalin's regime. By making everyone fear that he or she, too, could be arrested, the public could be controlled and even turned against itself, since everyone feared that they would be denounced by someone else. The use of arbitrary arrests, torture, disappearances, and murder continues to be common in many nondemocratic regimes.

Another important means of control is the ability to maintain a close watch over the population. Surveillance allows the government to prevent opposition from organizing and also instills uncertainty among the population—who is being watched? Surveillance may be conducted through the use of an internal security force, or "secret police," charged with monitoring public activity, spying on individuals, and interrogating members of the public suspected of political activity hostile to the regime. In some countries, surveillance has included widespread telephone tapping and the creation of a huge network of public informers, whereby nearly anyone may be the eyes and ears of those in power. With the rise of the Internet and cellular technology, surveillance has become more sophisticated, including the ability to monitor and control many forms of electronic communication, such as e-mail, social networking, and text messages.

Co-optation: Corporatism and Clientelism

The prevalence of coercion and surveillance in some nondemocratic regimes may give the impression that those in power must be ever vigilant against the public to prevent opposition or revolution, which might spring up at any time. But not all nondemocratic regimes need or choose to rely on punishment or surveillance as a central means of control. Another method they may use is co-optation, the process by which individuals outside an organization are brought into a beneficial relationship with it, making them dependent on the regime for certain rewards. Although co-optation is not unique to nondemocratic regimes, it tends to be much more widespread under such regimes than under democratic ones, where people are usually more suspicious of such favoritism, seeing it as contrary to the democratic process.

CORPORATISM

Co-optation can take many forms. The most structured form is corporatism. Recall from Chapter 4 the term *neocorporatism*, a system in which business, labor, and the state bargain over economic policy. In its earliest form, however, modern **corporatism** emerged as a method by which nondemocratic regimes attempted to solidify their control over the public by creating or sanctioning a limited number of organizations to represent the interests of the public and restricting those not set up or approved by the state. These organizations are meant to replace independent organizations with a handful that alone have the right to speak for various sectors of society. For example, under a corporatist regime, churches, labor unions, agricultural associations, student groups, neighborhood committees, and the like are all approved and funded by the state. Nonsanctioned, alternative organizations are not allowed.

Unlike the overlapping memberships, competition, and ever-changing nature of civil society and political parties in a pluralistic society, corporatism arranges society such that each organization is empowered by the state to have a monopoly of representation over a given issue or segment of society (meaning that no other organization may act in that area or speak on that issue). State, society, and the market under corporatism are viewed as a single organic body, with each institution cooperating and performing its own specific and limited role and subordinate to the state and regime.

Corporatism can be an effective form of control, as it gives the public a limited influence (or at least the pretense of influence) in the policy-making process. Farmers or students have an official organization with elected officers and resources that are meant to serve their interests. In return, the regime is able to better control the public through these institutions, which are funded and managed by the state, and civil society is marginalized or eliminated. For the average individual, a state-sanctioned organization is better than none at all, and many willingly participate in the hope that their needs will be met.

Many nondemocratic regimes have used variants of corporatism as a means of control. It is an integral part of totalitarianism, but it also existed in nontotalitarian Spain and Portugal up to the 1970s. In Spain, for example, a single political party organized most business and labor interests together into a limited number of "syndicates" that represented both owners and workers in different sectors of the economy. Communist regimes are similarly corporatist. In Cuba, for example, all labor is organized under a single union directly controlled by the state, and independent unions are illegal. Although corporatism differs in form and degree, in all corporatist regimes a limited number of organizations represent and direct societal interests, bringing the public under organized state control.

CLIENTELISM

A less structured means by which states may co-opt the public is **clientelism**, whereby the state co-opts members of the public by providing specific benefits to a person in return for public support (such as voting in elections). Unlike corporatism, clientelism relies on individual patronage rather than organizations that serve a large group of people, and it is more ad hoc than corporatism. Clientelism does not require a set of sanctioned and licensed organizations but allows those in power to target and respond to individuals and groups as they see fit, trading benefits for particular forms of support.

In both corporatism and clientelism, the state has a number of perquisites it can use in co-opting individuals. Jobs within the state or in state-run sectors of the economy, business contracts or licenses, public goods such as roads and schools, and kickbacks and bribes are a few of the tools in its arsenal. Such largesse often leads to rent seeking, a process in which political leaders essentially rent out parts of the state to their supporters, who as a result control public goods that would otherwise be distributed in a nonpolitical manner. For example, leaders might turn over control of a nationalized industry, providing supporters with jobs and the ability to siphon off public funds from that branch of the state.

In general, co-optation is likely to be much more successful than coercion at maintaining nondemocratic regimes, since many in the public may actively support the regime in return for the benefits they derive from it. Political opposition is dealt with not through repression and violence but by incorporating one's opponents into the system and making them dependent on it, or by withholding largesse. Such a regime, however, faces limitations. Corporatist and clientelist regimes can run out of benefits with which to pacify the public, especially if a great deal of the economy is built around state-controlled industries that provide rewards to the loyal rather than growth and increased employment. Also, in a regime that doles out economic resources for political reasons, problems may emerge as productive resources are siphoned off to secure the acquiescence of the public. At its worst, such a regime can decline into a **kleptocracy** (literally, "rule by theft"), where those in power seek only to drain the state of assets and resources. As these assets and resources dry up, co-optation can quickly unravel.

Personality Cults

Nondemocratic regimes may also reinforce their rule through emphasis on veneration of the leadership—essentially an emotional appeal to legitimize rule. The most extreme example is what is known as a personality cult. First used to describe Stalin's rule in the Soviet Union, a personality cult refers to the promotion of the image of a leader not merely as a political figure but as someone who embodies the spirit of the nation, possesses far more wisdom and strength than the average individual, and is thus portrayed in a quasi-religious manner as all-wise, all-seeing, all-knowing. In other words, personality cults attempt to generate a charismatic form of authority for the political leader from the top down by convincing the public of the leader's admirable qualities. In one recent example, Saparmurat Niyazov, president of Turkmenistan from 1990 until his death in 2006, built his personality cult by doing things like dubbing himself "Turkmenbashi," or "Father of the Turkmen," changing the months of the year (renaming April after his mother and January after himself), and constructing a large, gold-leaf statue of himself that rotated during the day to follow the sun.

The media and culture play a vital role in a personality cult: news reports, public rallies, art, music, films, and other means are used to spread flattering imagery of the leader. Successes in the country are attributed to the power of the leader, and mistakes are blamed on the mortal flaws of the public or on external enemies. Cults of personality may also be coupled to coercion; the public may not believe the praise, but no one is willing to say so. This is especially the case where charismatic power has faded over time to become little more than a facade, held up only by force. Under these conditions, there is always the chance that the cult will crack, leading to a rapid political decompression. This occurred in Romania in 1989, when Nicolae Ceaușescu, the self-styled "conductor" of his country, was shown on national television reacting in a stunned and confused manner when attendees at a public rally he was addressing suddenly grew hostile. Within hours, revolution had swept the country, and, within three days, Ceaușescu and his wife had been executed by firing squad.

Personality cults may also take a weaker but still powerful form. In Iran, the image of Supreme Leader Ayatollah Khamenei adorns shops and billboards around the country, and he is portrayed as an embodiment of the 1979 revolution and the country's Shia Muslim faith. Yet in spite of his power, few Iranians would view him as a kind of deity or believe that he has superhuman powers. In recent years, Latin America has produced a number of populist leaders whose personal charisma and symbolic power are significant. Most notable of these is Hugo Chávez in Venezuela, known for his regular presence in the media, including unscripted speeches on national television that can last for several hours. His personal popularity is strong and amplified by the state-run media, but it would be a stretch to call this a personality cult. Chávez remains, in the eyes of the public and in his own political communication, an exceptional, but still flawed, human being.

Looking back over what we have discussed so far, we find that nondemocratic regimes come to power and stay in power in various ways: some of these are "carrots" (rewards for compliance and support), others "sticks" (threatened or actual punishments). A combination of such carrots and sticks may cause some people, perhaps even a majority, to view the regime as legitimate. They may agree with the regime's ideology, directly benefit from its rule, venerate its leaders, or simply fear political change. The idea of nondemocratic legitimacy may be hard for us to accept. Particularly in Western democracies, there is an assumption that in every nondemocratic regime the people are simply waiting for the chance to install democracy. Yet nondemocratic regimes can be just as institutionalized and stable and legitimate as any democratic regime, enjoying some, or even a great deal of, public support, especially if benefits are widespread enough, coercion limited, and political change viewed as fraught with risk. Many, for example, would suggest that the current Chinese regime enjoys widespread public support and that the public has little interest in democratization, which many fear as a source of political and economic instability.

Models of Nondemocratic Rule

By now it should be clear that nondemocratic regimes emerge for different reasons and persist in different ways by using, to different degrees, tools of coercion and co-optation. Political scientists often classify such regimes according to how they use these tools. The most important forms of nondemocratic rule are personal and monarchical, military, one-party, theocratic, and illiberal or hybrid regimes. Personal and monarchical rule is based on the power of a single strong leader who typically relies on charismatic or traditional authority to maintain power. Under military rule, in contrast, the monopoly of violence that characterizes militaries tends to be the strongest means of control. One-party rule is often corporatist, creating a broad membership as a source of support and oversight. Theocracies derive their power from their claim to rule on behalf of God. Finally, in illiberal or hybrid regimes, the basic structures of democracy exist but are not fully institutionalized and often not respected. Across regimes, we find structures we are familiar with in liberal democracies: heads of state and government, judiciaries, legislatures and elections. But these are not subject to the rule of law, in the absence of which they reflect the preferences of those in power.

Personal and Monarchical Rule

Personal and monarchical rule is what usually comes to mind when people think of nondemocratic rule, perhaps because long before modern politics, states, and economies came into being, people were ruled by powerful figures—kings and caesars, emperors and sultans, chiefs and caudillos. Drawing on charismatic or traditional legitimacy, personal and monarchical rule often rests on the claim that one person alone is fit to run the country, with no clear regime or roles to constrain that person's rule. Under this form of rule, the state and society are commonly taken to be possessions of the leader, to be dispensed with as he (or, occasionally, she) sees fit. The ruler is not a subject of the state; rather, the state and society are subjects of the ruler. Ideology may be weak or absent, since rulers justify their control through the logic that they alone are the embodiment of the people and therefore uniquely qualified to act on the people's behalf. This claim may be coupled with a strong personality cult or a reliance on the traditional authority of bloodlines.

In some cases, personal and monarchical rule relies less on charismatic or traditional authority than on a form of co-optation known as patrimonialism. Patrimonialism can be seen as a form of clientelism, since a patrimonial leader trades benefits for political support. However, under **patrimonialism** the benefits are not distributed in an ad hoc way among individuals in society but are instead limited to a small group of regime supporters inside the state itself. This ruling group gains direct benefits in return for enforcing the ruler's will. The state elite swear allegiance to the leadership in return for personal profit. This is a form of co-optation, although under patrimonialism, it is only the ruler's own personal followers who benefit. All others in society tend to be held in check by force.

An example of personal rule based on patrimonialism was found in Zaire (now the Democratic Republic of Congo) under the rule of Mobutu Sese Seko from 1965 until 1997. Although he once commanded a great deal of charismatic legitimacy, over time Mobutu increasingly used patrimonialism as a way to maintain his power. In particular, Mobutu built his patrimonial regime around Zaire's abundant natural resources, such as diamonds, gold, copper, and cobalt. He used these resources not to benefit the country as a whole but to amass his personal fortune; he siphoned off the profits from these resources to enrich himself and his followers. The result was a coterie of supporters who were willing to defend Mobutu in order to maintain their economic privileges.[6] This system of dependence and economic reward helps explain how Mobutu maintained power for more than three decades while Zaire's per capita GDP dropped by two-thirds from the 1970s to the 1990s.

While monarchies have waned, they remain powerful in parts of the Middle East, such as Saudi Arabia and across the Persian Gulf. Even when they are not monarchies, regimes with a single ruler attempt to keep power within one family, typically transferring it from father to son. Leaders of such regimes may take on titles such as president, but in essence they function much like traditional monarchs. Personal rule remains common in Africa and is typically coupled to patrimonial regimes that are enriched through control over natural resources or trade.

Military Rule

A second form of nondemocratic regime is military rule. Once considered relatively unusual, military rule became much more common over the past 50 years, particularly in Latin America, Africa, and parts of Asia. Where governments and states are struggling with legitimacy and stability, often as a result of modernization, and where there is a high level of public unrest or violence, the military has sometimes chosen to intervene directly in politics, seeing itself as the only organized force able to ensure stability. This view is often combined with a sense among military leaders that the current government or regime threatens the military's or the country's interests and should be removed. Military rule may even have widespread public support, especially if people believe that the strong arm of the military can bring an end to corruption or political violence, prevent revolution, and restore stability.

Military rule typically emerges through a coup d'état, in which military forces take control of the government by force. In some cases, military actors may claim that they have seized control reluctantly, promising to return the state and government to civilian rule once stability has been restored. This was the case in Thailand in 2006 and following Egypt's revolution in 2011. Often, under military rule, political parties and most civil liberties are restricted; civilian political leaders or opponents of military rule are arrested and may be killed. The use of coercion is a common aspect of military rule, since by their nature militaries hold an overwhelming capacity for violence.

Military rule typically lacks both a specific ideology and a charismatic or traditional source of authority. Hence, if the military seeks legitimacy in the eyes of the people, it must often fall back on rational authority. One variant of military rule that reflects this logic is known as **bureaucratic authoritarianism**, a regime in which the state bureaucracy and the military share a belief that a technocratic leadership, focused on rational, objective, and technical expertise, can solve the problems of the country—unlike "emotional" or "irrational" ideologically based party politics. Public participation, in other words, is seen as an obstacle to effective and objective policy making and so is done away with. In the 1960s and 1970s, bureaucratic authoritarian regimes emerged in a number of less-developed countries as rapid modernization and industrialization generated a high degree of political conflict. State and industry, with their plans for rapid economic growth, clashed with the interests of the working class and peasantry, who sought greater political power and a larger share of the wealth. This increasing polarization in politics often led business leaders and the state bureaucracy to advocate military rule as a way to prevent the working class and the peasantry from gaining power over the government.

Over the past thirty years, many bureaucratic authoritarian regimes have transitioned to democracy. However, some noteworthy examples remain. Russia might be viewed as a bureaucratic authoritarian regime, where those in power have tended to come from within the secret service or military, including Vladimir Putin. Supporters of military rule believe that dispensing with democracy can help facilitate modernization and development; they point to cases like South Korea, Taiwan, and Chile as success stories. But this is a problem of selection bias (see Chapter 1), where people have only looked for cases of economic success. If we concentrate instead on military rule, we can find many more cases that led to poor economic development, such as much of Central America.[7]

One-Party Rule

Commonly associated with totalitarianism, one-party rule is a regime in which a single political party monopolizes politics and bans other parties or excludes them from power. The ruling party serves several functions. It helps to incorporate the people into the political regime through membership and participation. Typically, the party incorporates only a small minority of the population—in most communist countries, for instance, party membership has been less than 10 percent—but this still means that hundreds of thousands or millions of people are party members. One-party rule is often also combined with a corporatist regime of public control.

Through membership, the party can rely on a large segment of the public that is willing to help develop and support the policies of nondemocratic rule as well as to transmit information back to the leadership on developments in all aspects of society. Single-party regimes are often broken down into smaller units or "cells" that operate at the university, workplace, or neighborhood level. These cells report back to higher levels of the party, help deal with local problems and concerns, and keep tabs on society as a whole. No area is untouched by the presence of the party, and this helps to maintain control over the public.

In return for their support, members of the party are often granted privileges that are otherwise denied to the public at large. They may have access to certain resources (better health care or housing, for instance) that nonmembers do not; positions in government and other important areas of the economy or society are also reserved for party members. One important result of such membership is that a large group of individuals in society directly benefits from the regime and is therefore willing to defend it. This pragmatic membership, however, can backfire: those who embrace party membership only for the personal benefits and not out of any ideological conviction may quickly desert the leadership in a time of crisis.

Finally, the party serves as a mechanism of mobilization. The leadership uses the party as an instrument to deliver propaganda that extols the virtues of the current regime and government; it relies on its rank-and-file members, through demonstrations and mass rallies, to give the appearance of widespread public support and enthusiasm for the leadership. If necessary, it also uses party members to control and harass those who do not support the regime. However, co-optation is the primary mechanism that ensures compliance and support.

One-party regimes are often associated with communism and fascism and have been present in all cases of totalitarianism. However, they can also be found around the world in a variety of nondemocratic regimes. Other parties may exist, but they are typically highly restricted by the government so that they cannot challenge the current regime. For many years, this was the case in Mexico, which was dominated by the Institutional Revolutionary Party, or PRI. Cuba, North Korea, China, Vietnam, and Laos are other examples of one-party regimes, each controlled by a single communist party.

Theocracy

Theocratic rule is probably the hardest form of nondemocratic rule to describe and analyze, though it is likely one of the oldest forms of rule. *Theocracy* literally means "rule by God," and a theocratic regime can be founded on any number of faiths and variations within them. A Christian theocracy might look completely unlike a Jewish one, drawing on different beliefs, texts, and traditions. Another obstacle to describing theocracy is the paucity of current examples of such regimes. In fact, some scholars would say there are no remaining theocracies, which would make a discussion of the term in contemporary politics irrelevant. However, we can observe in several countries some elements of theocratic rule, even if such a system does not exist in pure form. In Chapter 3, we noted that one of the recent challenges to ideology has been the rise of fundamentalism, which we defined as the fusion of religion and politics into an ideology that seeks to merge religion and the state. Such a merger, where faith is the sole source of the regime's authority, would render democratic institutions subordinate or in contradiction to the perceived will of God. In the vast majority of cases, such a goal remains hypothetical. Yet we can note cases where theocratic institutions are present and powerful.

Iran is the best example of a country that could be described as a theocracy. In 1979, the existing secular monarchy was overthrown by an Islamic revolution, ushering in a new government headed by the cleric Ayatollah Khomeini. In the Iranian system, the traditional forms of secular government (executive, legislature, judiciary) are mirrored by unique institutions that are controlled by religious leaders. Thus, the Supreme Leader, a religious figure, holds power over the president, while a Guardian Council can reject legislation and candidates for office for being insufficiently Islamic, much like an upper house and constitutional court. Afghanistan between 1996 and 2001 could also be described as a theocracy, lacking any

Types of Nondemocratic Rule

TYPE	DEFINITION	PRIMARY TOOLS OF CONTROL
PERSONAL AND MONARCHICAL RULE	Rule by a single leader, with no clear regime or rules constraining that leadership	Patrimonialism: supporters within the state benefit directly from their alliance with the ruler (corruption)
MILITARY RULE	Rule by one or more military officials, often brought to power through a coup d'état	Control of the armed forces, sometimes also allied with business and state elites (bureaucratic authoritarianism)
ONE-PARTY RULE	Rule by one political party, with other groups banned or excluded from power	Large party membership helps mobilize support and maintain public control, often in return for political or economic benefits
THEOCRACY	"Rule by god"; holy texts serve as foundation for regime and politics	Religious leadership and political leadership fused into single sovereign authority
ILLIBERAL REGIMES	Rule by an elected leadership, through procedures of questionable democratic legitimacy	Manipulation of democratic procedures, such as vote rigging or harassment of opposition

constitution and relying instead on local clerics authorized by the Taliban to rule on judicial matters based on their interpretation of Islamic law.

Saudi Arabia combines monarchical and theocratic forms of rule. Politics is monopolized by the ruling family, and the king acts as the supreme religious leader. Judicial and other matters must conform to Islamic law and are enforced by the Mutawwai'in, or morality police.[8] Conversion from Islam in Saudi Arabia and Iran is punishable by death, and other religions and other sects within Islam are brought under strict control or banned outright. Some fear that other countries in the Middle East, such as Egypt, could become more theocratic following the 2011 uprisings. But as with fundamentalism in general, we should not confuse religiosity, or even a wish for religion to play a greater role in politics, with a desire for theocracy.

Illiberal and Hybrid Regimes

Our last example is perhaps the most important for us to consider, since it seems to be growing in prominence around the world. In fact, Figure 6.1, shown earlier on p. 173, includes a large group of countries, such as Colombia, Kenya, Lebanon, and Turkey, that are categorized as neither "free" nor "not free" but as "partially free," falling somewhere between democratic and nondemocratic regimes. These regimes go by a number of names, such as *electoral authoritarian* and *semi-democratic*. When scholars speak of **illiberal or hybrid regimes**, *illiberal* and *hybrid* both refer to the same regime type, though each term captures a different aspect of this particular form: illiberal, because such regimes do not fully institutionalize liberty; and hybrid, because they combine democratic and nondemocratic institutions and practices. The terms *illiberal* and *hybrid* will be used interchangeably here.

What do illiberal or hybrid regimes have in common? These regimes feature many of the familiar aspects of democracy, though with important qualifications. As a starting point, while the rule of law may be in place, it is weak. As a result, all the democratic institutions that rest upon the rule of law are weakly institutionalized and poorly respected. Executives, legislatures, and judiciaries have their respective arenas of authority; the public enjoys the right to vote; elections take place on a regular basis; and political parties compete. But these institutions and processes are circumscribed or unpredictable in ways inconsistent with democracy. Executives typically hold an overwhelming degree of power. This power is often concentrated in a presidency that limits the ability for removal. Moreover, presidents in illiberal systems often rely on referenda to bypass the state and confirm executive power. Legislatures in turn are less able to check the power of the executive, and judicial institutions such as constitutional courts are often packed with the supporters of those in power. In addition, while political competition may exist on paper, parties and groups are restricted or harassed. Government monopolies over print and electronic media are used to deny the opposition a public platform, while the judicial system is used to harass opponents. The military often is not subject to civilian control. Elections are manipulated through changing electoral rules, through vote buying, intimidation, or barring candidates from running.

Illiberal regimes in many ways represent a gray area between nondemocratic and democratic rule. Although these regimes look much like democracies on paper, they are much less so in practice. The big question here is whether illiberal regimes are transitional, in the process of moving from nondemocratic to democratic rule (or vice versa), or are a new form of nondemocracy that uses the trappings of democracy to perpetuate its control. We are seeing increasing examples of the latter: countries where the transition from authoritarianism to democracy has stalled and government institutions are democratic in name only, so that participation, competition, and liberty are severely curtailed.[9] We will gain a clearer answer to this question as we see how many of the Middle Eastern countries whose governments were overthrown in the recent revolutions transition into liberal democracies, become illiberal regimes, or turn into some other form of authoritarianism.

In Sum: Retreat or Retrenchment for Nondemocratic Regimes?

Although nondemocratic regimes exhibit an amazing diversity and flexibility in maintaining political control, the global trend has been away from this form of rule. In the early part of the last century, democratic countries were few and beleaguered, wracked by economic recession, whereas nondemocratic regimes and totalitarianism in particular, backed by communist and fascist ideologies, seemed to promise radically new ways to restructure state, economic, and societal institutions. The German philosopher Oswald Spengler summarized this view in his 1922 work *The Decline of the West*: "The era of individualism, liberalism and democracy, of humanitarianism and freedom, is nearing its end. The masses will accept with resignation the victory of the Caesars, the strong men, and will obey them. Life will descend to a level of general uniformity, a new kind of primitivism, and the world will be better for it."[10]

Yet the exact opposite has taken place. Figure 6.2 shows that in spite of the rise of illiberal and hybrid regimes, the number of countries classified as "not free" and "partly free" has declined dramatically over just the past four decades. In the early 1970s, less than a third of countries were democratic; now nearly half of them are. Why this decline in nondemocratic regimes? We have advanced economic, political, and societal arguments regarding the sources of nondemocratic rule and democratization. One final explanation may be ideological. Nondemocratic rule has lost much of its mobilizing power. Fifty years ago, ideologies predicated on nondemocratic regimes could mobilize people with visions of a world to be transformed. However, in the aftermath of the Cold War, there is no longer any strong ideology that combines the absence of individual freedom with some broader goal. Leaders may claim that limitations on political rights are necessary for political stability or economic development, but they no longer offer any real alternative vision for politics. It is increasingly difficult to justify nondemocratic regimes through any universal set of ideas.

What Explains the Different Paths of Zimbabwe and South Africa?

In Chapters 2 and 3 we looked at the different paths India and Pakistan took after gaining independence from British rule. Like those two countries, Zimbabwe and South Africa are neighbors whose historical, economic, racial, and political institutions are similar but whose political trajectories over the past three decades could not have been more different. South Africa's democratic transition is well-known and regarded as a triumph in the face of tremendous obstacles.

For a century, South Africa was controlled by a small white minority, which accorded itself political and economic privileges while oppressing the black majority. In response, a resistance movement, the African National Congress (ANC), formed, using peaceful and, later, violent means to bring down the regime. Its leader, Nelson Mandela, served nearly three decades in prison, and yet in spite of this and other repressive government actions the ANC grew in strength. Faced with international isolation and the growing power of the black majority, the government released Mandela from prison in 1990, conducted negotiations with the ANC and other political parties, and inaugurated full democratic elections in 1994. The result has been a stable liberal democracy for nearly two decades.

What is less well remembered is that South Africa's next-door neighbor Zimbabwe (formerly Rhodesia) confronted a similar set of conditions much earlier. Like South Africa, Rhodesia was controlled by a white minority that dominated the country's economy and politics. Its government was also challenged by a liberation movement, the Zimbabwe African National Union (ZANU), which relied on politics, guerrilla warfare, and terrorism to achieve majority rule. To defuse this conflict, the Rhodesian government began negotiations for a transition to democracy in 1978, and the first elections were held in 1980. Yet unlike South Africa, Zimbabwe never became an institutionalized democracy. It functioned as an illiberal regime for twenty years, eroding over time until eventually the country slid into authoritarianism in the early part of this century.

Why did these two countries take such different paths? The answers are unclear and at times seem contradictory. For many, the answer simply lies in leadership. Nelson Mandela's leadership of the ANC, even while in prison, was exceptional, combining charismatic authority with the organizational skills necessary to keep the movement alive in spite of his detention. His long period in jail only increased his stature at home and abroad, reinforcing the legitimacy of the struggle and helping to intensify international pressure on South Africa. In contrast, the resistance movement in Zimbabwe was led by several different and clashing figures, who divided rather than unified the movement. Robert Mugabe, who finally came to power and continues to rule Zimbabwe, was talented politically, but more interested in accumulating power than engendering democracy. This argument assumes that political change is essentially a function of individual leadership. Yet there are other institutional factors that set the stage on which such leadership can function.

In many respects, the paths of Zimbabwe and South Africa differ in degree rather than kind. ZANU was from its inception a highly authoritarian party, which allowed for no internal democratic practices and suppressed external opposition. The ANC was similarly undemocratic internally; however, the ANC worked to include other opposition groups under a common political umbrella. Scholars have also suggested that Zimbabwe's authoritarianism stemmed from its close alliance with China and the Soviet Union during the Cold War. This alliance radicalized ZANU's objectives, which came to entail a revolution against colonialism and capitalism. The ANC also benefited from close ties to the Soviet Union, and its founding charter similarly called for the nationalization of industry and land, but unlike ZANU its political platform did not call for a revolution against capitalism.

A farm in zimbabwe previously owned by a white farmer; it was appropriated in 2000 by veterans of the war against the previous regime.

An important difference between Zimbabwe's and South Africa's societies also has had a bearing on the divergence of their political paths. South Africa is a highly urbanized and relatively industrialized society, especially in comparison to Zimbabwe, whose economy has been largely based on agriculture. South Africa's urbanization, combined with its ethnic, religious, and cultural diversity, contributed to a strong civil society that gave rise to the ANC and helped create and institutionalize that organization's civic and democratic commitments. ZANU could not rely on such foundations, and became instead a largely rural military movement dominated by one ethnic group.

In part as a result of South Africa's civil institutions, the ANC was careful about how it used violence as part of its struggle. It consistently emphasized the primacy of politics over violence and the need to minimize the loss of life in spite of numerous deaths at the hands of the state. The ANC did not target white civilians, even though this would have been an easy way to terrorize that minority and mobilize the majority population. In Zimbabwe, by contrast, violence became the primary means toward revolution. When ZANU came to power in 1980, it continued to rely on violence to suppress its opponents. As the party faced growing opposition in the 1990s, it seized agricultural land held by white Zimbabweans, arrested oppositional leaders, and killed or tortured hundreds of people. The result was economic collapse and international isolation that continues to the present.

1. Which country has experienced greater modernization? What role has that played in their differing paths?

2. How might the presence of a vibrant civil society in South Africa have given it an advantage toward democratization over Zimbabwe?

3. Why might Zimbabwe's use of coercion make its regime more vulnerable?

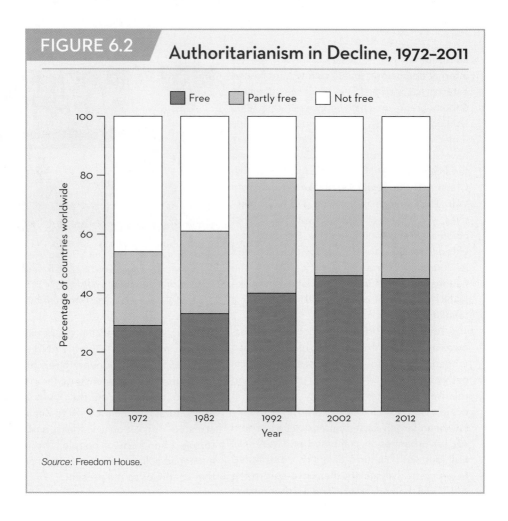

FIGURE 6.2 **Authoritarianism in Decline, 1972–2011**

Percentage of countries worldwide

- Free
- Partly free
- Not free

Year

Source: Freedom House.

Does this mean that the days of nondemocratic regimes are numbered? Perhaps we are coming to a time where nondemocratic rule is regarded as a global scourge rather than a legitimate practice. A shift in global values ended slavery; might a similar shift, a "moral revolution," be underway?[11] While such an imagined outcome may be attractive, we cannot know what new or perennial issues may again give power and purpose to nondemocratic rule. Will inequality clash with freedom? Will people someday come to see the absence of individual freedom as a benefit rather than a form of bondage? Might a new religious or secular vision of human life reject democracy as antiquated or profane? Perhaps what we now enjoy is simply a brief aberration in the long human history of nondemocratic rule.

For Further Reading

Appiah, Kwame Anthony. *The Honor Code: How Moral Revolutions Happen* (New York: W. W. Norton, 2010).

Arendt, Hannah. *Totalitarianism* (New York: Harcourt, Brace and World, 1951).

RS> Diamond, Larry. "The Rule of Law Versus the Big Man." *Foreign Affairs* 87, no. 2 (March/April 2008).

RS> Levitsky, Steven and Lucan A. Way. "The Rise of Competitive Authoritarianism." *Journal of Democracy* 13, no. 2 (April 2002).

Linz, Juan. *Totalitarian and Authoritarian Regimes* (Boulder, CO: Lynne Rienner, 2000).

RS> Linz, Juan J. and Alfred Stepan. *Problems of Democratic Transition and Consolidation: Southern Europe, South America, and Post-Communist Europe* (Baltimore: Johns Hopkins University Press, 1996).

RS> Weinthal, Erika and Pauline Jones Luong. "Combating the Resource Curse: An Alternative Solution to Managing Mineral Wealth." *Perspectives on Politics* 4, no. 1 (March 2008).

 Visit StudySpace for quizzes and other review material.
www.norton.com/studyspace

- **Vocabulary Flashcards of All Key Terms**
- **Chapter Review Quizzes**
- **Complete Study Reviews and Outlines**

RS >
Reader Selection

Highlighted selections are included in *Essential Readings in Comparative Politics*, Fourth Edition.

Terrorism entails politically motivated non-state violence toward civilians. The aftermath of a suicide car bomb in Abuja, Nigeria, is pictured here. The group Boko Haram, meaning "Western Education is Forbidden," claimed responsibility.

POLITICAL VIOLENCE

KEY CONCEPTS

- Political violence is violence outside of state control that is politically motivated.

- Institutional, ideational, and individual reasons may all contribute to political violence.

- Revolutions are public seizures of the state to overturn the government and regime.

- Terrorism is nonstate violence against civilians, often toward a revolutionary goal.

- Political violence may have a religious source when faith serves as an ideological force.

- Countering political violence raises questions about state power and individual liberty.

The turn of the century brought a new global threat. This danger was not surprising; for decades, loosely affiliated radicals had been staging attacks worldwide, killing civilians, government officials, and heads of state. These attacks were motivated by local grievances and bound by a common ideology that sought the destruction of states and regimes these radicals viewed as tyrannical and corrupt. Global connections helped facilitate the spread of this ideology and its followers, who moved from country to country, eluding detection and capture. Attacks in New York and Washington, D.C., directed at key symbols of America's national and global power, were another chapter in what had already been a long battle.

In response to these attacks, many citizens asked themselves to what extent freedom should be sacrificed for national security. Foreigners and those viewed as possible accomplices of or sympathizers with the perpetrators of the attacks became subject to public scrutiny, deportation, and, sometimes, questionable prosecution. Around the world, governments instituted policies that limited civil liberties in democratic countries and increased repression in authoritarian ones. Another concern was whether greater economic integration and higher immigration rates had made countries more vulnerable to such attacks.

The time we are speaking of is not today, and the violence was not religiously motivated. This wave of attacks began over a century ago, and they were carried out in the name of anarchism and communism. In 1881, anarchists killed the Russian czar Alexander II; in 1889, Empress Elizabeth of Austria; in 1894, the French president Carnot; and in 1901, the U.S. president William McKinley. In 1917, the communist Russian Revolution swept away the czarist regime, and short-lived revolutionary communist regimes followed in Hungary and Bavaria. In 1919, a series of mail bombs were sent by anarchists to political and economic elites across the United States, and shortly thereafter explosions were set off in seven American cities, including Washington, D.C., where the home of the attorney general was severely damaged. In 1920, a wagon carrying several hundred pounds of explosives and shrapnel was planted opposite 23 Wall Street, in New York City, the headquarters of J. P. Morgan, killing over thirty people when it was ignited. The government's response to this "Red Scare" was the Palmer Raids, in which thousands were arrested and many held without charge for long periods or deported.[1]

In previous chapters, we identified various institutions that define states, societies, and types of economic structures and regimes. We also saw how these institutions are constructed and function in different parts of the world. Power and legitimacy rest in these institutions, to varying degrees, but what happens when they lose power altogether, or when people seek to take them down by force?

This chapter will shed some light on this complex question, providing ways to think about political violence and its implications. We will begin by defining our terms: what do we mean by *political violence*, and how does it relate to the political institutions we have already covered? Next, we will look at some of the motivations of political violence, examining the different (and often conflicting) explanations for why such violence occurs. We will then concentrate on two important forms of political violence: revolution and terrorism. Each is a phenomenon that can threaten governments, regimes, and states. Each is also a loaded political term that stirs emotional responses, complicating analysis. We will look at some of the different ways revolution and terrorism can be defined and understood. In addition, we will explore the extent to which the two are related—how terrorism is often justified as a tool to achieve revolution. Once we have these concepts and arguments before us, we will look at them in the contemporary context of political violence motivated by religion. Finally, we will conclude with a discussion of how states and societies prevent or manage political violence and what this means for freedom and equality.

What Is Political Violence?

This textbook began with a focus on the state. This institution is the cornerstone of modern politics, one that we defined in its most basic terms as the monopoly of violence or force over a territory. Across human history, centralized political authority has been a part of this monopoly whereby states vanquish their domestic rivals, defend themselves from external threats, and establish order and security at home. This has been described as the shift from "private war" to "public war," meaning that individuals lose the freedom to use violence against one another, turning that right over to the state. This right is exchanged for a greater sense of security for all.

Of course, the state's monopoly of violence is never perfect or complete. Other states always represent a potential threat, given their own capacity for violence. Even at the domestic level, violence persists in such forms as murder and armed robbery. In many countries, such problems, though persistent, are manageable and do not threaten the stability and security of the state, society, or economy. But under certain conditions, this may not be true. Public violence may grow so pervasive or destructive that the state loses its control. Governments, regimes, states, and individuals are subject to attack, and sovereignty is weakened or lost. We have already seen this in some detail in our discussion of ethnic and national conflict in Chapter 3.

Political violence, or politically motivated violence outside of state control, is the focus of this chapter. Some political scientists see much of this political violence as part of a larger category of "contentious politics," or collective political struggle. This can include such things as revolutions, civil war, riots, and strikes, but also more-peaceful protest movements, some of which we will consider below. In the case of political violence, we are speaking of a phenomenon that operates beyond state sovereignty, neither war nor crime, and that seeks to achieve some political objective through the use of force. Such definitions are always cleaner in theory than in reality, of course. The lines between domestic and international and between war, crime, and contentious politics are often quite blurry.

Why Political Violence?

Although defining political violence presents some challenges, a more controversial issue is why political violence occurs. What leads civilians to take up arms against a state or its citizens toward some political aim? The reasons given by scholars are diverse and have changed over time, but we can group them into three basic categories: institutional, ideational (based on ideas), and individual. These three explanations overlap to some degree; where one explanation ends and the other begins is not always clear. At the same time, such explanations are often in contention, with scholars or policy makers tending to favor one explanation over others. We will examine each of these generally before we look at how each is used specifically in studies of revolution and terrorism. Each explanation seeks to answer the same questions. What motivates political violence, and toward what end is it perpetrated?

Institutional Explanations

Since we have covered institutions at length, what we mean by this term should be relatively clear; we are referring to self-perpetuating organizations or patterns of activity that are valued for their own sake. Institutions define and shape human activity, and institutional explanations argue that their specific qualities or combination are essential to political violence. The emphasis can be on political institutions, such as states and regimes; economic institutions, such as capitalism; or societal institutions, such as culture and religion. Moreover, these explanations can be based on either a constraining or an enabling argument. It may be that institutions contain values or norms that implicitly or explicitly encourage political violence, or that they constrain human activity, thus provoking political violence. For example, in the chapter on democratic institutions we covered variations in executive structures and electoral systems; it has been argued that variants that reduce the opportunity for power sharing—versions that produce "winner take all outcomes," like presidencies—increase the likelihood of marginalization and conflict. Under these conditions, political violence can be a logical reaction when other forms of participation are blocked. Institutional explanations can be seen as a quest for a "root source" for violence, a necessary condition for violent actions to take place, and a presumption that changes in the institutional structure would eliminate the motivation for this violence.

Ideational Explanations

If institutional explanations emphasize the impact of fixed organizations and patterns in fostering political violence, ideational explanations focus more on the rationale behind that violence. By **ideational** we simply mean having to do with ideas. Ideas may be institutionalized—concepts rooted in some institution such as a political organization or a religion—but just as often they are uninstitutionalized, with no real organizational base. The argument here is that ideas play an important role in political violence in the way they set out a worldview, diagnose a set of problems, provide a resolution, and describe the means of getting there. Any or all of these elements can be bound up with a justification of violence. These ideational factors take us back to our discussion of political attitudes in Chapter 3. As we noted there, political violence is more likely to be associated with attitudes that are radical or reactionary, since each attitude views the current institutional order as bankrupt and beyond reform. Hence, it is not only the content of the ideas that matters but also their relation to the domestic political status quo. Ideas seen as conservative in one context may become a source of radicalism or reaction, and perhaps violence, elsewhere.

IN FOCUS — Explanations for Political Violence

EXPLANATION	REASONING	EXAMPLE
INSTITUTIONAL	Existing institutions may encourage violence or constrain human action, creating a violent backlash.	Presidentialism
IDEATIONAL	Ideas may justify or promote the use of violence.	Some forms of religious fundamentalism; nationalism
INDIVIDUAL	Psychological or strategic factors may lead people to carry out violence.	Humiliation

Individual Explanations

Finally, individual explanations center on those who carry out the violence. Here the scholarship emphasizes the personal motivations that lead people to contemplate and carry out violence toward political ends. Scholars who study individual explanations of political violence usually follow one of two paths. One emphasizes psychological factors, conditions that draw individuals toward violence. Such factors can be a function of individual experiences, or they may be shaped by broader conditions in society, such as levels of economic development or gender roles. Such an approach tends to concentrate on how people may be driven to violence as an expression of desperation, the desire for liberation, or social solidarity. For example, some scholars of religious violence emphasize the role of humiliation as a motivating force, a sense that one's own beliefs are actively marginalized and denigrated by society. Revolutionaries or terrorists, in this view, see violence as a way to restore meaning to their lives and may be largely unconcerned with whether they are effectively achieving their goals.[2] A contrary approach, however, rejects this view, seeing political violence as a rational act, carried out by those who believe it to be an effective political tool. Strategy, rather than despair, drives these actions. Political violence is in this view not an expression of deviance but a strategy that is carefully wielded by those who understand its costs and potential benefits.[3]

Comparing Explanations of Political Violence

One important element of comparison across these three explanations is how they approach free will—that is, to what extent people are the primary actors in political violence. Institutional explanations often are quite deterministic, seeing people as shaped and directed by larger structures that they do not control. An individual's recourse to violence is simply the final step in a much larger process. In contrast, individual explanations place their focus squarely on people; they are the primary makers of violence because they choose to be. Ideational explanations lie somewhere in between. Ideas are influenced by institutions but are also actively taken up and molded by individuals to justify political violence.

A second element of comparison concerns universal versus particularistic explanations. Institutional explanations tend to be more particularistic, stressing the unique combination and role of institutions in a given case that are not easily generalized and applied elsewhere. Individual explanations typically center on those personal or psychological attributes common to all humans that can lead to violence. Ideational explanations, again, lie somewhere in the middle, generalizing the importance of ideas while noting the distinct lessons that different ideas impart.

Which explanation is most convincing: institutional, ideational, or individual? These explanations are often placed in competition with each other, but it may be that they actually work in conjunction. Institutional factors provide a context in which particular preconditions, problems, and conflicts may emerge. Ideational factors help describe and define those problems, ascribe blame, and provide solutions by calling for the transformation of the status quo. These ideas in turn influence and are shaped by individuals and groups that may already be prone to violent activity. Let's look at the case of the Basque independence group Euskadi Ta Askatasuna (ETA) in Spain, which used violence as a political tool for several decades. If we examine ETA, we can see institutional factors that include a long period of repression under authoritarian rule and its effects on the Basque region. There are ideational factors as well, such as a belief among ETA members and supporters that the Basque people face cultural extermination at the hands of the Spanish. Finally, individual factors include the role and motivations of many Basque youth in conducting "kale borroka" (urban struggle) in their support for an independent, revolutionary Basque state. This example helps illustrate the interconnection of these three factors and why political violence is relatively unpredictable and has emerged in a variety of contexts. We will consider these various explanations next as we look at revolution and terrorism.

Forms of Political Violence

So far, we have spoken of political violence in general terms, defining it as violence that is outside state control and politically motivated. This definition encompasses many forms of political violence: assassinations, riots, rebellions, military coups, civil war, and ethnic conflict, to name a few. We will concentrate on two forms of political violence: revolution and terrorism. Revolution is important to study because of its profound effects. Revolutions have ushered in sweeping changes in modern politics, overturning old institutions and dramatically transforming domestic and international relations. Terrorism, while less sweeping, holds our attention as a similar challenge to modern political institutions, one whose impact on domestic and international politics has spiked in recent years. Both are forces that seek dramatic change. Yet in many ways, revolution and terrorism are opposites. Revolution is an uprising of the masses, who take to the streets, seize control of the state, and depose the old regime. In contrast, terrorism is much more secret and hidden, a conspiratorial action carried out by a small group. But there are similarities in their sources and goals. As we analyze and compare the dynamics of revolution and terrorism, we will draw out some of these elements and show how these seemingly disparate forms of political violence can be linked.

Revolution

The term *revolution* has many connotations. Although we speak of revolution as a form of political violence, the word is also used much more indiscriminately. Any kind of change that is dramatic is often described as revolutionary, whether the change is political or technological, and the term has a generally positive connotation, one that evokes progress. People speak of dramatic change as positive, so "counterrevolution" is seen as an attempt to turn back the clock to a darker time. This should not be surprising; across much of the world, significant political change has been a result of revolution, and in countries where this is the case, revolution is often associated with independence, sovereignty, and development. Thus, revolution is a loaded term, albeit with mostly positive connotations.

For our purposes, we shall speak of revolution in a more limited manner. **Revolution** can be defined as a public seizure of the state in order to overturn the existing government and regime. There are several factors at work here. First, revolutions involve some element of public participation. To be certain, there are typically leaders, organizers, and instigators of revolution who play a key role. But unlike a coup d'état, in which elites overthrow the government, in a revolution the public plays an important role in seizing power. Russia is an interesting example. While we typically speak of communism's triumph in 1917 as a revolution, some scholars call it a coup, with Lenin and a handful of followers seizing power rather than some mass action toppling the government. Second, revolutions gain control of the state. This distinguishes these actions from such violence as ethnic conflict, through which groups may gain local control or even seek independence but do not or cannot take over the entire state. Finally, the objective of revolution is not simply the removal of those in power, but the removal of the entire regime. Protests or uprisings and other forms of contentious politics intended to pressure a leader to leave office are not necessarily revolutionary. At their core, revolutions seek to fundamentally remake the institutions of politics and often economic and societal institutions as well. As a result, scholars sometimes speak of "social revolutions" to indicate that they are referring to events that completely reshape society.

Must revolutions be violent? This is a tricky question. Given the dramatic goals of revolution, violence is often difficult to avoid. Governments will resist overthrow, and such conflict can often lead to the fragmentation of the monopoly of violence, with parts of the state (such as elements of the military) often siding with revolutionaries. The immediate aftermath of revolutions can also be very bloody, as the losers are killed or carry out a counterrevolutionary struggle against the new regime.

However, not all revolutions are violent. In 1989, communist regimes in Eastern Europe collapsed in the face of public pressure, sweeping away institutions that many thought immovable. In most cases, violence was limited; Romania is the only country that experienced a violent struggle between the communist regime and revolutionaries that led to numerous deaths. Because of this absence of violence, many scholars would resist calling the collapse of communism in Eastern Europe revolutionary, preferring instead to speak of these changes as political transitions. Yet in most important ways, specifically in the overturning of the government and regime, these events did fulfill our definition of revolution. South Africa is another case of regime change, from apartheid to multiracial democracy, that most scholars are uncomfortable calling a revolution, because it was an elite-driven, largely nonviolent, and slowly negotiated process. As we see, one of the problems here is whether we believe that violence is a necessary component to revolutionary outcomes.

What causes revolution? There is no agreement on this question, and the consensus has changed over time; scholars group studies of revolution into three phases. In the first phase, before World War II, scholars tended to describe rather than explain revolution. When causes were assigned, explanations were often unsystematic, blaming bad government policies or leaders. In the second phase, coinciding with the behavioral revolution of the 1950s and 1960s (see Chapter 1), social scientists sought more generalized explanations. Their new research efforts took on varied forms and areas of emphasis, but they shared a common view that dramatic economic and social change or disruption, such as modernization, was central in sparking revolutionary events. The views tended to focus on the role of individuals as potential revolutionaries and sought to understand what motivated them.

One of the main arguments that emerged out of this work was a psychological approach known as the **relative deprivation model**. According to this model, revolutions are less a function of specific conditions than of the gap between actual conditions and public expectations. Improving economic or political conditions might even help lead to revolution if, for example, such change causes increased public demands that go unmet, fostering discontent. It has sometimes been suggested that the 1979 Iranian Revolution and the 2011 Egyptian Revolution are examples of relative deprivation at work. As Iran experienced rapid modernization in the decades before the revolution, this only increased expectations for greater freedom and equality, especially among young adults. This is what is meant by relative deprivation: it is not absolute conditions that instigate revolution but rather how the public perceives them.

By the 1970s, these studies of revolution began to lose favor. In the third phase, critics argued that theories of revolution predicated on sudden change could not explain why some countries could undergo dramatic change without revolution (as in Japan during the early twentieth century) or what levels of change would be enough to trigger revolution. In the case of the relative deprivation model, there was little evidence that past revolutions were in fact preceded by rising expectations or discontent. Similarly, there were many cases when both expectations and discontent rose but revolution did not result. New studies of revolution took a more institutional approach, moving away from a focus on public reactions to a focus on the target of revolutions: the state.

Most influential in this regard has been the work of Theda Skocpol and her landmark book *States and Social Revolutions*. Focusing on France, China, and Russia, Skocpol argues that social revolutions require a very specific set of conditions. The first is competition between rival states as they vie for military and economic power in the international system through such things as trade and war. Such competition is costly and often betrays the weakness of states that cannot match their rivals. Second, as a result of this competition, weaker states often seek reform to increase their autonomy and capacity, hoping that changes to domestic institutions will boost their international power. These can include greater state centralization and changes in agriculture, industry, education, and taxation. Such changes, however, can threaten the status quo, undermining the power of entrenched elites, sowing discord among the public, and creating resistance. The result is discontent, political paralysis, and an opening for revolution. In this view, it is not change per se that is central to revolution, but the power and actions of the state. Other actors are of relatively little importance.

The institutional approach to revolution became the dominant view during the 1980s, paralleling a wider interest in institutions and the power of the state. Yet institutional approaches themselves are subject to questions and criticism. Some argue that an overemphasis on institutions ignores the role played by leadership or ideas in helping to catalyze and direct revolutionary action. In addition, if earlier approaches did not seem to fit with the historical record, institutional approaches are themselves hard to disprove, essentially asserting that where a revolution has occurred, the state must have been weak and under international pressure.

These criticisms were underscored by the revolutions in Eastern Europe in 1989, and again in the "Arab Spring" revolutions of 2011. In the case of Eastern

Shifting Views of Revolution

PHASE	APPROACH	CRITICISMS
FIRST: PRE-WORLD WAR II	Studies of revolutionary events	Unsystematic and descriptive
SECOND: POST-WORLD WAR II BEHAVIORAL REVOLUTION	Studies of disruptive change, such as modernization, as driving revolutionary action	Not clear why change or rising discontent leads to revolution in some cases and not others
THIRD: 1970S-PRESENT	Studies of domestic and international state power as providing the opening for revolution	Too focused on institutions, to the neglect of ideas and individual actors

Europe, there can be no doubt that changes in the international system, specifically the Cold War and the Soviet Union's loosening of control over Eastern Europe, led to conflict and paralysis within these states. At the same time, however, public action was mobilized and shaped by opposition leaders who were strongly influenced by the ideas of liberalism, human rights, and nonviolent protest. In addition, mass protest appeared influenced by strategic calculation: successful public opposition in one country changed the calculations of actors elsewhere, increasing their mobilization and demands. One can see similar events at work in the Middle East (see the "Institutions in Action" box, p. 204). A street vendor's death by self-immolation in Tunisia unleashed a cascade of protests across the region, mobilizing publics and revolutionary movements in Egypt, Yemen, Libya, and Syria. A key factor in determining the movements' outcome has been the degree to which the military and paramilitary forces have remained loyal to the state or shifted their allegiance to those seeking to bring down the regime.

Drawing on these events, some scholars have reintegrated individual and ideational approaches. While state actions do matter, so do the motivations of opposition leaders, elites, and the public as a whole; the views of all three groups regarding political change; and the tools used to mobilize the public. Small shifts in ideas and perceptions may have a cascading effect, bringing people into the streets when no one would have predicted it the day before—including the revolutionaries themselves.[4]

Why Did the "Arab Spring" of 2011 Occur?

Revolutions and transitions often seem to come out of the blue. Regimes that appeared impervious to change a year earlier are swept away before our eyes. No one expected that communism would collapse in Eastern Europe in the 1980s; at best, it seemed, reforms within the Soviet Union would lead to some modest liberalization, perhaps even reinvigorating the one-party regimes in the region. Just the opposite occurred. In the recent case of the Arab Spring in North Africa and the Middle East, the signs were even less promising. Recall from Chapter 6 some of the most common institutional factors in explanations for authoritarianism and democratization: modernization, elites, society, international forces, and culture. Each of these factors helps explain the perseverance of authoritarianism in the Middle East. Modernization in the region is often viewed as stunted; development is especially lagging in the areas of gender equality, education, and health. Among Middle Eastern countries, only Bahrain (at 49th) ranks in the top 50 best-educated countries in the world as defined by the UN's Human Development Index. In the area of health, no country in the region ranks in the top 35, and wealthy countries such as Saudi Arabia (at 77th) rank below the much poorer China.

Oil, as well as foreign aid from the United States in particular, has helped support many of these states, creating systems built around a coterie of supporters who benefit directly from the state. This elite has relied on various means of repression—harassing, jailing, and killing opponents—to maintain its control over the state and the benefits it has drawn from it.

Civil society in much of the region is weak and fragmented, a result of state repression and of the low levels of development. Democratization and liberalization are ideas tainted by their association with Western colonialism and U.S. foreign policy in the region, particularly after the invasion of Iraq; there is wariness of U.S. foreign policy, which for many years has been to support nondemocratic regimes in the region. Many inside and outside the region worried that political liberalization would provide an opening for Islamist groups to come to power. The chaos in Iraq and Afghanistan reinforced this fear and seemed to give authoritarianism in the Middle East a new lease on life. As the UN's Arab Development Report put it in 2009, the region's problems

> lie in the fragility of the region's political, social, economic and environmental structures, in its lack of people-centered development politics and in its vulnerability to outside intervention.... [T]hese characteristics undermine human security ... and its widespread absence in Arab countries has held back their progress.[5]

How, then, in the face of all these challenges, did the Arab Spring burst forth? Why revolutions break out when they do is beyond the understanding of social scientists, much as geologists cannot predict earthquakes. But to make some sense of these changes, we can turn to our institutional, ideational, and individual explanations, which overlap with each other and encompass the explanations for democracy and authoritarianism given above. These explanations are not comprehensive but rather point to the complexity of revolutionary change.

Institutional explanations for the Arab Spring focus on the nature of authoritarian rule; for example, while Tunisia functioned as a highly repressive one-party system that sought to co-opt or control civil society, its regime also maintained just a small military force and a limited degree of patrimonialism. Thus, when protests intensified, the military refused to fire on the population, paving the way for revolution with relatively few deaths. In contrast, Syria's highly patrimonial regime relies in large part on para-military forces directly controlled by the ruling Assad family, giving those in power both the desire and the means to use violence against protesters to quell revolution. This was also true of Libya, where political power was held by the Qaddafi family for four decades. Yet Libya, like Tunisia, also experienced revolution, though it took a very different, more violent path, and was abetted by international intervention. Institutions, in short, can't fully account for why revolution succeeded where it did, but they can be seen to have influenced the strategies of political elites across the various cases.

Ideational explanations are similarly useful. In the case of Egypt, many point to the role played by young people in shaping the message of the protests that brought down President Hosni Mubarak. Their "April 6 Youth Movement" studied how public protests brought down authoritarian regimes in Eastern Europe and drew on the civil disobedience work of the American political scientist Gene Sharp, among others. To mobilize the public, activists relied on Facebook and YouTube, prompting the regime to cut off Internet access in a failed last-ditch effort to fend off the revolution. This factor has institutional components as well: Egyptian society, two-thirds of which is under 30, can be viewed as a product of ongoing modernization and an emerging civil society.

Finally, we should not discount the role of individual action, which sparked these revolutions. Mohamed Bouazizi was a 26-year-old Tunisian man who had worked since a young age to support his family, selling produce as a street

Egyptian protestors gather at Tahrir Square, Cairo, at the start of the Egyptian Revolution in 2011.

vendor. Bouazizi was repeatedly harassed by the police, ostensibly for lacking a business license but in reality because he failed to pay bribes. These repeated assaults took their toll; as his sister later noted, "those with no connections and no money for bribes are humiliated and insulted and not allowed to live."[6] After a final clash in December 2010, Bouazizi stood before the local governor's office, amid the traffic, doused himself in gasoline and set himself alight. Protests began soon thereafter and spread across the region, with common demands: dignity and change. Large-scale, domestic and international, and state and societal forces were critical in explaining the Arab Spring (and all revolutions), but we should not forget the role that one apparently powerless person can play in shaping history.

1. What institutional factors help explain why Tunisia's revolution took such different shape from Libya's?

2. How did institutional and ideational factors combine in the case of Egypt to spur its revolution?

3. Why did revolution overturning authoritarian regimes in the Middle East seem so unlikely in the first plae?

As important as the cause of revolution is its impact. If a revolution does manage to sweep away the old regime and install a new one, the effects can be profound, but surprising continuities from the past can remain. The first major impact is that revolutionary regimes often institutionalize new forms of politics, transforming the existing regime. Revolutions help pave the way for new ideas and ideologies: republicanism, secularism, democracy, liberalism, communism, and Islamism were all marginal ideas until revolutions helped place them at the center of political life. Revolutions have destroyed well-entrenched regimes and legitimized new and radical alternatives. They have also been responsible for dramatic economic and societal changes, such as the end of feudalism and the development of capitalism. This is why we tend to think of revolutions as positive events: in hindsight, their effects frequently seem progressive. If ideational factors are often underplayed as a source of revolution, they are undeniably central in the successful institutionalization of revolutionary regimes.

Though revolutions may be instruments of progress, it is important to note what they do not achieve. In spite of the call for greater freedom and equality that is a hallmark of revolution, the result is often the reverse. Revolutionary leaders who once condemned the state quickly come to see it as a necessary tool to consolidate their victory, and they often centralize power to an even greater extent than before. This is not necessarily bad if the centralization of power can facilitate the creation of a modern state with a necessary degree of autonomy and capacity. Revolutions are often the foundation of a modern state. However, revolutionary leaders may seek a high degree of state power, rejecting democracy as incompatible with the sweeping goals of the revolution. Cuba, China, Russia, France, and Iran are all cases in which public demands for more rights ended with yet another dictatorship that uncannily echoed the previous authoritarian order. Mexico is another good example: the 1910 revolution swept away the previous, corrupt dictatorship but was soon replaced by a one-party regime, itself corrupt and dictatorial, that held power until 2000.

A second impact is the high human cost that revolutionary change can incur. Revolutions are often destructive and bloody, especially if removing those in power is a protracted affair. Moreover, in the immediate aftermath, revolutionary leaders and their opponents often use violence in their struggle over the new order. The Mexican Revolution led to the death of a million and a half people; the Russian Revolution and subsequent civil war may have claimed well over five million. This violence can become an end in itself, as in the case of the Reign of Terror that followed the French Revolution of 1789. Enemies, supporters, and bystanders alike may all be consumed by an indiscriminate use of violence. It has been suggested that revolutionary states are also more likely to engage in interstate war, whether to promote their revolutionary ideology or because other countries feel threatened or see an opportunity to strike during this period of turmoil.[7] Given the fragmentation of state power and the loss of the monopoly of force associated with revolution, the violence that follows in its wake is not surprising. One general observation we can make is that the greater the violence involved in bringing down the old regime, the more likely it is that violence will continue under the new one.

Terrorism

The word *terrorism*, like *revolution*, is loaded with meaning and used rather indiscriminately. However, the conceptual difficulties surrounding the two terms are diametrically opposed. While *revolution*'s conceptual fuzziness comes in part from its inherently positive connotation (which can lead people to associate the term with all sorts of things), the word *terrorism* carries a stigma and is a term no one willingly embraces. As a result, some confuse *terrorism* with a variety of other words, many of which are misleading, while others use the term indiscriminately to describe any kind of political force or policy they oppose. This has led some to conclude that it is effectively impossible to define terrorism, and they fall back on an old cliché: "One man's terrorist is another man's freedom fighter." Such a conclusion undercuts the whole purpose of political science, which is to define our terms objectively. We should therefore seek out a definition as precise as possible and use it to distinguish terrorism from other forms of political violence with which it might be confused.

Terrorism can be defined as the use of violence by nonstate actors against civilians to achieve a political goal. As with revolution, there are several components at work in this definition, and we should take a moment to clarify each. First, there is the question of nonstate actors. Why should the term not be applied to states as well? Do they not also terrorize people? Indeed, as we shall discuss later, the concept of terrorism originally referred to state actions, not those of nonstate actors. Over time, the term came to be associated with nonstate actors who used terrorism in part because conventional military force was not available to them. This, however, does not mean that states cannot terrorize. Rather, other terms have come to describe such acts. When states use violence against civilian populations, we speak of war crimes or human rights violations, depending on the context. Both can include such acts as genocide and torture. Finally, there is **state-sponsored terrorism**. States do sometimes sponsor nonstate terrorist groups as a means to extend their power by proxy, using terrorism as an instrument of foreign policy. For example, India has long faced terrorist groups fighting for control over Kashmir, a state with a majority Muslim population (unlike the rest of India, which is majority Hindu). These terrorists are widely thought to be trained and armed by Pakistan,

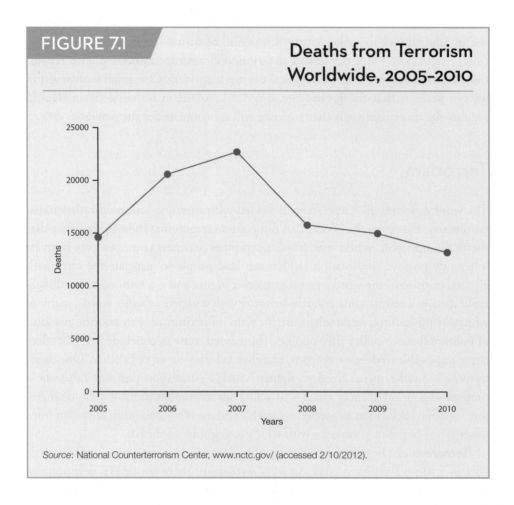

FIGURE 7.1

Deaths from Terrorism Worldwide, 2005–2010

Deaths (y-axis): 25000, 20000, 15000, 10000, 5000, 0

Years (x-axis): 2005, 2006, 2007, 2008, 2009, 2010

Source: National Counterterrorism Center, www.nctc.gov/ (accessed 2/10/2012).

whose state leaders contend that Kashmir should be joined to their country. In short, we speak of terrorism as a nonstate action not because states are somehow above such violence but rather because other terminology exists to describe forms of violence perpetrated by states (Figure 7.2).

Second, our definition of terrorism emphasizes that the targets of violence are civilians. Here the issue of intentionality is important. In violent conflicts, there are often civilian casualties. But terrorists specifically target civilians, believing that this is a more effective way to achieve their political ends than attacking the state. This allows us to distinguish terrorism from **guerrilla war**, something that came up in our last chapter's comparison of South Africa and Zimbabwe. In contrast to terrorism, guerrilla war involves nonstate combatants who largely accept traditional rules of war and target the state rather than civilians. In the case of South Africa, during the military struggle against the regime the African National Congress considered, and then explicitly rejected, targeting civilians. In contrast, the Zimbabwean African National Union engaged in both guerrilla warfare and terrorism to achieve power. However, the line between these two can often be blurry: is killing a policeman or a tax collector an act of terrorism or guerrilla warfare? Still, the central distinction remains, not only to observers but also, as suggested above, to those carrying out the violence. We will speak more of this in a moment.

Finally, there is the issue of the political goal. It is important to recognize that terrorism has some political objective; as such, it is not simply a crime or a violent act without a larger purpose. Here, too, the lines can be less than clear: terrorists may engage in crime as a way to support their activities, while criminal gangs may engage in terrorism if they are under pressure from the state. Groups can also

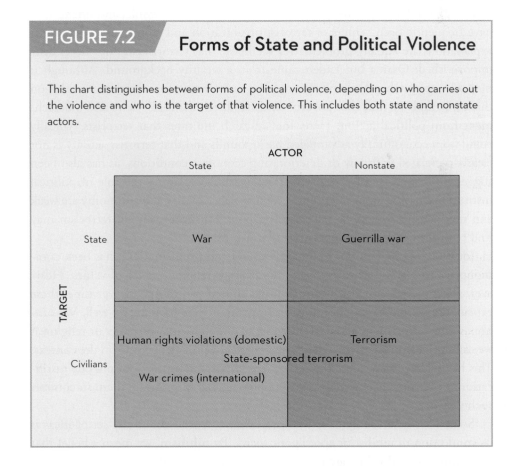

FIGURE 7.2 — Forms of State and Political Violence

This chart distinguishes between forms of political violence, depending on who carries out the violence and who is the target of that violence. This includes both state and nonstate actors.

| | ACTOR | |
	State	Nonstate
TARGET — State	War	Guerrilla war
TARGET — Civilians	Human rights violations (domestic) State-sponsored terrorism War crimes (international)	Terrorism

morph from one into the other. But in general, terrorism and other forms of violence can be sorted out by the primacy of political intent.

What are the causes of terrorism? As with revolution, there are varied and conflicting hypotheses, and these have changed over time as the nature of terrorism has shifted. In addition, because terrorism is so amorphous and shadowy, we find few of the comprehensive theories we see in studies of revolution, though we can again group these in terms of institutional, ideational, and individual explanations.

One of the most common responses to terrorism is to cast it in institutional terms, often with the assertion that economic and educational background are critical to understanding terrorist motivations. Poverty and the lack of education are commonly cited in this regard, with terrorism viewed as a tool of desperation when avenues for personal advancement (getting a job, starting a family) are absent or blocked. These arguments, while intriguing, don't have a great deal of evidence to back them up. Educational explanations do not appear to hold up, since terrorists tend to be better educated than the population as a whole, and universities have frequently been centers of terrorist organization and recruitment. Economic explanations are equally problematic. We know that terrorists are not necessarily impoverished; Osama bin Laden came from a wealthy background. Although it may seem reasonable that poverty would be a motivation for terrorism, research on this topic finds instead that poverty tends to foster apolitical views and a detachment from political action. Here, too, research indicates that terrorists typically come from economically advantaged backgrounds and that terrorist activity is not clearly correlated with low or deteriorating economic conditions, as has also been suggested in the case of revolution.[8] Explanations regarding the role of political institutions may be on firmer ground. Where state capacity and autonomy are weak and mechanisms for public participation poorly institutionalized, terrorism may find both the rationale and opportunity to use force.[9]

Ideational explanations are similarly useful and problematic. It has been commonplace to blame terrorism on some ideology, religion, or set of values. However, given the way in which terrorism has shifted and morphed over time, these explanations often cannot account for cause and effect particularly well. We cannot ascribe terrorism as a logical outcome of one particular ideology or religion if we can find terrorism associated across a range of values depending on the context. This having been said, ideas themselves are important, as they can provide justification for terrorist acts; groups need a political goal to motivate them to commit such violence.

Some have asserted that for terrorists what is crucial about any set of ideas is its connection to nihilist or apocalyptic views. By **nihilism**, we mean a belief that all institutions and values are essentially meaningless and that the only redeeming value one can embrace is violence. In this view, violence is desirable for its own sake. Nihilism can also be combined with utopian and apocalyptic views, generating a conviction that violence can destroy and thus purify a corrupted world, ushering in a new order. Interestingly, then, the actual content of the ideas themselves can change, even dramatically, so long as the justification for violence and the call for utopia remain intact. Indeed, in many cases terrorist organizations lack a clear articulation of the actual outcome they want to achieve; the means is more important than the message.

Finally, researchers have consistently turned to individual explanations in seeking to understand the personal motivations of terrorists. As mentioned earlier, one common explanation centers on feelings of injustice—that an individual's or community's self-worth has been denigrated by others—coupled with alienation or humiliation. Such feelings can generate frustration, anger, and, most important, a desire for vengeance. In addition, terrorist groups can provide a sense of identity and solidarity for alienated or humiliated individuals. Political violence can give a life meaning, a sense of greater purpose. In fact, it has been argued that terrorist groups resemble religious cults, with their emphasis on community, the purity of the cause, faith in the rectitude of the group's own beliefs and actions, and the conviction that retribution paves the way toward some utopian outcome.[10]

The effects of terrorism are harder to discern than the effects of revolutions. The first question to ask is whether terrorists are able to achieve their goals. In the case of revolution, the political violence is by definition successful—we study cases in which regimes have been successfully overthrown. In the case of terrorism, however, scholars often concentrate more on the actors with less of a focus on outcomes.

Terrorists are mostly unsuccessful in achieving their stated long-term outcomes. Terrorists often seek some dramatic change in the existing domestic or international order, and their actions usually do not achieve the goal they have in mind. In that sense, then, terrorism is not particularly strategic if its primary outcome is to usher in specific political changes. However, this is not to say that terrorism has no impact. Economically, terrorism can be highly successful in depressing tourism, foreign direct investment, stock markets, and other sectors of the economy. Society can be similarly impacted, not just by the effects of a weakened economy but also by increasing anxiety and insecurity that undermines people's sense of well-being.

Terrorism can also have a distinct effect on politics. Countering terrorism can be a costly and frustrating process with little to show for itself, diverting national resources while failing to address public concerns. An eroded sense of confidence in the state can be the result. In the quest for greater security, governments and their citizens may favor increasing state power and curtailing civil liberties in the hope that such steps will limit terrorists' scope for action. However, this can lead to a weakening of democratic institutions and civil rights. The result can be less trust in government and less public control over it. At an extreme, terrorism can help bring down a regime. In 1992, Alberto Fujimori, the president of Peru, dissolved the legislature and suspended the constitution, acts that he justified in part as necessary to battle two separate terrorist groups that had destabilized the country. Much of the public supported this action, seeing it as the only way to reestablish order. Terrorism in Russia by Chechen separatists similarly helped pave the way for Vladimir Putin to win the presidency in 2000, and subsequent attacks were used as a justification for removing democratic institutions and limiting civil liberties. And as we well know from Afghanistan, terrorism can also be used as a tool to provoke international conflict.

This destruction of a regime, of course, is precisely what terrorists seek. Terrorism uses violence against civilians to tear the institutional fabric of state, society, and economy, calling into question all those things we take for granted, including stability, security, and predictability. By disrupting these most basic elements of modern life and instilling fear, terrorists believe they will help pave the way for revolution.

Terrorism and Revolution: Means and Ends

The question of what terrorists want leads us to consider terrorism and revolution as related forms of political violence. While we might think of these two as quite separate, it was not always this way. In modern politics, the concepts of terrorism and revolution were initially bound together as parts of a single process, having their origins in the French Revolution. For revolutionary leaders like Maximilien Robespierre, terror was an essential part of revolution. Robespierre argued that "terror is nothing other than justice, prompt, severe, inflexible; it is therefore an emanation of virtue" in the service of revolutionary change.[11] Thus, terror was not only a positive act but also a tool in the service of the revolutionary state.

Over time, this concept of the relation between terrorism and revolution began to shift. Revolutionaries who embraced the lessons of Robespierre concluded that terror is not needed to consolidate revolution after a regime has been overthrown but can instead be used as the means toward that revolutionary end. A small group could speak for and lead the masses, instigating violence as a way to spark revolution. These revolutionaries thus openly embraced the name "terrorist" as an expression of their desire to use violence to achieve their political goals. Although the label *terrorist* has become stigmatized over time, this relationship between terrorism and revolution remains in place.

Terrorism can therefore be understood not simply in terms of who is directing political violence toward whom, but also in its revolutionary nature. Terrorists rarely seek limited goals, such as political or economic reform, since the entire political system is seen as illegitimate. Rather, they believe that through their seemingly indiscriminate use of violence, all the dominant institutions can be shattered and remade. Consider, for example, this passage from an early manifesto of the Peruvian terrorist group The Shining Path:

> The people rise up, arm themselves and rebel, putting nooses on the necks of imperialism and reaction. The people take them by the throat, threaten their lives and will strangle them out of necessity. The reactionary meat will be trimmed of fat, they will be torn to tatters and rags, the scraps sunk into mire, and the remainders burned. The ashes will be thrown to the winds of the world so that only the sinister reminder of what must never return will remain.[12]

This link between terrorism and revolution also helps to distinguish between terrorism and guerrilla war. We mentioned earlier that the line between these two forms of political violence is blurry, but that we can distinguish between them in terms of their targets. Guerrilla war seeks to abide by traditional rules of war, avoiding the targeting of civilians. This decision is driven by political goals. Guerrillas typically accept that their opponents are legitimate actors, and they themselves wish to be regarded as legitimate by their opponents and the international community. Their demands, while sometimes extensive (such as greater civil rights or independence for an ethnic group), do not deny the legitimacy of the other side, as is normally the case with terrorism. These distinctions matter, as such differences in means and ends will affect the degree to which states can negotiate with such groups to bring an end to conflict.

For example, during the civil conflict in Algeria in the 1990s, two nonstate groups were operating: the Islamic Salvation Front (FIS) and the Armed Islamic Group (GIA). Both opposed the Algerian regime, which suppressed Islamic fundamentalist groups, but they fought it in very different ways. The FIS created an armed wing that targeted specific parts of the state seen as directly supporting the regime. The FIS, which began as a nonviolent political movement, declared that they could come to a compromise with the regime if certain demands were met, such as holding democratic elections. In contrast, the GIA rejected the entire regime and political process as un-Islamic and argued that anyone they viewed as having cooperated with the state in any manner, such as voting, deserved to be killed. The GIA's killing was thus much more indiscriminate and widespread, directed at state, society, and the FIS. Jihad (war), they argued, was the only means to an Islamic state.[13]

In short, revolution and terrorism have close connections. Revolution is often the ultimate goal of terrorists, who believe that using violence will help set the stage for revolution. More limited use of force, as in guerrilla war, reflects a desire to participate in or work with existing institutions rather than overthrow them. The issue, then, for nonstate wielders of violence is whether they desire a seat at the political table or seek to knock the table over.

Political Violence in Context: Faith, Terrorism, and Revolution

Now that we have considered different ways to approach political violence, particularly revolution and terrorism, let us apply these ideas to the most pressing example in contemporary domestic and international politics: religious violence. In Chapter 3 we spoke about the rise of ideology as a challenge to religion in the modern world. Ideologies appropriated for themselves many of the same claims and values that belonged to religion in the past, forcing religion out of the public and political sphere and into private life. Ideology, in this sense, can be seen as a secular or civil religion. However, as ideology has waned, the role of religion has reemerged in the public realm. This religious resurgence is accompanied by a particular element of fundamentalism: the desire to unite faith and the state, transforming religion into the ideological foundation for a political regime. While such fundamentalism may be uncompromising (as with many ideologies), it is not necessarily violent. Many fundamentalists believe that reestablishing God's sovereignty can be done through nonviolent engagement in politics or by withdrawing from politics and instead working to increase the societal power of religion. But, as with ideologies, this form of religious fundamentalism contains a violent strain of thought.

What are the conditions under which religion becomes a source of political violence? As in our earlier discussion, they include institutional, ideational, and individual factors. First, one common factor is hostility to modernity. In this view, modern institutions, driven by states and nations, capitalism, ideology, secularism, individualism, and material prosperity, have stripped the world of greater meaning and driven people to alienation and despair. Indeed, political violence is often embraced by those who initially enjoyed modernity but at some point turned away from its "corrupt" lifestyle. This view has emerged in many different contexts but seems to be most powerful in societies where modern institutions are foreign in nature and poorly grafted onto traditional structures and values This often the case in less developed countries, which we will turn to in Chapter 10. It is at this border between traditional and modern institutions that the tension can be the greatest, which may explain why proponents of religious violence are often urban and well-educated individuals: such persons are frequently most deeply immersed in modernity and may feel its contradictions most sharply.

A second factor is what the sociologist Mark Juergensmeyer calls "cosmic war."[14] In this view, the modern world not only actively marginalizes, humiliates, and denigrates the views of the believers, but also seeks their outright extermination. Those who hold this view see themselves as soldiers in a struggle between the righteousness of faith and its enemies (modernity), a war that transcends space and time. This is often bound up in conspiracy theories that point to shadowy forces in league to exterminate the good. People holding these views can rationalize violence against civilians because they see the conflict not in terms of civilians versus combatants but in terms of the guilty versus the innocent: those who do not stand on the side of righteousness are by definition on the side of evil. Scholars note that this dehumanization of the enemy is an important component in justifying violence against civilians, since social or religious taboos against murder must be overcome.

Third, religion as a source of political violence is often connected to messianic, apocalyptic, and utopian beliefs. Although the forces of darkness (modernity) have gained the upper hand, the role of the righteous is to trigger events that will lead to the destruction of the modern world. Evil will be destroyed and justice served. These views of violent apocalypse are often tied to some messianic belief that links the apocalypse to a savior's return. Following the apocalypse, a new utopian order will be established, re-creating the sovereignty of God and reuniting humanity with the true faith. Violence is therefore not only acceptable but also a form of ritual, whether in the form of self-sacrifice (martyrdom) or the sacrifice of others.

Religious groups or movements that resort to violence represent an extreme form of fundamentalism, since their path to violence requires a dramatic reinterpretation of the faith in a way that sharply divorces it from its mainstream foundations. These groups or movements thus tend to break away from the mainstream faith and other fundamentalists, whom they accuse of having lost their way, presenting their radical alternatives as a restoration of religious truth. Most Muslim, Christian, and other fundamentalists would thus find many of these radical views to be horrific and far removed from their view of faith. To reiterate, it is a mistake to confuse fundamentalism with violence. Indeed, much of what we have described above—hostility toward rival institutions, dehumanization, and utopian views—can be found in modern political ideologies. We can see this in the bloody revolutions that established communism in the Soviet Union and China. Even the French Revolution of 1789 that helped usher in the modern era was described by Alexis de Tocqueville in 1856 as akin to a religious revolution directed toward "the regeneration of the human race" that "roused passions such as the most violent political revolutions had been incapable of awakening . . . able, like Islamism, to cover the earth with its soldiers, its apostles, and its martyrs."[15] Bearing this in mind, we can consider some specific examples where religion has intersected with politics to generate political violence.

Within Al Qaeda and similar jihadist groups, individuals like Osama bin Laden and Mohammed Atta (one of the leaders of the September 11 attacks) were steeped in modernity before turning to religion and religious violence. This violence is understood as part of a global struggle against infidels that goes back centuries. Hence, when bin Laden referred to the West as "Crusaders" in his 1996 manifesto, he was reaching back to the battles between the Islamic and Christian worlds in the Middle Ages. In the modern world, bin Laden argued, this crusade against Islam and its followers continues, though the West's conspiracies are often cloaked by international organizations like the United Nations. In the September 11 attacks, we can see how the logic of cosmic war also fits into apocalyptic beliefs. Al Qaeda carried out these attacks not simply to weaken the United States but also to provoke a backlash that they believed would intensify the conflict between the Islamic and non-Islamic worlds and would in turn lead to the overthrow of "un-Islamic" regimes in the Middle East and to the eventual collapse of the West.

In these circumstances, even Muslim civilians are fair targets, whether in the United States, Europe, or the Middle East. This is justified because their "collaboration" with the forces of evil means that they are not true Muslims and therefore can be killed, sacrificed to the cause. The jihadists' willingness to sacrifice civilian lives recalls our discussion of the GIA in Algeria, whose leader justified their widespread violence against the public by stating that "all the killing and slaughter . . . are an offering to God."[16]

Such views have strong parallels to certain violent strains drawn from Christianity. In the United States, racist groups assert that Western Christianity has been corrupted and weakened by a global Jewish conspiracy, and they seek to rebuild Western society on the basis of a purified white race. One particularly important figure in this ideology was William Pierce, who died in 2002. Pierce, who held a Ph.D. in physics and was at one time a university professor, formed the white supremacist organization The National Alliance in 1974. Pierce departed from Christianity altogether as a faith tainted by its association with Judaism, offering instead a "cosmotheist" faith that viewed whites as belonging to a superior evolutionary track, on the road to unity with God. In his novel *The Turner Diaries*, Pierce describes the creation of a dedicated underground that would attack symbols of American authority, seize territory, and eventually launch a nuclear attack against the country itself. This apocalypse would destroy the state, allowing the revolutionaries to exterminate all nonwhites and those who do not accept the new order. This genocide would eventually extend worldwide. Timothy McVeigh's bombing of the federal courthouse in Oklahoma City in 1995, which killed 167 people, was directly inspired by *The Turner Diaries* and Pierce's argument that terrorism could trigger revolution. Pierce, while dissociating himself from McVeigh's act, nevertheless stated that McVeigh was

> a soldier, and what he did was based on principle. . . . He was at war against a government that is at war against his people. . . . In this war the rule is: Whatever is good for our people is good, and whatever harms our people is evil. That is the morality of survival.[17]

Pierce's views and those of related movements continue to attract followers throughout North America and Europe; it is estimated that several hundred thousand copies of *The Turner Diaries* have been sold, and the book has been translated into a number of European languages. Anders Breivik, who carried out the horrific bombings and shootings in Norway in 2011, used similar language in his manifesto:

> Europe is being targeted for deliberate colonisation by Muslim states, and with coordinated efforts aimed at our Islamisation and the elimination of our freedoms. We are being subject to a foreign invasion, and aiding and abetting a foreign invasion in any way constitutes treason. If non-Europeans have the right to resist colonization and desire self-determination then Europeans have that right, too. And we intend to exercise it.[18]

This violence extends outside the monotheistic religions of the West. In the 1980s, Japan saw the emergence of a new religion, Aum Shinrikyo ("Supreme Truth"). Aum was headed by Shoko Asahara, a partially blind mystic who claimed that he had reconnected with the true values of Buddhism that had been lost in the modern world. Asahara claimed that the world had gone through a series of thousand-year stages since the time of Buddha, with each one moving further away from his teachings until the contemporary period of moral degeneration. Aum attracted thousands of well-educated members in Japan and Russia, including scientists and doctors, who felt alienated and in need of spiritual meaning. Asahara initially believed that the group should try to engage Japanese politics and fielded candidates for parliamentary elections in 1990. When all these candidates were defeated, however, Aum took on a more apocalyptic tone. Asahara claimed that a global war triggered by the United States would destroy the planet by the end of the decade, and he began to investigate how to construct weapons of mass destruction to trigger this event. The use of violence against civilians was justified with the argument that those who had not embraced Aum had already experienced a "karmic death," making violence more akin to a mercy killing.[19] In 1995, members of Aum placed bags of the nerve gas sarin in the Tokyo subway, killing 12 and injuring several thousand. Had the poison been more refined, the casualties would have been much higher.

In these three cases we see important similarities. First, these groups radically reinterpreted an existing faith by arguing that it had departed from the true path. Osama bin Laden, William Pierce, and Shoko Asahara each claimed for themselves the ability to reinterpret traditional faith in a new, overtly ideological manner. Second, through this reinterpretation, they recast the world in terms of a final showdown between good and evil, purity and corruption. Third, as the defenders of truth, they placed themselves in the role of warriors in the service of faith, able to mete out justice to all those who are seen as the enemy, whether state or society. Fourth, this violence was described not as an unfortunate necessity but as a sacrifice to the cause that would purify and bring forth or restore a higher order.

These kinds of religiously motivated political violence have many parallels with similar acts carried out by nonreligious groups. The failures and humiliations of modernity, the creation of a group of "true believers" who see the world in stark terms of good versus evil, the idea of a global apocalypse that will destroy the old order and usher in a utopia can all be ascribed to many forms of secular, even antireligious, political violence.

Do such conclusions give us any better understanding of how political violence will manifest itself in the future? There has been a sharp debate among scholars about whether environmental and animal-rights groups might become more violent. Some assert that these are inherently peaceful movements that would never tolerate such activity. Others point to arson and other property damage already committed by individuals associated with the Animal Liberation Front, the Animal Rights Militia, or the Earth Liberation Front. In fact, many of the elements we have considered—hostility to modernity, a struggle in which the fate of the planet hangs in the balance, the belief in apocalypse and utopia, and the need for violence—can be found in the writings of the more radical environmentalists.[20] Again we can see the parallels between ideology and religion and the similar ways in which both can be used to justify violence.

Countering Political Violence

Our discussion indicates that political violence is a varied and constantly shifting force in the modern world. As long as states monopolize force, there will be actors who seek to wrest this power from the state so they can use it to pursue their own political objectives. Violence can be motivated by institutional, ideational, and individual factors—most likely some combination of the three. Though religious violence is currently the most pressing concern, we see that in many ways the distinctions between ideological and religious violence are not as great as we might have supposed.

Given the amorphous nature of political violence, what can states do to manage or prevent it? This is difficult to answer, since the response partly depends on the nature of the political violence itself. Although violence differs across time and from place to place, we can nevertheless make a few tentative observations, understanding that these are not ironclad answers.

One observation is that regime type appears to make a difference; terrorism and revolution are less likely in democratic societies. Why? The simplest answer is that democracies allow for a significant degree of participation among a wide enough number of citizens to make them feel that they have a stake in the system. While democracies produce their own share of cynicism and public unrest, including political violence, they also appear to co-opt and diffuse the motivations necessary for serious organized or mass violence against the state and civilians. Again, this is not to say that democracies are impervious to political violence; Timothy McVeigh and Shoko Asahara have recently proved otherwise. Our observation is merely that democracies appear to be more effective at containing and limiting such groups by providing more options for political opposition.

Of course, one of the dangers is that terrorism and revolution sparked by one kind of regime can easily spill beyond its borders, particularly in such an interconnected world. While democracy may be an important factor in preventing violence carried out by its own citizens, it may not offer protection against political violence carried out by groups operating outside the state. Indeed, the paradox here is that open democratic societies may limit domestic conflict but make for a much more tempting target for globalized political violence.

Regime Type and Terrorism

REGIME TYPE	EFFECT ON TERRORISM	RESULT	RISK OF TERRORISM
AUTHORITARIAN	Authoritarianism may foster terrorism, but the state can repress domestic terrorists; the state is unhindered by civil liberties.	Limited terrorism, but may be redirected outside of the country toward more vulnerable targets.	Lower
DEMOCRATIC	Participatory institutions and civil liberties are likely to undercut public support for terrorism.	Domestic terrorism less likely, but country may be a target of international terrorism generated in nondemocratic regimes.	Moderate
ILLIBERAL/ TRANSITIONAL	Weak state capacity, instability, and limited democratic instutitions may generate both opportunities and motivations for terrorism.	Terrorism more likely, with domestic and/or international support.	Higher

One might conclude that if democracy is an important factor, regime change should be a central goal for reducing political violence. However, such a policy is fraught with problems. First, research indicates that the successful institutionalization of democracy is predicated on how that regime change takes place. Regime changes that are imposed from the top down (such as through external intervention) or involve societal violence are less likely to produce a democratic outcome in the long run (Figure 7.3).[21]

The result of top-down or violent regime change is instead more likely to lead to an illiberal regime where democracy is weakly institutionalized, or even to a failed state. And such conditions can provide both the motivation and the opportunity for political violence to emerge. In short, certains kinds of regime change can increase, not reduce, the number of regimes that foster political violence. Iraq and Afghanistan would appear to provide sad evidence of this. By this logic, we would expect that more-peaceful social revolutions, like the recent one in Egypt, will be less likely to lead to long-term political violence than armed uprisings like the one in Libya, where the conflict was both protracted and shaped by international intervention.

FIGURE 7.3

Regime Change and Freedom

These charts look at nearly seventy cases of regime change from authoritarianism between 1973 and 2002. Chart (a) shows that in those cases where societal actors led the transition, over 50 percent resulted in a free country with full civil and political rights. In contrast, less than 15 percent of transitions controlled by those in power or imposed by other states led to a free political regime. Chart (b) indicates that in those cases where societal actors refrained from violence, nearly 70 percent of transitions resulted in a free country with full civil and political rights. In contrast, only 20 percent of transitions with societal violence resulted in a free political regime.

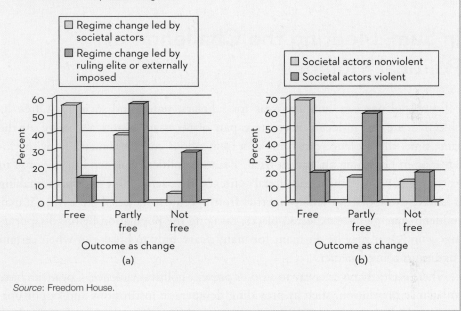

Source: Freedom House.

What about states that are already liberal democracies and yet face political violence from domestic or international actors? In this case, the classic dilemma of freedom versus security raises its head. In the face of threats, democratic states and their citizens will often favor limiting certain civil liberties and increasing state autonomy and capacity in order to bring an end to political violence. In the United States, the 2001 Patriot Act is an example of such counterterrorism, with its increased powers to conduct public surveillance. Suspects in the United Kingdom can be detained up to 28 days without charge, and individuals can be arrested for inciting or "glorifying" terrorism.

There are dangers here. An excessive focus on security over freedom may be dangerous to democracy. Placing too much power in the hands of the state to observe and control the public could seriously threaten to erode individual rights and with them democracy, creating what some have called a "surveillence state."[22] Such actions can in turn contribute to political violence, since they confirm the idea that the state is conspiring to destroy its opponents, thus justifying violent resistance. In spite of these dangers, people and politicians often seek dramatic and visible solutions because they provide a sense of security, although in reality they may have limited or even counterproductive effects. The old adage attributed to Benjamin Franklin is worth recalling: "Those who would give up essential liberty to purchase a little temporary safety deserve neither liberty nor safety."[23]

In Sum: Meeting the Challenge of Political Violence

Political violence is a complex issue for scholars, states, and societies. Often its objectives are cast in idealistic terms as part of necessary historical change. At the same time, this violence can come at a tremendous cost of human life, with violence often becoming an end in itself. Because political violence is a response to existing institutions, the institutional context differs across time and space, making it hard to extrapolate general properties from specific instances. Like a virus, it may suddenly emerge in unexpected places, ravaging the population before disappearing again. Or it may lie dormant for many years, only to break out when certain conditions come together.

There is clearly no one way to stop or prevent political violence. Countries have to balance prevention, such as providing democratic institutions and opportunities for political contention, with treatment, such as military and legal methods to counter terrorism. Treatment carries its own risk, and even the most comprehensive forms of prevention cannot guarantee that political violence will never break out.

For Further Reading

RS> Abrahms, Max. "What Terrorists Really Want: Terrorist Motives and Counterterrorism Strategy." *International Security* 32, no. 4 (Spring 2008).

RS> Crenshaw, Martha. "The Causes of Terrorism." *Comparative Politics* 13, no. 4 (July 1981).

RS> Goldstone, Jack. "Understanding the Revolutions of 2011: Weakness and Resilience in Middle Eastern Autocracies." *Foreign Affairs* (May/June 2011).

Haberfeld, M. R. and Agostino von Hassels, eds. *A New Understanding of Terrorism: Case Studies, Trajectories and Lessons Learned, ed.* (New York: Springer, 2009).

Juergensmeyer, Mark. *Terror in the Mind of God: The Global Rise of Religious Violence* (Berkeley: University of California Press, 2003).

Krueger, Alan B. *What Makes a Terrorist: Economics and the Roots of Terrorism* (Princeton: Princeton University Press, 2008).

RS> Kuran, Timur. "Now Out of Never: The Element of Surprise in the East European Revolution of 1989." *World Politics* 44, no. 1 (October 1991).

Pape, Robert. *Dying to Win: The Strategic Logic of Suicide Terrorism* (New York: Random House, 2005).

RS> Skocpol, Theda. "France, Russia, China: A Structural Analysis of Social Revolutions." *Comparative Studies in Society and History* 18, no. 2 (April 1976).

Tilly, Charles and Sidney Tarrow. *Contentious Politics* (Boulder: Paradigm Publishers, 2007).

Walt, Stephen M. *Revolution and War* (Ithaca: Cornell University Press, 1996).

 Visit StudySpace for quizzes and other review material.

www.norton.com/studyspace

- **Vocabulary Flashcards of All Key Terms**
- **Chapter Review Quizzes**
- **Complete Study Reviews and Outlines**

RS>
Reader Selection

Highlighted selections are included in *Essential Readings in Comparative Politics*, Fourth Edition.

8

The flags of the member states of the European Union, in front of the European Parliament in Brussels. The directly-elected parliament is intended to provide democratic accountability to an increasingly powerful supranational EU.

ADVANCED DEMOCRACIES

KEY CONCEPTS

- Advanced democracies are characterized by institutionalized liberal democracy and capitalism.

- Despite a set of shared core institutions, advanced democracies differ greatly in how their political, economic, and social institutions are constructed.

- All advanced democracies have faced changes in and challenges to sovereignty, in the forms of supranational integration and devolution.

- Many advanced democracies have seen a rise in postmodern values, though these may come into conflict with increased ethnic and religious diversity.

- Economic institutions in advanced democracies have become increasingly postindustrial and tied to large welfare states, which encounter demographic challenges as their populations grow older.

Now that we are familiar with various concepts that help us compare a range of political institutions, we can investigate how these institutions manifest themselves in the world. Instead of grouping countries by geographic location, we will look at countries whose political institutions resemble each other in some way. Our first group of countries is commonly known as the **advanced democracies**. This term is problematic since it is both value-laden and teleological—that is, "advanced democracies" connotes some "end stage" that other countries are heading toward. Recalling the hubris and disappointment of the behavioral movement and modernization theory, we should emphasize that the term can cover a diverse set of countries that may get only more diverse in the future. We use the term here to refer to countries that have institutionalized democracy and a high level of economic development and prosperity.

In this chapter, we will look at the basic institutions and dynamics that characterize advanced democracies, applying the concepts we have studied so far. What do the advanced democracies have in common with one another? What differences exist between them? This comparison will lead us to a discussion of the role of individual freedom and collective equality in the advanced democracies. How do these countries reconcile the two? Once we have a grasp of these ideas, we will move on to consider the challenges their institutions face in contemporary politics. The forces of integration and devolution—the transfer of power to international institutions or down to local ones—may challenge the notion of state sovereignty that has been at the core of modern politics. In economics, too, the emergence of postindustrial societies is transforming the very nature of wealth and labor. Similar changes can be seen in societal institutions, as old and new social values come into conflict. All of these issues are compounded by demographic challenges as the populations of the advanced democracies become older and more diverse.

Are the advanced democracies on the brink of transformation or are they approaching stagnation and decline? And what are the implications of either for comparative and international politics? This chapter will lay out evidence that will allow us to consider possible scenarios.

Defining Advanced Democracy

What, exactly, are advanced democracies? In the past, scholars typically spoke of economically developed countries as belonging to the "First World." They were contrasted with the countries of the "Second World," or communist states, and those of the "Third World," the vast body of less-developed countries. Dividing countries into these three "worlds" was always somewhat problematic, since even within each category there was a great deal of institutional diversity. With the end of the Cold War and the collapse of communism, the three-worlds approach became even less useful.

Instead of using this problematic three-worlds approach, this book will refer to "advanced democracies," "communist and postcommunist countries," and "developing and less-developed countries." These categories, too, have their limitations, and critics might say they differ from past approaches only in name. One difference, however, is that our groupings imply that movement takes place between the categories—that countries can industrialize or democratize, can move to or from communism, can develop or remain less developed. In Table 8.1 we have a list of what we can consider advanced democracies. At the same time, some of these countries will also appear in the subsequent chapters on post-communist and newly industrializing countries, especially those that lie in an area of transition from one category to the next.

How do we determine which countries are advanced democracies? In the area of democracy, we can rely on the factors discussed in Chapter 5, looking at the degree and institutionalization of participation, competition, and liberty in each. In the area of economic development and prosperity, we can consider the issues raised in Chapter 4: the presence of private property, open markets, and the level of gross domestic product (GDP) at purchasing-power parity (PPP). We might also consider the kind of economic output that countries produce. Advanced democracies tend to derive a relatively small portion of their GDP from agriculture and industrial production. During and after the Industrial Revolution, industry displaced agriculture in many of today's advanced democracies; today, industry itself is increasingly being displaced by the service sector, which includes such things as retail sales, information technology, and education. Finally, we should also consider the output of wealth by looking at the overall well-being of society (as measured by the Human Development Index [HDI]).

Table 8.2 provides measurements of some of these factors for several advanced democracies, as well as for a few non-advanced democracies. The advanced democracies share not only liberal democratic regimes but also capitalist economic systems (liberal, social democratic, or mercantilist) in which the service sector dominates; additionally, they have high HDI rankings. They contrast with countries that are poorer, have low HDI rankings, and lack a strong industrial and service sector, institutionalized liberal democracy, or both.

Given our definition of advanced democracies, the countries that we place in this category are diverse—and they have grown markedly more diverse over the past decade. For example, countries such as Poland and South Korea were historically categorized as part of the Second and Third Worlds, respectively. But with economic and political changes in both countries, it makes less and less sense to think of them in these terms. Postcommunist Poland now has much more in common economically and politically with Western European countries like Germany and France than with neighboring countries that were also once part of the communist world; South Korea has more in common with Japan and the United States than it does with other, less-developed countries in Asia.

TABLE 8.1

Advanced Democracies, 2011

NORTH AND SOUTH AMERICA	EUROPE	ASIA	MIDDLE EAST AND AFRICA
Argentina	Austria	Australia	Israel
Canada	Belgium	Japan	
Chile	Bulgaria	New Zealand	
Costa Rica	Cyprus	South Korea	
Bahamas	Czech Republic	Taiwan	
Barbados	Denmark		
Bermuda	Estonia		
Mexico	Finland		
Panama	France		
United States	Germany		
Uruguay	Greece		
	Hungary		
	Ireland		
	Italy		
	Latvia		
	Lithuania		
	Luxembourg		
	Malta		
	Netherlands		
	Poland		
	Portugal		
	Romania		
	Slovakia		
	Slovenia		
	Spain		
	Sweden		
	United Kingdom		
	Croatia*		
	Iceland*		
	Norway*		
	Switzerland*		

*Non-EU members.

TABLE 8.2

Economic Portraits, 2011

PERCENTAGE OF GDP CONTRIBUTED BY

COUNTRY	AGRICULTURE	INDUSTRY	SERVICES	GDP PER CAPITA (PPP IN US $)	DEMOCRACY?	HDI RANK
United States	1	22	77	50,300	Y	4
Canada	2	20	78	41,000	Y	8
Sweden	2	26	72	41,700	Y	9
United Kingdom	2	22	76	36,800	Y	26
Germany	1	28	71	38,800	Y	10
Japan	1	23	76	36,000	Y	11
France	2	19	79	35,800	Y	14
South Korea	3	39	58	33,100	Y	12
Saudi Arabia	3	62	35	25,900	N	55
Poland	4	32	64	20,900	Y	41
Mexico	4	33	63	15,800	Y	56
Iran	11	46	43	11,600	N	70
South Africa	3	31	66	11,300	Y	112
Brazil	6	26	68	12,300	Y	73
China	10	47	43	9,200	N	89
India	16	29	55	4,000	Y	121
Nigeria	32	33	35	2,700	N	142

Note: Countries in italics are NOT advanced democracies.

Sources: Central Intelligence Agency, International Monetary Fund, United Nations Development Program.

The countries listed as advanced democracies in Tables 8.1 and 8.2 have high levels of economic development (GDP per capita at PPP of over $12,000) and small agricultural sectors. They are also democratic regimes and are among the top third of countries on the HDI, classified as having very high or high human development. As we noted earlier, within this category are several recently democratized and postcommunist countries that also exhibit the hallmarks of economic development and democracy. This group is not meant to be exhaustive or definitive—no doubt many readers would add or remove some countries on the basis of other criteria. In fact, a number of them will be discussed again in the chapters on postcommunist countries and developing and less-developed countries. The central point for us to consider is that as a result of recent global economic and political changes, the camp of advanced democracies has expanded well beyond its traditional provinces of Western Europe and North America.

Freedom and Equality in Advanced Democracies

How do advanced democracies achieve a balance between freedom and equality? All such countries share an institutionalized liberal democracy, private property, free markets, and a high level of economic development based on industry and services. However, this similarity does not mean that these countries' approaches to reconciling freedom and equality are identical. Advanced democracies reconcile freedom and equality differently, particularly in the area of political economy. Countries with liberal economic systems are focused more on individual freedoms than on collective equality, limiting the role of the state in regulating the market and providing public goods, whereas social democratic systems normally do the opposite. Mercantilist systems, meanwhile, tend to focus more on development than either freedom or equality. In spite of this wide variation, however, these countries are united by common democratic and economic institutions.

First, consider the role of freedom: all advanced democracies are institutionalized liberal democracies, sharing a belief in participation, competition, and liberty. Yet they define these differently. For example, civil rights or liberties may be expanded or restricted without calling into question the democratic nature of a country. Take the case of abortion. Some advanced democracies, such as Sweden, Greece, and Canada, allow abortions during a pregnancy's first trimester with relatively few restrictions. In other countries, such as South Korea, Argentina, and Poland, abortions are more restricted. And some advanced democracies ban abortions altogether or allow them only in exceptional circumstances (Chile and Ireland, for example). We can find similar discrepancies in the regulation of prostitution, drugs, or hate speech, or in the degree to which privacy is protected from state or economic actors. The judicial systems of advanced democracies interpret and defend their citizens' rights in various ways. Some of these countries rely on vigorous constitutional courts whose wide array of powers allows them to overturn legislation; other courts play a more conservative role, circumscribed by the existing forms of abstract and concrete review (see Chapter 5).

The public's level of political participation also varies among advanced democracies. One or more of the electoral systems discussed in Chapter 5 can be found in all these countries. The use of referenda and initiatives differs greatly across these countries; most advanced democracies use them to some degree, although in a few countries (like the United States and Germany) such votes take place only at the local level, and in some others (like Japan) not at all. Nor is competition uniform across the advanced democracies. Its variations include the ways in which political parties and campaigns are funded: some countries limit the amount of money that can be contributed by private actors to any political party or candidate and require the disclosure of the source of private political contributions. Politics are also shaped by the electoral systems in use. The majority of advanced democracies rely on some form of proportional representation to elect their legislatures, while a minority (such as the United States, France, the United Kingdom, Australia, and Canada) rely on some form of single-member-district plurality or majority. Another group (including Mexico, Hungary, Italy, and Japan) uses mixed electoral systems that combine proportional representation and single-member districts. The role of the executive, too, differs; as we read in Chapter 5, prime ministers tend to be the dominant executive in most advanced democracies, though we find purely presidential systems in the United States, Chile, Mexico, and Taiwan, and semipresidential systems in France and South Korea. Some of these states have federal systems, while others are unitary; their legislatures may be bicameral or unicameral. All these institutions manage liberal democracy in different ways.

In short, the advanced democracies are politically diverse. They all guarantee participation, competition, and liberty, but they differ in where the boundaries of these elements are drawn and how they are exercised. Freedom is a basic guarantee of the state unto its citizens, but the form and content of freedom vary from case to case.

In addition to a commitment to freedom, advanced democracies also share a similar approach to equality that emphasizes capitalism—that is, private property and free markets. This approach appears to have generated a great deal of economic prosperity—basic standards of living are higher across the advanced democracies than in other countries, and life expectancy is over seventy years (closer to eighty in some countries). But this prosperity coexists with varying degrees of inequality, with the wealth sometimes concentrated disproportionately among certain ethnic groups. Recall from Chapter 4 that the Gini index, a measurement of inequality around the world, found a surprising amount of difference even among countries whose levels of economic development were roughly the same. For example, Germany, Canada, and the United States have comparable levels of economic development as measured by GDP but very different levels of inequality as measured by the Gini index.

This difference in equality is in part a function of the role of the state. Across the advanced democracies, the economic functions of the state, including its role in the distribution of wealth, differ greatly. In the United States, Mexico, and Japan, the state expends relatively little on social-welfare programs. Individuals or families have a greater responsibility for funding basic needs, and the total tax burden on the public in these countries is typically lower as a result. In social democratic systems, such as those in much of Europe, taxation is often higher, and the resulting revenues are used for income redistribution through an extensive system of social expenditures. Here too, social democratic systems

IN FOCUS | Political Diversity in Advanced Democracies

PARTICIPATION

- Standards of voter eligibility differ.

- Referenda and initiatives are used in varying degrees.

- Some, but not all, states automatically register all eligible voters.

- Voting is compulsory in some nations, but voluntary in most.

COMPETITION

- Different methods and levels of funding are used for political parties and campaigns.

- Separation of powers varies greatly and is based primarily on the relative strength of different branches of government.

LIBERTIES

- Distinctions exist in the regulation, allowance, or prohibition of activities such as abortion, prostitution, and hate speech.

- Different degrees of individual privacy are protected from state and corporate intrusion.

TABLE 8.3   Income Redistribution in Advanced Democracies

COUNTRY	POLITICAL-ECONOMIC SYSTEM	TAXES AS A PERCENTAGE OF GDP, 2009	GINI INDEX
Sweden	Social democratic	46	23
France	Social democratic	42	33
Germany	Social democratic	37	27
United Kingdom	Liberal	34	34
Canada	Liberal	31	32
United States	Liberal	24	45
Japan	Mercantilist	28	38

Sources: Central Intelligence Agency, Organization for Economic Cooperation and Development.

are not uniform; some have more job protection, unemployment insurance, or neocorporatist institutions. All of these variations do not change the fact that in each advanced democracy, private property and free markets are fundamental institutions (Table 8.3).

In short, the advanced democracies share a basic set of institutions through which they reconcile freedom and equality. These institutions include liberal democracy, with its emphasis on participation, competition, and liberty; and capitalism, with its emphasis on free markets and private property. Yet each of the advanced democracies has constructed these institutions in a different way, resulting in quite significant variations among them.

Advanced Democracies Today

The institutions that the advanced democracies share are part of what makes these countries **modern**—that is, secular, rational, materialistic, technological, bureaucratic, and concerned more with individual freedom than with collective equality.

But like any other group of countries, the advanced democracies are not only diverse but also dynamic; their institutions are subject to change under the influence of domestic and international forces. Indeed, many scholars argue that the advanced democracies are currently undergoing significant social, political, and economic changes. If true, this would mean that existing modern institutions may give way to new ones as these countries transition from modernity to something else. Those writing on this topic lack a proper word to describe this change, using instead the awkward term **postmodern**. Clearly, this word says more about what isn't than what is. We'll spend the remainder of this chapter considering the challenges to modernity in the advanced democracies and whether these challenges are indicative of dramatic change. If so, are the advanced democracies making a transition to postmodernity, and what would that mean? Or is change overstated or perhaps not in the direction we imagine? These are big questions that lie in the realm of speculation and rely on fragmentary evidence. We will look at them in the context of the categories that have defined our discussion up to this point: political, societal, and economic institutions.

Political Institutions: Sovereignty Transformed?

In Chapter 2, we discussed a number of ways in which states can be analyzed and compared. In particular, we spoke about state sovereignty and noted that state power can be viewed in terms of autonomy and capacity. Yet in recent decades, we have seen a movement toward greater integration between countries and greater devolution within countries. Integration is a process by which states pool their sovereignty, surrendering some individual powers in order to gain political, economic, or societal benefits in return. Integration blurs the line between countries by forging tight connections, common policies, and shared rules that bind them together. In contrast, devolution is a process by which political power is devolved, or "sent down," to lower levels of government. This process is intended to increase local participation, efficiency, and flexibility, as tasks once handled at the national level are managed by local authorities. Although both integration and devolution can be found to varying degrees around the world, such processes have brought the most profound change to the advanced democracies. While many have expected these twin processes of integration and devolution to effectively transform the modern state and sovereignty as we know it, countervailing processes may limit, or even end, these movements.

The European Union: Integration, Expansion, and Resistance

The best-known example of integration is the European Union (EU). While European unification may seem normal today, it came on the heels of a devastating war between European countries that left millions dead. In the aftermath of World War II, a number of European leaders argued that the repeated conflicts in the region were caused by a lack of interconnection between countries, which fostered insecurity, inequality, and nationalism. These leaders believed that if their countries could be bound together through economic, societal, and political institutions, they would reject war against each other as irrational. Moreover, they argued, a common political agenda would give European states greater international authority in a postwar environment that had become dominated by the Soviet Union and the United States. With these motivations, a core of Western European countries began the process of integration in the early 1950s. This was a radical step away from sovereignty and not an easy one for any state or society to take. As a result, integration moved forward slowly and in piecemeal fashion.[1]

As the time line on page 236 shows, the EU developed incrementally. It began as a small agreement among a handful of countries that dealt primarily with the production of steel and coal, expanding over time to become a body that included many more members and that held vastly greater responsibilities. Out of this expansion a basic set of institutions has developed that gives the EU increasingly sovereign power in many areas over the member states.

The European Council is charged with setting the "general political direction and priorities" of the EU, and with helping member states resolve the "complex or sensitive issues" that arise between them.[2] The council is comprised of the heads of state or government of every EU member; the EU's own president is elected for two-and-a-half year terms by the council to help manage its affairs. The president is not directly elected by the EU public, nor does the office hold the kind of executive power that its title suggests. The European Commission, in contrast, is a body made up of 27 members (one per member state), each responsible for some specific policy area, such as transport, environment, and energy. The commission, confusingly, has its own president, also chosen by the European Council, who serves a five-year term. The commission's president manages the work of the commission, which is to propose and enforce laws and treaties, as well as to manage the EU budget. A third body is the European Parliament. Unlike the council and commission, which are staffed, directed, or chosen by EU member governments, the European Parliament is a legislature whose 736 members are directly elected by the EU member states for five-year terms. The parliament passes legislation proposed

1951	European Coal and Steel Community (ECSC) founded by Belgium, France, Germany, Italy, Luxembourg, and the Netherlands
1957	European Economic Community (EEC) created from ECSC
1967	European Community (EC) created from EEC
1973	Denmark, Ireland, and the United Kingdom join EC
1979	Direct elections to the European Parliament
1981	Greece joins EC
1986	Spain and Portugal join EC
1993	European Union (EU) created from EC
1995	Sweden, Finland, and Austria join EU
1999	Monetary union created among most EU member states
2002	Euro currency enters circulation; most EU national currencies eliminated
2004	EU accepts ten new members, most former communist countries
2007	Bulgaria and Romania join EU
2009	Lisbon Treaty becomes new constitution of EU
2009	Iceland, Albania, and Serbia apply for membership

by the commission. It also passes the budget for the EU and approves members of the commission (and can call for their resignation). Each country's number of representatives is roughly proportional to the size of its population. Finally, the EU's Court of Justice, made up of one judge for each country, rules on EU laws and conflicts between EU laws and the laws of member states. Member countries, EU bodies, companies, and individuals may all appeal to the Court of Justice. EU laws supersedes national laws.

As these statelike institutions have gained power over time, many people no longer speak of the EU as an **intergovernmental system** like the United Nations, whose member countries cooperate on issues but may not be bound by the organization's resolutions, but as a **supranational system**, where sovereignty is shared between the member states and the EU. As a result, for most Europeans the reconciliation of freedom and equality has become as much an international task as a domestic one. Accordingly, member states still struggle to gain the benefits of integration into the EU without losing sovereignty. Britain, Denmark, and Ireland only joined in 1972; Austria, Sweden, and Finland only in 1995. Referenda in Norway have rejected membership twice, and Switzerland, too, has chosen not to join. For many countries, the benefits of membership have come at the cost of having to harmonize regulations and laws with other member states, as well as having to transfer certain economic powers, which we will touch on next.

The growing breadth and depth of the EU countries' integration have been underscored by two recent projects, each of which changed (or hoped to change) the EU in fundamental ways. The first was monetary union. On January 1, 1999, the majority of EU member states linked their currencies to the euro, a single currency eventually meant to replace those of the member states as a means to promote further economic integration and growth. The logic of monetary union was that a single currency would allow for one measure of prices and values across the EU, increasing competition by stimulating trade and cross-border investment within the EU. More generally, proponents hoped that by binding countries closer together, the euro would help foster a true European identity. Finally, a single currency backed by some of the world's wealthiest countries would increase the EU's power in the international system by creating what could become a "reserve currency" for other countries—that is, a currency with global legitimacy that central banks would use as part of their monetary holdings. Reserve currencies are also the main monetary standard for businesses and individuals around the world. The U.S. dollar has been the global reserve currency for decades, giving the United States certain benefits, so the euro represented a real challenge to its global authority. In short, monetary union was promised to have both domestic (intra-EU) and international benefits.

On January 1, 2002, all EU member states that joined the monetary union withdrew their own currencies from circulation and replaced them with the euro, under control of the European Central Bank. This monetary union represents the largest single transfer of power to date within the EU; it has also been extremely contentious. Some EU members, such as Sweden, Denmark, and the United Kingdom, have declined to join the monetary union. These countries have seen monetary union as an important loss of sovereignty that is unacceptable to their publics. In Denmark and Sweden, referenda on euro membership have failed, while in the United Kingdom, a promised referendum failed to materialize altogether. In total, ten of the 27 member states have not (yet) adopted the euro as their currency.

Has monetary union been a success? That depends on how we define it. The hope to make the euro a reserve currency appears to have been borne out, as the currency has become a serious rival to the U.S. dollar. Many countries and individuals who once held only dollars as a foreign reserve increasingly rely on the euro. However, since the creation of the euro, economists have been concerned that the economic diversity of EU member states works against the idea of a single currency, since it forces all members into a single set of monetary policies, such as interest rates, that may be unsuitable for different kinds of economies with different rates of growth or unemployment. In fact, these concerns have come to pass, particularly in the case of Greece after 2009. For a number of years following the adoption of the euro, the Greek government ran significant deficits and racked up debt as a result. Eventually, the Greek state simply ran out of money and was no longer able to borrow enough to meet its public needs or cover what it already owed. Fearing economic collapse, other EU members were forced to loan money to Greece to keep it afloat (see the "Institutions in Action" box, p. 240). This exposed key fears within the EU—not only that problems affecting one member of the euro or EU would ripple across the whole institution, but also that to ensure stability, member states would need to take financial responsibility for each other. Needless to say, significant tensions have emerged between the countries in the EU over their levels of debt and whether some EU members must bail out other members in financial crisis.

What is the solution? Some suggest that these monetary problems can only be solved through fiscal integration—in other words, that the EU needs to have more sovereignty over the budgets and broader economic policies of the member states. In fact, some EU supporters believe this crisis is precisely the catalyst needed to move the EU toward true federalism. Skeptics wonder whether member states will be inclined toward further integration if it means that more resources will go from richer to poorer states—a "transfer union," as some put it. It would be possible to limit greater integration to euro countries in good financial shape, but this would create tiers of richer and poorer states, with different levels of integration. The need for wealthier countries to subsidize poorer ones has long been a concern, especially since the EU took in poorer states from postcommunist Eastern Europe. The most skeptical observers suggest that the euro itself may eventually come to an end, as similar currency unions have in the past, or at least that several current members will have to exit. At least symbolically, this could be a huge setback for the European Union.

The second long-term project for the EU has been its ongoing expansion (Figure 8.1). From 1951 to 2004, the EU grew from six member states to 15, and with the collapse of communism in Eastern Europe, a new wave of mostly postcommunist

FIGURE 8.1

European Union Membership, 2012

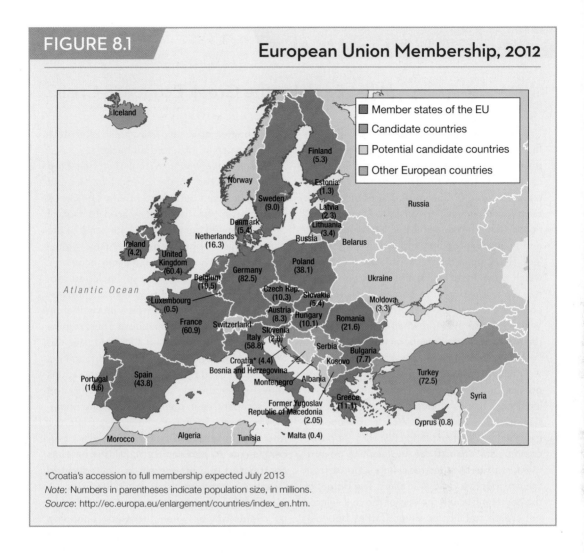

■	Member states of the EU
■	Candidate countries
□	Potential candidate countries
□	Other European countries

*Croatia's accession to full membership expected July 2013
Note: Numbers in parentheses indicate population size, in millions.
Source: http://ec.europa.eu/enlargement/countries/index_en.htm.

countries sought membership. After a long period of negotiation, between 2004 and 2007, 12 new countries were accepted, adding over 100 million people to the EU. This brought the total population of the EU to a half billion (the United States' population, by contrast, is just over 300 million) and made the EU's total GDP as large as that of the United States.

The EU's growth has created new issues and concerns. Most new member states are far poorer than the older EU member states. For example, while the per capita GDP at PPP of the EU as a whole is over $33,000, the figure for many newer members is half that amount. Although most of these newer members do not use the euro, the recent conflicts over the debt crisis have underscored the debate over

What Explains the Greek Economic Crisis?

As we discussed in Chapter 4, Japan has faced over a decade of decline after a long postwar boom that made it one of the richest countries in the world. This crisis has in many ways unfolded in slow motion—people use the term "lost decade" to refer to Japan's economic downturn and the inability of the state and economy to effectively resolve the problem. This is quite different from Greece's crisis, which seemed to come out of nowhere and quickly spiraled out of control, shaking that country and the rest of the EU. Why Greece? Why so suddenly? And what does it mean for the other advanced democracies?

To understand the Greek economic crisis, we need to understand the nature of Greek politics and the Greek state. Greece was a latecomer to both industrialization and liberal democracy; after World War II, the country experienced a devastating civil war that pitted communists against the monarchist government, with both sides receiving support from their respective Cold War allies. The defeat of the communists and the end of the civil war did not create stability, however. Battles between leftist and rightist parties eventually resulted in a military coup and a dictatorship that lasted from 1967 to 1974. Following the end of military rule, the political parties that came to dominate politics—particularly the Panhellenic Socialist Movement, which ruled for much of the next thirty years—used clientelism to institutionalize their support. As discussed in Chapter 6, clientelism is a means to co-opt members of the public by providing benefits to a person or group in return for public support. This was reinforced by the relatively underdeveloped economy. In the absence of private economic opportunities, political parties could offer state benefits, such as jobs, to their backers.

The result was a system that benefited those connected to the political parties but raised significant barriers to others. The Greek civil service grew large compared to that of other advanced democracies, with some of the highest levels of compensation. Many regulatory barriers were created, making economic development difficult. These included so-called "closed professions," in which firms or individuals were shielded from competition in return for their political support. Thus, regulations emerged that limited such things as the number of pharmacies, lawyers, and long-haul truckers allowed to operate. These regulations and closed economic sectors have contributed to discrepancies in unemployment; the unemployment rate for those under 25 is triple the rate for those above—approximately 50 percent versus 20 percent in 2012. This in turn has contributed to a brain drain as well-educated Greeks have moved elsewhere in the EU.

Finally, the deep connections created by clientelism between the state, economy, and political parties have led to widespread corruption. According to Transparency International, on its scale of corruption (with one being the least corrupt state) Greece ranks 78th, on par with China. In addition to bribe taking and the siphoning of resources from the state, Greece has suffered from widespread tax evasion. Many businesses function in a "gray" or informal sector (see Chapter 10), where they are unlicensed and can therefore avoid state regulations and tax obligations. By some estimates, this comprises over a quarter of the economy, functioning outside the law.

Individuals and formal businesses similarly evade taxes, often by bribing tax officials or simply counting on the fact that an overburdened tax-collection system cannot catch them. This points to a broader failure of state autonomy, capacity, and overall legitimacy; as we have noted earlier, tax compliance can be a function less of enforcement than of the public's general sense that taxation is acceptable and that most people are participating. In Greece, the *fakelaki*—a small envelope of cash, necessary to secure public services, from healthcare to building permits—has essentially replaced the tax system.

Graffiti on a shuttered bank in Athens says "Bring the stolen money back," a common chant from protestors who blame corruption for the country's economic crisis.

The combination of these institutional factors explains the Greek crisis. Of course, a corrupt or clientelist system is not necessarily headed for collapse. China's equally high level of corruption has not stopped it from enjoying heady economic growth. But in Greece, the weakness of the private economy combined with the state's corruption and outlays through clientelism have meant that the government has consistently faced a large budget deficit. Greece joined the euro in 2001 on the condition that it reduce its budget deficit. Instead, it fudged its books and continued to run high deficits, which as a euro member, it was easily able to cover by borrowing money. The Greek government essentially relied on the creditworthiness of the other euro member states, and lenders did not worry that deficits would hurt their investments through a weakening Greek currency (as would have been the case had Greece stayed outside of the euro). As deficits continued to grow, so did debt.

What finally triggered the Greek crisis was the recession in the United States. Once the U.S. housing bubble popped, investors grew nervous about investments elsewhere in the world—including Greece, whose debt and deficits were becoming clearer. Investors were no longer confident that Greece could sustain its eco-

nomic situation, or that the EU could or would bail the country out. Short of funds, the Greek government was forced into dramatic austerity measures: tax increases, a 15-percent pay cut for public-sector employees, a later retirement age, limits on pension benefits, and massive cuts to defense, healthcare, and education.

Greece's crisis has contributed to uncertainty about the long-term stability of the euro, and about whether a similar crisis may hit other advanced democracies carrying a high degree of public debt. Such uncertainty extends to the United States, whose $15 trillion debt is approximately 100 percent of the country's GDP.[3]

1. In what ways did the Greek government's use of clientelism hinder economic development?

2. What role did Greece's membership in the EU play in advancing its economic crisis? What concerns does this raise about the EU in general?

3. How has Greece's political and economic corruption impacted the state's capacity and legitimacy?

whether richer and poorer states will cooperate and share resources when times are tough. Related to this are questions of labor and capital. Many eastern Europeans have migrated westward looking for work, while many western European firms have relocated in eastern Europe to take advantage of lower wages. Both dynamics have raised tensions over immigration and jobs.

These tensions are heightened by the question of future enlargement. Given the fragile nature of Europe's economy, the further expansion of the EU might seem a distant issue. But enlargement has been a key factor in the development of EU authority. While the population of the United States has been steadily migrating toward and growing faster in the west, expansion of the EU has led to its population center shifting east.[4] If this trend eastward and southward continues, new questions and tensions will rise along the way.

Such a shift is not hypothetical. A number of other countries are either in the negotiation process or interested in beginning negotiations to join the EU in the next decade. Among these are Iceland, Croatia, Macedonia, Montenegro, and Serbia. The EU also recognizes as "potential candidates" Albania, Bosnia, and Kosovo. Among the applicants, the most important is Turkey, which after years of delays finally began accession negotiations in 2005. With a population of over 70 million, it is second in size only to Germany among EU member states, while its per capita GDP is less than a third of the EU average. It is also the only prospective EU member with a Muslim majority and a strong ruling party with a religious orientation. The possibility of Turkish membership has brought into focus a number of questions about the meaning of the EU. If the EU is a "European" organization, where exactly does Europe end? What would it mean to have a state with an overwhelmingly Muslim population alongside a community of states with largely Christian populations? What would it mean to have the borders of the EU stretch to Syria, Iraq, and Iran? Given the recent "Arab Spring," it is conceivable that a decade from now North African countries with Muslim majorities like Tunisia might also seek membership, as was the case with countries in eastern Europe after 1989. Is it possible to sustain integration when EU members are increasingly differentiated along economic, historical, cultural, and religious lines? EU membership and enlargement were easier when the members had relatively similar institutions and experiences. This is no longer so. Reflecting the growing complexity of EU integration, negotiations with Turkey have slowed, leading many (especially Turks) to ask whether the EU considers them part of Europe.[5]

The lessons here extend beyond Europe. The Free Trade Agreement of the Americas attempted to create a free-trade zone across North and South America, but this foundered in 2005 due to disagreements and general mistrust between the members.

Similar arrangements in Latin America and Asia have made further progress toward integration, but there is little evidence for now that the EU represents a model that other regions will follow. Even the EU is not certain where it may be heading.

Devolution and Democracy

Integration continues to exert a strong pull on many advanced democracies in spite of resistance. At the same time, many advanced democracies also face the tug of devolution from below. As mentioned above and in Chapter 3, devolution is a process by which powers and resources are transferred away from central state institutions and vested at a lower level. Interestingly, devolution reverses the historical development of the state, which is noteworthy for its centralization of power over time. Typically, power over institutions such as social welfare has increasingly moved from the local to the national level. Yet across the advanced democracies there have been moves of late to redirect power in the opposite direction.

Why this apparent reversal? Many political leaders in advanced democracies are concerned that the public mistrusts the state, viewing it as too large, too distant, and too inflexible. Devolution is seen as a way to counteract this distrust by bringing government closer to the public, thereby increasing local control and participation. Devolution can also help give voice to more-marginal communities, such as ethnic minorities, by giving them greater control over their local affairs. By increasing the public's voice and capacity to shape politics, it is hoped, democracy can be reinvigorated.[6]

How does devolution take shape in reality? One way is through the transfer of responsibility and funds to local authorities, giving them a greater say in how policies are crafted and executed. When local institutions have more control and responsibility, they can craft policy to meet their own particular conditions. One example of such devolution occurred in the United States in the 1990s, when welfare reform created bulk transfers of funds to the states, which could then use this money to design and implement their own particular social welfare policies. Another way to effect devolution is by creating wholly new political institutions to provide a greater level of public participation. An example of such innovation was seen in Canada in 1999, when a new province, Nunavut, was created out of a portion of the Northwest Territories. The creation of this new province was intended to give the native Inuit people self-government and control over the natural resources in the region where they lived. Similarly, in 1999 the United Kingdom created new, directly elected assemblies for the regions of Scotland, Wales, and Northern

Means of Devolution

- Transfer of policy-making responsibility to lower levels of government.

- Creation of new political institutions at lower levels of government.

- Transfer of funds and powers to tax to lower levels of government, affording them more control over how resources are distributed.

Ireland. The EU itself, as part of its integration process, has encouraged devolution as a way to give local and regional interests a greater voice in government even as more powers are transferred upward from the member states. Even Japan, well known for its highly centralized state, is currently struggling over whether to pursue greater devolution and regional autonomy. Across many of the advanced democracies, powers have been devolved to varying degrees.

As with integration, it is not certain whether devolution is a trend among the advanced democracies that will continue to spread and deepen, nor is it clear what the long-term implications of such a process would be. Devolution may be a means to rebuild democratic participation by making people more directly responsible for policy making. However, it may also undermine the capacity and autonomy of the central state, especially if coupled with integration. As we discussed in Chapter 3, when it is a response to ethnic conflict devolution may help resolve the problem or only increase demands for sovereignty, depending on how the institutional reforms are structured. In the United Kingdom, devolution has gone a long way toward bringing religious conflict between Catholics and Protestants in Northern Ireland to an end. However, devolution in Belgium has not resolved conflicts between the French- and Flemish-speaking populations, and the country has grown only more polarized over time. In 2010–11, Belgium actually went for over a year without a government, relying instead on a "caretaker" cabinet with minimal powers. Some wonder if Belgium will eventually divide in two. Finally, the trend toward devolution in the advanced democracies has perhaps reached its limits. In the aftermath of September 11 and terrorist attacks in Europe, a number of advanced democracies have moved away from devolution in important ways, centralizing and increasing capacity and autonomy as a way to fight the threat of terrorism and manage legal and illegal immigration (which are often conflated, as we shall discuss below). As with integration, devolution's pace and strength can be influenced by external and internal conditions. Not long ago, observers saw integration and devolution as inexorable processes that states and citizens could not stop. That no longer seems to be the case.

Societal Institutions: New Identities in Formation?

Just as advanced democratic states are facing a number of political challenges and changes in the new millennium, societies too are confronting change and are seemingly being pulled in two directions at once. Some political scientists point to a new set of shared norms and values emerging across the advanced democracies that are not bound to traditional identities of nation and state; others emphasize the strengthening of local identities that are turning these same societies inward. These processes are strongly connected to the struggle over integration and devolution. Whether these social forces are complementary or contradictory, and whether such developments are a sign of greater cooperation or conflict, is a matter of debate.

Postmodern Values and Organization

In recent years, a number of political scientists have begun to track the emergence and development of what they see as postmodern values in the advanced democracies.[7] In premodern societies, people were focused to a greater extent on traditional forms of authority and on basic survival; this focus often led to authoritarian systems with clear standards of obedience and collectivism. Starting in the eighteenth century, the countries that would become the advanced democracies began to embrace the notions of rationality and science, individualism and autonomy. The modern state, society, and economy promised a world of progress, development, and limitless possibilities, and they did enable unprecedented economic growth, material abundance, and improved standards of living for hundreds of millions of people.

Yet by the 1960s, modern values came under attack, just as they themselves had challenged premodern values more than two centuries earlier. These challenges took several forms. Questions were raised about the environmental cost of economic development. Modern values stressed the environment's utility for achieving material goals, but critics now argued that the environment should be valued for its own sake—a public good to be shared by all. Science, too, was viewed with greater skepticism. It was pointed out that technological innovation did not lead to unmitigated benefits but rather carried with it risks and uncertainty. Fears over nuclear power or chemical contamination led many to believe that "progress" was a questionable goal. In politics, too, nationalism and patriotism were challenged, and authority, hierarchy, and deference to the state were questioned. In general, these criticisms indicated the possible emergence of a new set of social norms and values.

Postmodern values differ from modern ones in a number of ways. As already indicated, postmodern values are much less focused on the idea of progress as embodied by material goods, technological change, or scientific innovation. Instead, they center on what have been called "quality of life" or "postmaterialist" issues, which primarily involve concerns other than material gain, including the environment, health, and leisure, as well as personal equality and diversity. Postmodern values are at the same time skeptical of state power and supportive of democracy, especially in the form of direct participation and action. These values in many ways reflect both integrationist and devolutionary tendencies, with their concern for tolerance among different kinds of people and their hostility toward centralized power.

We must be careful not to overstate these findings, however. The central assumption among scholars has been that all advanced democracies are converging toward a shared set of postmodern values. Moreover, as the camp of advanced democracies expands, its new members are also expected to trend in a postmodern direction.[8] Nevertheless, as we noted in our earlier discussion of political culture, research indicates that a society's religious heritage continues to shape societal values irrespective of the level of development. The role of religious heritage indicates that domestic factors in each country remain important in molding the value systems of societies, even as they undergo a general process of development and consequent change. At one time, scholars saw postmodernization as inexorable. Now, there are more doubts regarding the inevitability of a common set of postmodern values. As the camp of advanced democracies becomes religiously and culturally more diverse, we will see how these questions play themselves out.

Diversity, Identity, and the Challenge to Postmodern Values

There are reasons why scholars have become more tentative about the institutionalization of postmodern values. One is the lasting effect of religious and cultural institutions. Another is the changing nature of societies within the advanced democracies. More specifically, the twenty-first century has been marked by a wave of immigration to advanced democracies unseen for a century. In 1960, around four percent of the population of the United States was foreign born; today, that number is 13 percent. In Canada the percentage is 20, while in Australia over a quarter of the population is foreign born. In many larger countries of the EU (Germany, Spain, and the United Kingdom), over 10 percent of the population was born in other countries. This rapid increase in immigration is changing the ethnic, religious, and racial compositions of these countries; for example, forecasters have concluded that in thirty years, whites of European origin will comprise less than half of the U.S. population, compared to nearly 90 percent in 1960.[9] Moreover, the makeup of the immigrant population is quite different across the advanced democratic countries. In the United States, the largest proportion of these immigrants come from Latin America; in Canada, Australia, and New Zealand, the largest group comes from Asia; and in Europe, the largest group comes from North Africa and Turkey. Thus, while many advanced democracies are experiencing immigration, the nature of that immigration and the challenges or opportunities it brings are very different.

In many countries, growing numbers of immigrants have increased xenophobia—fear of foreigners—in the existing population. This xenophobia has economic, societal, and political dimensions. The economic dimension is perhaps most familiar to us. Although supporters of immigration note the benefits of new sources of labor and skills that can come from immigrants, critics view immigrants as a threat to existing workers, since they compete for scarce jobs and depress wages. Debates in Europe over the expansion and powers of the EU have turned in part on fears of immigration. Immigration has been a similar sticking point in United States–Mexican relations, and Australians, Canadians, and New Zealanders express concern over an influx of immigrants from Asia. Some countries, like Japan, have avoided this issue by strictly limiting immigration, though this brings with it its own problems, as we shall discuss shortly.

A more complicated issue is that of societal institutions. As more diverse groups of immigrants enter the advanced democracies, they raise questions about what it means to be American, Canadian, French, or European. Advanced democracies struggle with questions of assimilation and multiculturalism. How much leeway should new groups be given in deciding whether to participate in national institutions and take on national identities? At one end of the spectrum, arguments for multiculturalism assert that societies should help support these new groups, preserving what is distinct about them as a positive contribution to a diverse society. At the other end, arguments for assimilation hold that immigration implies an agreement to accept and adapt to the existing culture, values, and norms of a given society. For countries like the United States, Canada, and Australia, multiculturalism may be somewhat easier to embrace because the vast majority of citizens have come from somewhere else within the last two or three generations, so that the norm is for each person to bring a new contribution to society that can be incorporated into it. Yet even in these countries, there are strong tendencies toward assimilation and fears that the sheer number of immigrants makes assimilation, even if desired, impossible.[10]

If multiculturalism is a source of controversy in traditionally immigrant countries, it is an explosive subject in countries where ethnic and national identities are much more tightly fused, as in much of Europe. There, the influx of non-Europeans, especially Muslim North Africans and Turks, has raised even greater fears. Racially, religiously, and ethnically homogeneous populations now confront people whose cultural, religious, and historical traditions are quite different. The paradox that has emerged is uniquely postmodern. In the past, many European states prided themselves on their high degree of secularism and tolerance for different lifestyles. But how do they tolerate immigrant groups that may be much more religiously and socially conservative—immigrants coming from societies that are quite removed from postmodern values?

In Europe, this paradox has been most sharply defined by several events. In the Netherlands, the controversial writer and filmmaker Theo Van Gogh was murdered in 2004 after making a film critical of the role of women in Islam; his killer, born in Amsterdam to Moroccan parents, claimed that anyone who insulted God needed to be killed.[11] In 2005, a Danish paper sparked protests worldwide when it published editorial cartoons lampooning Mohammed and Islam. In these cases, the questions that arose turned on issues of tolerance. Postmodern societies emphasize individual tolerance and a skepticism of institutions; one result of this emphasis, however, is an incomprehension of (and often intolerance for) others who have strong religious, ethnic, or cultural identities. Some argue that the greatest virtue of a democracy is the ability to criticize and even offend others, and that limiting this is an attack on liberty. Reconciling such views with those of people who hold some values and beliefs sacred is not easy. Germany's Prime Minister Angela Merkel concluded that "the approach [to build] a multicultural [society] and to live side by side and to enjoy each other . . . has failed, utterly failed."[12]

Needless to say, such economic and social concerns work their way into politics. In many advanced democracies, growing ethnic and religious diversity has fueled the rise of anti-immigration, nationalist, and xenophobic movements that seek to restrict immigration, increase assimilation, and assert ethnic and national primacy. The most extreme example is Anders Breivik's horrific terrorist attack in Norway in 2011. In his manifesto, *2083: A European Declaration of Independence*, Breivik articulated his worldview, arguing, "The European Union—or the Eurabian Empire if you will—is a naked power grab by the elites in order to dismantle the nations [it is] supposed to serve. . . . Mass immigration is used to crush all nation states simultaneously so that the natives have no real alternatives to flee to, and no countries can come to the aid of others against the advancing Islamization."[13] Hostility toward immigrants often leads to their being marginalized and humiliated. Terrorist attacks in Spain and the United Kingdom in 2004, 2005, and 2007 were led in part by immigrants or native-born children of immigrants.

Finally, the new wave of immigrants will affect relations between the advanced democracies. Although most of these countries, as we noted, face similar questions regarding immigration and its effects, the source of migration differs from country to country or region to region. This growing difference between the advanced democracies may pull the West apart by shaping different cultural values and external orientations. In North America, migration from Latin America and East Asia may reorient these countries south and east, away from Europe, while in Europe, larger Muslim communities and EU expansion may draw these countries closer to the Middle East and South Asia. Faith may also come into play, with Hispanic immigrants into the United States bringing with them more-conservative Roman Catholic, Evangelical, or Pentecostal religious values, while Islam will grow more central to European life. The advanced democracies may see less and less of themselves in one another. This need not be a source of conflict; democratic values and a commitment to prosperity link very different countries together as part of the community of advanced democracies. But some speculate that a growing divergence of the advanced democracies may eventually mean an end to the idea of a single set of postmodern values that defines the advanced democracies.

Economic Institutions: A New Market?

Our discussion so far has asked to what extent postmodernity is changing state and societal institutions. Our last area of interest, economic development, is perhaps the most obvious. Dramatic changes have taken place in the economic structures of the advanced democracies over the past generation. Specifically, their reliance on traditional industries, such as manufacturing, has shifted to such an extent that it is no longer logical to refer to them as "industrial" at all. At the same time, long-standing assumptions about the role of the state in such areas as the redistribution of income and social expenditures have come into question, challenging the traditional functions of the welfare state. This may lead to an overturning of existing ideas and policies regarding the proper balance of freedom and equality in the advanced democracies.

Postindustrialism

So far, we have considered how postmodernity has affected advanced democratic states and societies. In both of these arenas, what is going on is open to interpretation. But in the economic realm the data are clearer: the advanced democracies have experienced a dramatic shift during the last half-century from economies based primarily on industry and manufacturing to postindustrial economies. In postindustrial countries, the bulk of profits are made and the majority of people are employed in the service sector—work that involves not the creation of tangible goods, such as cars or computers, but industries such as finance, insurance, real estate, education, retail sales, transportation, communication, high technology, utilities, health care, and business and legal services. As Table 8.4 indicates, this shift has been occurring across the advanced democracies over the past several decades. In these countries, around three-quarters of the working population are now employed in the service sector. This shift has occurred for a number of reasons. Much industrial production has migrated outside of the advanced democracies in search of lower labor and other costs. Globalization is accelerating this trend. Furthermore, technological innovation in the advanced democracies is changing the requirements of

TABLE 8.4	Employment by Economic Sector, 1960–2010			
PERCENTAGE OF TOTAL NATIONAL EMPLOYMENT IN				
	AGRICULTURE	INDUSTRY	MANUFACTURING	SERVICES
United States				
1960	8.4	33.4	26.1	58.1
2010	1.6	17.2	10.1	81.2
Canada				
1960	13.3	32.0	24.7	54.7
2010	2.2	19.0	10.3	78.9
Japan				
1960	29.5	28.5	21.7	41.9
2010	3.9	24.9	16.9	71.2
France				
1960	22.5	36.9	27.3	40.7
2010	2.8	20.6	13.1	76.6
Germany				
1960	13.8	46.0	34.4	40.2
2010	2.2	28.0	21.2	69.7

Source: U.S. Bureau of Labor.

labor. Employees are expected to have higher levels of education than in past; in the United States, 40 percent of those between the ages of 25 and 64 have a college degree; in Canada, 50 percent of them do.[14]

Postindustrialism in some ways reflects and may reinforce the political and social trends discussed earlier. The emergence of an information-based economy, for example, may contribute to a greater devolution of power within the economy as firms become less hierarchical and more decentralized, less physical and more "virtual," less national and more international, and as they grant their employees greater autonomy and flexibility. However, for those without specialized training and education, postindustrialism may mean less freedom and equality; the growing importance of knowledge may well marginalize these workers, creating an educational underclass whose prospects for upward mobility are limited. Technological advances can be highly disruptive, and we can recall from Chapter 4 that inequality in the United States in particular has risen over time. In 1969, the Gini index measurement for the United States was 36; in 2007, it was 45.

The future of postindustrialism is also clouded by the recent financial crisis. The reasons behind the downturn are complex and vary from country to country. However, the basic chronology is clear. Starting in the late 1990s, the United States, as well as some other advanced democracies (see the discussion of Japan in Chapter 4), experienced a housing "bubble"—a dramatic and unsustainable rise in real estate prices. Investors came to the conclusion that real estate was a safe and profitable investment. Government deregulation, combined with banks' desire to earn profits on housing loans, meant that millions of people and firms borrowed money, often more than they could repay, to build and buy real estate and borrow against its value. The borrowers' debts were sold to other investors, in the United States and abroad. As with past financial bubbles, people imagined that prices would rise indefinitely and cover their debts, but eventually overvalue and oversupply caused the bubble to burst. As prices declined, many borrowers lost their ability to repay their debt, sending banks in the United States and Europe into collapse and spreading panic throughout the financial markets. The result was a contraction in lending and spending, higher unemployment, and a decline in global GDP.

Whatever the primary cause, this economic downturn has raised significant questions about the long-term prospects of many postindustrial economies. To some, the recession merely revealed underlying weaknesses in the economies of the United States and many other advanced democracies, where large debts have been used to mask unemployment and inequality, and where globalization has amplified these problems. We will speak about this more in Chapter 11, when we ask to what extent this recession was caused by globalization. There are calls for greater domestic and international regulation of finance; a rethinking of how to invest public funds in education, infrastructure, and technology to meet the needs of the rapidly changing economic environment; and redesigned social safety nets that can protect the many individuals now on the margins of economic life. Some also go so far as to suggest that advanced democracies pursue greater protectionism, even default on debt, to recapture jobs and industries lost to countries like China.[15] Such actions have not been taken since the Great Depression in the 1930s.

Maintaining the Welfare State

This leads us to the final aspect of economic transformation in the advanced democracies: the future of the welfare state. As we discussed in Chapter 4, for the past half-century a defining element of the advanced democracies has been the development of social expenditures as a way to reduce inequality and provide public goods through such programs as national pension plans, public health care, education, and unemployment benefits. There can be no doubt that the welfare state has provided a wide array of benefits among the advanced democracies: extreme poverty, especially among the elderly, has been reduced; infant mortality has declined and life expectancy has increased; and literacy and education have improved dramatically. Social expenditures have played an important role in socializing risk—that is, making the uncertainties that come with work, health, and age a public, rather than a private, concern.

The welfare state has brought with it costs and controversies that have only been exacerbated by the global recession. First, although social expenditures have been lauded as an essential part of a humane society, they are increasingly expensive. During the early part of the twentieth century, social expenditures typically amounted to around 10 to 15 percent of advanced democracies' GDPs. Currently, however, in most of these countries social expenditures (not including education) consume between a quarter and a third of GDP. This increased spending has required a choice between two options. The first is to raise taxes, which among advanced democracies average close to 40 percent of GDP (closer to 50 percent in several social democracies). Of course, if the public is willing to pay higher taxes in return for benefits, this is not necessarily a problem, though liberals in particular argue that such large state expenditures reduce private income and profit and thus hinder growth. The second option, which has become more difficult in the global recession, is to borrow from the public or other states to cover budget deficits. Japan, whose public debt is now 225 percent of its GDP, is the most extreme example, but the debts of many advanced democracies are over 50 percent of their GDP.

These trends will be magnified by important demographic changes within the advanced democracies. In 1900, residents of these countries had an average life expectancy of around 40 to 50 years; by 2050, they can expect to live more than 80 years. As life expectancies have risen, birthrates have declined. In most of the advanced democracies, the birthrate is below the replacement level—more people die than are being born. There are two results from these demographic changes. First, the populations of many advanced democracies will eventually begin to shrink. For example, projections indicate that by the end of this decade deaths in the EU will exceed births and that in spite of immigration the population will peak around 2040 and then begin to decline. By 2060, the projected EU will have lost around 17 million people (the United States shows no such decline, because of higher birth and immigration rates). Second, all advanced democracies will see a growing elderly population. According to some estimates, by 2050 a third of the population in the advanced democracies will be over 65 years old, compared with around 15 percent in 2000. As an ever-larger proportion of the population, this older segment of society will seek more welfare benefits, such as healthcare, but declining birthrates mean there will be fewer working-age individuals to fill needed jobs and pay into these systems.[16]

The solutions are not easy. Increased immigration is one obvious solution, especially given that the world population, especially in Africa, will continue to grow. However, we've already noted the problems that accompany immigration, an issue that becomes even more contentious when social expenditures are involved, for while young immigrants may be needed to support the welfare of those who are older, the public is often unwilling to extend the benefits they enjoy to immigrants.[17] A second course is to cut back on benefits. However, politicians face well-organized opposition to welfare reform, and in many countries benefits have continued to increase even as revenues have shrunk, leading to deficits and debt. A third solution would be to expand the labor market. This could be done by raising the retirement age and making job markets more flexible, encouraging more part-time work among parents and younger or older workers. Although there is resistance, many European countries are now raising their retirement ages, which have typically been below 65. Some combination of increased immigration, reduced benefits, and later retirement will be necessary. Otherwise, the advanced democracies will borrow even more against the young and their future, cutting long-term investments in such areas as education and infrastructure in order to care for the elderly. Growing debt means that even if states do not default on their loans, they may be forced instead to print ever greater amounts of money to cover their debts. According to some economists, this could lead in extreme cases "to ever-higher inflation and interest rates, ever-lower growth or deeper recession, and eventually hyperinflation along with rapid currency depreciation."[18] Those results would, needless to say, be disastrous.

Japan provides an extreme example of the complexities involved in these demographic changes and policy responses. By current estimates, the population of Japan, around 127 million, has already peaked and is beginning to decline. By 2050, it is expected to have dropped to around 100 million, a loss of over 20 percent. Moreover, a third or more of the population will be over 65. To prevent population decline, the country would need to accept several hundred thousand immigrants every year, which would dramatically transform the composition of a country that is ethnically very homogenous. As can be imagined, there is little desire in Japan to follow such a course; in fact, during the recent economic downturns immigrants have been encouraged to leave. The alternative is for the country to shrink significantly in population and wealth. If solutions are not found for Japan and the other advanced democracies, many will find themselves unable to sustain some of the most basic elements of prosperity and risk management they have constructed over the past century, and they will face societal conflict that pits young against old and immigrant against native.

In Sum: The Advanced Democracies in Transition

Advanced democracies—their institutions and the challenges they face—are unlike other countries in many ways. Although there is variation among them, these countries are all characterized by liberal democracy and high levels of economic development. They represent what we consider modern social, economic, and political life. Yet their institutions are being directly challenged. State sovereignty is confronted by the twin dynamics of devolution and integration. Social norms are similarly in flux, as postmodern values challenge the status quo and are challenged in turn. Modern industrial structures have given way to a new, information-based economy that empowers some and dislocates others, and demographic changes will affect how countries provide public goods to their people. All these factors can affect general prosperity and shape the existing balance between freedom and equality.

In the coming chapters, we will turn to these same issues as they exist outside the advanced democracies. Communist, postcommunist, less-developed, and newly industrializing countries all confront issues of state sovereignty, social values, industrialization, and social welfare. The next two chapters will focus on the unique challenges these groups of countries face in these areas. Will these countries eventually join the ranks of the advanced democracies in a convergence of political, economic, and social institutions around the globe? This question will follow us through our remaining discussion.

For Further Reading

RS> Acemoglu, Daron, Simon Johnson, James A. Robinson, and Pierre Yared. "Income and Democracy." *American Economic Review* 98, no. 3 (2008).

Cooper, Robert. *The Postmodern State and the World Order* (London: Demos, 1996).

Crepaz, Markus. *Trust beyond Borders: Immigration, the Welfare State, and Identity in Modern Societies* (Ann Arbor: University of Michigan Press, 2007).

RS> de Tocqueville, Alexis. *Democracy in America* (New York: A. A. Knopf, 1945).

Diamond, Larry, ed. *Developing Democracy: Toward Consolidation* (Baltimore: Johns Hopkins University Press, 1999).

RS> Duverger, Maurice. *Political Parties: Their Organization and Activity in the Modern State* (New York: Wiley, 1954).

RS> Estévez-Abe, Margarita, Torben Iversen, and David Soskice. "Social Protection and the Formation of Skills: A Reinterpretation of the Welfare State." *Varieties of Capitalism: The Institutional Foundations of Comparative Advantage.* Peter A. Hall and David Soskice, eds. (New York: Oxford University Press, 2001).

Irwin, Derek. *The Community of Europe: A History of European Integration since 1945* (New York: Addison-Wesley, 1995).

RS> Iversen, Torben and David Soskice. "Electoral Institutions and the Politics of Coalitions: Why Some Democracies Redistribute More than Others." *American Political Science Review* 100, no. 2 (May 2006).

RS> Przeworski, Adam. "Conquered or Granted? A History of Suffrage Extensions." *British Journal of Political Science* 39, no. 2 (2009).

 Visit StudySpace for quizzes and other review material.
www.norton.com/studyspace

- **Vocabulary Flashcards of All Key Terms**
- **Chapter Review Quizzes**
- **Complete Study Reviews and Outlines**

RS>
Reader Selection

Highlighted selections are included in *Essential Readings in Comparative Politics*, Fourth Edition.

A Chinese poster from the cultural revolution, mid 1960s. This propaganda image captures communist ideology, where all sectors of society would move together toward economic prosperity and equality.

社 会 主 义 到 处 都 在 胜 利 地 前 进

Socialism Advances in Victory Every

COMMUNISM AND POSTCOMMUNISM

KEY CONCEPTS

- Communist ideology is founded on the understanding that politics stems from economic inequality.

- Communist systems sought to eliminate inequality by eliminating private property and market forces, under the direction of a one-party state.

- State control over markets and property proved too complex, and these systems eventually collapsed or radically reformed their institutions.

- Postcommunist states have had to transform their economic institutions to restore markets and private property, with mixed results.

- Postcommunist states have had to transform their political institutions, with some becoming liberal democracies and others remaining authoritarian.

The advanced democracies we studied in the last chapter have become the wealthiest and most powerful countries in the world. Yet these wealthy countries continue to struggle with the problems of poverty and inequality—both within their societies and between themselves and the rest of the world. Can poverty and inequality be solved? This concern goes to the heart of communist theory and practice, for communism has sought to create a system that limits individual freedoms in order to divide wealth in an equitable manner. This vision of a world without economic distinctions drove the formation of communist regimes around the world, eventually bringing hundreds of millions of people under its banner.

Yet in spite of the lofty ideals of communist thought, and in spite of the dramatic emergence of communism as a political regime in the early part of the twentieth century, within less than a century the majority of the world's communist regimes began to unravel. Why? In this chapter, we will look at how communism attempted to reconcile freedom and equality and why communist systems have largely failed at that endeavor. We will begin by looking at the original theories of modern communism, particularly the ideas of Karl Marx. From there we will investigate how communism progressed from theory into practice as communist regimes were built around the world, most notably in the Soviet Union, Eastern Europe, and China (See Table 9.1). How did these systems seek to create equality and bring Marx's ideas to life?

After examining the dynamics of communism in practice, we will study its demise. What were its shortcomings, and why could these limitations not be overcome? Our look at the downfall of communism will take us to our final questions:

TABLE 9.1   Communist Regimes in the 1980s

EUROPE	ASIA	AFRICA AND THE MIDDLE EAST	LATIN AMERICA
Albania	Afghanistan	Angola	*Cuba*
Bulgaria	Cambodia	Benin	
Czechoslovakia	*China*	Ethiopia	
East Germany	*Laos*	Mozambique	
Hungary	Mongolia	South Yemen	
Poland	*North Korea*		
Romania	*Vietnam*		
Soviet Union			
Yugoslavia			

Note: Countries still controlled by a communist party as of 2012 are shown in italics.

What comes after communism, and is communism dead? In addressing each of these questions, we will uncover the enormous scope and vision of communist thought, the tremendous challenges of putting it into practice, the serious flaws and limitations that this implementation encountered, and the daunting work of building new political, social, and economic institutions from the rubble of communism's demise.

Communism, Equality, and the Nature of Human Relations

Communism is a set of ideas that view political, social, and economic institutions in a manner fundamentally different from most political thought, challenging much of what we have studied so far. At its most basic level, it is an ideology that seeks to create human equality by eliminating private property and market forces.

Communism as a political theory and ideology can be traced primarily to the German philosopher Karl Marx (1818–83).[1] Marx began with a rather straightforward observation: human beings impart value to the objects they create by investing their own time and labor in them. This value can be greater than the cost of creating the object—for example, a chair maker may spend $20 on materials to build a chair that would sell for $30. The extra $10 reflects the added value of the maker's time and energy. This "surplus value of labor" stays with the object, making it useful to anyone, not just the maker. This ability to create objects with their own innate value sets humans apart from other animals, but it also inevitably leads to economic injustice, Marx concluded. He argued that as human beings develop their knowledge and technological skills, an opportunity is created for those with political power to extract the surplus value from others, enriching themselves while impoverishing others. In other words, once human beings learned how to produce things of value, others found that they could gain these things at little cost to themselves simply by using coercion to acquire them. Using the example above, if the chair maker were employed by a "capitalist," it would be this employer who would benefit from the surplus value of labor, getting to keep the extra $10.

For Marx, then, the world was properly understood in economic terms; all human action flowed from the relations between the haves and the have-nots. Marx believed that structures, rather than people or ideas, made history. Specifically, Marx spoke of human history and human relations as functions of what he termed the base and the superstructure. The **base** is the system of economic production, including the level of technology (what he called the "means of

Surplus value of labor The value invested in any human-made good that can be used by another individual. Exploitation results when one person or group extracts the surplus value from another.

Base The economic system of a society, made up of technology (the means of production) and class relations between people (the relations of production).

Superstructure All noneconomic institutions in a society (e.g., religion, culture, national identity). These ideas and values derive from the base and serve to legitimize the current system of exploitation.

False consciousness Failure to understand the nature of one's exploitation; essentially amounts to "buying into" the superstructure.

Dialectical materialism Process of historical change that is not evolutionary but revolutionary. The existing base and superstructure (thesis) would come into conflict with new technological innovations, generating growing opposition to the existing order (antithesis). This would culminate in revolution, overthrowing the old base and superstructure (synthesis).

Dictatorship of the proletariat Temporary period after capitalism has been overthrown during which vestiges of the old base and superstructure are eradicated.

Proletariat The working class.

Bourgeoisie The property-owning class.

Communism According to Marxists, the final stage of history once capitalism is overthrown and the dictatorship of the proletariat destroys its remaining vestiges. In communism, state and politics would disappear, and society and the economy would be based on equality and cooperation.

Vanguard of the proletariat Lenin's argument that an elite communist party would have to carry out revolution, because as a result of false consciousness, historical conditions would not automatically lead to capitalism's demise.

production") and the kind of class relations that exist as a result (the "relations of production"). Resting on the base is the **superstructure**, which represents all human institutions—politics and the state, national identity and culture, religion and gender, and so on. Marx viewed this superstructure as a system of institutions created essentially to justify and perpetuate the existing order. People consequently suffer from "false consciousness," meaning that they believe they understand the true nature of the world around them, but in reality they are deluded by the superstructure imposed by capitalism. Thus, liberal democracy was rejected by

Marx and most other communists as a system created to delude the exploited into thinking they have a say in their political destiny, when in fact those with wealth actually control politics.

Revolution and the "Triumph" of Communism

Having dissected what he saw as the nature of politics, economics, and society, Marx used this framework to understand historical development and to anticipate the future of capitalism. Marx concluded that human history developed in phases, each driven by a particular kind of exploitation. In each phase, he argued, the form of exploitation was built around the existing level of technology. In early agrarian societies, for example, feudalism was the dominant political and economic order; the rudimentary technology available tied individuals to the land so that their labor could be exploited by the aristocracy. Although such relations may appear stable, technology itself is always dynamic. Marx recognized this and asserted that the inevitable changes in technology would increase tensions between rulers and ruled as these changes empowered new groups who clashed with the base and the superstructure. In the case of feudalism, emerging technology empowered an early-capitalist, property-owning middle class or **bourgeoisie**, whose members sought to gain political power and to remake the economic and social order in a way that better fit capitalist ambitions.

Eventually, the tensions resulting from technological advances would lead to revolution; those in power would be overthrown, and a new ruling class would come to power. In each case, change would be sudden and violent and would pave the way for a new economic base and superstructure. Marx called this entire process **dialectical materialism**. "Dialectic" is the term he used to describe history as a struggle between the existing order (the thesis) and the challenge to that order (the antithesis), resulting in historical change (the synthesis). Materialism simply refers to the fact that this tension is over material factors, specifically economic ones. Revolutions inevitably result from this dialectic process.

On the basis of these ideas, Marx concluded that capitalist democracy, which had displaced feudalism, would itself be overthrown by its own internal flaws. As capitalism developed, competition between firms would intensify. The working class, or **proletariat**, would find itself on the losing end of this process as firms introduced more and greater technology to reduce the number of workers and as unprofitable businesses began to go bankrupt in the face of intense competition.

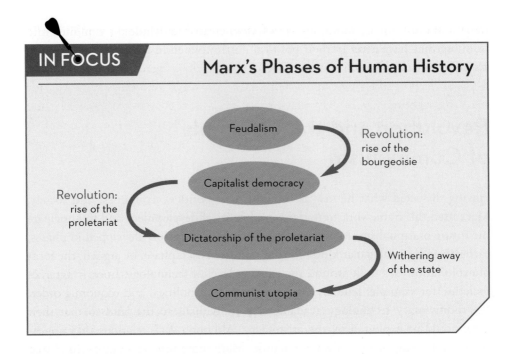

IN FOCUS

Marx's Phases of Human History

Feudalism

Revolution:
rise of the
bourgeoisie

Capitalist democracy

Revolution:
rise of the
proletariat

Dictatorship of the proletariat

Withering away
of the state

Communist utopia

The bourgeoisie would grow smaller and smaller as the wealth of society became concentrated in fewer and fewer hands, and large monopolies would come to dominate the economy. The oversupply of labor created by these factors would drive down the wages of the working class and swell the ranks of the unemployed.

Alienated and driven to desperation by these conditions, the proletariat would "gain consciousness" by realizing the true source of their poverty and rise up in rebellion. They would carry out a revolution, seizing control of the state and the economy. Marx saw this process not simply as a national phenomenon but also as an international one. When the conditions were right, he hypothesized, revolution would spread among all the capitalist countries, sweeping away this unjust order.

Once world revolution had taken place, Marx foresaw, there would be a temporary "dictatorship of the proletariat," during which the last vestiges of capitalism, particularly the old remnants of the superstructure, would be swept away. After the institutions of capitalism had been decisively eliminated, the institutions of the state itself would begin to "wither away." There would be no more need for laws or police, because all people would share equally in the fruits of labor. No longer would there be a need for armies or flags, because people would be united in equality rather than blinded by the false consciousness of nationalism. People would live in a stateless world, and history, which in Marx's view had been driven by exploitation and class struggle, would essentially come to an end. Only then could one actually speak of "communism"—which is why communist parties would usually describe their own countries as "socialist," since they were still controlled by the state. Adding to this confusion is the fact that in the advanced democracies, the word *socialism* is often used interchangeably with *social democracy*. However, for most contemporary social democrats, socialism is seen as an end stage, where the state exercises significant but not total control over the economy. For communists, however, socialism is a transitional phase toward a time when private property and the state no longer exist.

Putting Communism into Practice

Communism thus provides an entire worldview, explaining the course of human history and the inevitable ascent into utopia as the products of economic interaction. As we know, such a sweeping theory has proved compelling for many people, especially those who sought to put Marx's ideas into practice. Two of the most notable followers of Marx's ideas were Vladimir Ulyanov, more commonly known as Lenin, and Mao Zedong, who came to lead communist revolutions in Russia (1917) and China (1949), respectively. Yet although both Mao and Lenin were inspired by Marx, they departed from his ideas by seeking to carry out revolution in two countries that were weakly industrialized and far from being capitalist. Marx had argued that revolution would occur only where and when capitalism was most advanced and thus most prone to collapse; however, at the end of his life, he did hold out the possibility that revolution could occur in less developed Russia, in contradiction to his own theories.[2] Lenin in particular believed that revolution could be carried out in less advanced countries if leaders constructed a "**vanguard of the proletariat**"—his term for a small revolutionary movement that could seize power on behalf of the people, who may lack the consciousness necessary to rise up.[3] This approach meant that in reality, communism spread where the level of economic development was relatively low—exactly the opposite of what Marx had originally theorized.

Yet even as the number of communist regimes grew, they faced a common quandary: how exactly to go about building communism. Marx had left no blueprint for what to do once the revolution had succeeded. In many ways, communists assumed that the revolution was the difficult part and that what should occur afterward would unfold as a matter of course. In part because Marx provided no specific outline for how communism should be built, the institutions that were created varied widely. Most were based on forms first built in the Soviet Union after 1917. Because they desired to fundamentally reshape human relations, communist states

Important Figures in Communism

Karl Marx (1818–83) First philosopher to systematically construct a theory explaining why capitalism would fail and be replaced by communism; father of modern communist thought.

Lenin (Vladimir Ulyanov) (1870–1924) Applied Marxist thought to Russia, leading a successful revolution in 1917; modified Marxist ideas by arguing that revolution would occur not in most-developed societies, but rather in struggling countries such as Russia.

Stalin (Josef Dzhugashvili) (1879–1953) Succeeded Lenin as leader of the Soviet Union; embarked on rapid industrialization of the country, modifying Marxism to argue that socialism could be built within just a single country; extended communism to Eastern Europe after World War II; denounced by Nikita Khrushchev in 1956 for his use of a personality cult and terror.

Mao Zedong (1883–1976) Led the Chinese Communist Party and fought against Chinese rivals and Japanese occupiers during World War II; modified communism to focus on the peasantry instead of the working class, given the primarily agrarian nature of China; unleashed the Cultural Revolution in 1966 to weaken the party and increase his own power.

Deng Xiaoping (1905–97) Fought with Mao Zedong against Chinese nationalists and Japanese occupiers during World War II; named general secretary of the Chinese Communist Party in 1956; stripped of all posts during the Cultural Revolution, but emerged as the country's leader after Mao's death; pursued economic liberalization in the 1980s and supported repression of the Tiananmen Square protests.

Fidel Castro (1926–) Led the Cuban Revolution in 1959 and defended the communist system against anticommunist forces and U.S. opposition; continues to defend Cuban socialism in spite of the collapse of the Soviet Union and other communist regimes in Eastern Europe.

Mikhail Gorbachev (1931–) Made general secretary of the Communist Party of the Soviet Union in 1985; initiated the twin policies of perestroika (economic restructuring) and glasnost (political liberalization), which eventually led to increasing discord within the country and a failed coup attempt by hard-line communists who opposed further reform; the resulting dissolution of the Soviet Union left Gorbachev without a country to lead.

accrued a high level of autonomy and capacity; their regimes have at times become totalitarian in their drive to transform virtually all basic human institutions.

The task of this transformation was entrusted to the communist elite who came to direct and staff the state.[4] At its apex, political power rested within the Communist Party, a relatively small "vanguard" organization (typically comprising less than 10 percent of the population) whose leading role in the country was typically written directly into the constitution—meaning that there was no constitutional way to remove the party from power. Because the Communist Party embodied what it saw as the "correct" view of human history and future relations, alternative organizations and ideologies making up civil society were seen as hostile to communism and were repressed.

But as we discussed in Chapter 6, on nondemocratic regimes, no system of rule can survive through the threat of force alone. Communist parties maintained control over society not only through repression but also by carefully allocating power throughout the country's various political, social, and economic institutions—a thorough form of co-optation. This can be seen clearly in the ***nomenklatura***, politically sensitive or influential jobs in the state, society, or economy that were staffed by people chosen or approved by the Communist Party. The *nomenklatura* encompassed a wide range of important positions: the head of a university, the editor of a newspaper, a military officer, a film director. Not surprisingly, party approval often required party membership, making joining the party the easiest way to prove one's loyalty and rise up the career ladder. Party membership could also bring other benefits: better housing, the ability to travel abroad, or access to scarce consumer goods. As a result, party membership was often driven more by opportunism than by idealism; many joined so that they could pursue certain careers or simply gain the benefits that party membership could buy.[5]

The dominant role played by the Communist Party and the *nomenklatura* created a power relationship different from those in democratic and many other nondemocratic systems. Rather than being centered within the state and government, power rested within the party. For example, when observers referred to the "leader" of a communist country, they were usually referring not to a government official but to the general secretary of the Communist Party. Indeed, top party leaders often did not hold any important formal position within the state. Though the political systems in communist countries by and large resembled those we see elsewhere in the world, typically with a prime minister or president, a parliament, a judiciary, and local government, all these positions were part of the *nomenklatura* and thus staffed by party members appointed by the party leaders. Although the trappings of democracy, such as parliamentary elections, typically existed, electoral candidates were almost exclusively Communist Party members with no real competition. Moreover, parliaments and other organs of power were little more than "rubber-stamp" institutions, approving decisions sent down the party hierarchy.

As for the party itself, in many ways it intentionally mirrored the state, with a general secretary serving as chief executive, and a **Politburo** (short for "Political Bureau") and **Central Committee** acting as a kind of cabinet and legislature, respectively, shaping national policy and confirming the decisions of the party leadership. Below the Central Committee, various other bodies extended all the way down to individual places of work or residence, where party members were assigned to basic party organizations called "cells." These cells were ostensibly intended to represent the interests of the people, but they were primarily mechanisms by which the party could closely monitor the population. Traditionally, the party held a congress every few years, at which its leadership was elected by delegates sent from the party cells, but these elections were little more than confirmations of those already in power. Outside the party and state, a limited number of organizations, such as unions, were allowed to function; these were in turn linked to the state and party, completing this highly corporatist structure, with sanctioned organizations for all facets of society.

While the party and its *nomenklatura* controlled key organizations, communist ideology shaped policy and sought to legitimize authoritarian control. Based fundamentally on the theories of Marx as adapted by Lenin and Mao, communist ideology focused on the elimination of inequality and the promotion of economic development. Because of the expansive nature of communist ideology and its promise of a future utopia, it was, perhaps more than the other ideologies we discussed in Chapter 3, a secular "religion," requiring unquestioning faith in a set of beliefs and sacrifice for a future reward, and boasting its own collection of holy texts, shrines, saints, martyrs, and devils. Adherents venerated charismatic leaders who served as prophets of communism, such as Lenin, Mao, Josef Stalin, and Fidel Castro. Many charismatic communist leaders reinforced their position through elaborate personality cults, as we discussed earlier.

The quest for and exercise of this monopoly on power, as expressed through the *nomenklatura* and through the deep penetration of the state and society by the party, down to the most basic level of home and work, proved to be dangerous and even lethal. In the first decades of communist rule in the Soviet Union, China, and Eastern Europe, terror was used to eliminate opposition and to maintain control. Tens of millions perished, especially in the Soviet Union under Stalin and in China under Mao. Under the rule of Stalin, many people were purged from the Soviet Communist Party and executed for imaginary crimes. These were not cases of mistaken punishment: Stalin used terror and victimized symbolic "criminals" as a way to intimidate the Communist Party and the population as a whole.[6] Similarly, in China, Mao unleashed the Cultural Revolution in the late 1960s, encouraging the public (students, in particular) to attack any institution or individual that was either a remnant of precommunist China or lacked revolutionary zeal. Mao's targets included the **party-state**; which he believed had grown conservative over time and was restricting his power, indeed, his notable slogan was "bombard the party headquarters." During the next decade, not only did countless Chinese die but books were burned, art destroyed, and cultural relics demolished—all for the crime of being "reactionary."[7]

Communist Political Economy

If the Communist Party's singular quest for power led in the cases of Stalin and Mao to its gross abuse, the centralization of economic power similarly created problems that Marxist theory did not anticipate. Communist political-economic systems shared a set of institutions fundamentally different from liberal, mercantilist, or social democratic alternatives, as both markets and property were essentially absorbed by the state.[8] With the means of production held by the state, many of the typical aspects of capitalism that we take for granted—individual profit, unemployment, competition between firms, bankruptcy—were eliminated. Individuals lost their right to control property, including their own labor; the party-state made the decisions about how these resources should be used. Communist leaders redirected national wealth toward the goal of collective equality through such mechanisms as industrialization and social expenditures. Several million died in the Soviet Union in the 1930s during the forced collectivization of agriculture, while an attempt at rapid industrialization and the collectivization of agriculture during the Great Leap Forward in China (1959–61) led to some 45 million famine deaths. As Mao himself put it, "When there is not enough to eat people starve to death. It is better to let half of the people die so that the other half can eat their fill."[9]

Alongside private property, communist systems also eliminated the market forces of supply and demand, believing that they were incapable of equitably distributing wealth. Communist countries by and large chose to replace the market with the state bureaucracy, which explicitly allocated resources by planning what should be produced and in what amounts, setting the final prices of these goods, and deciding where they should be sold. This system is known as **central planning**.

As one might imagine, planning an entire economy is an extremely difficult task. As communist planners found, matching up all the inputs and outputs necessary for producing goods is overwhelming. There are simply too many things to plan—in the Soviet Union, for instance, there were some 40,000 to 50,000 kinds of physical items—and too many unforeseen outcomes, such as a factory failing to deliver its full output, or a change in demand. Because most entities in an economy are interdependent, small problems can have a huge effect on the entire plan. A miscalculation resulting in the underproduction of steel, for example, would have disastrous effects on all those goods dependent on steel, some of which would themselves be components in other finished goods, such as wheels or bolts.

Another problem encountered in centrally planned economies was the lack of worker incentives. Factories and farms were unconcerned about the quality of their goods, since central planners simply indicated a numerical quota they had to fulfill.

Communist Political Economy

- Markets and property are wholly absorbed by the state.

- Central planning replaces the market mechanism.

- Individual property rights, individual profit, unemployment, competition between firms, and bankruptcy are all virtually eliminated.

- Most of the nation's means of production are nationalized.

- The economy functions in essence as a single large firm, with the public as its sole employees.

- The state provides extensive public goods and social services, including universal systems of public education, health care, and retirement.

Workers did not have to fear losing their jobs or factories going out of business as a result of shoddy work, because under communism employment was guaranteed and firms, being owned by the state, could not go bankrupt. This explains in part why all communist countries eventually fell behind economically. In the absence of competition and incentives, innovation and efficiency disappeared, leaving these systems to stagnate.

Societal Institutions under Communism

In addition to reengineering politics and economics to eliminate the inequality and exploitation associated with capitalist systems, communist parties also sought to reorder human relations, hoping to sweep away the old superstructure held responsible for generating false consciousness. One aspect of this superstructure viewed with particular hostility was religion. Marx is known for his oft-cited statement that "religion is the opiate of the masses"—like a drug, religion numbs its practitioners to their pain, in this case by promising them they will be rewarded in the afterlife for enduring their present suffering, legitimizing the inequality and poverty perpetuated by the superstructure. As a result, in most communist countries religion was strongly suppressed. In the Soviet Union, most places of worship were closed, converted to other uses, or torn down. In China during the Cultural Revolution, temples and other religious shrines were destroyed. Even where religion was tolerated to a greater extent, it was directly controlled or its practitioners were harassed by the Communist Party.

Traditional gender relations were also seen by Marxists as a function of capitalism—specifically, as a microcosm of class relations. Men exploit women through the family structure, just as the bourgeoisie exploit the proletariat, and sexual morality serves as a means to perpetuate this gender inequality. Communism envisioned complete economic, social, and political equality between men and women. Even the repressive institution of marriage, like the state, would fade away, replaced by what Marx called "an openly legalized community of free love."[10]

In spite of Marxist ideals, gender relations only partially changed under communist rule. In most communist countries, women were given much greater opportunities than they had experienced previously. To promote industrialization, communist parties encouraged women to enter the workforce and to increase their education. Most countries also enacted liberal divorce and abortion laws and provided social benefits such as state-run child care. In spite of these changes, however, women's traditional roles as housekeepers and mothers did not change. The "new socialist woman" was not complemented by a "new socialist man"; traditional patterns of sexism persisted, and women found themselves burdened by the double duty of work inside and outside the home. In addition, while many women worked in important occupations, few rose to positions of any significant political or economic power. The top ranks of the party membership, the state, and the economy remained dominated by men.[11]

IN FOCUS

Societal Institutions under Communism

IDEAL	REALITY
Religion, the "opiate of the masses," will disappear.	Religion was suppressed but not eliminated.
Men and women will be economically, socially, and politically equal.	Opportunities for women increased, but women were still expected to fulfill traditional duties in the home.
Repressive institutions such as marriage will be replaced by "an openly legalized system of free love."	Many communist countries remained very sexually conservative.
Nationalism, exposed as part of the elite's "divide and conquer" strategy, will be eliminated.	Though discouraged from doing so, people clung to old national and ethnic identities.

A final aspect of society that communist countries sought to change was national and ethnic identity. As part of the superstructure, nationalism and ethnicity were seen as mechanisms by which the ruling elite pit the working classes of different countries against one another to divide and rule them. With the advent of the world communist revolution, such divisions were expected to disappear, to be replaced by equality and harmony among all peoples. As a result, communist parties tended to reject any overt expressions of nationalism and ethnicity, though national and ethnic identities often lurked beneath the surface. For example, encompassed within the vast Soviet Union were many ethnic groups, although the Communist Party tended to be dominated by Russians, who made up the single largest ethnic group. Many non-Russians resented this Russian domination. Many Eastern Europeans also viewed communist rule as little more than Russian imperialism; their national identities were therefore sharpened, not erased. This simmering nationalism played an important role in the fall of communism in Eastern Europe and the Soviet Union.

The Collapse of Communism

In retrospect, it may seem obvious that communism was bound to fail, and yet on the eve of its collapse in Europe few expected that it would happen anytime soon. Two factors played an important role in bringing about its sudden decline.

The first was the reemergence of Cold War struggles between the Soviet Union and the United States. After the tense decades of the 1950s and 1960s, which were marked by international competition, arms races, and harrowing events such as the Cuban Missile Crisis, the United States and the Soviet Union settled into a period of détente, in which peaceful coexistence became the main goal. But détente lasted less than a decade. The Soviet Union's invasion of Afghanistan in 1979 to prop up a failing communist regime there and the election of Ronald Reagan as president of the United States in 1980 soured relations between the two countries. Reagan, who viewed the Soviet Union as an "evil empire," embarked on a new policy of military buildup. Growing economic stagnation made it difficult for the Soviet Union to meet this expensive challenge.

At the same time that the United States and the Soviet Union entered a new and costly stage of the Cold War, a new generation of political leaders rose to power in the Soviet Union, among them Mikhail Gorbachev, who was chosen as general secretary of the Communist Party in 1985. Unlike his predecessors, Gorbachev recognized the stagnation of the Soviet system and understood the cost of a new arms race. He thus proposed reforming international relations and domestic politics, revitalizing both the Soviet Union and communist thought.

At the domestic level, Gorbachev initiated the twin policies of glasnost (openness) and perestroika (restructuring), with the intention of liberalizing and reforming communism. **Glasnost** encouraged public debate, with the hope that a frank discussion of the shortcomings of the system would help foster change and increase the legitimacy of the regime. **Perestroika**, or actual institutional reforms in the economy and political system, would flow from this critique. These reforms were expected to include some limited forms of democratic participation and market-based incentives in the economy. Moderate reform, not wholesale transformation, was Gorbachev's goal.[12]

In the international arena, Gorbachev similarly proposed widespread, if moderate, changes. To reduce the Soviet Union's military burdens and improve relations with Western countries, he began to loosen his country's control over Eastern Europe, which had been under the thumb of the Soviet Union since the end of World War II. Gorbachev hoped that some limited liberalization in the region would ease tensions with Europe and the United States, enabling expanded trade and other economic ties.

But as Alexis de Tocqueville famously wrote with regard to the French monarchy, the most dangerous moment for a bad government is usually when it begins to reform itself. Glasnost encouraged public debate, but rather than simply criticize corruption or the quality of consumer goods, as Gorbachev expected, the public began to challenge the very nature of the political system. Ethnic groups within the Soviet Union and citizens of Eastern European states also used glasnost to agitate for greater freedom from Russian domination.

Perestroika had similarly unexpected effects. By seeking political and economic reform, Gorbachev threatened those within the party who had long benefited from the status quo. Political leaders, administrators, factory bosses, and many other members of the *nomenklatura* resisted reform, leading to infighting and instability. This problem was compounded by the uncertainty over how far Gorbachev's reforms would go. Confusion deepened within the party, the state, and society about where communism and the Soviet Union were heading.

Meanwhile, among the Soviet Union's satellite states, change was proceeding faster than anyone expected. In 1989, civil society rapidly reasserted itself across Eastern Europe and used Gorbachev's new hands-off policy to oppose their countries' communist regimes, demanding open elections and an end to one-party rule. Eastern European Communist Party leaders, realizing that the Soviet Union would no longer intervene militarily to support them, had little choice but to acquiesce. As a result, by 1990 communists had been swept from their monopolies on power across the region. In most cases, this regime change was largely peaceful.

The Soviet Union would not be far behind. By 1991, the country was in deep turmoil: limited reforms had increased the public's appetite for greater change;

Communist History

1848	Karl Marx and Friedrich Engels write *The Communist Manifesto*, a central document in communist thought.
1917	Vladimir Lenin leads the Russian Revolution, creating the Soviet Union as the world's first communist country.
1930s	Josef Stalin begins to arrest and execute Soviet Communist Party members and others to consolidate power and terrorize the population.
1945	The Soviet Army occupies Eastern Europe, imposing communist regimes; tensions between the United States and the Soviet Union lead to the Cold War.
1949	The Chinese Communist Party, led by Mao Zedong, gains control over mainland China after a long struggle against local opposition and Japanese occupiers.
1953	Stalin dies.
1956	Nikita Khrushchev denounces Stalin's use of terror and allows limited open debate; debate turns to unrest in parts of Eastern Europe; protests in Hungary lead to open revolution against communism; Hungarian revolution put down by the Soviet army.
1966–76	Mao unleashes the Cultural Revolution in China; the student "Red Guard" attacks symbols of precommunism and party leaders accused of having grown too conservative; the Cultural Revolution used to eliminate Mao's political rivals.
1976	Mao Zedong dies; China and the United States begin to improve relations; Deng Xiaoping rises to power and starts to enact widespread economic reforms.
1979	The Soviet Union invades Afghanistan, worsening relations between the United States and Soviet Union; the Cold War reintensifies.
1985	Mikhail Gorbachev becomes general secretary of the Soviet Communist Party and begins to carry out economic and political liberalization.
1989	Student protests for political reform in China's Tiananmen Square crushed by the military.

| 1989–90 | Eastern Europeans seize on reforms in the Soviet Union to press for dramatic political change; largely peaceful political protests lead to free elections and the elimination of communist rule in Eastern Europe. |
| 1991 | Increasing turmoil in the Soviet Union leads communist conservatives to oust Gorbachev and seize power; coup fails because of weak military support and public demonstrations; the Soviet Union breaks into fifteen separate states. |

the end of communism in Eastern Europe further emboldened opposition within the Soviet Union; and ethnic conflict and nationalism were on the rise as various groups sought political power.[13] Communist hard-liners eventually tried to stop the reform process through a coup d'état, seizing power and detaining Gorbachev. However, these leaders lacked the support of important actors, such as the military, and public demonstrations helped bring the poorly planned coup to an end.[14]

In the aftermath of the 1991 coup and in response to their own ethnic constituents, the individual republics that formed the Soviet Union broke up, forming fifteen new independent countries, of which Russia is but one. But communism did not collapse everywhere. Although 1989 marked liberalization and the first moves toward democracy in Eastern Europe and the Soviet Union, similar protests in China that year, led by students and encouraged by Gorbachev's example, were met with deadly military force in Tiananmen Square, Beijing. Communist leaders in China did not heed public demands for reform and political liberalization and showed themselves both willing and able to use the army to violently quell peaceful protests. Why did the Soviet Union and China go down such different paths? We will turn to this question at the end of the chapter (see the "Institutions in Action" box, p. 286).

The Transformation of Political Institutions

So far, we have discussed the communist theory regarding the origins of and solutions to inequality, the difficulties in translating theory into reality, and how institutions controlled by the state unraveled across most of the communist world. Yet although the downfall of communism was dramatic, what followed was no less awesome. Postcommunist countries faced, and continue to face, the challenge of building new political, economic, and social institutions to strike a new balance between freedom and equality. No country had ever made such a dramatic change in all three areas at once, and this task has met with varying degrees of success.

Reorganizing the State and Constructing a Democratic Regime

An underlying task in the transition from communism has been to reorganize the state in terms of its autonomy and capacity. Under communism, the party-state was able to dominate virtually all aspects of human relations without any effective check. But with the collapse of communism, the party was ejected from its leading role in political life. This left many formerly communist countries with a sprawling, if not always powerful or particularly legitimate, postcommunist state, which did not embody the rule of law.

Postcommunist countries have also faced the prospect of building a democratic regime where authoritarianism has long been the norm. This project requires numerous tasks: revising or rewriting the constitution to establish civil rights and freedoms; creating a separation of powers between branches of government; choosing between different kinds of executive and legislative institutions; establishing electoral laws and regulating political parties; and doing all of this in a way that generates support among the majority of actors in society.

Civil rights have been a final area of concern. Under communism, constitutions typically established an elaborate set of civil liberties, though in reality such liberties were largely ignored by those in power. With the collapse of communism, the challenge has been to expand and protect civil liberties. This has meant not only strengthening the rule of law so that those once-hollow rights could be enforced, but also deciding what kinds of rights should be enshrined in the constitution and who should be the final arbiter of disputes over these rights. The role of constitutional courts has been an important issue in countries where traditionally the judiciary had been neither powerful nor independent.

Evaluating Political Transitions

Over twenty years have passed since communism began to collapse in Eastern Europe and the former Soviet Union. How have the postcommunist countries' political transitions fared? The picture is mixed. Freedom House, a nongovernmental organization in the United States that studies democracy around the world, ranks countries on a one-to-seven freedom scale, the most-free countries given a one and the least-free a seven. This ranking is based on such considerations as electoral competition, freedoms of speech and assembly, rule of law, levels of corruption, and protection of human and economic rights.

As Table 9.2 shows, a number of postcommunist countries have made dramatic strides toward democracy and the rule of law, to such an extent that Freedom House now considers them consolidated democracies—meaning that their democratic regimes have been ranked highly on the Freedom House scale for a decade or so and are therefore stable and largely institutionalized. The majority of these consolidated democracies can be found in central Europe (such as Hungary, Poland, and the Czech Republic) and the Baltics (Estonia, Latvia, and Lithuania), areas that share a precommunist history of greater economic development, civil society, democratic institutions, and experience with the rule of law; they also enjoyed more contact with Western Europe and a shorter period of communist rule. All of these factors may help explain why democratic transition in these regions has been more successful and culminated in EU membership. Even the Balkans, which experienced widespread violence and civil conflict less than two decades ago, have seen their democratic practices improve markedly since then, and the EU continues to expand into this region. Many of these countries were listed in our previous chapter, having made the transition to advanced democracies. This is not to say that the legacies of communism have faded entirely away. In Chapter 5, we discussed Hungary's recent constitutional changes, driven by polarization in that country over the communist past, which many have argued could weaken democracy there.

As we move eastward, the situation is less promising. In many of the former Soviet states, including Russia, democracy is illiberal and weakly institutionalized or completely absent. These countries tend to be poorer, with little historical experience of democracy and a long period of Soviet control. In many of them, authoritarian leaders, often from the communist *nomenklatura*, have consolidated power in strong presidencies. Democratic rights and freedoms are restricted, civil society is weak, and those in power have enriched themselves through corrupt practices. Support for democracy is often very weak (Table 9.3).

Outside of Eastern Europe and the former Soviet Union, democracy has been slow to spread, and several communist regimes continue to hold on to power: China, Laos, Vietnam, North Korea, and Cuba. Elsewhere in Asia and in Africa, communist regimes have given way, but this has often resulted in state collapse and civil war. Most notable is Afghanistan; upon the Soviet Union's withdrawal from that country in 1989, civil war raged until 1996, when the Taliban gained power over most of the country, paving the way for the eventual establishment of Al Qaeda.

TABLE 9.2 — Freedom in Selected Communist and Postcommunist Systems, 2011

(1 MOST FREE, 7 NOT FREE)

	POLITICAL RIGHTS	CIVIL LIBERTIES	REGIME TYPE
Poland	1	1	Liberal democracy
Hungary	1	1	Liberal democracy
Estonia	1	1	Liberal democracy
Czech Republic	1	1	Liberal democracy
Croatia	1	2	Liberal democracy
Latvia	2	2	Liberal democracy
Bulgaria	2	2	Liberal democracy
Romania	2	2	Liberal democracy
Albania	3	3	Illiberal democracy
Moldova	3	3	Illiberal democracy
Ukraine	3	3	Illiberal democracy
Georgia	4	3	Illiberal democracy
Kyrgyzstan	5	5	Authoritarian
Russia	6	5	Authoritarian
Tajikistan	6	5	Authoritarian
Belarus	7	6	Authoritarian
China	7	6	Authoritarian
Uzbekistan	7	7	Authoritarian

Source: Freedom House.

TABLE 9.3

Support for Authoritarianism, 2005–08

HAVING A STRONG LEADER WHO DOES NOT HAVE TO BOTHER WITH PARLIAMENT AND ELECTIONS IS ... (PERCENT ANSWERING)

COUNTRY	VERY/FAIRLY GOOD	BAD/VERY BAD
Slovenia	20	80
Poland	30	70
Serbia	32	68
China	36	64
Georgia	54	46
Russia	57	43
Ukraine	65	35
Moldova	67	33
Bulgaria	68	32
Romania	78	22

Source: World Values Survey.

Thus, not everywhere has the end of communism been peaceful or democratic, and in some ways, it created a path for the rise of terrorism and the wars in Afghanistan and Iraq. The legacies of communism and the Cold War in these regions are significant.

The Transformation of Economic Institutions

In addition to transforming the state and the regime, transitions from communism have also confronted the task of reestablishing some separation between the state and the economy. This involves two processes: privatization, or the transfer of state-held property into private hands, and marketization, or the re-creation of market forces of supply and demand. In both cases, decisions about how to carry out these changes and to what end were influenced by different political-economic alternatives. Let's consider the ways in which privatization and marketization can be approached before we investigate the different paths postcommunist countries have taken in each area.

Privatization and Marketization

The transition from communism to capitalism requires a redefinition of property. To generate economic growth and limit the power of the state, the state must reentrust economic resources to the public, placing them back into private hands. But the task of privatization is neither easy nor clear. In fact, before 1989 no country had ever gone from a communist economy to a capitalist one, so no model existed.

Among the many questions and concerns facing the postcommunist countries was how to place a price on the various elements of the economy—factories, shops, land, apartments. To privatize these assets, the state first must determine their values, something difficult in a system where no market has existed. And who should get these assets? Should they be given away? Sold to the highest bidder? Made available to foreign investors? Each option has its own advantages in developing a thriving economy but also risks increasing inequality and generating public resentment.

Privatization was carried out in a number of different ways, depending on the country and its economic assets. Small businesses, like restaurants or retail shops, were often sold directly to their employees, and some countries also sold many large businesses, like automobile manufacturers, to the highest bidder, often foreign investors. Other countries essentially distributed shares in firms to the public as a whole. Scholars debated the benefits of each model, but in the end each form, whether alone or in combination, was shown to work well in some circumstances and badly in others.

IN FOCUS

Reestablishing Separation of State and Economy

- Privatization: the transfer of state-held property into private hands.

- Marketization: the re-creation of the market forces of supply and demand.

No matter what the privatization process, ultimately there were many firms in postcommunist countries that were overstaffed, outdated, and unable to turn a profit in a market economy. Most problematic were very large industrial firms, such as coal mines and steel plants built in the early years of industrialization; these antiquated behemoths could not compete in the international market. Such firms often needed to be sold or radically downsized, leading to unemployment in a society where employment had previously been guaranteed. Such firms sometimes employed thousands of people and represented the main source of work in a city or region. As a result, in some countries privatization proceeded slowly for fear of widespread unemployment and resulting social unrest.

In addition to re-creating private property, states needed to re-create a market in which property, labor, goods, and services could all function in a competitive environment that would determine their value. On the surface, marketization appears easier than privatization—a simple matter of eliminating central planning and allowing the market to resurface naturally. But marketization, too, is a complicated process. One issue of debate concerned how rapidly marketization should take place. Some argued that given the profound nature of the economic transformation in postcommunist states, changes should be gradual to minimize any social disruptions that might undermine these fledgling economies and democracies. In particular, supporters of this "gradualism" feared that sudden marketization would lead to a wild jump in prices as sellers became able to charge whatever they wanted for their goods. Inflation and even hyperinflation could result, undermining confidence in the transition process and generating widespread poverty. Others rejected these arguments, advocating rapid market reforms that would free prices and bring an end to central planning and state subsidies for businesses virtually overnight—a policy known as **shock therapy**. Such changes would be painful and might initially trigger high rates of inflation, but the pain would be shorter than that accompanying gradualism.

In choosing particular forms of privatization and marketization, postcommunist countries adopted new political-economic models—some gravitating toward the social democratic models of Western Europe, others to the liberalism of the United States and the United Kingdom, and still others to more mercantilist policies.

Evaluating Economic Transitions

How successful have all of these reforms been? The answer again depends on what country you are looking at. Table 9.4 shows some of the results of 20 years of transition. In Eastern Europe and the Baltics, economic reforms have borne fruit—in some cases, dramatically so. Slovenia is now as wealthy as Greece; Slovakia and

TABLE 9.4

Economic Indicators in Selected Communist and Postcommunist Countries, 2010

	PER CAPITA GDP, 2010 (PPP US $)	2010 GDP AS A PERCENTAGE OF 1989 GDP	TRANSPARENCY INTERNATIONAL CORRUPTION RANKING (1=LEAST CORRUPT)
Slovenia	28,200	150	27
Hungary	18,800	130	50
Poland	18,800	190	41
Croatia	17,400	100	62
Russia*	15,900	100	154
Latvia*	14,700	90	59
Romania	1,600	120	69
Azerbaijan*	10,900	210	134
Serbia	10,900	70	78
Cuba	9,900	153	69
Albania	8,000	170	87
China	7,600	1,200	78
Ukraine*	6,700	60	134
Armenia*	5,700	140	123
Georgia*	4,900	60	68
Moldova*	2,500	50	105

*Former republic of the Soviet Union

Sources: CIA, World Bank, European Bank for Reconstruction and Development.

Hungary are comparable to Portugal. In contrast, many of the former Soviet republics have not done nearly as well, some having GDPs that are actually lower than they were in 1989. Why this variation? The countries that have done particularly well have benefited from many of the factors we discussed earlier: shorter periods of Soviet control; more precommunist experience with industrialization, markets, and private property; closer ties with Western Europe; and strong support from the European Union (EU), including membership. The countries that have done less well have experienced just the opposite. In these countries, freeing up markets often led to uncontrollable inflation and a rapid decline in the standard of living. These problems were compounded by the way privatization was carried out, with many of the most valuable assets falling into the hands of the old *nomenklatura* or a few private individuals, typically supported by corrupt political leaders. Even countries that have done well, such as Azerbaijan, owe their economic success to natural resources (oil and gas) rather than the development of a private sector. One theme that runs through all these cases is the correlation between economic growth and the rule of law. Where the rule of law is weak, economic transition is much less successful, because entrepreneurs (both domestic and international) lack a predictable environment in which to invest, while political leaders and state officials use their positions to siphon off resources for themselves.

Overall, postcommunist countries have seen an increase in inequality, poverty, and unemployment, which is to be expected as markets and private property become central economic forces. Where this has been balanced by economic prosperity for the majority of the population, support for change has been stronger. When the majority of the population feels worse off, as in much of the former Soviet Union, economic change has bred resentment, nostalgia for the old order, and obstacles to democratization. A notable example is Russia, where during the last decade many large industries and natural resources have been renationalized and mercantilist economic policies have been adopted.

Outside of Eastern Europe and the former Soviet Union, the success rate of economic transition has been equally varied. Much attention has been focused on China, which is still controlled by a communist party but in many ways can be thought of as "postcommunist" in its economic system. Since the 1970s, China's reforms have included a dramatic expansion of private business and agriculture, all with the support of the Chinese Communist Party. The slogan of this set of economic reforms—"to get rich is glorious"—sounds anything but Marxist, and it is rooted in the practical realization that earlier drives for rapid economic growth led to disaster. Some observers argue that these reforms have succeeded where those in many other communist and postcommunist countries have failed because the Chinese introduced economic transition while restricting political change, so as to better manage the course of reform. Indeed, since 1989 the Chinese economy has grown by leaps and bounds, lifting hundreds of millions out of poverty and dramatically transforming the country, not to mention world trade.

Yet the Chinese model has its own problems. Alongside economic growth and the development of a free market and private property, problems such as inflation, corruption, unemployment, and growing inequality have also surfaced, often exacerbated by the still-powerful presence of the state in the Chinese economy. The weakness of the rule of law—a system where both individuals and the government are accountable to the law—only compounds these problems. China's rapid development has been profound; the question is to what extent this will continue into the future. Some see in China a growing economic superpower that will eclipse the economies of much of Asia and perhaps the world. This development could, in turn, foster a middle class that would pave the way for the democratization of one-fifth of the world's population. Others believe that the Chinese "miracle" covers up serious problems, like conflict between urban and rural, rich and poor, as well as significant environmental problems. China could see a future of greater development, greater liberty, and greater conflict, all at the same time.[15]

The Transformation of Societal Institutions

Like political systems and economies, societies, too, have been fundamentally transformed in postcommunist countries. Where once communist control asserted a single unquestionable understanding of human relations and development, people now face a world much more uncertain and unclear. Individuals in postcommunist societies have the freedom to act more independently, but this potential carries with it greater risk. The elimination of an all-encompassing ideology from people's lives has created a social vacuum that must be filled. In all of these countries, the transition from communism has been a wrenching process as people adjust to new realities and seek new individual and collective identities.

Re-creating Identities

This transformation of society has manifested itself in a number of different ways. Religion, once suppressed by Communist parties, has resurfaced in many countries. In Eastern Europe and parts of the former Soviet Union, various Christian groups from western Europe and the United State have made many new converts. In other parts of the former Soviet Union, such as central Asia, Islam has reemerged as a powerful force, with thousands of mosques and religious schools built in part with funds from other Muslim countries, such as Saudi Arabia. In many countries, this return to religion has helped rebuild social norms and values and has also led to the emergence of fundamentalism and increased conflict between politics and religion. In China, too, new and old religious movements are gaining strength. For example, the spiritual group Falun Gong, which attracted between 70 million and 100 million followers in the 1990s, was the target of a harsh crackdown by government authorities, who feared any organization that could command greater loyalty than the regime.[16] Underground Christian churches in China may claim a similar number of members, and Islam is a strong and perhaps growing religion in far-western China among Turkic peoples. In the face of economic hardship, corruption, and often still-oppressive regimes, this religious resurgence should not be surprising: religion can play an important role in providing people with a sense of community and purpose.

Like religion, ethnic and national identities have reemerged as potent forms of group identification. In many postcommunist countries, both leaders and publics have sought to reinstill national pride and resurrect the values, symbols, and ideas that bind people together. The scope of this task varies among the postcommunist countries. In much of Eastern Europe, a clear sense of ethnic and national identity has existed for many generations, and in spite of communist rule, many of these social structures not only remained intact but were reinforced as a form of resistance. In contrast, across the diverse ethnic groups of the former Soviet Union, national identity has historically been much weaker. Many of these peoples have few ethnic or national institutions to draw on, and their identities are being not so much resurrected as created from scratch, with new words, anthems, symbols, and myths. All such identities can be a double-edged sword, of course. Although they can help mobilize the public and provide stability in a time of great transition, religious, ethnic, and national identities can also generate division and conflict, particularly when several identities coexist in one country or in opposition to the state or regime.

The changes underway in social identities cannot help but affect gender relations as well. Recall our earlier discussion of how communist theory advanced the radical notion of gender equality. Although equality was not realized in practice, women were incorporated into the workforce and provided with social benefits that generated new opportunities for them. With the end of communism, however, many of these policies and institutions have been weakened or challenged. Critics have attacked many communist-era practices such as easy access to abortions, while economic reforms have cut back much of the elaborate social safety net that once benefited women and families. The reemergence of religion has also challenged women's roles in society in some cases.

Evaluating Societal Transitions

New societies in postcommunist countries have developed in very different ways. In some, the emergence, or reemergence, of religious and national identities has contributed to violence and civil war. In Eastern Europe, the dissolution of Yugoslavia pitted ethnic and religious groups against one another, claiming more than 200,000 lives. Parts of the former Soviet Union, such as the nations of Tajikistan, Uzbekistan, Moldova, Azerbaijan, and Armenia, as well as the Russian region of Chechnya, have also seen violent religious and ethnic conflicts, in which thousands have been killed. Many of these conflicts continue. Finally, the almost endless wars in Afghanistan since the 1970s are yet another tragedy whose consequences have rippled throughout the domestic and international communities. In Afghanistan during the 1980s, volunteers from numerous Muslim countries, such as Osama bin Laden, fought alongside Afghan guerrillas against Soviet occupation in what they saw as a need to defend Muslims from atheist communism. At the end of that conflict and with the dissolution of the Soviet Union, some of these fighters turned their attention toward the postcommunist world, taking up the causes of Muslim populations in Central Asia, the Caucasus, and the Balkans. What were regional and ethnic conflicts quickly became international and religious ones.[17] Other fighters would later regroup in Afghanistan, forming, under bin Laden's leadership, Al Qaeda—"the base"—as a launching pad for this international jihad.

However, much of the postcommunist world has been largely peaceful over the past decade, with ethnic and religious conflicts resolved or averted. While data indicate that nationalism is strong in many postcommunist countries, in most cases this has not directly translated into nationalist movements that threaten democracy or ethnic minorities. In the area of religion, too, surveys show that in many postcommunist countries people do not believe that faith is an important precondition for political leadership or that religion is a necessary foundation for morality. An important distinction appears to be Central Asia, where religion has become an important force since the breakup of the Soviet Union.

Of particular concern are the futures of Russia and China. In both countries nationalism has been growing, generated partly by the government as a way to shore up legitimacy in the absence or waning of communist ideology. This nationalism, which emphasizes mistreatment by the West and the unique nature of Chinese and Russian identity, may be part of the difficult transition these countries are making. It may fade in time, but it has complicated relations with the rest of the world, particularly over such issues as Russian influence over postcommunist countries and Chinese authority over Tibet and Taiwan.[18] Given the size and power of these two countries, their evolving national identities will strongly affect the rest of the world.

Gender relations in postcommunist countries are equally interesting. The UN uses several indicators to measure the standard of living and differences in that standard between genders. The UN's Gender Inequality Index (Table 9.5) measures inequality between women and men in three areas: health (maternal mortality and adolescent fertility), empowerment (share of parliamentary seats and secondary and higher education levels) and labor (women's participation in the workforce). When

TABLE 9.5 — Gender Inequality Index, 2011

Country	Rank	Country	Rank
Sweden	1	Vietnam	48
Germany	7	Azerbaijan	50
France	10	Romania	55
Japan	14	Kazakhstan	56
Czech Republic	17	Ukraine	57
Canada	20	Russia	59
Poland	25	Armenia	60
Croatia	27	Tajikistan	61
Slovenia	28	Georgia	73
United Kingdom	34	Mexico	79
China	35	Brazil	80
Latvia	36	South Africa	94
Hungary	39	Iran	98
Bulgaria	40	Laos	107
Moldova	46	India	122
United States	47	Afghanistan	141

Note: The Gender Inequality Index is a composite measure reflecting inequality in health, education, participation in legislature, and participation in the workforce. Countries are ranked from 1 to 145; countries in italics are included for comparison.

Source: UN Development Program.

Why Did Reform Fail in the Soviet Union but Succeed in China?

One of the greatest puzzles regarding the collapse of communism has to do with a revolution that did not happen. In 1989, as communism was coming to an end in Eastern Europe and the Soviet Union was on the verge of breaking up, China, too, was experiencing a wave of political protests that threatened to bring down the communist regime. Most notably, student protesters occupied Tiananmen Square in Beijing, the political center of China, calling for liberalization and political reform. At its peak, these protests numbered in the tens of thousands in Beijing alone, and spread to other cities throughout the country. Many observers believed that China, like the Soviet Union and Eastern Europe, was at a turning point. The movement expanded from students to professionals and the working class, and the protests were amplified by the widespread presence of the international media, which in turn influenced the actions of the movement.

However, the revolution never occured. After several weeks of protest, the Chinese leadership declared martial law. Although there were massive public protests to block the approach of the military, army units violently forced their way into Tiananmen Square, dispersing the protestors. Estimates are that several hundred died, and thousands were arrested. This outcome is puzzling in comparison to what happened in the Soviet Union and Eastern Europe, where most regimes were overwhelmed by, and capitulated to, largely nonviolent protests not unlike those in China. What led to such different outcomes?

While a combination of factors helps explain the diverging paths, we can outline a few individual explanations here, relying on the institutional categories we discussed in Chapter 5: modernization, elites, society, international relations, and culture.

In Eastern Europe and the Soviet Union, modernization under communism had generated a well-educated class of professionals who were able to articulate their desires for greater political and economic independence. This nascent civil society reacted to a centrally planned economy that was increasingly unable to deliver economic growth or even maintain existing standards of living. Elites in power lost legitimacy—not just in the eyes of society at large, but also amongst themselves. Gorbachev initiated reforms precisely because he faced this crisis of legitimacy and realized that even the ranks of the party no longer had faith in the viability of communism.

As these reforms began to accelerate faster and go further than elites anticipated, international factors amplified this process. Civil society in Eastern Europe looked to the rest of Europe and the EU as a model to emulate. Moreover, Gorbachev's desire to end the Cold War led him to release the Soviet Union's military control over Eastern Europe, emboldening opposition forces there into challenging and toppling those in power. Cultural forces also played a role, as many Eastern European societies viewed their protests as part of a quest to "return to Europe," from which they felt they had been separated while under Soviet rule. At the same time, rival nationalisms within the Soviet Union led to violent clashes, even outright war, between different ethnic groups that helped bring down the country as a whole.

Meanwhile, China in 1989 could not have been more different. Modernization was far behind the levels of the Soviet Union or Eastern Europe. The country remained overwhelmingly agricultural, and while the student protests did contain the seed of civil society, it was small relative to the size of the Chinese public as a whole. Further, while economic reforms in the Soviet Union in the 1980s were a late and limited response to the stagnation of a centrally planned industrial economy, China's reforms had begun earlier and had led to the doubling of their economy over the course of that same decade. Given the chaos and economic disasters that accompanied the Great Leap Forward and the Cultural Revolution, many Chinese could look upon the country in 1989 as finally moving in the right direction, with their lives showing substantial improvement. This in turn bolstered the government's legitimacy both within and outside the regime. Public support for the Communist Party remained strong, and party members and leaders retained a firm conviction that the Tiananmen Square protests would only undermine the country's progress.

With regard to international factors, while it is true that the student protests were widely covered by the foreign media, the Chinese leadership did not need to worry that the use of force would jeopardize the country's future in the same way that Gorbachev believed that the use of force would prevent any integration with Europe or an end to the Cold War. Gorbachev and others argued that communist reforms would mean that Russia and Eastern Europe could "return to Europe" or "rejoin the west." There was no similar sentiment in China, which, if anything, sought recognition as a power unto itself.

Finally, cultural factors may have played some role as well. The absence of any tradition of democratic practices in China made it difficult for student leaders to clearly articulate their objectives for reform and led to factions and disorder within the movement itself.

Protestors burning a Communist Party flag in Romania, 1989. Romania was unusual in that the Communist regime fell only through a violent revolution in which hundreds were killed.

This kind of comparative analysis of these differing institutional trends and state trajectories helps make sense of this puzzle, but we should be careful not to assume we can fully explain the outcomes in either of these cases. Chinese liberalization akin to that in the Soviet Union was perhaps closer to occuring than it seems. Documents leaked from the Chinese government suggest that party leader Deng Xiaoping had to push the government and military toward the use of force. In his absence, might Tiananmen have become the starting point for political change? If so, what kind of government would we see in China today?

1. How did the level of modernization in the Soviet Union versus that in China contribute to differences in civil society?

2. How might economic performance explain the difference in the public's view of party elites between the Soviet Union and China?

3. In what way was the "Return to Europe" sentiment an international factor in the Soviet Union's path to reform? In what way was it a cultural factor?

we look at the data, we see that many postcommunist countries perform well, ranking higher on the index than the United States or the United Kingdom. However, many others lag further behind, particularly in the Caucasus (Georgia, Armenia) and Central Asia (Azerbaijan, Tajikistan). This range of rankings confirms that as we move further away from communism and its legacies, these states will resemble each other less and less, as some continue to develop while others stagnate or even decline.

In Sum: The Legacy of Communism

According to Marxist thought, capitalism would inevitably lead to great industrialization but also to great injustice, a contradiction that would result in its downfall. On the ruins of capitalism, communism would build a society of total equality. But constructing communism proved to be a daunting task. People in communist systems found little incentive for hard work and innovation and had little freedom to express themselves individually.

For the Soviet Union and Eastern Europe, attempts to solve these problems led to outright collapse. One might find an apt analogy in attempts to renovate a dilapidated house that reveal the whole structure to be unsound and that only make the situation worse. At that point, one has to either demolish the whole structure or be demolished by it. In 1989, people in a number of Eastern European countries chose to demolish the institutions of communism. Communist structures in the Soviet Union eventually collapsed on the Communist Party and Soviet society. China seems to be in a process of endless (and perhaps precarious) remodeling, while other communist countries, such as North Korea, have yet to carry out any major reforms.

It is not clear what the coming decades will bring to the postcommunist world. All of the societies in this world are attempting to grapple again with the challenge of balancing freedom and equality. New political, economic, and social institutions are needed, but in many cases they must be forged out of the rubble of the old order, a situation that is creating unique difficulties and contradictions. Over the past decade, both individual freedom and collective inequality have grown in many countries. Increased civil liberties have arisen alongside poverty, and society has been reborn alongside conflict and hostility.

The results of this diverse process have been dramatically different across the communist and postcommunist world. In some countries, we see the institutionalization of democracy and capitalism; in others, authoritarianism and state-controlled economies remain in place. Moreover, it is apparent that over time these countries will grow increasingly dissimilar. Democratic consolidation and economic growth in Eastern Europe appear to have placed many of these countries on the path to becoming advanced democracies. Within parts of the former Soviet Union, however, economic stagnation or decline, political instability, and nondemocratic rule are more common; those countries more closely resemble the less-developed world. China and Russia remain question marks.

Communism as a set of political institutions may now be finished. Yet even if this is the case, the motivation that drove their creation—the desire to eliminate inequality—remains. And in fact, these concerns have fed a recent wave of populist ideas in Latin America, inspired in part by Marxist and Leninist thought. As long as inequality and poverty remain, there will be room for ideologies that seek to use politics and the state to create economic justice.

For Further Reading

RS> Bunce, Valerie and Sharon Wolchik. *Defeating Authoritarian Leaders in Postcommunist Countries* (New York: Cambridge University Press, 2011).

Darden, Keith and Anna Grzymala-Busse. "The Great Divide: Literacy, Nationalism, and the Communist Collapse." *World Politics* 59, no. 1 (October 2006).

RS> Gat, Azar. "The Return of Authoritarian Great Powers." *Foreign Affairs* (July/August 2007).

RS> He, Baogang and Mark E. Warren. "Authoritarian Deliberation: The Deliberative Turn in Chinese Political Development." *Perspectives on Politics* 9, no. 2 (June 2011).

RS> Krastev, Ivan. "Paradoxes of the New Authoritarianism." *Journal of Democracy* 22, no. 2 (April 2011).

RS> Marx, Karl and Friedrich Engels. "Manifesto of the Communist Party." *Selected Works in Three Volumes*, Vol. 1 (Moscow, USSR: Progress Publishers, 1969).

McAuley, Marcy. *Soviet Politics 1917–1991* (New York: Oxford University Press, 1992).

 Visit StudySpace for quizzes and other review material.
www.norton.com/studyspace

- **Vocabulary Flashcards of All Key Terms**
- **Chapter Review Quizzes**
- **Complete Study Reviews and Outlines**

RS>
Reader Selection

Highlighted selections are included in *Essential Readings in Comparative Politics*, Fourth Edition.

Women receiving a microcredit loan from the Grameen Bank in Bangladesh. These small loans have been lauded by many as a key instrument in alleviating poverty, though others question microcredit's efficacy.

LESS-DEVELOPED AND NEWLY INDUSTRIALIZING COUNTRIES

KEY CONCEPTS

- Less-developed and newly industrializing countries have struggled with both economic and political development.

- Imperialism and colonialism strongly affected less-developed and newly industrializing countries' state, societal, and economic institutions.

- Many postimperial countries have suffered from ethnic and national division, limited economic growth, and weak states.

- Scholars and policy makers are increasingly turning to civil society, small-scale economic development, and political decentralization as pathways to development and democracy.

So far, we have investigated two major kinds of countries—the advanced democracies, often described as the First World; and communist and postcommunist countries, which have been known as the Second World. But these two categories leave out much of Latin America, Asia, and Africa. Many of the countries in these regions have had neither liberal democratic nor communist regimes. Of these countries, the vast majority have levels of economic industrialization far below those in the advanced democracies or the communist and postcommunist world. The traditional labeling of these countries as belonging to the Third World unhelpfully grouped together a diverse range of people and political systems according to what they were not, rather than what they were—what we call a residual category.

How, then, should we understand these countries? Whereas the advanced democracies are noted for their early modernization and capitalist development, and the communist states for their later, rapid, state-directed modernization and industrialization, the countries discussed in this chapter are characterized by their mixture of premodern and modern institutions and their hybrid forms of economic, societal, and political institutions, both foreign-imposed and indigenous.

In this chapter, we will attempt to develop some ideas and categories to investigate and understand these countries. We will begin by distinguishing between newly industrializing and less-developed countries and examining the relationship between freedom and equality in both groups. From there we will look at some of the fundamental experiences and institutions that these countries share, particularly those associated with imperialism and colonialism. Although imperialism had different effects in different parts of the world, we can generalize about its legacies. Next we will consider what challenges and obstacles these countries have faced after gaining independence. How does a country reconcile freedom and equality when the conditions may favor neither? And how is it that some countries have managed to enjoy economic and political development while others have stagnated or declined? These topics will lead us into a final discussion of the prospects for political, economic, and societal development in newly industrializing and less-developed countries. What policies might help generate greater democracy, political stability, and economic prosperity in these countries? The difficulties they face are great and the tasks daunting. But out of such challenges can emerge new ideas and innovations with the potential for bringing about positive change.

Freedom and Equality in the Newly Industrializing and Less-Developed Countries

The countries of what was traditionally referred to as the Third World are often divided into two groups that indicate important differences in their levels of development. Over the past fifty years, some of these countries, particularly in Asia and parts of Latin America, have experienced dramatic rates of economic growth and democratization, to the point that they now resemble the advanced democracies in many ways. These are typically known as **newly industrializing countries (NICs)**. Although this name emphasizes their rapid economic growth, in recent years many

NICs have also shown a marked tendency toward democratization and political and social stability, such that many of them are also listed in Chapter 8 as moving into the category of advanced democracies, such as Mexico and South Korea. In other cases, economic and political structures have remained weak or grown weaker over the past decades; some of these countries have slid into poverty, violence, and civil conflict. They are often referred to as the **less-developed countries (LDCs)**, a term that implies a lack of significant economic development or political institutionalization (Table 10.1).

As with postcommunist countries, newly industrializing and less-developed countries have grown increasingly dissimilar, making it difficult to place them in a single category. However, comparisons can help us understand these variations. Why have some countries broken out of the trap of underdevelopment and others not? Is it a question of how states are constructed? Of the kinds of regimes or political-economic systems they have? Of the absence or presence of democracy? Of their ethnic, national, or religious institutions? Of culture? Are there lessons that could be drawn from the NICs and adapted by LDCs?

Before we address present problems, we should turn to history. Despite differences in their current conditions, less-developed and newly industrialized countries share a legacy of colonialism and imperialism and the experience of belonging to large empires, possessions of more-powerful states. Imperial rule, which lasted for decades or even centuries, dramatically and often rapidly transformed economic, political, and societal institutions in the colonized countries. Although resistance eventually brought down imperial rule, the changes wrought by this system could not be easily unmade. To better understand these institutional legacies, it is worth looking at them in some detail, though we should also keep in mind that history is not destiny—imperialism matters, but it is only one factor in explaining the problems of the postimperial world.

Imperialism and Colonialism

In the first three chapters of this book, we saw that over the past millennium, Europe, the Middle East, and Asia embarked on a series of dramatic societal, economic, and political changes that formed the outlines of what are now recognized as the hallmarks of modern society: ethnic and national identity, technological innovation, and political centralization. The growing power of modern societies was soon projected outward to conquer and incorporate new lands and peoples that could contribute to their rapid development. The result was the emergence of **empires**, which are defined as single political authorities that have under their

TABLE 10.1

Less-Developed and Newly Industrializing Countries, 2012

CENTRAL AND SOUTH AMERICA	ASIA	NORTH AFRICA AND MIDDLE EAST	SUB-SAHARAN AFRICA (CONTINUED)
Antigua & Barbuda	Afghanistan	Algeria	Equatorial Guinea
Argentina	Bahrain	Egypt	Gabon
Belize	Bangladesh	Eritrea	Gambia
Bolivia	Bhutan	Ethiopia	Ghana
Brazil	Brunei	Iran	Guinea
Chile	Burma (Myanmar)	Iraq	Guinea-Bissau
Colombia	Cambodia	Jordan	Ivory Coast
Costa Rica	Cyprus	Lebanon	Kenya
Dominica	Fiji	Libya	Lesotho
Dominican Republic	India	Morocco	Liberia
Ecuador	Indonesia	Oman	Madagascar
El Salvador	Kiribati	Qatar	Malawi
Grenada	Korea (South)	Saudi Arabia	Mali
Guatemala	Kuwait	Syria	Mauritania
Guyana	Laos	United Arab Emirates	Mauritius
Haiti	Malaysia	Yemen	Mozambique
Honduras	Maldives		Namibia
Jamaica	Marshall Islands	SUB-SAHARAN AFRICA	Niger
Mexico	Micronesia		Nigeria
Nicaragua	Nauru		Rwanda
Panama	Nepal	Angola	São Tomé and Príncipe
Paraguay	Palau	Benin	Senegal
Peru	Pakistan	Botswana	Seychelles
St. Kitts & Nevis	Papua New Guinea	Burkina Faso	Sierra Leone
St. Lucia	Philippines	Burundi	Somalia
St. Vincent & the Grenadines	Samoa	Cameroon	South Africa
Suriname	Singapore	Cape Verde	Sudan
Trinidad & Tobago	Solomon Islands	Central African Republic	Swaziland
Uruguay	Sri Lanka	Chad	Tanzania
Venezuela	Taiwan	Comoros	Togo
	Thailand	Congo (Republic of)	Tunisia
	Tonga	Congo (Democratic Republic of)	Uganda
EUROPE	Turkey	Djibouti	Zambia
	Tuvalu		Zimbabwe
Turkey	Vanuatu		
	Vietnam		

sovereignty a large number of external regions or territories and different peoples. Although this definition might lead one to conclude that any large, diverse country is an empire, central to the definition is the idea that lands and peoples that are not seen as an integral part of the country itself are nonetheless under its direct control. The term **imperialism** describes the system whereby a state extends its power to directly control territory, resources, and people beyond its borders. *Imperialism* is often used interchangeably with the term *colonialism*, though they are different. **Colonialism** indicates to a greater degree the physical occupation of a foreign territory through military force, businesses, or settlers. Colonialism, then, is often the means for consolidating an empire.

Although imperialist practices began many thousands of years ago, modern imperialism can be dated from the fifteenth century, when technological development in Europe, the Middle East, and Asia—advanced seafaring and military technology in particular—had advanced to such an extent that these countries were able to project their military might far overseas. In Asia, the powerful Chinese Empire turned away from this path. Having consolidated power hundreds of years before the states of Europe did, the Chinese state grew conservative and inflexible, interested more in maintaining the status quo than in striking out to acquire new lands. Indeed, at the same time that Europeans were setting out for the Americas, the Chinese were actually retreating from overseas voyages; by 1500, it had become illegal for Chinese subjects to build oceangoing vessels. Similarly, while the powerful Ottoman Empire in the Middle East expanded its power over much of the Arab world and into Asia, North Africa, and parts of Europe, nearly conquering Vienna in 1683, it also turned inward and lost interest in technological innovation and in expanding power beyond the Islamic world, for reasons that are open to debate. In contrast, the Europeans saw imperialism as a means to expand their resources,

---

IN FOCUS

Imperialism . . .

- Is a system in which a state extends its power beyond its borders to control other territories and peoples.

- Was propagated by European powers from the sixteenth to the twenty-first centuries.

- Is driven by economic, strategic, and religious motives.

- Often led to colonialism, the physical occupation of foreign territories.

markets, number of subjects, and territory in order to gain the upper hand in their frequent battles with one another.

What should be made clear is that the peoples who became subject to modern imperialism were not a blank slate, without any of their own institutions. On the contrary, many of the regions that were so dominated already possessed their own highly developed economic, political, and societal systems, in some cases as sophisticated as those found in Europe, or even more advanced. Nevertheless, they lacked the military power to withstand European imperial pressure.

Thus, in the 1500s Europe began a process of imperial expansion that would continue for nearly five centuries. Driven by economic and strategic motives as well as by a belief that Christianity and Western culture needed to be brought to the rest of the world, European empires stretched their power around the globe. First, Spain

TIMELINE — Modern Imperialism

1494	Following European discovery, Spain and Portugal partition the Americas between their two empires.
1519–36	Indigenous groups (Aztecs, Incas) are defeated by imperial powers in South America.
1602–52	Dutch begin to establish control over parts of Indonesian archipelago and southern Africa. English settlement begins in North America.
1810–25	Wars of independence in Latin America; Spanish and Portuguese rule is brought to an end.
1839–58	United Kingdom expands control into Asia, notably Hong Kong and India.
1884	The Berlin Conference; Africa is rapidly divided among European powers, notably France, Portugal, and Belgium.
1939–45	World War II catalyzes the eventual decolonization of Asia and Africa.
1947	Independence of India; first major decolonization of twentieth century.
1956–68	Independence of most British, French, and Belgian colonies in Africa after local rebellions against imperial rule.
1975	Independence of most former Portuguese colonies in Africa and Asia.
1997–99	Hong Kong (United Kingdom) and Macau (Portugal) returned to China.

and Portugal gained control over South and Central America. By the seventeenth century, British, French, and other settlers began to arrive in North America, displacing the local population. In the eighteenth century, Europeans started to assert control over parts of North Africa and the Middle East, shocking Ottoman elites who had long viewed Europeans as technologically and culturally backward. Their shock was shared by the Chinese in the nineteenth and early twentieth centuries as European imperialism rapidly expanded into Asia. Nearly all of Africa, too, was eventually divided up by the European states. This European imperialist expansion was joined briefly by Japan, which in the early twentieth century established its own empire across parts of Asia. In each of these cases, imperial powers possessed well-organized political systems and military structures, technological advances, and economic resources; these advantages were combined with a belief that imperial control was not only possible but also necessary, just, and willed by God.[1]

Institutions of Imperialism

The effect that imperialism had on the societies that came under foreign rule differed across time and place, but some common elements resulted from the imposition of modern political, societal, and economic systems onto largely premodern societies. As we shall see, this imposition had a dramatic (and often traumatic) effect that continues to the present.[2]

Exporting the State

One of the first major effects of imperialism was the transfer of the state to the rest of the world. Recall from Chapter 2 how the modern state that we take for granted today emerged as a result of a long historical process in Europe; before that time, political units tended to have much weaker control over land and their subjects, and territorial sovereignty and the rule of law was tenuous. States, however, eventually succeeded in consolidating power over other forms of political organization, eliminating their rivals, clearly delineating their borders, and establishing sovereignty.

When European empires began to expand around the world, new territories were incorporated into these state structures, territories carved up by rival states in the quest for economic resources and strategic advantages. The borders drawn by imperial states therefore often reflected the shape of their colonial ambitions rather than existing geographic, religious, or linguistic realities. The borders of 80 percent of African states are drawn according to longitude and latitude, not local geography or population groups. Many of these externally imposed and arbitrary boundaries became the demarcations for independent countries once imperial rule ended. Even countries that were able to resist direct imperial rule, such as Iran, Thailand, and Ethiopia, found themselves under the continuous influence and pressure of these empires.

Having conquered these territories, imperial powers went about establishing state power and authority. In many empires, this meant creating bureaucratic structures similar to those found in the home country in an attempt to "civilize"—to modernize and Westernize—the local population. These institutions commonly included a national language (typically that of the imperial power), police and a military, taxation and legal systems, and basic public goods such as roads, schools, and hospitals. How new institutions were established and new laws enforced differed. Some empires relied on local leaders to enforce their will, whereas others bypassed indigenous elites in favor of their own centralized forms of authority. These differences tended to reflect the degree of state capacity and autonomy found in the imperial country itself. In both cases, few if any democratic practices were introduced, even if they were the norm in the home country. Individuals under colonial rule were considered subjects, not citizens, and thus had few political rights.

This imposition of the state had mixed effects. Many subject peoples experienced increased education and the benefits of a basic infrastructure that improved communication and transportation. Life expectancies rose and infant mortality rates declined, although when those trends were combined with traditional family practices, they produced a population explosion that in many poor countries continues today. Traditional institutions such as local religions and customs were eroded and replaced by or fused with modern practices and institutions. This transition was incomplete and uneven. Imperial territories remained economically and politically underdeveloped, placing many subject peoples in a kind of limbo—no longer part of a premodern system but not fully incorporated into the modern one. The frustration that grew out of this conflicted identity helped fan the flames of anti-imperialism, the desire for freedom from foreign control.

Social Identities

The imposition of organizational forms from outside included various new identities that often displaced or were incorporated into existing social institutions. Among these were ethnic and national identities. In much of the world that came under imperial control, people had identified themselves by tribe or religion, by economic position, or by vocation rather than by some ethnic or national identity (essentially modern institutions). But just as empires brought their own political institutions with them, the concepts of ethnicity and nation were also introduced by the new ruling powers. Imperial elites, themselves shaped and defined by national and ethnic identities, took great interest in identifying and classifying different ethnic groups in the regions they came to occupy and structuring their political and economic control around these classifications. Ironically, even as groups were subject to Western classification, they were often divided across imperial borders that had been drawn with little regard for their tribal, religious, or any other identities.

Suddenly, people who had never thought of themselves as being part of an ethnic group found that their basic rights were tied to how they were ethnically defined by the empire. In some cases, this ethnic classification was determined by early pseudoscientific notions of race, which held that certain ethnic groups were naturally superior to others. The European and Japanese empires were influenced by the assumption that the colonizing race was superior to the colonized and thus destined to rule them. Different peoples within the empire, too, were subject to hierarchical classification. Certain ethnic groups were promoted to positions of power and economic advantage while other groups were marginalized. Colonialism often exacerbated these hierarchies as nonindigenous peoples migrated to colonies. Sometimes these migrants were settlers from the home country; in other cases, they were peoples from other parts of the empire or beyond (e.g., Indians migrating to Africa or African slaves being brought to Brazil). These foreign presences further sharpened ethnic and racial divisions, especially when such groups were accorded specific economic or political privileges. In short, inequality became tightly interconnected with ethnicity or race.

In addition to ethnicity, imperial powers also introduced the idea of national identity. During the late nineteenth and early twentieth centuries, in particular, national identity grew to be a powerful force in the industrializing world, helping drive competition between the industrial powers and in turn advancing the imperialist cause. But the peoples brought under imperial control had little familiarity with national identity, little notion of any right to a sovereign state. This combination of nationalism and imperialism proved to be unstable. Empires viewed the peoples living in their overseas possessions as inferior subjects and gave them only a limited ability to improve their standing within the empire. Yet the imperial powers' own concept of nationalism provided these subject peoples with the very means to challenge foreign rule. If nationalism meant the right for a people—any people—to live under their own sovereign state, did this not mean that subject peoples had a right to rule themselves? Empires thus provided the ideological ammunition that their subjects would eventually use to overturn imperialism.

Colonialism also affected gender roles in the colonies. It is hard to make generalizations in this area, since in each region existing gender roles differed greatly and

Political and Social Institutions of Imperialism

- The state, as a form of political organization, was imposed on much of the world outside of Europe.

- Ethnic and national identities were created where none had existed before colonization.

- Gender roles from the imperial country were often imposed on colonies.

each imperial power viewed gender somewhat differently. Some scholars argue that imperialism brought a number of benefits to women, increasing their freedom and equality by improving their access to health care and education. Others reject this argument, asserting that in many cases colonialism restricted women's role in society. In many premodern societies, gender roles may have been much less fixed than those found in the modern world, allowing women particular areas of individual freedom, equality, and autonomy. Imperial powers brought with them their own assumptions regarding the status of women, views that were shaped in part by their religious values. These views were imposed through such institutions as education and the legal system. The economic systems imposed by the colonizers marginalized women in many ways.

One example can be found in research on agriculture and gender equality. Recent studies suggest that in societies where farming was done through "shifting cultivation" (performed with hoes and hand weeding rather than ploughs, which require greater upper-body strength), women more actively participated in the agricultural economy as equals with men. These norms of equal participation extended outward into other areas, such as politics. However, with the advent of imperialism, such practices were transformed by agricultural modernization and industrial development, shifting participatory power away from women and toward men.[3]

Dependent Development

Just as imperialism transformed political and social institutions in colonial areas, creating an amalgam of premodern and modern forms, economic change occurred in a similarly dramatic and uneven way.[4] The first important change in most imperial possessions was the replacement of a traditional agricultural economy with one driven by the needs of the industrializing capitalist home country. Systems based largely on subsistence agriculture and barter were transformed into cash economies, in which money was introduced as a means to pay for goods and labor.

Alongside this introduction of a cash-based economy came the transformation of economic production. Using a mercantilist political-economic system (see Chapter 4), empires sought to extract revenue from their colonies while at the same time using these territories and their people as a captive market for finished goods from the home country. Free trade thus did not exist for the colonies, which were obliged to sell and buy goods within the confines of the empire. In addition, colonial production was organized to provide goods that were not easily available in the home country. Rather than finished goods, local economies were rebuilt around primary products such as cotton, cocoa, coffee, tea, wood, rubber, and other valuable commodities that could be extracted from the natural environment. Large businesses were established to oversee these so-called extractive economies, which were often dominated by a single monopoly. For example, in Indonesia the United East India Company, a Dutch firm, gained control over lucrative spice exports while monopolizing the local market for finished goods from Europe, thereby destroying indigenous trade networks that had existed in the region for centuries. Similarly, the British East India Company functioned virtually as a state of its own, controlling a large portion of the Indian economy and much of its foreign trade. Export-oriented imperialism also led to the creation of large plantations that could produce vast quantities of rubber, coffee, or tobacco.

This form of economic organization was quite different from that of the home countries and in many respects was ill suited to domestic development. Infrastructure was frequently developed only to facilitate effective extraction and export rather than to improve communication or movement for the subject peoples; jobs were created in the extractive sector, but local industrialization and entrepreneurialism

IN FOCUS — Economic Institutions of Imperialism

- Traditional agricultural economies were transformed to suit the needs of the imperialist power.

- Economic organization under imperialism impeded domestic development in the colonies.

- Free trade was often suppressed as colonies were forced to supply goods only to the imperial country, creating extractive economies in the colonies.

were limited; the development of agriculture for export instead of for subsistence damaged the ability of these peoples to feed themselves; and the creation of large-scale agricultural production drove many small farmers off the land. Many colonies saw a resulting boom in urbanization, typically in the colonial capital or other cities central to imperial politics and trade. By the late 1500s, for example, the Spanish had established more than 200 cities in Latin America, which to this day remain the central urban areas in the region.

Let us take a moment to summarize what we have considered so far. By virtue of their organizational strengths, modern states expanded their power around the globe, establishing new political, economic, and social institutions and displacing existing ones. In some cases, these institutions were reflections of the home country; in others, they were designed specifically to consolidate imperial rule. The result was an uneasy mixture of indigenous and foreign structures, premodern and modern. New political institutions and new societal identities were introduced or imposed while participation and citizenship were restricted; economic development was encouraged but in a form that would serve the markets of the home country. Imperialism thus generated new identities and conflict by classifying people and distinguishing between them—between rulers and ruled and between subject peoples themselves. At the same time, the contradictions inherent in this inequality and restriction of freedom became increasingly clear to subject peoples as they began to assimilate modern ideas and values. By the early twentieth century, the growing awareness of this system and its inherent contradictions helped foster public resistance to imperialism and paved the way for eventual independence.

The Challenges of Postimperialism

Despite the power of empires to extend their control over much of the world, their time eventually came to an end. In Latin America, where European imperialism first emerged, Napoleon's invasion of Spain and Portugal in 1807–08 led to turmoil in the colonies and a series of wars for independence, which freed most of the region by 1826. In Africa and Asia, where imperialism reached its zenith only in the nineteenth century, decolonization came after World War II. Numerous independence movements emerged within the Asian and African colonies, catalyzed by the weakened positions of the imperial powers and promoted by a Western-educated indigenous leadership able to articulate nationalist goals and organize resistance. Some imperial powers resisted bitterly: Portugal, for example, did not fully withdraw from Africa until 1975. Hong Kong was returned to China by the United

Kingdom in 1997. For the most part, however, colonies in Africa and Asia gained independence in the 1950s and 1960s.

The elimination of imperialism, however, did not bring a sudden end to the problems of the newly industrializing and less-developed countries. These countries have continued to struggle with political, social, and economic challenges to development and stability, freedom and equality. In many cases, these problems are a legacy of imperial rule, although in other cases they stem from particular domestic and international factors that have developed in the years since independence. But herein lies an important puzzle. If we consider the development of successful economic, social, and political institutions over the past 50 years, Asia has fared the best, Africa the worst, while the picture in Latin America is mixed. What accounts for these differences? Let's first consider some of the more common problems faced across postimperial countries, and then return to this question to see if the answer can provide some strategies for development and democracy.

Building State Capacity and Autonomy

One central problem that many NICs and LDCs have faced in the years after imperialism has been the difficulty in creating effective political institutions. In Chapter 2, we distinguished between weak states and strong states and noted that many scholars look at state power as consisting of state capacity and state autonomy. Capacity refers to a state's ability to fulfill basic policy tasks, and autonomy refers to its ability to act independently of the public and foreign actors. Both are necessary to carry out policy, and both have been difficult for postimperial countries to achieve.

In terms of capacity, LDCs are frequently unable to perform many of the basic tasks expected by the public, such as creating infrastructure, providing education and health care, or delivering other public goods. This lack of capacity stretches back to the absence of a professional bureaucracy; the foreigners who ran the imperial bureaucracies in the colonies typically left as soon as the colonies gained independence, precluding an effective transition to a local bureaucracy. These initial problems of capacity have since been exacerbated by the politicization of the state; in many cases, the bureaucracy has become an important source of jobs, resources, and benefits that are doled out by political leaders as a way to solidify control. Civil servants thus become part of a system of clientelism, patrimonialism, and rent seeking, in which they assist by providing goods and benefits to certain members of the public in return for political support.[5]

Autonomy has been equally problematic in the postimperialist world. On the surface, many of these countries appear to be highly autonomous, able to function without consulting the population at all. The prevalence of nondemocratic regimes in much of the newly industrializing and less-developed world only seems to reinforce this impression. Indeed, many of these states can repress or terrorize the population as they see fit, but this autonomy is quite limited, built largely (and dangerously) around force alone. In many cases, the state is not a highly independent actor but is instead penetrated by actors and organizations that see it as a resource to be exploited rather than a tool for achieving policy. Frequently, the result of such penetration is high levels of corruption—as we noted, this is sometimes called *kleptocracy*, or government by theft. For example, during military rule in Nigeria in the 1990s, officials stole more than $1 billion from the state treasury. Similarly, in oil-rich Angola, several billion dollars appear to have been siphoned off by its leadership just in the past few years. Studies of corruption indicate that the most corrupt

TABLE 10.2		Corruption Index, 2011	
COUNTRY	SCORE (10 = LEAST CORRUPT) ▼	COUNTRY	SCORE (10 = LEAST CORRUPT) ▼
Finland	9.4	China	3.6
Canada	8.7	India	3.1
Japan	8.0	Indonesia	3.0
United Kingdom	7.8	Mexico	3.0
United States	7.1	Bolivia	2.8
France	7.0	Iran	2.7
Taiwan	6.1	Philippines	2.6
Botswana	6.1	Nigeria	2.4
South Korea	5.4	Kenya	2.2
South Africa	4.1	Venezuela	1.8
Brazil	3.8	Myanmar	1.5

The corruption index is based on national surveys regarding the overall extent of corruption (size and frequency of bribes) in the public and political sectors.

Source: Transparency International.

countries in the world are less-developed and postcommunist countries, and there is a clear correlation between the level of development and the degree of corruption.

In addition to facing constraints on autonomy from domestic sources, the states of the newly industrializing and less-developed world are often limited in their autonomy by international factors. Less-developed and newly industrializing countries are subject to pressure from other, more powerful states and international actors such as the UN, the World Bank, multinational corporations, and nongovernmental organizations like Amnesty International and the Red Cross. Frequently wielding much greater economic and political power than the states themselves, these actors can significantly influence the policies of these countries, shaping their military and diplomatic alliances, trade relations, local economies, and domestic laws. Sovereignty is thus compromised.

These constraints on state capacity and autonomy have clear implications for freedom and equality. A state with weak capacity and autonomy is unlikely to be able to establish the rule of law. Laws will not be respected by the public if the state itself is unwilling or unable to enforce and abide by them. Freedom is threatened by conflict and unpredictability, which in turn hinder economic development. A volatile environment and the absence of basic public goods such as roads or education will dissuade long-term investment. Wealth flows primarily into the hands of those who control the state, generating a high degree of inequality. There is no clear regime, and no rules or norms for how politics is to be played.

Unfortunately, where instability is so high, there is often only one institution with a great deal of capacity and autonomy: the military. Where states are weak, military forces often step in and take control of the government themselves, either

---

IN FOCUS

Challenges to Building State Autonomy and Capacity in Less-Developed Countries

- Absence of professional bureaucracy (following departure of foreign imperial bureaucrats).

- Clientelism, rent seeking, and corruption in the handling of state jobs and revenue.

- Sovereignty often compromised by external actors (other states, international organizations).

to stave off disorder or simply to get a turn at draining the state. Military rule has been common in the newly industrializing and less-developed countries. Even where it has ended, as in many Latin American countries, the military often remains a powerful actor with its own political and economic interests.

Forging Social Identities

In the aftermath of colonialism, many less-developed and newly industrializing countries have struggled with the challenge of forging a single nation out of highly diverse societies. Initially, where centralized political authority did not exist before imperialism, societies were not homogenized. Their diversity became problematic when imperial powers began categorizing societal groups and establishing political boundaries and economic and social hierarchies. Migration within empires further complicated relations among these groups. When colonies gained independence, several problems rose to the surface.

First, group divisions often have economic implications, just as they did under colonial rule. Some ethnic or religious groups favored under colonialism continue to monopolize wealth in the postindependence society. For example, in Malaysia and Indonesia, ethnic Chinese hold a disproportionate share of national wealth, generating resentment. Similarly, in some African countries Indian immigrants—often brought in by the British as indentured labor—came to control a large portion of the business sector. At the other end of the spectrum, many indigenous populations, such as those in Latin America, are among the poorest in the world, a situation that has sparked ethnically based political movements in several of these countries. Many civil conflicts in the less-developed and newly industrializing countries are driven in large part by economic concerns that intersect with ethnic or religious differences.

Second, ethnic and religious divisions can similarly complicate politics. In countries where populations are heterogeneous, the battle for political power often falls along ethnic or religious lines, with each group seeking to gain control over the state in order to serve its own particular ends (see Chapter 3). Each ethnic or religious group competes for its share of public goods or other benefits from the state. This struggle may foster authoritarian rule, for a group that gains control over the state may be unwilling to relinquish or share it, and no one group can be confident that it could successfully dominate politics simply through the democratic process. As a result, where ethnic or religious divisions are strong we often see the state dominated by one group while others are effectively frozen out of the political process.[6] In some countries, a majority or plurality may dominate politics, as people of

European origin do in Mexico, where the minority indigenous population has little political power. In other cases, a minority may dominate a much larger majority; in Iraq, though the majority of the population belong to the Shia sect of Islam, those in power have traditionally been members of the minority Sunni sect. With the overthrow of Saddam Hussein, conflict has emerged between Sunnis and Shias over the future control of the country.

The economic and political difficulties that arise from such social divisions make the creation of a single national identity difficult. Amid such ethnic and religious diversity, many populations are much less inclined to see the postcolonial state as a true representation of their group's wishes, and states themselves have little beyond the initial struggle for independence on which to build a shared political identity for their people. When ethnic and religious conflicts are extreme, disaffected groups may seek to secede and create their own independent countries. The most recent example of this was the creation in 2011 of South Sudan, which separated from Sudan following a long civil war that pitted a black African south against an Arab north. Under the British Empire, they had been administered as two separate political entities. In advance of their withdrawal in 1956, Britain oversaw the unification of these two areas in spite of southern Sudanese opposition.

Gender is another important social issue in less-developed and newly industrializing countries. Gender roles imposed or strengthened by colonial rule persisted in many societies following independence, reinforced by rapid urbanization and the commercialization of agriculture, which tended to favor male labor and property rights. Because males have been privileged in this way, society has tended to view them as a more valuable addition to a family than females, an attitude that can limit women's access to important resources such as education. At its most extreme, this favoritism can be deadly, taking the form of female infanticide. Estimates indicate that in India alone, some 600,000 girls a year "go missing," having been aborted

IN FOCUS

Challenges to Building a Unified Nation-State

- Ethnic and religious divisions among different groups in heterogeneous societies (often exacerbated by economic inequality).

- Arbitrary political boundaries imposed by imperial powers.

following the use of ultrasound to determine the gender of the child. Vietnam, Pakistan, China, and other countries have faced similar issues, either through sex-selective abortions or through deliberate neglect of girl babies. This has led to a gender imbalance, with potentially dangerous implications. Some scholars have already noted that civil conflict in part results when there is a large number of unemployed and unmarried young men—a worrying thought when one considers that the some of the highest gender imbalances are found in the two most populous countries in the world, China and India. In the coming years, the security of women may be a key variable in predicting the security of states.[7]

Generating Economic Growth

Economic growth attracts the most focus among those who study the less-developed and newly industrializing countries. Indeed, when we think of development, it is typically economic progress that first comes to mind. Because of imperialism, instead of undergoing economic modernization on their own terms, these countries experienced rapid changes directed by the imperial powers to serve their own needs. As a result, on gaining independence many of these countries found themselves in a continued state of economic dependency on their former empire. But such dependent relationships did not bode well for long-term development, since they stressed the production of agricultural and other basic commodities in return for finished products. For many less-developed countries, this unequal relationship was simply a new, indirect form of imperialism, or what has been called **neocolonialism**. Breaking this cycle of dependent development was thus the greatest concern for the less-developed countries following independence.

The former colonies' need to break this cycle resulted in two distinct mercantilist economic policies that were applied throughout the less-developed world.[8] The first is known as **import substitution**. Under import substitution, countries restrict imports, raising tariff or nontariff barriers to spur demand for local alternatives. To fill this demand, new businesses are built with state funds by creating subsidized or parastatal (partially state-owned) industries. Patents and intellectual property rights are weakly enforced to tap into foreign innovations. Eventually, the hope goes, these firms will develop the productive capacity to compete domestically and internationally. Following World War II, import substitution was commonly used across Latin America and was also taken up in Africa and parts of Asia.

How successful was import substitution? Most observers have concluded that it did not produce the benefits expected, creating instead a kind of "hothouse economy." Insulated from the global economy, the state-supported firms could dominate the local market, but, lacking competition, they were much less innovative or efficient than their international competitors. The idea that these economies would eventually be opened up to the outside world became hard to envision; the harsh climate of the international market, it was thought, would quickly kill off these less competitive firms.

Import substitution thus resulted in economies with large industries reliant on the state for economic support and unable to compete in the international market. Such firms became a drain on state treasuries, compounding the problem of international debt in these countries, for states had to borrow from other countries to build and subsidize their industries. Uncompetitiveness was compounded by debt, leading to economic stagnation.

Not all postcolonial countries pursued import substitution, however. In several Asian countries, import substitution was eventually discarded in favor of what has been termed **export-oriented industrialization**. Countries that pursued an export-oriented strategy sought out technologies and developed industries that were focused specifically on export, capitalizing on what is known as the "product life cycle." Initially, the innovator of a good produces it for the domestic market and exports it to the rest of the world. As this product spreads, other countries find ways to make the same good more cheaply or more efficiently, eventually exporting their own version back to the country that originated the product. Thus, in South Korea initial exports focused on basic technologies such as textiles and shoes but eventually moved into more complex areas such as automobiles and computers. This policy was not without its own problems: countries that pursued export-oriented industrialization also relied on high levels of government subsidies and tariff barriers. Yet overall, this strategy has led to levels of economic development much higher than those achieved through import substitution (see Table 10.3). Some Asian export-oriented countries originally had per capita GDPs far below those of many Latin American and even some African countries. The question of why Latin America pursued a path of import substitution while Asia focused on export-led growth is an interesting puzzle, and one that we will turn to at the end of the chapter (see the "Institutions in Action" box, p. 318).

In recent years, both import substitution and export-oriented industrialization have been challenged. Although import substitution has long been criticized by liberals as inefficient and prone to corruption, the downturn of many Asian economies in the 1990s, including Japan's, has also led to critiques of export-oriented industrialization. In the wake of these economic difficulties, many less-developed and newly industrializing countries have adopted more liberal economic policies, often at the behest of the advanced democracies or international agencies. These policies of liberalization—often known as **structural-adjustment programs**, or

TABLE 10.3 — Import Substitution versus Export-Oriented Industrialization

PER CAPITA ANNUAL GROWTH RATE, 1990–2007 (PERCENT)

Brazil	Import substitution	1.2
Argentina	Import substitution	1.5
Ghana	Import substitution	2.1
Thailand	Export-oriented	2.9
Malaysia	Export-oriented	3.4
South Korea	Export-oriented	4.5
Vietnam	Export-oriented	6.0
China	Export-oriented	8.9

Source: Human Development Report 2010.

the **Washington Consensus**, since they reflect the wishes of institutions based in Washington, D.C., such as the World Bank and International Monetary Fund—have typically required countries to privatize state-run firms, end subsidies, reduce tariff barriers, shrink the size of the state, and welcome foreign investment. These reforms are controversial, and their benefits have been mixed. We will discuss this in greater detail when we consider future directions for economic prosperity in the poorer countries.

Puzzles and Prospects for Democracy and Development

We have covered some of the common challenges that postimperial countries face in developing institutions that will generate economic development and political stability. At the same time, we noted that in the face of these challenges, different parts of the world have had very different experiences. Asia has done the best, with

Three Paths to Economic Growth

IMPORT SUBSTITUTION	Based on mercantilism. State plays a strong role in the economy. Tariffs or nontariff barriers are used to restrict imports. State actively promotes domestic production, sometimes creating state-owned businesses in developing industries. Criticized for creating "hothouse economies," with large industries reliant on the state for support and unable to compete in the international market.
EXPORT-ORIENTED INDUSTRIALIZATION	Based on mercantilism. State plays a strong role in the economy. Tariff barriers are used to protect domestic industries. Economic production is focused on industries that have a niche in the international market. Seeks to integrate directly into the global economy. Has generally led to a higher level of economic development than import substitution.
STRUCTURAL ADJUSTMENT	Based on liberalism. State involvement is reduced as the economy is opened up. Foreign investment is encouraged. Often follows import substitution. Criticized as a tool of neocolonialism and for its failure in many cases to bring substantial economic development.

rapid growth among many of these countries and a trend toward effective states and democratization. Several countries in Latin America have also made progress, but this has often been accompanied by greater political difficulties and slower economic growth. Africa has done worst, with the lowest rankings on the Human Development Index and high levels of civil conflict and corruption.

Why this variation? Scholars increasingly agree on some of the major factors at work, though their assessments of how to solve the problems differ widely. One important factor we have discussed is the interplay between ethnic divisions and borders. Deep ethnic divisions appear to correlate with greater economic and political instability. As we noted earlier, in such cases it may be much more difficult to forge a sense of national identity or national welfare, when economic and political institutions are viewed as a means for one group to dominate others rather than as instruments to share power and wealth. This difficulty forging national identities can be compounded by borders, which may exacerbate conflict by dividing ethnic or religious groups across international boundaries. Such conditions are particularly difficult in Africa, with its ethnically fragmented states; in Kenya, for example, which recently saw severe ethnic conflict, no one group counts for more than a quarter of the population.

A second factor is resources. In Chapter 6, we spoke about the resource trap theory of development, which argues that countries with natural resources are hindered from political and economic development because the state or political actors can rely on these resources and effectively ignore public demands or needs. This can further polarize politics when combined with ethnic divisions, since each group will seek to control those assets at the expense of others. Again, while natural resources are relatively scarce in Asia, they are a central part of African economies, where resources like timber, oil, and diamonds not only lead to conflict but also fuel it, generating revenue for private militias and civil war.

Third, there is the question of governance. This is the hardest factor of the three to get a handle on, though it is perhaps the most important. It is evident to scholars that the obstacles discussed above, among others, cannot be addressed unless there is an effective state able to establish sovereignty and develop public goods and property rights, while resisting corruption and allowing for the transfer of power between governments over time. But what here is cause and what is effect? Are states weak because of ethnic division and resource traps, or do weak states facilitate these outcomes? This confusion has generated a great deal of controversy in the policy realm, as scholars remain divided over the extent to which political, social, and economic reforms need to be piecemeal and initiated locally or comprehensive and driven by international actors.[9] The remainder of our chapter will look at some possible solutions and the debates that surround them.

Forging States and Institutionalizing Democracy

The view of the state as an aid or obstacle to development in the postcolonial world has shifted over time. In the immediate postwar era, modernization theory focused on the importance of the state in economic and political development, seeing it as generating industrialization and modern citizens. Aid agencies and developed countries relied on states to be conduits for aid, often directing funds toward large-scale, top-down development projects like dams or health care. Over the next 40 years, some $2 trillion was funneled into Africa. However, many African states failed to live up to expectations, as corruption siphoned off resources and many development goals went unrealized. Large but inefficient states, often abetted by foreign funds, were common. As a result, by the 1980s the Washington Consensus took a different tack, encouraging (or pressuring) many less-developed countries to roll back state power, promote private industry, and limit regulation in the belief that market forces could succeed where states had failed. But while the Washington Consensus viewed states as too big and interventionist, others asserted that the power of these states needed to be redirected rather than reduced. Smaller would not be better if basic public needs still could not be met. As a result, attempts at liberalization have provided mixed results and generated skepticism of the Washington Consensus.[10]

What then should be done? Scholars are increasingly looking at the configuration and location of state power in less-developed countries, drawing from the experiences of democratization in Eastern Europe as well as changes in Latin America and Asia. In the past, studies of less-developed and newly industrializing countries were not particularly interested in how political institutions were arranged, focusing instead on imperial legacies or these countries' position in the global economy. However, studies focused on institutions have turned attention toward many of the concerns we have already addressed, such as executive-legislative relations and local versus national power.[11] A number of studies note that many less-developed countries rely on presidential rather than parliamentary systems, institutions that, as we noted in Chapter 5, are zero-sum offices that limit power sharing or make it hard to remove leaders from office. While most of these offices are sufficiently institutionalized that they would be difficult to replace entirely, research indicates that some basic reforms can have a large impact on governability. These can include greater limits on presidential power, specified in constitutions and backed by strong constitutional courts. Similarly, although there has been much interest in devolving power as a way to tackle corruption and increase state legitimacy, devolution, as we saw in Chapter 8, can in fact intensify conflicts if it encourages regional or ethnic parties that can increase political polarization. In general, there is a great deal of discussion in political science over whether democracy in poorer countries leads to greater instability and, as a result, lower prosperity.

Finally, there are questions about the very nature of sovereignty in less-developed and newly industrialized countries. The success of many newly industrialized countries may be due in part to their having effective states with a high degree of capacity. In many other countries, though, the state is weak and its capacity low, to such an extent that it is debatable whether sovereignty exists there at all—as in the case of civil conflicts and failed states. As a result, some scholars have raised the idea of "shared sovereignty," an arrangement in which international organizations would play a more direct role in building and maintaining political institutions.[12] For example, this can take the form of "conditionality," whereby other countries or organizations provide support (such as aid) only if particular outcomes have been met. International organizations can also oversee the management of natural resources or taxation and the distribution of revenue. Most dramatically, international institutions can step in to provide the core element of sovereignty, the monopoly of violence, intervening in domestic conflicts and serving, at least temporarily, as the central coercive power. The UN played this role in East Timor during its transition toward independence in 1999, and there have been calls for it to play a similar role in the newly independent South Sudan. The expansion of the International Court of Justice can be seen in this light as well.

It is easy to see the difficulty that shared sovereignty raises. While the term may be new, many of the ideas suggested above are not, and are often associated with imperialism. Few countries welcome the direct intervention of foreign organizations or countries in their domestic politics. At the same time, such arrangements require that the international community not only commit resources but also accept that for every state, sovereignty is not absolute.

In the case of state building, we can see important differences in how reforms can be achieved. Some calls for institutional reform imply that less-developed countries can make political improvements with relatively small changes that could be led from within the country. Other arguments emphasize the role of international actors in driving a much larger process of state reform forward.

Building Society

While scholars and policy makers have been debating how to improve states, a similar discussion has concerned improving social conditions in the less-developed world. Much of this is rooted in discussions of economics, which we will consider next. But there is also the realization that countries cannot simply focus their efforts on economic development alone, assuming that such development will resolve all major social issues. Earlier we spoke of the three central problems of ethnic conflict, resources, and governance. What steps can be taken at the societal level to address these concerns? Again, the debate turns in part on the scope and source of reforms.

Much scholarship over the last decade or so has emphasized the role that small-scale social organization can play in improving governance and contributing to social stability. Influenced in part by experiences in Eastern Europe and Latin America, this scholarship emphasizes building civil society in countries where social organization is poor and often polarized along ethnic, religious, class, or gender lines. Civil society, which we defined in Chapter 5 as organized life outside the state, accomplishes three important things: it binds people together, creating a web of interests that cuts across class, religion, ethnicity, and other divisions; it forms a bulwark through activism and organization against the expansion of state power that might threaten democracy; and it inculcates in citizens a sense of democratic politics based on interaction, negotiation, consensus, and compromise. In the absence of civil society, states can become enmeshed in clientelist relationships that prevent the formation of policies that serve society as a whole.

Alongside state reform, building civil society has become a focal point for scholars and political actors involved in development.[13] No longer is the state seen as the sole instrument for democracy and development; public activity is now viewed as a vital part of the equation. A first step in the development of civil society is civic education, in which communities learn their democratic rights and how to use those rights to shape government policy. Beyond education, organizational skills must be strengthened so that the public is able to mobilize effectively and make its voice heard. These efforts need to go hand in hand with state reform; changes require participation not just from political elites but from the public as well.

Other scholars, however, have argued that this emphasis is for now misplaced. Stressing grassroots organization is well meaning but unlikely to lead to any real outcomes as long as the country's basic social conditions are dire. Moreover, where civil society is built in the absence of political institutions that can process people's desires and demands, the result can be frustration and greater instability. Some scholars believe that responses to social issues in the less-developed countries require a massive international effort rather than a focus on local small-scale activism. The UN's Millennium Development Goals (MDGs) partly reflects this viewpoint, with proposals to improve education, health, agriculture, and gender equality and to reduce poverty. A number of "Millennium Villages" have already been set up in Africa to put these policies into practice, with the idea that these would eventually be scaled up to regional and national projects. Critics of the MDGs program charge that such an ambitious goal is not cheap; each of the villages requires $300,000 per year, and estimates are that a worldwide implementation of the MDGs would require close to $200 billion by 2015.[14] Some argue that such large-scale, top-down programs are little different from the international programs tried in the past, where billions of dollars poured into the less-developed world yielded limited results, and that such programs fail to reflect real needs on the ground.[15] Proponents of the MDGs approach claim that it is in fact local and community-led in nature.

Promoting Economic Prosperity

Economic prosperity is the third crucial need in the less-developed world. Above all, the diverse countries that fall into this category are defined by their lack of economic development and the pressing problems of poverty and inequality. And as with political and social reform, there are sharply contrasting views over how to improve economic conditions in these countries.

A central problem is that for many less-developed countries, much of the economy exists in the "informal" sector. By informal sector we mean a segment of the economy that is not regulated, protected, or taxed by the state. Typically, the **informal economy** is dominated by the self-employed or by small enterprises, such as an individual street vendor or a family that makes or repairs goods out of its home. In some cases, the informal economy may represent over half of a country's GDP, with women playing a large role. According to some research studies, in many less-developed countries up to 90 percent of women working outside the agricultural sector are part of the informal economy.

Why does the informal economy dominate many less-developed countries, and why does this matter? Corrupt and highly bureaucratic state controls over the economy often deter individuals from starting formal businesses; in addition, certain social institutions, such as hostility toward women in the workplace, may discourage women's employment outside the home. And while informal employment can be better than no employment at all, this "gray market" does not generate tax revenue, is not subject to state protection or regulation, and often lacks the capital necessary to grow since it lacks assets and collateral. Businesses operating in the informal economy are thus unable to grow into larger businesses and thereby enter the formal economy.

How can a small-scale, informal economy be transformed into a larger, formal one? Some scholars emphasize the need for localized reform and opportunities within state and society to improve economic opportunities. One important argument is that economic underdevelopment has been in large part a function of weak property rights in many of these countries. This idea, pioneered by the Peruvian economist Hernando De Soto, emphasizes the need to develop stronger property rights in the less-developed world. In all informal economies, De Soto argues, there is a vast amount of "dead capital"—that is, land, homes, and businesses whose owners lack basic property rights such as clear title to ownership. Codifying existing informal institutions and ensuring effective state protection of them would allow people to tap into these resources more easily. Formal property rights would allow for the development of credit as well as allow states to tax and regulate the economy. Here again we see a need not for less state power but for its redirection, in this case toward establishing and institutionalizing property rights.[16]

Similarly, others scholars have emphasized the need to improve access to capital that is normally unavailable to the informal economy except at exorbitant rates. A much-discussed alternative is microcredit or microfinance. Though these terms are often used interchangeably, there is a difference. **Microcredit** refers to a system where small loans (often less than $1,000) are made available to small-scale businesses that otherwise lack access to capital. **Microfinance** covers a much broader spectrum, including credit, savings, insurance, and financial transfers. Microcredit is often funded through nonprofit organizations, and in some cases the borrower is also held accountable to other borrowers in a local association, in that a failure of one individual to repay limits further loans that can be taken out by the members in that association. This increases the desire for members to vet loans and over-see their use within the association. There are, however, also private microcredit organizations, something that has raised concerns (see below). With globalization, microcredit has expanded; now organizations like the United States–based Kiva allow individuals around the world to make loans to those in need. As of 2011, Kiva had over half a million lenders, and had loaned $235 million to half a million individuals.[17] The Grameen Bank in Bangladesh, which first pioneered microcredit, has loaned over $10 billion since its inception, and 97 percent of those loans have gone to women. Grameen's founder, Muhammad Yunus, won a Nobel Peace Prize in 2006 for his work, and the bank has even expanded into the United States.

As promising as these developments are, they are not a cure-all.[18] Critics of microcredit note that while these small loans may help small entrepreneurs, they have not created a way for firms to grow and take on employees—a critical step in development and the creation of a middle class. Others have criticized microcredit programs for charging high interest rates or failing to screen borrowers properly, problems that can lead to indebtedness and default (this has been a particular prob-lem in India). The Grameen Bank has been criticized for economic improprieties, though this appears to have stemmed more from internal Bangladeshi politics than from the bank's practices. And while Kiva helps link people in rich and poor coun-tries, it provides only a small slice of the billions of dollars in credit needed each year. In short, there are clearly benefits to be gained from small-scale and bottom-up programs that provide opportunities for poor people to participate in their economy and to protect and use their profits and investments. However, broader state institu-tions must also be in place to help "scale up" these activities into wider prosperity.

Not surprisingly, then, other scholars have focused more on large-scale economic issues as a solution to development. One particular focus has been on trade liberali-zation that would favor agricultural and other exports from the poorest countries, tied to the goals of the MDG. However, many countries, rich and poor alike, resist opening up their markets, especially to agricultural imports. For example, the United States maintains a range of quotas and tariffs on sugar, keeping prices on imports high to protect domestic producers of sweeteners like corn syrup. At the same time, the United States has also mandated the development of biofuel alternatives to gasoline, setting a goal to increase the use of ethanol in particular as part of the country's fuel supply. The result of this combination of tariffs and government energy goals is prob-lematic. In 2010, approximately 40 percent of corn production in the United States

Why Did Asia Industrialize Faster than Latin America?

The rise of Asia over the past four decades as a global exporter, producing increasingly sophisticated goods over that time, presents an interesting puzzle, which deepens when we compare the region's economic development to Latin America's. In 1970, Brazil's and Argentina's per capita GDP at PPP was between $2,500 and $3,500, higher than South Korea's or Taiwan's. By 2010, while these Latin American countries had GDPs between $11,000 and $15,000, the GDPs of South Korea and Taiwan had soared to between $30,000 and $35,000. How did these Asian countries come from behind and grow so much wealthier than many of their Latin American counterparts within forty years? A simple explanation—such as a correlation between democracy and speed of economic growth—does not work, since all of these states were authoritarian during most of the last 50 years. What then might be the explanation?

There are several competing theories regarding Asia's faster growth. According to one argument, which we can describe as geostrategic, the major difference between Latin America and Asia lays in their relationships to the United States, and how their political-economic institutions were shaped by these relationships. Latin America's experience of the United States' influence during much of the nineteenth and early twentieth century has been described as neocolonial. In this interpretation, the subordinate relationship of Latin America to the United States effectively prevented the development of industries that could reach an export capacity and be competitive in world markets. Instead, economic development was dominated by foreign (U.S. and European) goods and foreign

investments that concentrated on the production of consumer goods for the small upper and middle classes rather than on broader industrialization.

In contrast, following China's 1949 revolution, the United States viewed Asia as under direct threat from communism, and as a result supported industrialization policies—through preferential trade agreements—that limited foreign direct investment and promoted export-led growth. Whereas Latin American markets were influenced (if not dominated) by Western investments, Asia's drive toward industrialization and export-led growth was fueled by state investments. While this argument can help explain why the regions' economies developed so differently, it doesn't account for a country like Mexico, where for much of the early twentieth century foreign investment was limited by the state and rapid industrial development resembled that of Asia later in the century.

A second argument thus concentrates to a greater extent on domestic politics and institutions within these regions. One area that has attracted a great deal of attention is land ownership and land reform. In many countries, agriculture is a powerful economic and political force. This is especially the case where agriculture takes the form of large landholdings, which concentrate power in relatively few hands, so that much of the population works land they do not own. Where such landowners are powerful, states may find it difficult to raise funds and build capacity and autonomy. Urbanization and industrialization are held back by the interests of landed elites (who often oppose the rise of both).

In the case of Latin America, economies dominated by large landholders and estates—known as latifundia, or *haciendas*, in Spanish—developed as part of Spanish and Portuguese colonialism to produce commodities on a large scale for export (such as sugar and coffee). Independence from imperialism did not destroy this agricultural system, however, and latifundia economies remained in Latin America, with landed elites continuing to dominate economic and political institutions. Latin America's economy developed more slowly, therefore, not because it lacked integration with the global economy or exported fewer goods but because the nature of its exports, agriculture and natural resources, did not provide a strong foundation for industrial development.

In Asia as in Latin America, much of the agricultural land was originally concentrated in a small number of estates. However, in places like South Korea and Taiwan, one of the first steps the state took on gaining independence was to enact widespread agricultural reform to break the landed elites' monopoly and empower the peasantry. A major motivating factor was the desire to stave off a peasant-backed communist revolution, like the ones that happened in China and North Korea (where land reform was a key promise of the Communist Party). This argument in many ways takes us back to the geostrategic issue, though what is critical here is the role of political elites in Asian countries in bringing the old feudal order to an end. As in the case of the earlier explanation, however, there are problems with this argument. The emphasis on the overwhelming power of the latifundia needs to be balanced by a consideration of the fact that Latin America has become an overwhelmingly urban region—nearly 80 percent of its population lived in cities as of 2009. Moreover, as mentioned earlier, many Latin American

Coffee pickers at a hacienda in Colombia. These large landholdings are central to the region's agricultural exports.

countries did develop a significant industrial base, even in the absence of land reform.

What, then, is the solution to our puzzle? We cannot draw clear conclusions, though certain factors seem significant. The institutional legacies of imperialism do appear to be stronger in Latin America than in Asia, while the economic policies in the two regions have been influenced differently by postwar international politics. This intersection of institutions and policies may explain what moved Asia and Latin America down different paths of development, which will continue to influence their future.[19]

1. What role did foreign direct investment in Latin America versus state investment in Asia play in the regions' differing paths?

2. How did the legacy of colonialism and its institutions impact Latin America's industrial development?

3. How did concerns about communism influence both the Asian countries' relationship with the U.S. and their own approach to land reform?

went into ethanol production, which some have argued has driven up food prices in both richer and poorer countries. In addition, corn production for ethanol leads to environmental damage (through fertilizer use, for example) while producing a product that is less energy-dense than gasoline. There is a much better alternative: for years, Brazil has been developing a sophisticated ethanol program based on waste from its sugar cane industry, which is more environmentally friendly than corn-based ethanol. However, Brazil finds that it cannot export its ethanol to the European Union because of its protectionism. The same barriers existed in the United States until 2012. While advanced democracies have called for poorer countries to reform their economies, many continue to place trade barriers before them.[20] In the meantime, new economic players, such as China, are rapidly investing in natural resources, businesses, and infrastructure in Africa and elsewhere, raising questions about whether less-developed countries will find themselves in yet another dependent relationship—albeit with a new partner.

In Sum: The Challenges of Development

Although newly industrializing and less-developed countries differ in their levels of development, almost all share the legacies of imperial rule. The fusion of local institutions with those of the imperial power created challenges as these countries sought to chart their own independent courses. Weak states; conflicts over ethnicity, nation, religion, and gender; and incomplete and distorted forms of industrialization all contributed to instability, authoritarianism, economic stagnation, and overall low levels of freedom and equality. The newly industrializing countries seem to have overcome many of these obstacles, but it is unclear whether their strategies and experiences provide lessons that can be easily applied elsewhere in the world.

There is no consensus on how to tackle the most pressing problems of the less-developed world. Some emphasize the power of small-scale, piecemeal, local, and bottom-up solutions, arguing against the grand plans that in the past consumed time and money with little to show for it. Others, who support larger-scale aid programs, argue that the problem with these initiatives in the past was a lack of concerted effort and a unified vision of what needed to be done. They call for a new investment of resources to lift the poorest countries out of poverty. Who is right? Do the solutions lie in a patchwork of reforms or a comprehensive plan for change? Proponents of both approaches are competing for the attention of donors and policy makers in the hope of leading the way in the coming decades. And globalization, which we will turn to in the next chapter, may complicate the questions and possible solutions even further.

For Further Reading

RS> Acemoglu, Daron and Simon Johnson. "Disease and Development: The Effect of Life Expectancy on Economic Growth." *Journal of Political Economy* 115. no. 6 (2007).

RS> Arnold, Wayne. "Vietnam Holds Its Own within China's Vast Economic Shadow." *New York Times* (1 January 2011).

RS> Collier, Paul and Jan Willem Gunning. "Why Has Africa Grown Slowly?" *Journal of Economic Perspectives* 13, no. 3 (Summer 1999).

RS> Easterly, William. "To Help the Poor." *The Elusive Quest for Growth: Economists' Adventures and Misadventures in the Tropics* (Cambridge, MA: MIT Press, 2011).

Eberly, Don. *The Rise of Global Civil Society* (New York: Encounter, 2008).

Fukuyama, Francis. *State Building: Governance and World Order in the 21st Century* (Ithaca, NY: Cornell University Press, 2004).

Gann, L.H. and Peter Duignan, eds. *Imperialism in Africa, 1870–1960* (Cambridge: Cambridge University Press, 1969–75).

Haggard, Stephan. *Pathways from the Periphery: The Politics of Growth in Newly Industrializing Countries* (Ithaca: Cornell University Press, 1990).

Kaplan, Seth. *Fixing Fragile States: A New Paradigm for Development* (Westport, CT: Praeger, 2008).

RS> Krugman, Paul. "The Myth of Asia's Miracle." *Foreign Affairs* 73, no. 6 (November/December 1994).

 Visit StudySpace for quizzes and other review material.
www.norton.com/studyspace

- **Vocabulary Flashcards of All Key Terms**
- **Chapter Review Quizzes**
- **Complete Study Reviews and Outlines**

RS>
Reader Selection

Highlighted selections are included in *Essential Readings in Comparative Politics*, Fourth Edition.

An advertisement for McDonald's in Kuwait. While McDonald's is often cited as an example of the downsides of globalization as a homogenizing force, this ignores the ways in which it adapts to local cultural norms.

GLOBALIZATION AND THE FUTURE OF COMPARATIVE POLITICS

KEY CONCEPTS

- Globalization is a process whereby extensive and intensive webs of relationships connect people across time and space.

- Political globalization challenges sovereignty.

- Economic globalization can transform markets and property within and between countries.

- Societal globalization may undermine old identities and create new ones.

- Scholars debate the nature of globalization: is it new? exaggerated? irreversible?

The central theme of this textbook has been the struggle to balance freedom and equality. When societies clash over how to reconcile these two values, states must confront the problems using their capacity to generate and enforce policy. Democratic institutions presume that freedom and equality are best reconciled through public participation, whereas nondemocratic regimes significantly restrict such rights. The variety of institutional tools available has led to a diverse political world, where freedom and equality are combined and balanced in many different ways. Here, in essence, is the core of comparative politics: the study of how freedom and equality are reconciled around the world.

Over the past two decades or more, this dynamic has become more international in scope. Of course, domestic politics has always been shaped by international forces, such as war and trade, empires and colonies, migration and the spread of ideas. But to some observers, this interconnection between countries is changing in its scope, depth, and speed. Linkages between states, societies, and economies appear to be intensifying, and at an increasingly rapid pace, challenging long-standing institutions, assumptions, and norms. This process, still ill-defined and unclear, is commonly known as **globalization**, a term that fills some with a sense of optimism and others with dread. Although the extent of globalization and its long-term impact remain unclear, behind it lies the sense that the battle over freedom and equality is becoming international, no longer a concern to be solved by each country in its own way.

What does this mean for comparative politics? At the end of Chapter 1, we discussed how comparative politics (and political science) remains hindered by problems of data and theory that are often unable to predict, much less explain, human behavior. Comparative politics has suffered in the past from scholars understanding too few cases, thus making comparisons difficult. But if globalization is transforming domestic politics, the very idea of comparative politics could be open to question. To play devil's advocate, wouldn't studying Brazil's energy-export sector be more valuable than investigating the internal workings of its legislature? Wouldn't a study of Internet traffic in the European Union (EU) yield better puzzles and answers than a study of German political culture? Wouldn't comparativists learn more from studying transnational crime networks than judicial politics in South Africa? Of course, we can argue that "globalized" questions need not come at the expense of comparative politics, but there remains the question of whether scholars of political science are missing the big questions that lie in the space between comparative politics (the study of politics within countries) and international relations (the study of politics between them). The above questions of course present a false dilemma, as we needn't choose between these areas of research. However, such questions help us consider the issue that comparative politics as it is structured now may not be geared to important puzzles and institutions currently in formation. In summary, is there even such a thing as domestic politics any longer? Is everything that we've read in this book up to this point becoming obsolete or irrelevant? And if so, how are we to study politics in a globalized world?

In this chapter, we will look at the concept of globalization and its potential impact on both comparative politics and the ongoing struggle over the balance of freedom and equality. We will begin by defining globalization and determining how we might measure it. Next, we will consider some of the possible effects of globalization, including how it may change political, economic, and societal institutions at the domestic level. We will also ask some questions about the progress of globalization—whether it is in fact something fundamentally new, profound, and inevitable. We will then conclude with a discussion of how the old dilemma of balancing freedom and equality may change in a globalized world.

What Is Globalization?

We could argue that we have lived in a globalized world for millennia. Even as early humans dispersed around the world tens of thousands of years ago, they maintained and developed long-distance connections among one another through migration and trade. Such contacts helped spur development through the dissemination of knowledge and innovations; for example, it is speculated that the technology of written language was created independently only three or four times in human history: in the Americas, in Asia, and in the Middle East. All other written languages were essentially modeled after these innovations as the idea of writing things down spread to other communities.[1] Thousands of years ago empires stretched from Asia to Europe, and people moved between these areas, exchanging goods and ideas. Trade routes forged even more far-flung connections between people who were only dimly aware of each other's existence. For example, in the first century C.E. the Romans treasured silk imported from distant China, although they did not fully understand how it was made or where it came from. Were these, then, "globalized" societies?

When we speak about globalization, we don't simply mean international contacts and interaction, which have existed for tens of thousands of years. According to the political scientists Robert Keohane and Joseph Nye, one important distinction between globalization and these earlier ties is that many of these past relationships were relatively "thin," involving a small number of individuals. Although such connections may have been extensive across a vast region, these connections did not directly affect large numbers of individuals. In contrast, globalization can be viewed as a process by which global connections grow increasingly "thick," creating an extensive and intensive web of relationships between many people across vast distances. In the twenty-first century, people are not distantly connected by overland routes plied by traders, diplomats, and missionaries; they are directly participating in a vast and complex international network through travel, communication, business, and education. Globalization is a system in which human beings are no longer part of isolated communities that are linked through narrow channels of diplomatic relations or trade. Entire societies are now directly connected to global affairs. Thus, globalization represents a change in human organization and interconnection.[2]

Globalization has a number of potential implications for comparative politics. First, because of the thickening of connections between people across countries, globalization breaks down the distinction between international relations and domestic politics, making many aspects of domestic politics subject to global forces. Debates over environmental policy become linked to global warming; struggles over employment are framed by concerns about trade, offshore outsourcing, and immigration; health care is influenced by the threat of pandemics. As a result, political isolation becomes difficult or even impossible.

Second, globalization can also work in the other direction, essentially "internationalizing" domestic issues and events. Given that globalization deepens and widens international connections, local events, even small ones, can have ripple effects throughout the world. A flood in Thailand can disrupt computer production worldwide; a panicky stock market in the United States can contribute to an economic crisis in Europe. These interconnections across space are further amplified by the speed of today's world. Whereas technological change once took years or centuries to spread from region to region, today a new piece of software or video can be downloaded or viewed at the same time everywhere. The Internet allows the rapid dissemination of news and information from every corner of the globe, no matter how remote. The world seems to live increasingly in the same moment—what happens to someone in one place immediately affects others around the world.

In short, globalization is a process that creates intensive and extensive international connections, changing traditional relationships of time and space. Will globalization overturn or transform the very foundations of politics? Would such a change make the world a better place—more prosperous, stable, and democratic— or just the opposite? And finally, is any of this inevitable? These are big questions of profound significance that have found little consensus. Let us first consider how we can think about the nature of institutions in a globalizing world.

Institutions and Globalization

We have spoken of globalization as a process, one that creates more extensive and intensive connections across the globe. These changes can, in turn, change the institutions of economics, politics, and society. At the start of this textbook, we spoke of institutions as being a key reference point for modern life. Institutions are organizations or patterns of activity that are self-perpetuating and valued for their own sake. The modern world is codified by them. Institutions such as states, culture, property, and markets establish borders, set boundaries for activity and behavior, and allocate authority, norms, rights, and responsibilities. Moreover, by doing so they establish local identity and control—a particular state, religion, or set of cultural values holds sway over the land and people here, but not there. Space and time are thus understood and measured through institutions.

The question we now ask is whether this will still be true in the future. It may be that before long, domestic institutions will not be the most important actors in people's lives. Long-standing institutions like states, cultures, national identities, and political-economic systems now face a range of international forces and organizations that transform, challenge, or threaten their traditional roles. Let's look at some of the reasons this might be the case.

To begin with, globalization is associated with the growing power of a host of nonstate or suprastate entities. Most can be grouped into three categories that we touched on in previous chapters: **multinational corporations (MNCs)**, **nongovernmental organizations (NGOs)**, and **intergovernmental organizations (IGOs)**. All three organizational forms are decades if not centuries old, but their role and impact are rapidly expanding as they benefit from and contribute to globalization. MNCs are firms that produce, distribute, and market goods and services in more than one country. They wield assets and profits far larger than the gross domestic products (GDPs) of most countries in the world and are able to influence politics, economic developments, and social relations through the goods and services they produce and the wealth at their disposal. NGOs, as we discussed in the last chapter, are national and international groups that are independent of any state and pursue policy objectives and foster public participation. Some, such as Greenpeace and Amnesty International, can shape domestic and international politics by mobilizing public support across the globe. IGOs, groups created by states to serve particular policy ends, include the United Nations, the World Trade Organization, the EU, and the Organization of American States. In some cases, these forms of organizations are part of a broader **international regime**. The use of this term in the study of international relations is similar to our use of *regime* in comparative politics. Recall from Chapter 2 that in comparative politics regimes are defined as the fundamental rules and norms of politics, a set of institutions that empower and constrain states and governments. International regimes function in the same way, but they link states together through rules and norms that shape their relationships to one another, usually regarding some specific issue (such as greenhouse gases or trade).

In addition to MNCs, NGOs, and IGOs, technology-driven organizations also play a role in globalization. This is not new; all earlier waves of human interconnection were dependent on technological changes, such as the domestication of plants and animals, the creation of the wheel, advances in seafaring, and the invention of the telegraph. Technology is not inherently globalizing or globalized, though in many cases technology and globalization can reinforce each other. In the last

25 years, one of the most important examples of such reinforcement has been the development of the Internet. Originally created by the United States government as a way to decentralize communications in the event of a nuclear war, the Internet has grown far beyond this initial limited objective to become a means through which people exchange goods and information, much of it beyond the control of any one state or regulatory authority. As bandwidth has increased and more information has been digitized, the Internet has transformed from a tool into an entity in its own right, holding a tremendous amount of content. Unlike MNCs, NGOs, or IGOs, the Internet has no single "location" to speak of—indeed, we hardly even speak of "the Internet" any longer, so ubiquitous is its presence. The Internet is also unlike a typical regime, in that while it has technical standards, it does not have norms that link states together to address a specific issue or meet a specific goal; it is not the means toward any one end. Discussions of authority, sovereignty, and control become problematic. But as technological change facilitates the growing reach of nonstate or suprastate actors, these actors in turn tend to foster further technological change.

Are these organizations, whether the UN or the Internet, indeed institutions? This is an important question, for as we have noted, institutionalization carries with it authority and legitimacy. Many MNCs, IGOs, and NGOs are legitimate and highly valued, a seemingly indispensable part of the global system. The same could be said of the Internet or other forms of technology, such as satellite television or GPS. As institutions, then, they can call on a degree of influence and power. This may augment and improve the workings of domestic institutions; it may also conflict with or undermine them. Let us consider this idea further through the familiar categories of states, economies, and societies.

IN FOCUS — Nonstate Organizations and Globalization

ORGANIZATION	DEFINITION	EXAMPLE
Multinational corporations (MNCs)	Firms that produce, distribute, and market their goods or services in more than one country	Microsoft, General Electric
Intergovernmental organizations (IGOs)	Groups created by states to serve particular policy ends	United Nations, European Union
Nongovernmental organizations (NGOs)	National and international groups, independent of any state, that pursue policy objectives and foster public participation	Greenpeace, Red Cross

Political Globalization

In Chapter 2, we noted that in historical terms, the state is relatively new, a form of political organization that emerged only in the past few centuries. Because of their unique organization, states were able to spread quickly across the globe, supplanting all other forms of political organization. Yet we also noted that if states have not always been present, there may come a time when they will no longer be the dominant political actor on the face of the earth. States may at some time cease to exist. Some see globalization as the force that will bring about this dramatic political change, but whether such a change is to be welcomed or feared is uncertain.

At the core of this debate is the fact that globalization and globalized institutions complicate the ability of states to maintain sovereignty. In some cases, states may abdicate sovereignty intentionally—giving up authority to IGOs, for instance, to gain some benefit or alleviate some existing problem. The EU is an excellent example of this, though, as we have seen, even under these conditions sovereignty is often given up reluctantly. The economic difficulties in Europe over the past few years remind us how sovereignty and integration can clash, and that the former does not easily give way to the latter. In other cases, the loss of sovereignty may be unintentional. The growth of the Internet, for example, has had important implications for states regarding legal authority in many traditional areas, since it does not readily conform to international boundaries or rules. It can circumvent legal restrictions on certain forms of speech in a way in which traditional newspapers or television cannot, through e-mail, Web sites, social networks, or blogs. Developments such as electronic currency may further erode the powers of states by undercutting their ability to print money, levy taxes, or regulate financial transactions—all critical elements of sovereignty.

What do these changes mean for state autonomy and capacity? One possible scenario is that states will become bound to numerous international institutions that will take on many of the tasks that states normally conduct. In this scenario, a web of organizations, public and private, domestic and international, would shape politics and policy, set standards, and enforce rules on a wide range of issues where states lack effective authority. The rule of law would become a preserve less of individual states than of a set of global institutions created for and enforced by a variety of actors.

With this diffusion of responsibility, sovereignty would decline. States would be "hollowed out," constrained by their reliance on the globalized world. This includes the use of force. One cannot arrest computer viruses or enact sanctions against global warming, and despite the United States' call for a "war on drugs" and a "war on terror," one cannot declare war on such threats in the conventional sense. For globalized states, then, war may become largely ineffective and too risky, as it may undermine vital international connections. This narrowing of state sovereignty as a result of globalization is what the *New York Times* columnist Thomas Friedman has referred to as a "golden straitjacket."[3] In this view, political globalization may bring about a more peaceful world order, constraining states' tendencies toward violent conflict by dispersing sovereignty among numerous actors while diminishing the capacity and autonomy of states.

It has also been argued that globalization will change not only the utility of force but also the nature of public participation and democracy. The increasing interconnection between domestic and international institutions makes it more difficult for sovereign actors to function without oversight from other organizations and to hide their actions from others. An example here is the development of the International Criminal Court, which has been charged with holding state leaders accountable for human rights violations in Libya, Sudan, and the former Yugoslavia. NGOs, such as Wikileaks and Transparency International (an anticorruption NGO), can play a similarly powerful watchdog role. Globalization will thus make politics less opaque and more open to scrutiny by domestic and international communities.

In contrast to these optimistic views, others see political globalization not as a pathway to peace and participation but as a source of dangerous fragmentation and weakened democracy. First, in their view, violence will not lose its utility in the international system as optimists hope; it will simply change form, much as it did when states themselves first appeared. According to this argument, globalization is fostering not only cooperation but also violent international actors and movements that in many ways are the exact opposite of the modern state. These groups are decentralized and flexible, hold no territory, and exercise no sovereignty, and they are able to draw financial and other support from across the globe. In many ways, then, they are not unlike other nonstate actors. Yet unlike NGOs and MNCs, these groups seek to achieve their objectives through the acquisition and use of force, applying it in ways that may be difficult for states or other international actors to counter.

Globalized criminal organizations and terrorist groups are perfect examples of this new threat. These are decentralized groups empowered by globalized technology, such as cell phones, encrypted e-mail, Web sites, and satellite television, which allows them to communicate, disseminate propaganda, access money, and recruit new members. Indeed, many argue that such groups look more like a social network than any formal nonstate actor. Although states may at times be able to use conventional force against such groups where they have a physical presence, there is no central location to attack nor any easy way to keep individuals and information from simply dispersing and regrouping elsewhere. States, whose military capacity is geared toward fighting other states, may be ill-equipped to battle small groups that can take advantage of globalization to attack and undermine existing institutions.[4]

Second, many question how a more globalized political system can be more democratic. Although deeper international connections may increase transparency, this does not necessarily lay out a mechanism by which individuals can act on that information. As we noted in Chapter 5, modern liberal democracy is based on republicanism, the ability to choose one's representatives through a competitive process. But who votes for international organizations? These bodies may be indirectly elected or appointed from the member states—or they may not be directly accountable to anyone at all. Thus, while one may laud the work of Greenpeace or the World Wildlife Fund, it is instructive to note that these organizations are not subject to popular democratic control nor necessarily more transparent than states themselves. This raises the concern of a "democratic deficit," an idea first raised with regard to the EU. If power moves to global institutions, representation and democratic control may grow weaker, since citizens lack the ability to control these bodies, which grow distant from the citizenry and their preferences. At an extreme, this could lead to a new form of global illiberalism, such as we discussed in Chapter 6, whereby representative institutions exist but have been hollowed out by the loss of sovereignty and by the power of global technocratic institutions and elites.[5]

These are two starkly different visions of politics in a globalized world. In both scenarios, states and state functions become more diffused as power shifts to the global level. For optimists, international cooperation follows, with these developments undermining the logic of war and increasing transparency. For pessimists, deepening international connections facilitate new violent organizations and weaken democratic ties between the people and their representatives. Some combination of both scenarios is also possible.

Economic Globalization

Politics is not the only realm in which globalization is taking place; in fact, when many people think about globalization, economics is what comes to mind, and it is this area that generates the most controversy and debate. In the area of economic globalization, there are several distinct but interrelated elements that we should take into consideration. While the development of political globalization may be thought of as piecemeal or incremental, scholars tend to point to several specific institutions and regimes as vital components of economic globalization. First is the **Bretton Woods System**, an economic regime created in 1944. The Bretton Woods System was created to manage international economic relations, whose instability was commonly cited as a driving force behind the Great Depression and World War II. Three important institutions emerged from the Bretton Woods System: the International Monetary Fund (IMF), the World Bank, and the General Agreements on Tariffs and Trade (GATT), later replaced by the World Trade Organization (WTO). The objectives of these three institutions were to expand and manage economic relations between countries. The IMF helps manage exchange rates between countries and provide loans to states in financial difficulty. The World Bank provides loans and technical assistance to advance development in less-developed countries. The WTO oversees trade agreements between the member states to lower tariffs and remove other nontariff barriers. For the past 60 years, these organizations have been at the center of a global liberal-economic regime. The Bretton Woods System also helped facilitate the policies of the Washington Consensus, which we referred to briefly in our discussion of structural adjustment in Chapter 10. The Washington Consensus emphasized rolling back the state's control over the market, through privatization, deregulation, trade, and financial liberalization. Many assert that the deepening of economic globalization, or "hyperglobalization," over the past two decades was enabled by the Bretton Woods System and catalyzed by the policies of the Washington Consensus.

Observers point to several important facets of economic globalization that are directly or in part related to the emergence of the Bretton Woods System and the Washington Consensus. First, and perhaps most obvious, is the globalization of international trade. Trade has always had a strong international component, driven by one country's advantage over another in producing a given good. However, globalized trade has become increasingly extensive and intensive, tying markets, producers, and labor together in a new way. The production and marketing of goods is more mobile—goods can be made by workers, and sold to consumers, in many more places around the world. The second facet of economic globalization is less visible but no less profound. Financial globalization is the integration of capital and financial markets—markets for money—around the world. Banking and credit, stocks and foreign direct investment all fall under this category. Money, too, is more mobile—investments and loans can be made from, and to, many more places around the world. Globalization deepens the connections between workers, goods, and money.

Some examples can provide perspective on the growth of economic globalization. In 1992, world exports in merchandise came to approximately $3 trillion; in

2010, they had grown to $12 trillion. **Foreign direct investment** (the purchase of assets in a country by a foreign firm) was under $200 billion in 1992; by 2007, it had reached approximately $2 trillion (though it has fallen back to about $1.24 trillion as of 2011—see Figure 11.1).[6] As mentioned earlier, economic globalization is also associated with the emergence of a number of MNCs that dominate global markets. Assisted by more-open markets and reduced transportation costs, large firms make profits in the billions of dollars, often rivaling the GDPs of many countries in which they do business. For example, General Electric's total profits in 2010 were approximately $14 billion, which is more than Haiti's entire GDP at purchasing-power parity. The company also paid no U.S. taxes, since its profits came from production overseas. Another commonly noted example of financial globalization is China's investment in U.S. assets. China now owns over $1 trillion in U.S. treasury securities, or about 25 percent of the total foreign loans made to the U.S. state to cover its debts. Finally, to place a human face on these statistics,

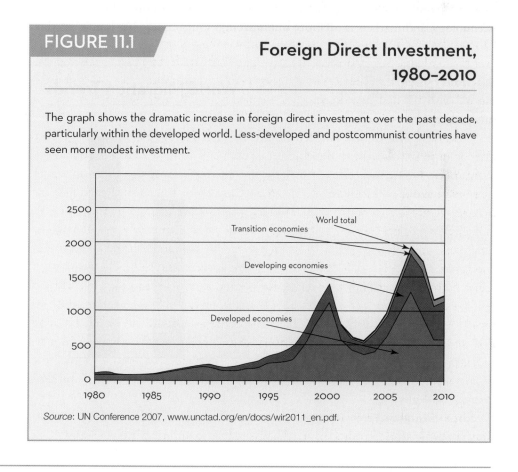

FIGURE 11.1

Foreign Direct Investment, 1980–2010

The graph shows the dramatic increase in foreign direct investment over the past decade, particularly within the developed world. Less-developed and postcommunist countries have seen more modest investment.

Source: UN Conference 2007, www.unctad.org/en/docs/wir2011_en.pdf.

deepening globalization can transform the mobility not simply of production and capital but also of labor, as people move to adapt to changing economic circumstances. In 2010, nearly a quarter of a billion people moved across international borders, more than double the number in 1980.[7]

These economic developments are amplified by expanding global communication, which we spoke of above, transforming the way in which markets, firms, and individuals interact. Technological innovations, alongside economic liberalization, have reduced many traditional economic barriers. People are able to buy goods and services from around the world using fewer or no intermediaries. As a result, markets are more open and firms and workers face greater competition. In the area of investment, too, changes allow firms, states, and individuals to move their money internationally and rapidly, jumping in and out of markets as they see fit. Many people liken these changes to the creation of railroads and the telegraph in the nineteenth century, which helped transform the way in which economies were networked.

Perhaps the best-known example of this intersection among globalized labor, technology, and markets is **offshore outsourcing**. Outsourcing has long existed, as

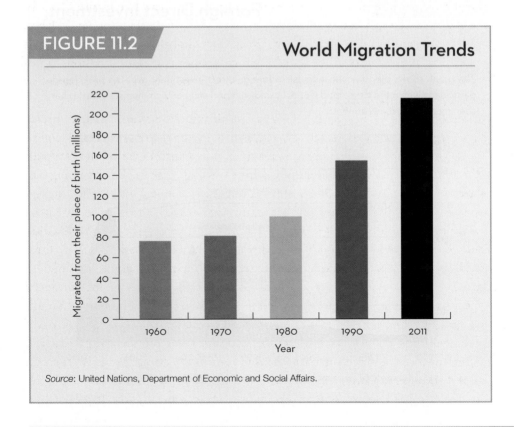

FIGURE 11.2 — **World Migration Trends**

Source: United Nations, Department of Economic and Social Affairs.

it is simply a process by which a firm moves some of its work to a secondary business that can do the work more efficiently or cheaply. However, in the past much of this outsourcing was done inside domestic or regional economies. The rise of a postindustrial and information-based economy, however, has meant that many jobs can now be moved a great distance away, to wherever the cost advantage can be found. Examples include call centers, data processing, animation, and software programming. In 2002, offshore outsourcing accounted for around $1.3 billion in economic activity; by some estimates, the current figure is around $400 billion. India is often noted as a major provider of outsourced labor, but Eastern Europe, Latin America, and even Africa have been active as well.

For optimists, economic globalization is a vehicle for global prosperity. Through the expansion of international economic connections, goods and services, labor, and finance can be allocated through a broader market, unfettered by tariff barriers and other obstacles that states might erect. Countries are able to export what they produce best, encouraging innovation, specialization, and lower costs. Jobs are also created as capital flows and transnational corporations take advantage of new markets and new opportunities. People, too, can move to where there is work, whether domestically or internationally, and work can move to them (see Figure 11.2). In the end, wealth is diffused more effectively through open markets for goods, labor, and capital, raising standards of living worldwide. Globalization is thus viewed as a positive, liberalizing trend, a global division of labor that can lift billions out of poverty and generate greater prosperity by allowing more people to be a part of an international marketplace for goods and labor.[8]

Others view economic globalization with more suspicion. Some equate increased trade with increased dependence, arguing that trade creates conditions whereby some countries will gain monopoly control over particular goods vital in the international economy, such as software, energy, biotechnology, or pharmaceutical products. The resulting unequal relationships in the international system will allow countries in control of crucial resources to dominate countries whose goods are less critical to the world economy. The globalization of investment and labor markets is also criticized as a system in which firms invest in countries with cheap labor and weak labor regulations in order to increase profits; these moves eliminate manufacturing jobs in the advanced democracies and undermine organized labor. The rise of information technology and globalization has even affected more-educated workers, moving traditional white collar jobs, such as editing and computer programming, overseas. Increased trade, foreign investment, and offshore outsourcing hurt workers around the globe as firms and countries engage in a "race to the bottom," driving down wages and weakening regulations. More generally, the fragmentation of firms, markets, and labor raises the fear that globalized businesses are increasingly able to avoid government taxation, oversight, and public accountability. In this view, as economic globalization weakens state capacity and autonomy, it is replaced not with a global rule of law but rather with a small cartel of powerful corporations that lack any national or democratic control and are able to wipe out existing economic, political, and social institutions—what one writer calls "disaster capitalism."[9] Freedom and equality are thus compromised.

Societal Globalization

Whether globalization and the political and economic transformations it brings become instruments of greater cooperation and prosperity or sources of conflict and hardship may depend on how societies themselves are transformed by globalization.

We have explored how political globalization may challenge state sovereignty and power and how economic globalization binds markets for goods, labor, and capital. Societal globalization is a similar process, in which traditional societal institutions are weakened, creating new identities that do not belong to any one community or nation. As we know from previous chapters, in the premodern world people's identities were rather limited and narrow, focused on such things as family, tribe, village, and religion. Only with the rise of the state did national identities begin to emerge, such that individuals began to see themselves tied to a much larger community of thousands, or millions—strangers bound together by complex myths and symbols, including flags, legends, and anthems. This transformation coincided with the development of sovereignty, whereby borders and citizenship reinforced the notion of national identity—one people, one state.

Some argue that as globalization proceeds, these central aspects of individual and collective identity are giving way. Just as the state and domestic economic institutions are being challenged, so, too, are traditional identities. New technologies, waves of migration, trade, and communication link people across vast distances, forging relationships between people on the basis of common interests and ideas rather than shared national symbols. Many find the Internet particularly powerful in this regard, in its ability to spread information, ideas, and cultural products to billions of individuals around the globe (Table 11.1). Even where Internet penetration has been weaker, cell phone use continues to expand; in Africa, there are nearly half as many cell phone subscriptions as there are people, and in Europe, there are more subscriptions than people (Figure 11.3). As electronic communications continue to grow by leaps and bounds, people find ways to link up with one another across time

TABLE 11.1 — World Internet Usage, 2000–11

REGION	PERCENT OF POPULATION	PERCENT GROWTH 2000–11
Africa	11	2,527
Asia	24	707
Europe	58	353
Middle East	32	1,987
North America	78	152
Latin America	36	1,037
Oceania/Australia	60	179
World	**30**	**480**

Source: www.internetworldstats.com.

and space, building and deepening connections. Text messaging, Web sites, blogs, and social networks are all examples of virtual interconnections that have become integral to, or perhaps have even displaced, physical spaces and relationships.

How might this process shape societal institutions and identities? We can point to two possible trajectories. The first is that societal globalization engenders global multiculturalism. The deepening of international connections and the exchange of ideas between people will transfer the dynamics of multiculturalism from the national to the international level, with different cultures linking and combining more through connections that are not bound by traditional barriers of time and space. This means not only that a globalized society will draw from many sources but also that the interconnection of domestic institutions at the global level will create new values, identities, and culture—a "creative destruction" that will enrich all cultures.[10] One result of this outcome could be a global *cosmopolitanism*—a term that comes from the Greek *kosmos*, or universe, and *polis*, or state. Cosmopolitanism is thus a universal, global, or "worldly" political order that draws its identity and values from everywhere. Historically, the cosmopolis was the physical space where disparate ideas usually came together, notably the city. In a globalized world, however, there is the potential for an international cosmopolitanism that binds people together irrespective of where they are.[11]

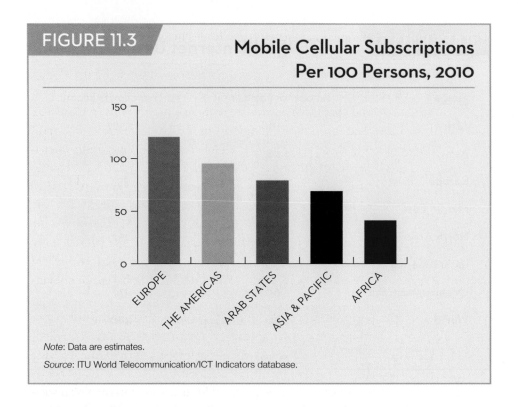

FIGURE 11.3

Mobile Cellular Subscriptions Per 100 Persons, 2010

Note: Data are estimates.

Source: ITU World Telecommunication/ICT Indicators database.

Parallel to a global cosmopolitanism is the idea of globalized democracy. We have already spoken of how globalization might shape political institutions at the domestic and international levels, though we focused largely on the development of nonstate and suprastate organizations as rivals to the state. When we focus on societal globalization and its effects on democracy, however, we return to our notion of civil society. The argument here is that growing international connections at the societal level would generate not only a form of cosmopolitanism but also a civic identity that stretches beyond traditional barriers and borders. This global civil society—organized life stretching beyond and above the state—can take shape in formal organizations like NGOs, as well as in such informal manifestations as social movements or more basic grassroots connections between people drawn together by shared interests and values. This global civil society could in turn shape politics by creating new opportunities for concerted public action and new ways of thinking about politics and participation at the domestic and international levels.[12] Finally, this development of global cosmopolitanism and civil society could help facilitate democratic change across countries by informing and amplifying local political action. For example, the 2011 revolution in Egypt has been characterized as a "Twitter Revolution," in which globalized social media helped catalyze and sustain democratization. International conflict, too, could decline where people are bound by a global civil society.

As you might expect, there are critics of such views, skeptical of the notion that increased globalization will benefit social progress. Their criticisms are two-fold. First, some contend that globalization overwhelms people with innumerable choices, values, ideas, and information that they are unable to understand, evaluate, or escape—especially those not part of the globalized elite. Confusion, alienation, and a public backlash can emerge as people seek to hold onto their identities in the face of these changes. Nationalism and fundamentalism can be viewed as reactions to a globalized society that people find alien and hostile to their own way of life. The September 11 attacks can be viewed in this light—as a strike against the values (and perceived source) of globalization rather than against the United States itself. A possible result of societal globalization is atomization or a retreat into old identities, rather than the creation of some kind of widespread global cosmopolitanism or civil society.

A second criticism emphasizes not the reaction to societal globalization but rather its eventual outcome. Even in the absence of a backlash against globalization, the critics contend, societal globalization will not generate a richer global culture and cosmopolitanism but will rather trigger cultural and intellectual decline. Societies will trade their own cultures, institutions, and ideas for a common global society shaped not by values or worldliness but by speed and consumption. The things that make each society unique—languages, food, music, history, customs, values, and norms—will be absorbed, rationalized, and packaged for mass consumption everywhere. Such critics would note that it is not accidental that after the U.S. and Chinese militaries, the third- and fourth-largest employers in the world (and the largest private employers) are Walmart and McDonalds. This view of globalization sees a process whereby what is unique in each society is repackaged and sold to the rest of the planet, while those things that lack mass appeal are thrown away or driven out, replaced by what satisfies the widest public and the lowest common denominator. This process can be thought of as a disenchantment of the world, what one scholar calls "the globalization of nothing."[13]

Taking Stock of Globalization

These are very different views of globalization. From the optimistic perspective, globalization will be the instrument of dramatic human progress, spreading prosperity, enriching cultures, and expanding democracy, peace, and civil society. This utopian view has its dystopian alternative, in which globalization is marked by poverty and inequality, violence, tyranny, and the destruction of culture. Embedded in both of these visions is the idea that globalization is a major and inevitable turning point in history. But what is the evidence for this? Our task now is to match evidence against argument and consider what impact globalization has had on the world to date, and whether, as is often assumed, this is truly something new that will transform humanity and politics.

Is Globalization New?

We can begin by questioning the assumption that globalization is a fundamentally new development in human history. As we noted earlier, for thousands of years humanity was linked across great distances, spreading people, goods, and ideas around the world. Scholars, however, have noted that such connections were often extensive but not intensive. But we should not underestimate how deep many of these connections were for their time. Medieval Europe was tightly interconnected through political, economic, and societal institutions, while a thousand years earlier the Persian Empire bound together people from Europe to North Africa and as far as India, shaping cultural values and human development. In many of these cases, war was an important component, disrupting old institutions and propelling change.[14]

Let us look at a more recent phenomenon: the development of modern imperialism. The spread of European power into Latin America, Africa, the Middle East, and Asia profoundly reshaped domestic and international relations as Western political, economic, and social systems were transplanted into these parts of the world. Imperialism and the declining costs of transportation also helped facilitate the migration of millions of Europeans to these regions. By comparison, the current world of passports, visas, and immigration in some ways constrains human mobility far more than other factors did just a century ago.

The late nineteenth century saw the rise of the first NGOs and IGOs, such as the Red Cross, founded in 1863, and the International Telegraph Union (ITU), in 1865. And those who marvel at the advent of Internet communication forget that the first transatlantic cable connected Europe and North America by telegraph in 1866, spurring a global system of rapid communications and trade.[15] In his famous work *The Economic Consequences of the Peace*, the economist John Maynard Keynes wrote of the dramatic impact of such changes:

> The inhabitant of London could order by telephone, sipping his morning
> tea in bed, the various products of the whole earth, in such quantity

as he might see fit, and reasonably expect their early delivery upon his doorstep; he could at the same moment and by the same means adventure his wealth in the natural resources and new enterprises of any quarter of the world, and share, without exertion or even trouble, in their prospective fruits and advantages; or he could decide to couple the security of his fortunes with the good faith of the townspeople of any substantial municipality in any continent that fancy or information might recommend.[16]

This may sound like the current global economy, but Keynes was actually writing about the period before World War I. Indeed, the rise of electronic commerce, often heralded as a central piece of globalization, would not be possible without the previous establishment of such institutions as the telephone, national postal services, passable roads, ports, and commercial shipping—all things that far predate globalization.

At that time, many observers believed that globalization would lead to the abolition of war and the spread of international law and world government. For others, however, these rapid changes also brought with them concerns and dangers not unlike those discussed today. Migration and trade triggered not only fears of cultural destruction but also violent resistance, including nationalism and fascism. And as we saw earlier, Marxist and anarchist ideas also attracted followers around the world, some of whom sought revolution and engaged in terrorism. In these confusing and often violent developments, some predicted the decline and collapse of Western society, not unlike some of the gloomier prognostications we hear today.

These examples suggest that it may be shortsighted of us to think that today's global interconnections are more dramatic than any that came before or that they portend changes that are beyond our power to control. History may help us better understand the present; we should not assume that what is occurring now is so unique that the past has nothing to teach us.

Is Globalization Exaggerated?

We considered earlier globalization's impact on political, economic, and societal institutions, and whether it is making the world better or worse. Is its impact as great as many of its supporters or critics assert? In the light of the recent global recession, it may seem obvious that globalization is very real and can be very dangerous. But given the different ways in which we can think about globalization, the situation is more complicated than that.

As is often the case, the data present a mixed picture. Let us begin with political globalization: some have suggested it would lead to greater transparency and global democratic institutions, while others have worried that the result would be an important loss of democratic participation and the rise of rival nonstate and nondemocratic actors. In both of these cases the assumption is essentially that globalization means the eclipse of the state; yet there is still not a great deal of evidence showing that either scenario is taking place. At the most basic level, even as globalization has spread, so too have the number of states; sovereignty has remained a critical demand for people around the world, from Kosovo to South Sudan. While observers of globalization commonly point to the EU as evidence that globalization is reducing state sovereignty, they fail to point out that fifty years after the EU was created, no other part of the world has shown a desire or ability to replicate this model, while the EU itself faces unprecedented difficulties.

Indeed, over the past decade sovereign authority has reasserted itself in some areas. For instance, while many have assumed that the stateless, almost anarchic nature of the Internet and electronic communications would virtually displace the state, governments have found ways to regulate content and limit access. Chinese and Iranian censorship of Web sites and social media like Facebook and European internet privacy laws are good examples, challenging what some scholars have called "the illusion of a borderless world."[17] There is little comprehensive evidence that states are becoming more transparent or hollowed out under globalization; rather, it seems that the nature of their capacity and autonomy is changing to meet new challenges and needs, especially in the face of the current economic challenges.

At the same time, the idea that stateless actors such as terrorists are beyond the reach of states seems exaggerated—new technologies can weaken or empower states and nonstate actors alike. Terrorist groups may have a global reach, but they are often more centralized than globalization suggests, and therefore can be targeted— as the killing of Osama Bin Laden demonstrates. Information gathered from his compound suggests that he remained deeply involved in the worldwide direction of Al Qaeda, in contrast to the view it had become a highly decentralized and essentially "leaderless" group.[18] In other words, while globalization may have extended the reach of Al Qaeda, the group has functioned much like a traditional state. For now, at least, states still matter.

If the picture of states and globalization is not clear, one might expect that in the area of economic globalization our evidence would be more comprehensive. While people may not agree on the effects of economic globalization, even the limited data we have regarding trade and foreign direct investment do indicate a profound change over the last two decades. But here too, caveats are in order. For example, in spite of impressive growth, the total levels of international trade represent only about a quarter of global GDP. Ninety percent of all fixed investment (investment in physical assets) in the world is still domestic; investors buy relatively few foreign stocks; and in contrast to our notion of the agglomeration of far-flung businesses, the merger of firms continues to be heavily driven by such factors as physical proximity and cultural connections. There continues to be a strong "home bias" in economic activity, much more so than we expect.[19] Not just states, but distance itself still matters.

What about prosperity and poverty? Has globalization made a difference? In Chapter 4, we saw that in China, India, and the United States inequality has increased during the past few decades. We might then correlate economic globalization with greater inequality. However, as we noted in Chapter 4, it has been suggested that total global inequality does not appear to have moved since the 1980s, when globalization started to flourish. At the same time, data indicate that poverty has fallen as a percentage of the world population since the 1980s, from a third to around 20 percent. Most of this reduction has occurred in China and India. Indeed, some scholars suggest that much of what we think of as economic globalization has been driven by domestic reforms in China and their subsequent integration into the global market, and that much of China's reform (which began in the late 1970s) occurred well before the current wave of economic globalization.[20] What we see now as a uniform and inexorable process of globalization may be more effectively viewed through the lens of traditional comparative politics: changes in the political and economic institutions first in China and, more recently, in India.

So far we've found no unequivocal evidence regarding political or economic globalization. What about at the level of society? Here, too, we confront the limitations of our data. Both supporters and opponents of societal globalization start from the proposition that national and local identities are giving way in the face of a broader global identity. Whether this will be a peaceful process and a positive outcome is the basis of their disagreement. But again we must ask: is this process actually taking place? Discussions of societal globalization often turn on the role of electronic communication, such as the promise of global social networks and the perils of cultural homogeneity. We have spoken a great deal about the rise of information technology, and while this is not the same as globalization it is easy to conflate the two. But as in our discussions above, when we dig a bit deeper into the data, the evidence for globalization is not clear. For example, in the area of telephony, while total international phone traffic has grown from 50 billion minutes in 1990 to 400 billion minutes in 2010, this still represents only about two percent of total phone traffic around the world. Even in countries that we might imagine are heavily integrated into global institutions—such as an EU country like France—international inbound calls make up only about five percent of total phone minutes.[21] Even this data can be interpreted in different ways. If, for example, international phone traffic in France is largely between immigrants and their home countries, we could argue that such connections do not foster a broader global identity, but reinforce national identities in spite of distance. Along these lines, some observers speak of "dish cities," immigrant communities that rely heavily on satellite television in their native language; it can be argued that such forms of globalization can in fact reinforce closed ethnic enclaves.[22]

This ties into the broader question of national identity. Are more people seeing themselves today as global cosmopolitans? The answer appears to be no. One recent survey indicates that when publics are asked to define themselves as citizens either of their nation or of their world, very few opt for the latter. Even when given the option to choose both, fewer than a quarter on average select this option (Table 11.2). It has, however, been suggested that there are important differences between those who have come of age during the era of globalization and older generations. According to this argument, basic public opinion surveys fail to capture a greater sense of global identity among the youth. This is intriguing, and there are some indications in the World Values Survey that more young people view themselves as "world citizens" than those over age 30. However, the difference is modest, and these same young people also strongly identify themselves as citizens of their nation—as strongly as those over 30. Even more interesting, while many scholars believe that globalized cosmopolitanism is a preserve of elites, levels of education do not appear to be an important predictor of whether young people identify themselves as world citizens. These findings discourage us from making any strong claims about global identity. Finally, even if we do determine that there is a greater sense of global identification among the young, does this reflect a generational shift toward global cosmopolitanism, or is it rather a function of youth—a perspective one is likely to abandon as one gets older? We'll get a better handle on these questions only as we track this generation across time.

Is Globalization Inevitable?

Let us for the sake of argument reject all of the qualifiers raised above and assume that globalization is a fundamentally new phenomenon whose effects are profound. For those who make this assumption, it often follows that globalization is a juggernaut that people, groups, societies, and states cannot stop. Is this true? To illustrate this point, let us return to history, and to Keynes. After noting the profound economic changes that occurred before World War I, he remarked that, above all, the average individual regarded these changes as "normal, certain, and

TABLE 11.2

Globalization and National Identity, 2009

DO YOU CONSIDER YOURSELF MORE A CITIZEN OF [COUNTRY], MORE A CITIZEN OF THE WORLD, OR BOTH EQUALLY?

	CITIZEN OF [COUNTRY]	CITIZEN OF THE WORLD	BOTH EQUALLY
Argentina	64	10	24
Mexico	56	9	35
United States	72	5	22
France	48	14	37
Germany	59	19	18
Great Britain	59	9	29
Italy	51	21	27
Russia	79	5	13
Ukraine	81	6	10
Azerbaijan	89	4	5
Egypt	73	13	13
Jordan	80	8	7
Palestinian ter.	70	14	13
Turkey	80	9	10
Kenya	88	9	3
Nigeria	69	11	19
China	35	6	44
India	40	14	32
Indonesia	68	2	27
South Korea	83	5	11
Thailand	48	15	23
Average	66	10	20

Source: WorldPublicOpinion.org.

permanent, except in the direction of further improvement, and any deviation from it as aberrant, scandalous, and avoidable."[23]

Yet this state of affairs was not permanent. International trade was disrupted by the onset of World War I, the effects of which were further compounded by a subsequent world depression. Keynes himself came to play a role in the Bretton Woods system precisely because he noted that global economic development was fragile and required the active role of states. History suggests, then, that globalization is not unstoppable; deglobalization can occur as well, as it has in the past.

Globalization can be limited or reversed in a number of ways. One is through economic crisis. The heady period of economic development a hundred years ago was finally undermined by financial collapse in the 1930s. In its immediate aftermath, trade, investment, and immigration across the globe declined, often as a result of new national barriers that reflected increased isolationism, protectionism, and nationalism. To take one example, between 1901 and 1910 the United States accepted nearly one million immigrants a year; it would not reach even half that level again until the 1970s. Ongoing global economic difficulties could continue to work against globalization, reducing economic ties, migration, or other forms of globalization.

Indeed, recent global economic turmoil has pointed to this very possibility. As we noted in previous chapters, much of what has developed in comparative politics over the past decade has taken place in the context of rapid global economic growth. The rise of China as a major exporting power, Russia and Brazil as suppliers of energy and other natural commodities, and India as a hub for outsourcing, as well as the integration of global markets for investment, are a few examples of this rapid economic growth that have had important political implications. Now a good portion of this development has been blunted by an economic crisis of a severity unseen since the 1930s. Exporters have faced weakened overseas markets and increased trade barriers; foreign investments in the developed and developing world have lost much of their value; businesses and banks large and small have reeled and collapsed; and migration to rich countries have plateaued or declined, in part because barriers to entry have increased. These difficulties portend a weakening of the web of interconnections that define globalization. This may last only a short time, or stretch on for many years.

This crisis may also increase public opposition to globalization. Many people's concerns about how globalization might affect such things as the environment, labor standards, and democratic practices around the world are being translated into antiglobalization activism—aided, ironically, by new technology such as the Internet. The protests against the WTO in Seattle in 1999 are perhaps the most notable example of such activism: there, for the first time in the WTO's history, members were unable to begin negotiations on a new round of trade liberalization measures. Although this failure was not simply, or even primarily, due to public protests, widespread opposition in the street by activists from around the world certainly helped to complicate matters.[24] Since 1999, the WTO has failed to regain momentum and faced another collapse of trade talks in 2008; opposition has grown in the EU to transferring more powers away from the member states; and there has been increased resistance toward expanding regional free-trade agreements. Such opposition to increased integration and globalization can be found across the political spectrum and around the world. A 2009 survey showed that in many countries (such as Mexico, India, Indonesia, Egypt, and Russia) half of the public supported the creation of trade barriers. In the United States, 40 percent supported such barriers.[25] At the same time, the survey showed widespread support for greater global financial regulation. The current crisis could pave the way for a new Bretton Woods System, whereby globalization would continue, but under greater state control. The result could be a "semiglobalized" world, where states, national identities, and domestic economic structures are linked across borders but remain powerful institutions in their own right.[26]

Whatever the outcome, it seems premature to declare that either a world of states or globalization has come to an end. Certainly it is more provocative to claim that a new age is upon us, whether a utopia of prosperity and peace or a dystopia of poverty and conflict. As we learned in our first chapter, politics is one arena where new activities emerge, are institutionalized, and come to define our lives. But the resulting institutions can become ossified and break down, leading to turmoil. New institutions emerge to take their place—some of which can produce more human happiness, and some less. Wherever we find ourselves now, it is not certain that we face major changes in our political institutions. And even if we do, it is not clear whether such changes will be a pathway to progress or a setback for humanity. So long as domestic political institutions, in whatever form, matter, the study of comparative politics remains a critical endeavor. And you, too, are now a participant in that important work.

In Sum: The Future of Freedom and Equality

Our world may now be undergoing a profound change in institutions, though this is subject to debate. One result of this transformation could be an evolution of the struggle over freedom and equality. Both values can be measured not just within states but also between them. Does one country's freedom or equality come

Did Globalization Cause the Economic Recession of 2008?

The economic recession that struck the United States and Europe in 2008 continues to reverberate worldwide; at the time of this writing, it is unclear when, and how, this crisis—the worst since the Great Depression—will come to an end. In Chapters 4 and 8 we talked about the long economic stagnation of Japan and the more recent Greek crisis, and in both cases we emphasized how political institutions shaped their predicaments. But if the earlier Japanese case can be understood largely though domestic politics, the more recent Greek case is deeply tied to global economic developments, shaped by forces outside of that country and resonating far past its borders. This raises a question: is globalization in general to blame for the current economic crisis? If it is, what does this mean for the future of globalization and global economic growth? A few pages (or a few hundred) can't fully cover this dramatic event. That said, we can examine the institutions of domestic and international finance to take a stab at answering these questions.

In order to consider the relationship between globalization and economic recession, we need to look at how the current difficulties unfolded. To begin with, we should consider what we mean when we say that globalization "caused" the current recession. It is not enough to simply say that this recession was linked to global economic forces; if that were the case, then any major economic downturn—such as the one beginning in 1929—could be seen as a product of globalization, since then as now forces like trade and international finance were involved. If we believe that globalization is a causal factor, we need to determine which global relationships, intensified over the past decades, created conditions that contributed to the eventual downturns in the United States, Europe, and elsewhere.

What exactly happened? Most observers trace the crisis to the United States (and, to a lesser extent, Europe) and its real estate market. This housing boom—a rapid increase in housing prices and housing stock—can be seen as a market "bubble." Market bubbles can occur in any area of an economy where prices rise rapidly and higher than their traditionally understood values. Prices rise dramatically because the public begins to see a particular market as generating almost limitless growth and profits. This can occur in virtually any market, from housing to stocks; most famously, in Holland in the 1600s a bubble formed in the market for tulips. While such bubbles can have global factors (the tulip bubble was fueled in part by trade), psychological factors are more important, since they drive mass expectations of profits, the rapid inflation of prices, and the eventual bursting of the bubble and resulting panic. To return to our discussion in Chapter 1, an understanding of cognitive, often seemingly irrational factors may tell us more in this regard than any consideration of global forces.

But it would be too simple to conclude that the psychology of the masses—the foolishness of crowds, if you will—can alone explain major economic declines. While a bubble in housing prices was a catalyst for the current recession, this does not take into consideration what led to the rise in housing prices or stocks to begin with, or why the impact spread so far. To account for the broader causes and effects of the housing bubble and its collapse, many would point to the international liberalization of finance (in other words, the global movement of money) over the past few decades.

We noted earlier in the chapter the rise of IGOs like the IMF and the World Bank, and the role that the Bretton Woods System played in the process of economic liberalization. These institutions originated immediately after World War II, but it was primarily after the Cold War that restrictions on capital began to be eased, allowing finance to move unimpeded around the world. Money could go where it wanted, investing in stocks or providing loans worldwide to people, firms, and countries. But easy movement in could also mean easy movement out. It was already clear a decade ago that liberalized finance could lead to "capital flight" if international investors grew jittery about a country's economic or political situation. In the late 1990s, investors fled from many East Asian markets following the collapse of a market bubble in the region. But global liberalization continued, increasing the possibility that, as the system of global finance expanded, a problem in one part of the world would radiate across countries and markets. Thus, as the housing bubble in the United States began to deflate, this affected not only American but also European banks that had invested in this area. And as American and European banks began to wobble, investors began to withdraw from stock markets around the world. Shrinking values of real estate and stocks eliminated wealth, dried up credit, decreased demand, and increased unemployment in the advanced democracies and beyond. However, countries whose exposure to global finance was more limited, like China and India, have so far suffered much less.

In short, we could conclude that while economic recession is not itself a function of globalization, the globalization of finance cre-

The global economic downturn was particularly stressful on the euro, a single currency perhaps ill-suited for the European Union's many members and varied economies.

ated a much riskier world economy. It is likely that in the future, global finance will become more regulated in order to prevent similar bubbles and panics. But does this mean less globalization? Is it possible to have a more globalized, more integrated, and at the same time more regulated world? Perhaps if globalization continues to expand, it will do so under the guidance of restrengthened states and international institutions. This chapter is yet to be written.

1. How has the increasingly unrestricted flow of money made economies more vulnerable to "capital flight"?

2. Why did the deflation of the housing bubble in the United State also affect European banks?

3. In what sense does economic globalization come at the expense of strong state autonomy?

at the expense of another's? How can freedom or equality be balanced globally in the absence of any single sovereign power or dominant regime? The very meanings of freedom and equality may evolve as new ways of thinking about individual choice and collective aspirations emerge. These changes could lead to greater stability, peace, and prosperity for humanity, or to greater conflict and misery. Whatever the path, states and nations, regimes and ideologies, and culture continue to play the dominant role in driving domestic politics, and domestic politics in driving world affairs. Comparative politics gives us the power to analyze the present, glimpse the future, and play a role in shaping the course of human progress.

For Further Reading

Findlay, Ronald and Kevin H. O'Rourke, *Power and Plenty: Trade, War, and the World Economy in the Second Millennium* (Princeton: Princeton University Press, 2007).

RS> Florida, Richard. "The World Is Spiky: Globalization Has Changed the Economic Playing Field, But Hasn't Leveled It." *The Atlantic Monthly* 27, no. 9 (October 2005).

Ghemawat, Pankaj. *World 3.0: Global Prosperity and How to Achieve It* (Boston: Harvard Business Review Press, 2011).

RS> Jiang, Min. "Authoritarian Informationalism: China's Approach to Internet Sovereignty." *SAIS Review of International Affairs* 30, no. 2 (2010).

Keynes, John Maynard. *The Economic Consequences of the Peace* (New York: Harcourt, Brace and Howe, 1920).

Klein, Naomi. *The Shock Doctrine: The Rise of Disaster Capitalism* (New York: Picador, 2008).

RS> "Leviathan Stirs Again." *The Economist* (21 January 2010).

RS> Rodrik, Dani. *The Globalization Paradox: Democracy and the Future of the World Economy* (New York: W. W. Norton, 2011).

Sageman, Mare. *Leaderless Jihad: Terror Networks in the Twenty-First Century* (Philadelphia: University of Pennsylvania Press, 2008).

Wolf, Martin. *Why Globalization Works* (New Haven: Yale University Press, 2005).

RS>

Reader Selection

Highlighted selections are included in *Essential Readings in Comparative Politics*, Fourth Edition.

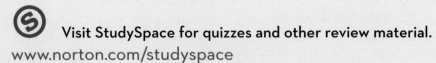

Visit StudySpace for quizzes and other review material.
www.norton.com/studyspace

- Vocabulary Flashcards of All Key Terms
- Chapter Review Quizzes
- Complete Study Reviews and Outlines

NOTES

CHAPTER 1: INTRODUCTION

1. Gary King, Robert Keohane, and Sidney Verba, *Designing Social Inquiry* (Princeton: Princeton University Press, 1994).

2. Gerardo Munck and Richard Snyder, "Debating the Direction of Comparative Politics: An Analysis of Leading Journals," *Comparative Political Studies* 40 (January 2007): 10.

3. Adam Przeworski, "Is a Science of Comparative Politics Possible?" and Robert J. Franzese, Jr., "Multicausality, Context-Conditionality, and Endogeneity," in *The Oxford Handbook of Comparative Politics*, ed. Charles Boix and Susan Stokes (Oxford: Oxford University Press, 2007).

4. Aristotle, *The Politics*, trans. T. A. Sinclair (New York: Viking, 1992).

5. Niccolò Machiavelli, *The Prince*, trans. W. K. Marriott (New York: Knopf, 1992).

6. For more on the behavioral revolution, see Robert A. Dahl, "The Behavioral Approach in Political Science: Epitaph for a Monument to a Successful Protest," *American Political Science Review* 55 (December 1961): 763–72.

7. David Laitin, "Comparative Politics: The State of the Subdiscipline," in *Political Science: The State of the Discipline*, ed. Ira Katznelson and Helen V. Milner (New York: W. W. Norton, 2002); James D. Fearon and David Laitin, "Integrating Qualitative and Quantitative Methods," in *The Oxford Handbook of Political Methodology*, ed. Janet M. Box-Steffensmeier, Henry E. Brady, and David Collier (Oxford: Oxford University Press, 2008).

8. Munck and Snyder, "Debating the Direction of Comparative Politics," 11.

9. Philip Tetlock, *Expert Political Judgment* (Princeton: Princeton University Press, 2005).

CHAPTER 2: STATES

1. U.S. history explains why *state* has different connotations for Americans. During the period of revolutionary struggle and the creation of a federal system, the former British colonies in America viewed themselves as independent political units—that is, as states. With the creation of a federal system of government, however, their individual powers were subordinated to a central authority. The United States of America, in other words, eventually became a system of national government, with the term

state left as a remnant of the brief period when these units acted largely as independent entities.

2. Max Weber, "Politics as a Vocation," in *From Max Weber: Essays in Sociology*, ed. and trans. H. H. Gerth and C. Wright Mills (New York: Oxford University Press, 1958), 77–128.

3. This idea has been developed by Charles Tilly, "War Making and State Making as Organized Crime," in *Bringing the State Back In*, ed. Peter Evans, Dietrich Rueschemeyer, and T. Skopol (New York: Cambridge University Press, 1985), 169–91.

4. The continuing power of states as institutions can be attested to in part by the fact that the number of states keeps increasing: Montenegro in 2006, Kosovo in 2008, South Sudan in 2011.

5. Azar Gat, *War in Human Civilization* (New York: Oxford University Press, 2006); Lawrence Keeley, *War Before Civilization: The Myth of the Peaceful Savage* (New York: Oxford University Press, 1997).

6. Angus Maddison, *Contours of The World Economy, 1–2030 AD* (New York: Oxford University Press, 2007).

7. Charles Tilly, *Coercion, Capital, and European States: 990–1990* (Oxford: Blackwell, 1990).

8. Jared Diamond, *Guns, Germs, and Steel: The Fates of Human Societies* (New York: W. W. Norton, 1997); Francis Fukuyama, *The Origins of Political Order: From Prehuman Times to the French Revolution* (New York: Farrar, Straus and Giroux, 2011).

9. Mancur Olson, "Democracy, Dictatorship, and Development," *American Political Science Review* 87 (September 1993): 567–76; Margaret Levy, "The State of the Study of the State," *Political Science: The State of the Discipline*, ed. Ira Katznelson (New York: W. W. Norton, 2002), 40–43.

10. For the cultural explanation, see David Landes, *The Wealth and Poverty of Nations: Why Some Are So Rich and Some So Poor* (New York: W. W. Norton, 1999), as well as Fukuyama, *Origins of Political Order*.

11. Stephen Krasner, "The Case for Shared Sovereignty," *Journal of Democracy* 16 (2005): 69–83.

12. Bruce Gilley, *The Right to Rule: How States Win and Lose Legitimacy* (New York: Columbia University Press, 2009), 4.

13. Weber, "Politics as a Vocation."

14. Robert I. Rotberg, ed., *When States Fail: Causes and Consequences* (Princeton: Princeton University Press, 2003).

15. Olaf J. de Groot and Anja Shortland, "Gov-aargh-nance—'Even Criminals Need Law and Order,'" CEDI Discussion Paper Series, Center for Economic Development and Institutions (February 2011), available at www.cedi.org.uk (accessed 2/6/2012).

16. Christophe Jafferlot, "India and Pakistan: Interpreting the Divergence of Two Political Trajectories," *Cambridge Review of International Affairs* 15 (July 2002): 253–67; Philip Oldenburg, *India, Pakistan and Democracy: Solving the Puzzle of Divergent Paths* (New York: Routledge, 2010).

CHAPTER 3: NATIONS AND SOCIETY

1. See, e.g., J. Philippe Rushton, "Ethnic Nationalism, Evolutionary Psychology and Genetic Similarity Theory," *Nations and Nationalism* 11 (2005): 489–507.

2. Edward L. Glaeser, "Inequality," KSG Working Paper No. RWP05-056 (October 2005), available at SSRN: http://ssrn.com/abstract=832653; see also Marc Hooge, et al, "Ethnic Diversity and Generalized Trust in Europe: A Cross-National Multilevel Study," *Comparative Political Studies* 42 (February 2009): 198–223.

3. Jack Jedwab, "Quebecers, Canada and Questions of Attachment: New Report of the Association for Canadian Studies," March 14, 2011, www.acs-aec.ca (accessed 2/6/2012).

4. Charles Tilly, ed., *The Formation of National States in Western Europe* (Princeton: Princeton University Press, 1975); see also Reinhard Bendix, *Nation-Building and Citizenship* (Berkeley: University of California Press, 1964); Douglass C. North and R. P. Thomas, *Rise of the Western World: A New Economic History* (New York: Cambridge University Press, 1976).

5. Stathis Kalyvas, "Civil Wars," in *The Oxford Handbook of Comparative Politics*, ed. Carles Boix and Susan C. Stokes (New York: Oxford University Press, 2007); James D. Fearon and David Laitin, "Ethnicity, Insurgency, and Civil War," *American Political Science Review* 97 (February 2003): 75–90.

6. Stefan Wolff, "Building Democratic States after Conflict: Institutional Design Revisited," *International Studies Review* 12 (March 2010): 128–41.

7. Alfred Stepan, Juan Linz, and Yogendra Yadav, *Crafting State-Nations: India and Other Multinational Democracies* (Baltimore: Johns Hopkins University Press, 2011).

8. Destutt de Tracy, *A Treatise on Political Economy* (New York: Kelley, 1970).

9. Thomas Jefferson, *Notes on the State of Virginia: Query XVII: Religion*, available at http://teachingamericanhistory.org/library/index.asp?document=291 (accessed 2/6/2012).

10. Qtd. in George Plechanoff, *Anarchism and Socialism* (Chicago: Kerr, 1909), 80.

11. Bruce Lawrence, *Defenders of God: The Fundamentalist Revolt against the Modern Age* (New York: Harper and Row, 1989), 78.

12. For an excellent discussion of fundamentalism in Christianity, Islam, and Judaism, see Karen Armstrong, *The Battle for God* (New York: Ballantine, 2001).

13. Gilles Kepel, *Revenge of God: The Resurgence of Islam, Christianity and Judaism in the Modern World*, trans. Alan Brayley (University Park: Pennsylvania State University Press,

1994); see also Daniel Philpott, "Has the Study of Global Politics Found Religion?" *Annual Review of Political Science* 12 (2009): 183–202.

14. Samuel P. Huntington, *The Clash of Civilizations and the Remaking of World Order* (New York: Simon and Schuster, 1996).

15. Ronald Inglehart and Christian Wetzel, "How Development Leads to Democracy," *Foreign Affairs* 88 (March–April 2009): 33–48.

16. Pippa Norris and Ronald Inglehart, *Sacred and Secular: Religion and Politics Worldwide* (New York: Cambridge University Press, 2004).

CHAPTER 4: POLITICAL ECONOMY

1. For a discussion of the difficulties inherent in providing public goods, see Mancur Olson, *The Logic of Collective Action: Public Goods and the Theory of Groups* (Cambridge: Harvard University Press, 1965).

2. On deflation see Nouriel Roubini and Stephen Mihm, *Crisis Economics: A Crash Course in the Future of Finance* (New York: Penguin, 2010).

3. Clyde E. Dankert, ed., *Adam Smith, Man of Letters and Economist* (Hicksville: Exposition Press, 1974), 218.

4. Edward Bernstein, *Evolutionary Socialism: A Criticism and Affirmation* (New York: Schocken, 1961).

5. OECD Tax Database, available at www.oecd.org/ctp/taxdatabase (accessed 2/6/2012).

6. For more on the variation within social democratic systems, see Gosta Esping-Anderson, *The Three Worlds of Welfare Capitalism* (Princeton: Princeton University Press, 1990).

7. For a discussion of communist political economies, see Robert W. Campbell, *The Socialist Economies in Transition: A Primer on Semi-Reformed Systems* (Bloomington: Indiana University Press, 1991).

8. The classic work on mercantilism is Friedrich List, *The National System of Political Economy* (New York: Kelley, 1966).

9. For a recent defense of mercantilism, see Ha-Joon Chang, *Bad Samaritans: The Myth of Free Trade and the Secret History of Capitalism* (New York: Bloomsbury, 2007).

10. Charles I. Jones and Peter Klenow, "Beyond GDP? Welfare across Countries and Time," NBER Working Paper no. 16352 (September 2010).

11. For calculation of global Gini index, see Branko Milanovic, *The Haves and the Have-Nots: A Brief and Idiosyncratic History of Global Inequality* (New York: Basic Books, 2011); on poverty, see Xavier Salai-i-Martin and Maxim Pinkovskiy, "Parametric Estimations of the World Distribution of Income," NBER Working Paper no. 15433 (October 2009).

12. The United Nations Human Development Indicators can be accessed at http://hdr .undp.org.

13. Richard A. Easterlin, *Happiness, Growth and the Life Cycle* (New York: Oxford University Press, 2011).

14. For crossnational comparisons of happiness and a critique of Easterlin's views, see Ruut Veenhoven, World Database of Happiness, Distributional Findings in Nations, Erasmus University Rotterdam, available at http://worlddatabaseofhappiness.eur.nl (accessed 2/6/2012); on Latin America in particular, see *Beyond Facts: Understanding Quality of Life* (Washington: Inter-American Development Bank, 2008).

15. This section draws heavily from Steinmo, *The Evolution of Modern States*.

16. Fraser Institute, *Economic Freedom of the World Annual Report 2010,* available at www .freetheworld.com; see also Heritage Foundation, *Index of Economic Freedom 2011*, available at www.heritage.org (accessed 2/6/2012).

17. Sven Steinmo, *The Evolution of Modern States: Sweden, Japan and the United States* (New York: Cambridge University Press, 2010).

18. Joseph Stiglitz, *Freefall: America, Free Markets, and the Sinking of the World Economy* (New York: W. W. Norton, 2010); Ian Bremer, *The End of the Free Market: Who Wins the War between States and Corporations?* (New York: Penguin, 2010).

CHAPTER 5: DEMOCRATIC REGIMES

1. C. B. MacPherson, *The Life and Times of Liberal Democracy* (New York: Oxford University Press, 1977).

2. Christopher Blackwell, ed., *Demos: Classical Athenian Democracy*, www.stoa.org/ projects/demos/home (accessed 1/1/12).

3. For details, see Charles Tilly, "War Making and State Making as Organized Crime," in *Bringing the State Back In*, ed. Peter B. Evans, Dietrich Rueschemeyer, and Theda Skocpol (New York: Cambridge University Press, 1985), 165–91; see also Francis Fukuyama, *The Origins of Political Order* (New York: Farrar, Straus and Giroux, 2011).

4. Adam Przeworski and Fernando Limongi, "Modernization: Theories and Facts," *World Politics* 49.2 (1997): 155–183.

5. Daron Acemoglu and James A. Robinson, *Economic Origins of Dictatorship and Democracy* (New York: Cambridge University Press, 2007).

6. Alexis de Tocqueville, *Democracy in America*, vol. 2, trans. Henry Reeve (New York: Henry G. Langley, 1845) 125, Google Books.

7. Vladimir Tismaneanu, *In Search of Civil Society: Independent Peace Movements in the Soviet Bloc* (London: Routledge, 1990).

8. David S. Law and Mila Versteeg, "The Evolution and Ideology of Global Constitutionalism," Legal Studies Research Paper Series Paper no. 10-10-01, October 4, 2010.

9. William T. Hutchinson, et al., eds., *The Papers of James Madison*, vol. 14 (Chicago: University of Chicago Press, 1985), 197–98.

10. An exhaustive discussion of the different forms of electoral systems and other facets of voting and elections can be found at the ACE Electoral Knowledge Network Web site, www.aceproject.org (accessed 2/6/2012)

11. Maurice Duverger, *Political Parties: Their Organization and Activity in the Modern State* (New York: Wiley, 1964).

12. Advocates for majority SMDs in the United States can be found at the Center for Voting and Democracy Web site, www.fairvote.org (accessed 2/6/2012).

13. For more on this debate, see the ACE Electoral Knowledge Network Web site (www.aceproject.org), as well as *Electoral System Design: The New International IDEA Handbook* (Stockholm: International Institute for Democracy and Electoral Assistance, 2005).

14. For a critique of the use of direct democracy, see Fareed Zakaria, *The Future of Freedom: Illiberal Democracy at Home and Abroad* (New York: W. W. Norton, 2003).

15. Patrick H. O'Neil, "Revolution from Within: Institutional Analysis, Transitions from Authoritarianism, and the Case of Hungary," *World Politics* 48.4 (1996): 579–603.

16. Council of Europe Venice Commission, Opinion on the New Constitution of Hungary, Opinion 618, June 20, 2011.

CHAPTER 6: NONDEMOCRATIC REGIMES

1. See the Freedom House Web site, www.freedomhouse.org (accessed 2/6/2012).

2. For an excellent discussion of the bewildering varieties of nondemocratic rule, see Juan Linz, *Totalitarian and Authoritarian Regimes* (Boulder: Lynne Rienner, 2000).

3. Linz, *Totalitarian and Authoritarian Regimes*.

4. Hannah Arendt, *Totalitarianism* (New York: Harcourt, Brace and World, 1951).

5. Mahathir Mohamad and Shintaro Ishihara, *Voice of Asia: Two Leaders Discuss the Coming Century* (Tokyo: Kodansha International, 1996), 82.

6. Michael Bratton and Nicholas Van de Walle provide details of Mobutu's rule in "Neopatrimonial Regimes and Political Transitions in Africa," *World Politics* 46.4 (1994): 453–89.

7. See Guillermo O'Donnell, *Modernization and Bureaucratic Non-democratic Regimes: Studies in South American Politics* (Berkeley: Institute of International Studies, 1973);

see also Hristos Doucouliagos and Mehmet Ali Ulubasoglu, "Democracy and Economic Growth: A Meta-Analysis," *American Journal of Political Science* 52.1 (2008): 61–83.

8. Muhammad Al-Atawneh, "Is Saudi Arabia a Theocracy? Religion and Governance in Contemporary Saudi Arabia," *Middle Eastern Studies* 45.5 (2009): 721–37.

9. See Arch Puddington, "Freedom in the World 2011: The Authoritarian Challenge to Democracy," www.freedomhouse.org (accessed 6/15/2011).

10. Oswald Spengler, *The Decline of the West* (New York: Knopf, 1928), 347.

11. Kwame Anthony Appiah, *The Honor Code: How Moral Revolutions Happen* (New York: W. W. Norton, 2010).

CHAPTER 7: POLITICAL VIOLENCE

1. M. J. Heale, *American Anticommunism: Battling the Enemy Within, 1830–1970* (Baltimore: Johns Hopkins University Press, 1990).

2. Max Abrams, "What Terrorists Really Want," *International Security* 32 (Spring 2008): 78–105.

3. Robert Pape, *Dying to Win: The Strategic Logic of Suicide Terrorism* (New York: Random House, 2005).

4. Timur Kuran, "Now out of Never: The Element of Surprise in the East European Revolution of 1989," *World Politics* 44 (October 1991): 7–48. See also Charles Tilly and Sidney Tarrow, *Contentious Politics* (Boulder: Paradigm Publishers, 2007).

5. *Arab Human Development Report 2009: Challenges to Human Security in the Arab Countries* (New York: United Nations, 2009), 2. See also Eva Bellin, "The Robustness of Authoritarianism in the Middle East: Exceptionalism in Comparative Perspective," *Comparative Politics* 36 (January 2004): 139–57.

6. Lin Noueihed, "Peddler's Martyrdom Launched Tunisia's Revolution," Reuters Africa, Jan. 19, 2011, http://af.reuters.com (accessed 1/31/2012).

7. Stephen M. Walt, *Revolution and War* (Ithaca: Cornell University Press, 1996).

8. Alan B. Krueger, *What Makes a Terrorist: Economics and the Roots of Terrorism* (Princeton: Princeton University Press, 2008).

9. Alberto Abadie, "Poverty, Political Freedom, and the Roots of Terrorism," NBER Working Paper No. W10859, October 2004, papers.ssrn.com (accessed on 1/31/2012). See also Krueger, *What Makes a Terrorist.*

10. Randy Borum, *Psychology of Terrorism* (Tampa: University of South Florida, 2004).

11. Maximilien Robespierre, *On the Moral and Political Principles of Domestic Policy,* 1794, www.fordham.edu (accessed 1/31/2012).

12. *We Are the Initiators*, Shining Path Manifesto, Shining Path Central Committee, 1980, www.presidentegonzalo.org (accessed 1/31/2012).

13. Mohammed M. Hafez, "Armed Islamist Movements and Political Violence in Algeria," *Middle East Journal* 54 (Autumn 2000): 572–91.

14. Mark Juergensmeyer, *Terror in the Mind of God: The Global Rise of Religious Violence* (Berkeley: University of California Press, 2003). See also David Livingstone Smith, *Less than Human: Why We Demean, Enslave, and Exterminate Others* (New York: St Martin's, 2011).

15. Alexis de Tocqueville, *The Old Regime and the Revolution* (New York: Harper and Brothers, 1856), 27.

16. Quoted in Hafez, "Armed Islamist Movements," 590.

17. William Pierce, "The Morality of Survival," May 2001, www.natvan.com (accessed on 1/31/2012). See also Brad Whitsel, "*The Turner Diaries* and Cosmotheism: William Pierce's Theology," *Nova Religio* 1 (April 1998): 183–97.

18. Anders Breivik, "2083: A European Declaration of Independence," 2011, www.archive .org (accessed on 1/31/2012).

19. Daniel A. Metraux, "Religious Terrorism in Japan: The Fatal Appeal of Aum Shinrikyo," *Asian Survey* 35 (December 1995): 1140–54.

20. Kirsten Christiansen, "When Radical Becomes Terrorist: Law Enforcement and Eco-Sabotage," in *A New Understanding of Terrorism: Case Studies, Trajectories and Lessons Learned*, ed. M. R. Haberfeld and Agostino von Hassels (New York: Springer, 2009).

21. "How Freedom Is Won: From Civic Resistance to Durable Democracy," Freedom House Special Report, 2005, www.freedomhouse.org (accessed 8/15/2009).

22. Shane Harris, *The Watchers: The Rise of America's Surveillance State* (New York: Penguin, 2010).

23. *An Historical Review of the Constitution and Government of Pennsylvania* (London, 1759), i.

CHAPTER 8: ADVANCED DEMOCRACIES

1. For details on the historical development of the EU, see Derek Irwin, *The Community of Europe: A History of European Integration since 1945* (New York: Addison-Wesley, 1995).

2. See the Web site of the EU: http://europa.eu/about-eu/.

3. For discussions of clientelism and its effect on the Greek economy, see Dimitri A. Sotirpoulos, "Democratization, Administrative Reform and the State in Greece, Italy, Portugal and Spain: Is There a 'Model' of South European Bureaucracy?," Hellenic

Observatory, April 2004; and Kevin Featherstone, "Varieties of Capitalism and the Greek Case: Explaining the Constraints on Domestic Reform," Hellenic Observatory, February 2008.

4. "Mean Center of Population for the United States, 1790 to 2000," United States Census, https://ask.census.gov (accessed 2/14/2012).

5. Vincent Morelli, "European Union Enlargement: A Status Report on Turkey's Accession Status," Congressional Research Service, March 15, 2011, www.fas.org/sgp/crs/row/RS22517.pdf (accessed 2/15/2012).

6. For a broader discussion of devolution, see Larry Diamond with Svetlana Tsalik, "Size and Democracy: The Case for Decentralization," in *Developing Democracy: Toward Consolidation*, ed. Larry Diamond (Baltimore: Johns Hopkins University Press, 1999).

7. Robert Cooper, *The Postmodern State and the World Order* (London: Demos, 1996).

8. For further discussion, see Pippa Norris and Ronald Inglehart, *Sacred and Secular: Religion and Politics Worldwide* (New York: Cambridge University Press, 2004).

9. "The Next Four Decades: The Older Population in the United States, 2010–2050," U.S. Census Department, www.census.gov/prod/2010pubs/p25-1138.pdf (accessed 2/14/2012).

10. For a controversial work on this topic, see Samuel Huntington, *Who Are We? The Challenges to America's National Identity* (New York: Simon and Schuster, 2004); on immigration and assimilation in Canada, see Jeffrey G. Reitz, et al., *Multiculturalism and Social Cohesion: Potentials and Challenges of Diversity* (New York: Springer, 2009).

11. See Ian Buruma, *Murder in Amsterdam: The Death of Theo Van Gogh and the Limits of Tolerance* (New York: Penguin, 2006).

12. "Germany's Angela Merkel: Multiculturalism Has 'Utterly Failed,'" *Christian Science Monitor*, October 17, 2010.

13. Anders Breivik, "2083: A European Declaration of Independence," 2011, www.archive.org (accessed 1/31/2012).

14. *OECD Factbook 2010: Economic, Environmental, and Social Statistics* (Paris: OECD, 2010).

15. See Dambisa Moyo, *How the West Was Lost: Fifty Years of Economic Folly—and the Stark Choices Ahead* (New York: Farrar, Straus and Giroux, 2011).

16. For data on population trends worldwide, see Population Reference Bureau, World Population Data Sheet, www.prb.org (accessed 2/14/2012).

17. Markus Crepaz, *Trust beyond Borders: Immigration, the Welfare State, and Identity in Modern Societies* (Ann Arbor: University of Michigan Press, 2007).

18. For a discussion of this scenario, see Joseph E. Gagnon and Marc Hinterschweiger, "The Global Outlook for Government Debt over the Next 25 Years: Implications for the Economy and Public Policy," Peterson Institute for International Economics, June 2011.

CHAPTER 9: COMMUNISM AND POSTCOMMUNISM

1. For a good overview of communist theory, see Alfred Meyer, *Communism* (New York: Random House, 1984).

2. See Marx's 1882 preface to the Russian translation of the *Communist Manifesto*, www .marxists.org (accessed 2/15/2012).

3. See V. I. Lenin, *What Is to Be Done? Burning Questions of Our Movement*, trans. Joe Fineberg and George Hanna (New York: International Publishers, 1969).

4. For a comparative discussion of different communist systems, see Stephen White et al, *Communist and Post-Communist Political Systems* (New York: St. Martin's Press, 1990).

5. See Michael Voslensky, *Nomenklatura: Anatomy of the Soviet Ruling Class* (Garden City: Doubleday, 1984).

6. See Robert Conquest, *The Great Terror: A Reassessment* (New York: Oxford University Press, 1990).

7. See Lowell Dittmer, *China's Continuous Revolution: The Post-Liberation Epoch, 1949–1981* (Berkeley: University of California Press, 1987).

8. Robert W. Campbell, *The Socialist Economies in Transition: A Primer on Semi-Reformed Systems* (Bloomington: Indiana University Press, 1991).

9. Quoted in Frank Dikotter, *Mao's Great Famine: The History of China's Most Devastating Catastrophe, 1958–62* (New York: Bloomsbury, 2010), 88.

10. Karl Marx and Friedrich Engels, *Manifesto of the Communist Party*, www.marxists.org/ archive/marx/works/1848/communist-manifesto/ (accessed 2/15/2012).

11. Joni Lovenduski and Jean Woodall, *Politics and Society in Eastern Europe* (Bloomington: Indiana University Press, 1987), s158.

12. Marcy McAuley, *Soviet Politics 1917–1991* (New York: Oxford University Press, 1992).

13. The best retrospective studies of the collapse of communism in Eastern Europe and its effects in the Soviet Union can be found in Mark Kramer, "The Collapse of East European Communism and the Repercussions within the Soviet Union," parts 1–3, *Journal of Cold War Studies* (Fall 2003, Fall 2004, and Spring 2005).

14. On the collapse of communism in Eastern Europe, see Timothy Garton Ash, *The Magic Lantern: The Revolution of 1989 Witnessed in Warsaw, Budapest, Berlin and Prague* (New York: Random House, 1990); on the collapse of communism in the Soviet Union, see David Remnick, *Lenin's Tomb: The Last Days of the Soviet Empire* (New York: Random House, 1993).

15. See Minxin Pei, *China's Trapped Transition: The Limits of Developmental Autocracy* (Cambridge: Harvard University Press, 2006).

16. See the Web site of Falun Gong at www.faluninfo.net/.

17. This idea is articulated in Abdullah Azzam, *Join the Caravan* (London: Azzam, 2001).

18. See, for example, Christopher Hughes, "Reclassifying Chinese Nationalism: The Geopolitik Turn," *Journal of Contemporary China* 20.17 (2011): 601–20; and Marlene Laurelle, *Russian Nationalism in Putin's Russia* (New York: Routledge, 2009).

CHAPTER 10: LESS-DEVELOPED AND NEWLY INDUSTRIALIZING COUNTRIES

1. For two excellent studies of imperialism in practice, see L. H. Gann and Peter Duignan, eds., *Imperialism in Africa, 1870–1960* (Cambridge: Cambridge University Press, 1969–75); and Nicolas Tarling, ed., *The Cambridge History of Southeast Asia* (Cambridge: Cambridge University Press, 1992).

2. A general discussion of the impact of imperialism can be found in Paul Cammack, David Pool, and William Tordoff, *Third World Politics: An Introduction* (Baltimore: Johns Hopkins University Press, 1993); see also Philip D. Curtin, *The World and the West: The European Challenge and the Overseas Response in the Age of Empire* (Cambridge: Cambridge University Press, 2000).

3. Alberto F. Alesino, Paola Giuliano, and Nathan Nunn, "On the Origins of Gender Roles: Women and the Plough," NBER Working Paper No. 17098, May 2011; Elizabeth Schmidt, *Peasants, Traders and Wives: Shona Women in the History of Zimbabwe, 1870–1939* (New York: Heinemann, 1992).

4. For a Marxist analysis of dependent development as it applies to Latin America, see Eduardo H. Galeano, *Open Veins of Latin America: Five Centuries of the Pillage of a Continent*, trans. Cedric Belfrage (New York: Monthly Review Press, 1998).

5. See Joel S. Migdal, *Strong Societies and Weak States: State-Society Relations and State Capabilities in the Third World* (Princeton: Princeton University Press, 1988).

6. For a discussion of these issues, see Dennis L. Thompson and Dov Ronen, eds., *Ethnicity, Politics, and Development* (Boulder: Lynne Rienner, 1986).

7. Valerie Hudson et al, "The Heart of the Matter: The Security of Women and the Security of States," *International Security* 33 (Winter 2009): 7–45; Valerie Hudson and Andrea M. Den Boer, *Bare Branches: The Security Implications of Asia's Surplus Male Population* (Cambridge: MIT Press, 2005).

8. For a discussion of different paths of industrialization, see Stephan Haggard, *Pathways from the Periphery: The Politics of Growth in Newly Industrializing Countries* (Ithaca: Cornell University Press, 1990).

9. For a good overview of these issues and responses, see Paul Collier, *The Bottom Billion: Why the Poorest Countries Are Failing and What Can Be Done about It* (Oxford: Oxford University Press, 2007).

10. Francis Fukuyama, *State Building: Governance and World Order in the 21st Century* (Ithaca: Cornell University Press, 2004).

11. See, e.g., Seth Kaplan, *Fixing Fragile States: A New Paradigm for Development* (Westport: Praeger, 2008).

12. Stephen Krasner, "The Case for Shared Sovereignty," *Journal of Democracy* 16 (January 2005): 69–83.

13. Don Eberly, *The Rise of Global Civil Society* (New York: Encounter, 2008).

14. For more on the Millennium Development Goals, see www.unmillenniumproject.org.

15. See, e.g., William Easterley, *The White Man's Burden: Why the West's Efforts to Aid the Rest Have Done So Much Ill and So Little Good* (New York: Penguin, 2006).

16. Hernando De Soto, *The Mystery of Capital: Why Capitalism Triumphs in the West and Fails Everywhere Else* (New York: Basic Books, 2000); see also De Soto's work at the Institute for Liberty and Democracy at www.ild.org.pe.

17. See www.kiva.org.

18. One evaluation of microcredit can be found in Abhijit Banerjee et al, "The Miracle of Microfinance? Evidence from a Randomized Evaluation," Massachusets Institute of Techology, Department of Economics, http://econ-www.mit.edu/files/4162 (accessed 2/15/2012).

19. Atul Kohli, *State Directed Development: Political Power and Industrialization in the Global Periphery* (New York: Cambridge, 2004).

20. Laura Ruth, "Bio or Bust? The Economic and Ecological Cost of Biofuels," *European Molecular Biology Organization Reports* 9.2 (2008): 130–33; David Biello, "Intoxicated on Independence: Is Domestically Produced Ethanol Worth the Cost?," *Scientific American* July 28, 2011.

CHAPTER 11: GLOBALIZATION AND THE FUTURE OF COMPARATIVE POLITICS

1. Jared Diamond, *Guns, Germs and Steel: The Fate of Human Societies* (New York: W. W. Norton, 1997).

2. See Robert O. Keohane and Joseph S. Nye, Jr., "Introduction," in *Governance in a Globalizing World*, ed. Nye and John D. Donahue (Washington: Brookings Institution Press, 2000), 1–41.

3. Thomas Friedman, *The Lexus and the Olive Tree* (New York: Farrar, Straus and Giroux, 2000).

4. Mare Sageman, *Leaderless Jihad: Terror Networks in the Twenty-First Century* (Philadelphia: University of Pennsylvania Press, 2008).

5. John Fonte, "Democracy's Trojan Horse," *National Interest* 76 (Summer 2004): 117–27.

6. *World Investment Report 2011*, www.unctad.org (accessed 2/17/2011).

7. Martin Wolf, *Why Globalization Works* (New Haven: Yale University Press, 2005).

8. World Migration Report 2010, International Organization for Migration, www.iom .int (accessed 2/27/2012).

9. Naomi Klein, *The Shock Doctrine: The Rise of Disaster Capitalism* (New York: Picador, 2008).

10. Tyler Cowen, *Creative Destruction: How Globalization Is Changing the World's Cultures* (Princeton: Princeton University Press, 2004).

11. David Held, *Democracy and the Global Order* (Cambridge: Polity Press, 1995).

12. Manuel Castells, "The New Public Sphere: Global Civil Society, Communication Networks, and Global Governance," *Annals of the American Academy of Political and Social Science* 16 (March 2008): 78–93.

13. George Ritzer, *The Globalization of Nothing* (Thousand Oaks: Pine Forge Press, 2007), and *Enchanting and Disenchanted World: Continuity and Change in the Cathedrals of Consumption* (Thousand Oaks: Pine Forge Press, 2009).

14. Ronald Findlay and Kevin H. O'Rourke, *Power and Plenty: Trade, War, and the World Economy in the Second Millennium* (Princeton: Princeton University Press, 2007).

15. Tom Standage, *The Victorian Internet: The Remarkable Story of the Telegraph and the Nineteenth Century's On-Line Pioneers* (New York: Berkley, 1998).

16. John Maynard Keynes, *The Economic Consequences of the Peace* (New York: Harcourt, Brace and Howe, 1920), 11–12.

17. Jack Goldsmith and Tim Wu, *Who Controls the Internet? The Illusions of a Borderless World* (Oxford: Oxford University Press, 2006).

18. Bruce Hoffman, "The Leaderless Jihad's Leader: Why Osama Bin Laden Mattered," *Foreign Affairs* May 13, 2011.

19. See Pankaj Ghemawat, *World 3.0: Global Prosperity and How to Achieve It* (Boston: Harvard Business Review Press, 2011); Piet Sercu and Rosanne Vanpee, "Home Bias in International Equity Portfolios; a Review," Katholieke Universiteit Leuven, Faculty of Economics and Applied Sciences, August 2007.

20. Martin Ravallion, "Looking beyond Averages in the Trade and Poverty Debate," *World Development* 34 (August 2006): 1374–92.

21. Thanks to TeleGeography Research for this information; on telephony in France, see "The Electronic Communications Services Market in France," ARCEP, February 2010, www.arcep.fr (accessed 2/14/2012).

22. Muhammad A. Shuraydi, "Feeling at Home Away from Home: The Pioneering Role of Al-Jazeera and Other Arab Transnational Satellite Channels in the Maintenance and Change of Arab Diasporic Enclaves," *Arab World Geographer* 9 (Spring 2006): 1–22.

23. Keynes, *The Economic Consequences of the Peace*, 12.

24. Jeffrey J. Schott, "The WTO after Seattle," in *The WTO after Seattle*, ed. Schott (Washington: Institute for International Economics, 2000), 5.

25. "Publics Want More Aggressive Government Action on Economic Crisis: Global Poll," WorldPublicOpinion.org, July 21, 2009, http://worldpublicopinion.org (accessed 2/14/2012).

26. The idea of semiglobalization is discussed in detail in Ghemawat, *World 3.0*.

GLOSSARY

ABSTRACT REVIEW Judicial review that allows the constitutional court to rule on questions that do not arise from actual legal disputes

ADVANCED DEMOCRACY A country with institutionalized democracy and a high level of economic development

ANARCHISM A political ideology that stresses the elimination of the state and private property as a way to achieve both freedom and equality for all

AREA STUDIES A regional focus when studying political science, rather than studying parts of the world where similar variables are clustered

ASYMMETRIC FEDERALISM When power is divided unevenly between regional bodies; for example, some regions are given greater power over taxation or language rights than others—a more likely outcome in a country with significant ethnic divisions

AUTHORITARIANISM A political system in which a small group of individuals exercises power over the state without being constitutionally responsible to the public

AUTONOMY The ability of the state to wield its power independently of the public

BASE The economic system of a society, made up of technology (the means of production) and class relations between people (the relations of production)

BEHAVIORAL REVOLUTION A movement within political science during the 1950s and 1960s to develop general theories about individual political behavior that could be applied across all countries

BICAMERAL SYSTEM A political system in which the legislature comprises two houses

BOURGEOISIE The property-owning class

BRETTON WOODS SYSTEM An economic regime that manages international economic relations; this includes the International Monetary Fund (IMF), the World Bank, and the World Trade Organization (WTO)

BUREAUCRATIC AUTHORITARIANISM A system in which the state bureaucracy and the military share a belief that a technocratic leadership, focused on rational, objective, and technical expertise, can solve the problems of the country without public participation

CAPACITY The ability of the state to wield power to carry out basic tasks, such as defending territory, making and enforcing rules, collecting taxes, and managing the economy

CAPITALISM A system of production based on private property and free markets

CENTRAL BANK The state institution that controls how much money is flowing through the economy, as well as how much it costs to borrow money in that economy

CENTRAL COMMITTEE The legislature-like body of a communist party

CENTRAL PLANNING A communist economic system in which the state explicitly allocates resources by planning what should be produced and in what amounts, the final prices of goods, and where they should be sold

CHARISMATIC LEGITIMACY Legitimacy built on the force of ideas embodied by an individual leader

CITIZENSHIP An individual's relationship to the state, wherein citizens swear allegiance to that state and the state in return is obligated to provide rights to those citizens

CIVIL LIBERTIES Individual rights regarding freedom that are created by the constitution and the political regime

CIVIL RIGHTS Individual rights regarding equality that are created by the constitution and the political regime

CIVIL SOCIETY Organizations outside of the state that help people define and advance their own interests

CLIENTELISM A process whereby the state co-opts members of the public by providing specific benefits or favors to a single person or a small group in return for public support

COERCION Compelling behavior by threatening harm

COLONIALISM An imperialist system of physically occupying a foreign territory using military force, businesses, or settlers

COMMUNISM (1) A political-economic system in which all wealth and property are shared so as to eliminate exploitation, oppression, and, ultimately, the need for political institutions such as the state; (2) A political ideology that advocates such a system

COMPARATIVE ADVANTAGE The ability of one country to produce a particular good or service more efficiently relative to other countries' efficiency in producing the same good or service

COMPARATIVE METHOD The means by which social scientists make comparisons across cases

COMPARATIVE POLITICS The study and comparison of domestic politics across countries

CONCRETE REVIEW Judicial review that allows the constitutional court to rule on the basis of actual legal disputes brought before it

CONSERVATIVES Those with a political attitude that is skeptical of change and supports the current order

CONSTITUENCY A geographical area that an elected official represents

CONSTITUTIONAL COURT The highest judicial body in a political system that decides whether laws and policies violate the constitution

CO-OPTATION The process by which individuals are brought into a beneficial relationship with the state, making them dependent on the state for certain rewards

CORPORATISM A method of co-optation whereby authoritarian systems create or sanction a limited number of organizations to represent the interests of the public and restrict those not set up or approved by the state

CORRELATION An apparent relationship between two or more variables

COUNTRY Term used to refer to state, government, regime, and the people who live within that political system

COUP D'ÉTAT A move in which military forces take control of the government by force

CULTURE Basic institutions that define a society

DEDUCTIVE REASONING Research that works from a hypothesis that is then tested against data

DEFLATION A period of falling prices and values for goods, services, investments, and wages

DEMOCRACY A political system in which political power is exercised either directly or indirectly by the people

DEVOLUTION A process in which political power is "sent down" to lower levels of state and government

DIALECTICAL MATERIALISM Process of historical change that is not evolutionary but revolutionary; the existing base and superstructure (thesis) would come into conflict with new technological innovations, generating growing opposition to the existing order (antithesis)—this would culminate in revolution, overthrowing the old base and superstructure (synthesis)

DIRECT DEMOCRACY Democracy that allows the public to participate directly in government decision making

ECONOMIC LIBERALIZATION Changes consistent with liberalism that aim to limit the power of the state and increase the power of the market and private property in an economy

ELECTORAL SYSTEM A set of rules that decide how votes are cast, counted, and translated into seats in a legislature

EMPIRE A single political authority that has under its sovereignty a large number of external regions or territories and different peoples

ENDOGENEITY The issue that cause and effect are not often clear, in that variables may be both cause and effect in relationship to one another

EQUALITY A shared material standard of individuals within a community, society, or country

ETHNIC CONFLICT A conflict in which different ethnic groups struggle to achieve certain political or economic goals at each other's expense

ETHNIC IDENTITY/ETHNICITY Specific attributes and societal institutions that make one group of people culturally different from others

EXECUTIVE The branch of government that carries out the laws and policies of a state

EXPORT-ORIENTED INDUSTRIALIZATION A mercantilist strategy for economic growth in which a country seeks out technologies and develops industries focused specifically on the export market

FAILED STATE A state so weak that its political structures collapse, leading to anarchy and violence

FASCISM A political ideology that asserts the superiority and inferiority of different groups of people and stresses a low degree of both freedom and equality in order to achieve a powerful state

FEDERALISM A system in which significant state powers, such as taxation, lawmaking, and security, are devolved to regional or local bodies

FIRST PAST THE POST An electoral system in which individual candidates compete in single-member districts; voters choose between candidates, and the candidate with the largest share of the vote wins the seat

FOREIGN DIRECT INVESTMENT The purchase of assets in a country by a foreign firm

FORMAL INSTITUTIONS Institutions usually based on officially sanctioned rules that are relatively clear

FREEDOM The ability of an individual to act independently, without fear of restriction or punishment by the state or other individuals or groups in society

FUNDAMENTALISM A view of religion as absolute and inerrant that should be legally enforced by making faith the sovereign authority

GAME THEORY An approach that emphasizes how actors or organizations behave in their goal to influence others. Built upon assumptions of rational choice

GINI INDEX A statistical formula that measures the amount of inequality in a society; its scale ranges from 0 to 100, where 0 corresponds to perfect equality and 100 to perfect inequality

GLASNOST Literally, openness. The policy of political liberalization implemented in the Soviet Union in the late 1980s

GLOBALIZATION The process of expanding and intensifying linkages between states, societies, and economies

GOVERNMENT The leadership or elite in charge of running the state

GROSS DOMESTIC PRODUCT (GDP) The total market value of all goods and services produced by a country over a period of one year

GUERRILLA WAR A conflict whereby nonstate combatants who largely abide by the rules of war target the state

HEAD OF GOVERNMENT The executive role that deals with the everyday tasks of running the state, such as formulating and executing policy

HEAD OF STATE The executive role that symbolizes and represents the people both nationally and internationally

HUMAN DEVELOPMENT INDEX (HDI) A statistical tool that attempts to evaluate the overall wealth, health, and knowledge of a country's people

HYPERINFLATION Inflation of more than 50 percent a month for more than two months in a row

IDEATIONAL Having to do with ideas

ILLIBERAL/HYBRID REGIME Rule by an elected leadership through procedures of questionable democratic legitimacy

IMPERIALISM A system in which a state extends its power to directly control territory, resources, and people beyond its borders

IMPORT SUBSTITUTION A mercantilist strategy for economic growth in which a country restricts imports in order to spur demand for locally produced goods

INDIRECT DEMOCRACY Democracy in which representatives of the public are responsible for government decision making

INDUCTIVE REASONING Research that works from case studies in order to generate hypotheses

INFLATION An outstripping of supply by demand, resulting in an increase in the general price level of goods and services and the resulting loss of value in a country's currency

INFORMAL ECONOMY A segment of the economy that is not regulated or taxed by the state

INFORMAL INSTITUTIONS Institutions with unwritten and unofficial rules

INITIATIVE A national vote called by members of the public to address a specific proposal

INSTITUTION An organization or activity that is self-perpetuating and valued for its own sake

INTEGRATION A process by which states pool their sovereignty, surrendering some individual powers in order to gain shared political, economic, or societal benefits

INTERGOVERNMENTAL ORGANIZATION (IGO) Group created by states to serve certain policy ends

INTERGOVERNMENTAL SYSTEM A system in which two or more countries cooperate on issues

INTERNATIONAL REGIME The fundamental rules and norms that link states together and shape their relationships to one another, usually regarding some specific issues (such as greenhouse gases or trade)

INTERNATIONAL RELATIONS A field in political science which concentrates on relations between countries, such as foreign policy, war, trade, and foreign aid

JUDICIAL REVIEW The mechanism by which courts can review the actions of government and overturn those that violate the constitution

KLEPTOCRACY "Rule by theft," where those in power seek only to drain the state of assets and resources

LAISSEZ-FAIRE The principle that the economy should be "allowed to do" what it wishes; a liberal system of minimal state interference in the economy

LEGISLATURE The branch of government charged with making laws

LEGITIMACY A value whereby an institution is accepted by the public as right and proper, thus giving it authority and power

LESS-DEVELOPED COUNTRY (LDC) A country that lacks significant economic development or political institutionalization or both

LIBERAL DEMOCRACY A political system that promotes participation, competition, and liberty and emphasizes individual freedom and civil rights

LIBERALISM (1) A political attitude that favors evolutionary transformation; (2) An ideology and political system that favors a limited state role in society and the economy, and places a high priority on individual political and economic freedom

MARKET The interaction between the forces of supply and demand that allocates resources

MARKETIZATION The creation of the market forces of supply and demand in a country

MERCANTILISM A political-economic system in which national economic power is paramount and the domestic economy is viewed as an instrument that exists primarily to serve the needs of the state

MICROCREDIT A system in which small loans are channeled to the poor through borrowing groups whose members jointly take responsibility for repayment

MICROFINANCE A loan system covering a broad spectrum, including credit, savings, insurance, and financial transfers

MILITARY RULE Rule by one or more military officials, often brought to power through a coup d'état

MIXED ELECTORAL SYSTEM An electoral system that uses a combination of single-member districts and proportional representation

MODERN Characterized as secular, rational, materialistic, technological, and bureaucratic, and placing a greater emphasis on individual freedom than in the past

MODERNIZATION THEORY A theory asserting that as societies developed, they would take on a set of common characteristics, including democracy and capitalism

MONOPOLY A single producer that is able to dominate the market for a good or service without effective competition

MULTICAUSALITY When variables are interconnected and interact together to produce particular outcomes

MULTIMEMBER DISTRICT (MMD) An electoral district with more than one seat

MULTINATIONAL CORPORATION (MNC) Firm that produces, distributes, and markets its goods or services in more than one country

NATION A group that desires self-government through an independent state

NATIONAL CONFLICT A conflict in which one or more groups within a country develop clear aspirations for political independence, clashing with others as a result

NATIONAL IDENTITY A sense of belonging to a nation and a belief in its political aspirations

NATIONALISM Pride in one's people and the belief that they have a unique political destiny

NATION-STATE A state encompassing one dominant nation that it claims to embody and represent

NEOCOLONIALISM An indirect form of imperialism in which powerful countries overly influence the economies of less-developed countries

NEOCORPORATISM A system of social democratic policy making in which a limited number of organizations representing business and labor work with the state to set economic policy

NEWLY INDUSTRIALIZING COUNTRY (NIC) A historically less-developed country that has experienced significant economic growth and democratization

NIHILISM A belief that all institutions and values are essentially meaningless and that the only redeeming value is violence

nomenklatura Politically sensitive or influential jobs in the state, society, or economy that were staffed by people chosen or approved by the Communist Party

NONDEMOCRATIC REGIMES A political regime that is controlled by a small group of individuals who exercise power over the state without being constitutionally responsible to the public

NONGOVERNMENTAL ORGANIZATION (NGO) A national or international group, independent of any state, that pursues policy objectives and fosters public participation

NONTARIFF REGULATORY BARRIERS Policies and regulations used to limit imports through methods other than taxation

OFFSHORE OUTSOURCING A process by which a firm moves some of its work to a secondary business outside the home country that can do the work more efficiently or cheaply

ONE-PARTY RULE Rule by one political party, with other parties banned or excluded from power

PARASTATAL Industry partially owned by the state

PARLIAMENTARY SYSTEM A political system in which the roles of head of state and head of government are assigned to separate executive offices

PARTY-STATE A political system in which power flows directly from the ruling political party (usually a communist party) to the state, bypassing government structures

PATRIMONIALISM An arrangement whereby a ruler depends on a collection of supporters within the state who gain direct benefits in return for enforcing the ruler's will

PATRIOTISM Pride in one's state

PERESTROIKA Literally, restructuring; the policy of political and economic liberalization implemented in the Soviet Union in the late 1980s

PERSONALITY CULT Promotion of the image of an authoritarian leader not merely as a political figure but as someone who embodies the spirit of the nation and possesses endowments of wisdom and strength far beyond those of the average individual and is thus portrayed in a quasi-religious manner

PERSONAL/MONARCHICAL RULE Rule by a single leader, with no clear regime or rules constraining that leadership

POLITBURO The top policy-making and executive body of a communist party

POLITICAL ATTITUDE Description of one's views regarding the speed and methods with which political changes should take place in a given society

POLITICAL CULTURE The basic norms for political activity in a society

POLITICAL-ECONOMIC SYSTEM The relationship between political and economic institutions in a particular country and the policies and outcomes they create

POLITICAL ECONOMY The study of the interaction between states and markets

POLITICAL IDEOLOGY The basic values held by an individual about the fundamental goals of politics or the ideal balance of freedom and equality

POLITICAL VIOLENCE Violence outside of state control that is politically motivated

POLITICS The struggle in any group for power that will give one or more persons the ability to make decisions for the larger group

POPULISM A political view that does not have a consistent ideological foundation, but that emphasizes hostility toward elites and established state and economic institutions and favors greater power in the hands of the public

POSTINDUSTRIALISM The shift during the last half century from an economy based primarily on industry and manufacturing to one in which the majority of people are employed in the service sector, which produces the bulk of profits

POSTMODERN Characterized by a set of values that center on "quality of life" considerations and give less attention to material gain

POWER The ability to influence others or impose one's will on them

PRESIDENTIAL SYSTEM A political system in which the roles of head of state and head of government are combined in one executive offices

PRIVATIZATION The transfer of state-owned property to private ownership

PROLETARIAT The working class

PROPERTY Goods or services that are owned by an individual or group, privately or publicly

PROPORTIONAL REPRESENTATION (PR) An electoral system in which political parties compete in multimember districts; voters choose between parties, and the seats in the district are awarded proportionally according to the results of the vote

PUBLIC GOODS Goods, provided or secured by the state, available to society and which no private person or organization can own

PURCHASING-POWER PARITY (PPP) A statistical tool that attempts to estimate the buying power of income across different countries by using prices in the United States as a benchmark

QUALITATIVE METHOD Study through an in-depth investigation of a limited number of cases

QUANTITATIVE METHOD Study through statistical data from many cases

QUOTA A nontariff barrier that limits the quantity of a good that may be imported into a country

RADICALS Those with a political attitude that favors dramatic, often revolutionary change

RATIONAL CHOICE Approach that assumes that individuals weigh the costs and benefits and make choices to maximize their benefits

RATIONAL-LEGAL LEGITIMACY Legitimacy based on a system of laws and procedures that are highly institutionalized

REACTIONARY Someone who seeks to restore the institutions of a real or imagined earlier order

REFERENDUM A national vote called by a government to address a specific proposal, often a change to the constitution

REGIME The fundamental rules and norms of politics, embodying long-term goals regarding individual freedom and collective equality, where power should reside, and the use of that power

REGULATION A rule or order that sets the boundaries of a given procedure

RELATIVE DEPRIVATION MODEL Model that predicts revolution when public expectations outpace the rate of domestic change

RENT SEEKING A process in which political leaders essentially rent out parts of the state to their patrons, who as a result control public goods that would otherwise be distributed in a nonpolitical manner

REPUBLICANISM Indirect democracy that emphasizes the separation of powers within a state and the representation of the public through elected officials

REVOLUTION Public seizure of the state in order to overturn the existing government and regime

RULE OF LAW A system in which all individuals and groups, including those in government, are subject to the law, irrespective of their power or authority

SELECTION BIAS A focus on effects rather than causes, which can lead to inaccurate conclusions about correlation or causation

SEMIPRESIDENTIAL SYSTEM An executive system that divides power between two strong executives, a president and a prime minister

SEPARATION OF POWERS The clear division of power between different branches of government and the provision that specific branches may check the power of other branches

SERVICE SECTOR Work that does not involve creating tangible goods

SHOCK THERAPY A process of rapid marketization

SINGLE-MEMBER DISTRICT (SMD) An electoral district with one seat

SOCIAL DEMOCRACY (SOCIALISM) (1) A political-economic system in which freedom and equality are balanced through the state's management of the economy and the provision of social expenditures; (2) A political ideology that advocates such a system

SOCIAL EXPENDITURES State provision of public benefits, such as education, health care, and transportation

SOCIETY Complex human organization, a collection of people bound by shared institutions that define how human relations should be conducted

SOVEREIGNTY The ability of a state to carry out actions or policies within a territory independently from external actors or internal rivals

STATE (1) The organization that maintains a monopoly of force over a given territory; (2) A set of political institutions to generate and execute policy regarding freedom and equality

STATE-SPONSORED TERRORISM Terrorism supported directly by a state as an instrument of foreign policy

STRONG STATE A state that is able to fulfill basic tasks, such as defending territory, making and enforcing rules, collecting taxes, and managing the economy

STRUCTURAL-ADJUSTMENT PROGRAM/WASHINGTON CONSENSUS A policy of economic liberalization adopted in exchange. for financial support from liberal international organizations; typically includes privatizing state-run firms, ending subsidies, reducing tariff barriers, shrinking the size of the state, and welcoming foreign investment

SUPERSTRUCTURE All noneconomic institutions in a society (e.g., religion, culture, national identity); these ideas and values derive from the base and serve to legitimize the current system of exploitation

SUPRANATIONAL SYSTEM An intergovernmental system with its own sovereign powers over member states

TARIFF A tax on imported goods

TERRORISM The use of violence by nonstate actors against civilians in order to achieve a political goal

THEOCRACY A nondemocratic form of rule where religion is the foundation for the regime

THEORY An integrated set of hypotheses, assumptions, and facts

TOTALITARIANISM A nondemocratic regime that is highly centralized, possessing some form of strong ideology that seeks to transform and absorb fundamental aspects of state, society, and the economy, using a wide array of institutions

TRADITIONAL LEGITIMACY Legitimacy that accepts aspects of politics because they have been institutionalized over a long period of time

UNICAMERAL SYSTEM A political system in which the legislature comprises one house

UNITARY STATE A state in which most political power exists at the national level, with limited local authority

VANGUARD OF THE PROLETARIAT Lenin's argument that an elite communist party would have to carry out revolution, because as a result of false consciousness, historical conditions would not automatically lead to capitalism's demise

VOTE OF NO CONFIDENCE Vote taken by a legislature as to whether its members continue to support the current prime minister; depending on the country, a vote of no confidence can force the resignation of the prime minister and/or lead to new parliamentary elections

WEAK STATE A state that has difficulty fulfilling basic tasks, such as defending territory, making and enforcing rules, collecting taxes, and managing the economy

CREDITS

PHOTOS:

Page 2: © Sampics/Corbis; p. 26: Sabah Arar/AFP/Getty Images; p. 51: © Rehan Khan/epa /Corbis; p. 56: Pedro Ladeira/AFP/Getty Images; p. 71: Naveen Jora/India Today Group /Getty Images; p. 90: © travelib asia/Alamy; p. 121: Mark Henley/AgeFotostock; p. 126: Bechir Taieb/AFP/Getty Images; p. 157: Szilard Koszticsak/epa/Corbis; p. 162: Daniel Mihailescu/AFP/Getty Images; p. 189: Odd Andersen/AFP/Getty Images; p. 192: Afolabi Sotunde/Reuters; p. 205: Miguel Medina/AFP/Getty Images; p. 224: Deleu/AgeFotostock; p. 241: Milos Bicanski/Getty Images; p. 256: © Swim Ink 2, LLC/CORBIS; p. 287: Bernard Bisson/Sygma/Corbis; p. 290: Phillipe Lissac/Godong/Corbis; p. 319: Jane Sweeney/JAI /Corbis; p. 322: Todd Maisel/NY Daily News Archive via Getty Images; p. 349: AP Photo /Peter Morrison.

TABLE:

INDEX

Page numbers in **boldface** refer to in-text glossary definitions. Page numbers in *italics* refer to figures and tables.

New Zealand:
 electoral system in, 155
 female suffrage in, 132
 happiness of, *117*
 immigration to, 247
 liberalism in, 104
Nigeria, 38
 constituencies in, 147, 148
 corruption in, 304–5, *304*
 economic liberalization in, *119*
 economic portrait of (2011), *229*
 electoral system in, 147, 148
 ethnic conflict in, 66, 67
 happiness of, *117*
 size of economy of, *113*
 wealth and prosperity compared in, *115*
 wealth distribution in, *113*
nihilism, **210**, 210–11
Niyazov, Saparmurat "Father of the
  Turkmen," 178
nomenklatura, 265–66, **265,** 271, 275, 281
nondemocratic regimes, **164**
nondemocratic rule, 163–90
 coercion and surveillance in, 174–76
 co-optation in, 176–78
 decline of, 187, 190, *190*
 defined, 164–65
 economic sources of, 168–74
 by illiberal regimes, 185, 186–87
 by military, 181–83, 185
 one-party, 183–84, 185, 205
 personal and monarchical, 180–81, 185, 205
 personality cults and, 175, 178–80
 political control and, 174–80
 by region, *173*
 societal sources of, *173*
 theocracy, 184–85
 types of, 180–87
 see also authoritarianism; totalitarianism
nongovernmental organizations (NGOs), **327**
 globalization and, 327–28, 330, 338, 340
nontariff regulatory barriers, **101,** 109, 110
nonviolence, 201

North Africa:
 immigrants from, 247, 248
 imperialism in, 296, 297
North America, 36, 325, 340
 advanced democracies in, *228*
 ideology and political attitudes in, 81
 imperialism in, 296, 297
 Internet use in, *337*
 see also specific countries
Northern Ireland, 149
 devolution and, 243–44
North Korea, 6, 7, 135, 275, 288
 one-party rule in, 184
 state power in, 52
 totalitarianism in, 167
Norway, 237
 constituencies in, 147
 happiness of, *117*
 HDI ranking of, 114
 political-economic system in, 114, *115*
 public goods in, 95
 2011 shootings in, 217
Nunavut Province, 243
Nye, Joseph, 325

oil:
 democracy and, 133, 134, 169, 170, 320
 as public good, 95
Oklahoma City bombing (1995), 217
one-party rule, 183–84, 185, 205
Organization of American States, 327
Ottoman Empire, 296, 297
outsourcing, 334–35, 346

Pakistan, 71
 as failing state, 50–51, 52, 70
 gender imbalance in, 308
 happiness of, *117*
 secession of, 50–51, 61, 70
 terrorism and, 207–8
Palestine, happiness of, *117*
Palestinians, 19, 63–64
Palmer Raids, 194

defined, 28–32, **28**

globalization and, 329–30, 344

government distinguished from, 31–32, *32*

identity and, 64–66

imperialism and the exportation of, 297–98

inflation and, 99

modern, rise of, 35–40, 80, 82

origins of political organization and, 33–35

postcommunist reorganizing of, 274

postimperialism and, 303–6, *304*

regime distinguished from, 29–31, *32*

revolution and, 203, 207

studying of, 52–53

state power, comparing, 40–52

centralization vs. decentralization and, 44–52

legitimacy and, 40–44

States and Social Revolutions (Skocpol), 202

state-sponsored terrorism, 207–8, **207**

strong states, 45, **45,** 48

structural adjustment programs, 309, **309**

Sudan, 307

ethnic conflict in, 67

suffrage, 132

see also voting

Sunni Muslims, 307

superstructure, 260, 262

supranational system, **237**

surplus value of labor, 259

surveillance, 175–76

counterterrorism and, 221–22

Sweden:

as advanced democracy, 230, *233*

constitution of, 158

economic liberalization in, *119*

economic portrait of (2011), *229*

in European Union, 237

happiness of, *117*

political-economic system in, 107, 111, *113,* 114, *115*

political parties in, 146

size of economy of, *113*

social democracy in, 107, 114, 158, *233*

taxation in, *98*

wealth and prosperity compared in, 114, *115*

wealth distribution in, *113*

Switzerland, 237

referendum in, 155

Syria, 30, 203

patrimonial regime in, 205

Taiwan:

democracy in, 129

military rule in, 182

nondemocratic rule in, 182

presidential system in, 144, 231

Tajikistan:

postcommunist political transition in, *276*

postcommunist social transition in, 284, 288

Taliban, 50, 275

tariffs, 100–102, **100,** 109

taxes:

in advanced democracies, 232, *233,* 252

democracy and, 20, 130

as institution, 20

international organizations in oversight of, 314

political economy and, 96–97, *98*

technological innovation, 3, 13

communist revolution and, 261

culture and, 84

in rise of state, 37

risks and uncertainty of, 245

see also Internet

terrorism, 50, 70, 188, 199–200, 207–19, *209,* 341

advanced democracies and, 248

causes of, 210–13

communism and, 266, 272

deaths from, *208*